THE RATIONALISTS

·ANCHOR·PRESS·
·DOUBLEDAY·

THE RATIONALISTS

RENÉ DESCARTES
Translated by John Veitch

DISCOURSE ON METHOD

MEDITATIONS

BENEDICT DE SPINOZA
Translated by R. H. M. Elwes

THE ETHICS

GOTTFRIED WILHELM
FREIHERR VON LEIBNIZ

Translated by George Montgomery,
with Revisions by Albert R. Chandler

DISCOURSE ON METAPHYSICS

THE MONADOLOGY

Anchor Books
Doubleday & Company, Inc.
Garden City, New York

The Anchor Books edition is the same as original Dolphin Books edition first published in 1960.

Anchor Books edition: 1974

ISBN: 0-385-09540-6
Printed in the United States of America

CONTENTS

DESCARTES (1596–1650)

SPINOZA (1632–1677)

LEIBNIZ (1646–1716)

RENÉ DESCARTES

DISCOURSE ON METHOD

MEDITATIONS

DISCOURSE

ON THE

METHOD OF RIGHTLY CONDUCTING THE

REASON AND SEEKING TRUTH

IN THE SCIENCES

PREFATORY NOTE

BY THE AUTHOR

If this Discourse appear too long to be read at once, it may be divided into six parts: and, in the first, will be found various considerations touching the Sciences; in the second, the principal rules of the Method which the Author has discovered; in the third, certain of the rules of Morals which he has deduced from this Method; in the fourth, the reasonings by which he establishes the existence of God and of the Human Soul, which are the foundations of his Metaphysic; in the fifth, the order of the Physical questions which he has investigated, and, in particular, the explication of the motion of the heart and of some other difficulties pertaining to Medicine, as also the difference between the soul of man and that of the brutes; and, in the last, what the Author believes to be required in order to greater advancement in the investigation of Nature than has yet been made, with the reasons that have induced him to write.

A DISCOURSE ON METHOD

PART I

Good sense is, of all things among men, the most equally distributed; for every one thinks himself so abundantly provided with it, that those even who are the most difficult to satisfy in everything else, do not usually desire a larger measure of this quality than they already possess. And in this it is not likely that all are mistaken: the conviction is rather to be held as testifying that the power of judging aright and of distinguishing truth from error, which is properly what is called good sense or reason, is by nature equal in all men; and that the diversity of our opinions, consequently, does not arise from some being endowed with a larger share of reason than others, but solely from this, that we conduct our thoughts along different ways, and do not fix our attention on the same objects. For to be possessed of a vigorous mind is not enough; the prime requisite is rightly to apply it. The greatest minds, as they are capable of the highest excellences, are open likewise to the greatest aberrations; and those who travel very slowly may yet make far greater progress, provided they keep always to the straight road, than those who, while they run, forsake it.

For myself, I have never fancied my mind to be in any respect more perfect than those of the generality; on the contrary, I have often wished that I were equal to some others in promptitude of thought, or in clearness and distinctness of imagination, or in fulness and readiness of memory. And besides these, I know of no other qualities that contribute to the perfection of the mind; for as to the reason or sense, inasmuch as it is that alone which constitutes us men, and distinguishes us from the brutes, I am disposed to believe that it is to be found complete in each individual; and on this point to adopt the common opinion of philosophers, who say that the difference of greater and less holds only among the *accidents*, and not among the *forms* or *natures* of *individuals* of the same *species*.

I will not hesitate, however, to avow my belief that it has been my singular good fortune to have very early in life fallen in with certain tracks which have conducted me to considerations and maxims, of which I have formed a method that gives me the means, as I think, of gradually augmenting my knowledge, and of raising it by little and little to the highest point which the mediocrity of my talents and the brief duration of my life will permit me to reach. For I have already reaped from it such fruits that, although I have been accustomed to think lowly enough of myself, and although when I look with the eye of a philosopher at the varied courses and pursuits of mankind at large, I find scarcely one which does not appear vain and useless, I nevertheless derive the highest satisfaction from the progress I conceive myself to have already made in the search after truth, and cannot help entertaining such expectations of the future as to believe that if, among the occupations of men as men, there is any one really excellent and important, it is that which I have chosen.

After all, it is possible I may be mistaken; and it is but a little copper and glass, perhaps, that I take for gold and diamonds. I know how very liable we are to delusion in what relates to ourselves, and also how much the judgments of our friends are to be suspected when given in our favour. But I shall endeavour in this discourse to describe the paths I have followed, and to delineate my life as in a picture, in order that each one may be able to judge of them for himself, and that in the general opinion entertained of them, as gathered from current report, I myself may have a new help towards instruction to be added to those I have been in the habit of employing.

My present design, then, is not to teach the method which each ought to follow for the right conduct of his reason, but solely to describe the way in which I have endeavoured to conduct my own. They who set themselves to give precepts must of course regard themselves as possessed of greater skill than those to whom they prescribe; and if they err in the slightest particular, they subject themselves to censure. But as this tract is put forth merely as a history, or, if you will, as a tale, in which, amid some examples worthy of imitation, there will be found, perhaps, as many more which it were advisable not to follow, I hope it will prove useful to some without being hurtful to any, and that my openness will find some favour with all.

From my childhood, I have been familiar with letters; and as I was given to believe that by their help a clear and certain knowledge of all that is useful in life might be acquired, I was ardently desirous of instruction. But as soon as I had finished the entire course of study, at the close of which it is customary to be admitted into the order of the learned, I completely changed my opinion. For I found myself involved in so many doubts and errors, that I was convinced I had advanced no farther in all my attempts at learning, than the discovery at every turn of my own ignorance. And yet I was studying in one of the most celebrated schools in Europe, in which I thought there must be learned men, if such were anywhere to be found. I had been taught all that others learned there; and not contented with the sciences actually taught us, I had, in addition, read all the books that had fallen into my hands, treating of such branches as are esteemed the most curious and rare. I knew the judgment which others had formed of me; and I did not find that I was considered inferior to my fellows, although there were among them some who were already marked out to fill the places of our instructors. And, in fine, our age appeared to me as flourishing, and as fertile in powerful minds as any preceding one. I was thus led to take the liberty of judging of all other men by myself, and of concluding that there was no science in existence that was of such a nature as I had previously been given to believe.

I still continued, however, to hold in esteem the studies of the schools. I was aware that the languages taught in them are necessary to the understanding of the writings of the ancients; that the grace of fable stirs the mind; that the memorable deeds of history elevate it; and, if read with discretion, aid in forming the judgment; that the perusal of all excellent books is, as it were, to interview with the noblest men of past ages, who have written them, and even a studied interview, in which are discovered to us only their choicest thoughts; that eloquence has incomparable force and beauty; that poesy has its ravishing graces and delights; that in the mathematics there are many refined discoveries eminently suited to gratify the inquisitive, as well as further all the arts and lessen the labour of man; that numerous highly useful precepts and exhortations to virtue are contained in treatises on morals; that theology points out the path to heaven; that philosophy affords the means of discoursing with an appearance of truth on all matters, and commands the admiration of the more simple; that jurisprudence, medicine, and the other sciences, secure for their cultivators honours and riches; and, in fine, that it is useful to bestow some attention upon all, even upon those abounding the most in superstition and error, that we may be in a position to determine their real value, and guard against being deceived.

But I believed that I had already given sufficient time to languages, and likewise to the reading of the writings of the ancients, to their histories and fables. For to hold converse with those of other ages and to travel, are almost the same thing. It is useful to know something of the manners of different nations, that we may be enabled to form a more correct judgment regarding our own, and be prevented from thinking that everything contrary to our customs is ridiculous and irrational,—a conclusion usually come to by those whose experience has been limited to their own country. On the other hand, when too much time is occupied in travelling, we become strangers to our native country; and the overcurious in the customs of the past are generally ignorant of those of the present. Besides, fictitious narratives lead us to imagine the possibility of many events that are impossible; and even the most faithful histories, if they do not wholly misrepresent matters, or exaggerate their importance to render the account of them more worthy of perusal, omit, at least, almost always the meanest and least striking of the attendant circumstances; hence it happens that the remainder does not represent the truth, and that such as regulate their conduct by examples drawn from this source, are apt to fall into the extravagances of the knight-errants of romance, and to entertain projects that exceed their powers.

I esteemed eloquence highly, and was in raptures with poesy; but I thought that both were gifts of nature rather than fruits of study. Those in whom the faculty of reason is predominant, and who most skilfully dispose their thoughts with a view to render them clear and intelligible, are always the best able to persuade others of the truth of what they lay down, though they should speak only in the language of Lower Brittany, and be wholly ignorant of the rules of rhetoric; and those whose minds are stored with the most agreeable fancies, and who can give expression to them with the greatest embellishment and harmony, are still the best poets, though unacquainted with the art of poetry.

I was especially delighted with the mathematics, on account of the certitude and evidence of their reasonings; but I had not as yet a precise knowledge of their true use; and thinking that they but contributed to the advancement of the mechanical arts, I was astonished that foundations, so strong and solid, should have had no loftier superstructure reared on them. On the other hand, I compared the disquisitions of the ancient moralists to very towering and magnificent palaces with no better foundation than sand and mud: they laud the virtues very highly, and exhibit them as estimable far above anything on earth; but they give us no adequate criterion of virtue, and frequently that which they designate with so fine a name is but apathy, or pride, or despair, or parricide.

I revered our theology, and aspired as much as any one to reach heaven: but being given assuredly to understand that the way is not less open to the most ignorant than to the most learned, and that the revealed truths which lead to heaven are above our comprehension, I did not presume to subject them to the impotency of my reason; and I thought that in order competently to undertake their examination, there was need of some special help from heaven, and of being more than man.

Of philosophy I will say nothing, except that when I saw

that it had been cultivated for many ages by the most distinguished men, and that yet there is not a single matter within
its sphere which is not still in dispute, and nothing, therefore,
which is above doubt, I did not presume to anticipate that my
success would be greater in it than that of others; and further,
when I considered the number of conflicting opinions touching a single matter that may be upheld by learned men, while
there can be but one true, I reckoned as well-nigh false all that
was only probable.

As to the other sciences, inasmuch as these borrow their
principles from philosophy, I judged that no solid superstruc-
tures could be reared on foundations so infirm; and neither
the honour nor the gain held out by them was sufficient to
determine me to their cultivation: for I was not, thank Heaven,
in a condition which compelled me to make merchandise of
science for the bettering of my fortune; and though I might
not profess to scorn glory as a cynic, I yet made very slight
account of that honour which I hoped to acquire only through
fictitious titles. And, in fine, of false sciences I thought I knew
the worth sufficiently to escape being deceived by the profes-
sions of an alchemist, the predictions of an astrologer, the im-
postures of a magician, or by the artifices and boasting of any
of those who profess to know things of which they are ignorant.

For these reasons, as soon as my age permitted me to pass
from under the control of my instructors, I entirely abandoned
the study of letters, and resolved no longer to seek any other
science than the knowledge of myself, or of the great book of
the world. I spent the remainder of my youth in travelling,
in visiting courts and armies, in holding intercourse with men
of different dispositions and ranks, in collecting varied experience, in proving myself in the different situations into which
fortune threw me, and, above all, in making such reflection on
the matter of my experience as to secure my improvement.
For it occurred to me that I should find much more truth in
the reasonings of each individual with reference to the affairs
in which he is personally interested, and the issue of which
must presently punish him if he has judged amiss, than in
those conducted by a man of letters in his study, regarding
speculative matters that are of no practical moment, and fol-

lowed by no consequences to himself, farther, perhaps, than that they foster his vanity the better the more remote they are from common sense; requiring, as they must in this case, the exercise of greater ingenuity and art to render them probable. In addition, I had always a most earnest desire to know how to distinguish the true from the false, in order that I might be able clearly to discriminate the right path in life, and proceed in it with confidence.

It is true that, while busied only in considering the manners of other men, I found here, too, scarce any ground for settled conviction, and remarked hardly less contradiction among them than in the opinions of the philosophers. So that the greatest advantage I derived from the study consisted in this, that, observing many things which, however extravagant and ridiculous to our apprehension, are yet by common consent received and approved by other great nations, I learned to entertain too decided a belief in regard to nothing of the truth of which I had been persuaded merely by example and custom; and thus I gradually extricated myself from many errors powerful enough to darken our natural intelligence, and incapacitate us in great measure from listening to reason. But after I had been occupied several years in thus studying the book of the world, and in essaying to gather some experience, I at length resolved to make myself an object of study, and to employ all the powers of my mind in choosing the paths I ought to follow, an undertaking which was accompanied with greater success than it would have been had I never quitted my country or my books.

PART II

I was then in Germany, attracted thither by the wars in that country, which have not yet been brought to a termination; and as I was returning to the army from the coronation of the emperor, the setting in of winter arrested me in a locality where, as I found no society to interest me, and was besides fortunately undisturbed by any cares or passions, I remained the whole day in seclusion, with full opportunity to occupy my attention with my own thoughts. Of these one of the very first that occurred to me was, that there is seldom so much perfection in works composed of many separate parts, upon which different hands had been employed, as in those completed by a single master. Thus it is observable that the buildings which a single architect has planned and executed, are generally more elegant and commodious than those which several have attempted to improve, by making old walls serve for purposes for which they were not originally built. Thus also, those ancient cities which, from being at first only villages, have become, in course of time, large towns, are usually but ill laid out compared with the regularly constructed towns which a professional architect has freely planned on an open plain; so that although the several buildings of the former may often equal or surpass in beauty those of the latter, yet when one observes their indiscriminate juxtaposition, there a large one and here a small, and the consequent crookedness and irregularity of the streets, one is disposed to allege that chance rather than any human will guided by reason must have led to such an arrangement. And if we consider that nevertheless there have been at all times certain officers whose duty it was to see that private buildings contributed to public ornament, the difficulty of reaching high perfection with but the materials of others to operate on, will be readily acknowledged. In the same way I fancied that those nations which, starting from a semi-barbarous state and advancing to civilisation by slow degrees, have had their laws successively determined, and, as it were, forced upon them simply by experience of the hurtfulness of particular crimes and disputes, would by this process come to be possessed of less perfect institutions than those which, from the commencement of their association as communities, have followed the appointments of some wise legislator. It is thus quite certain that the constitution of the true religion, the ordinances of which are derived from God, must be incomparably superior to that of every other. And, to speak of human affairs, I believe that the past pre-eminence of Sparta was due not to the goodness of each of its laws in particular, for many of these were very strange, and even opposed to good morals, but to the circumstance that, originated by a single individual, they all tended to a single end. In the same way I thought that the sciences contained in books (such of them at least as are made up of probable reasonings, without demonstrations), composed as they are of the opinions of many different individuals massed together, are farther removed from truth than the simple inferences which a man of good sense using his natural and unprejudiced judgment draws respecting the matters of his experience. And because we have all to pass through a state of infancy to manhood, and have been of necessity, for a length of time, governed by our desires and preceptors (whose dictates were frequently conflicting, while neither perhaps always counselled us for the best), I farther concluded that it is almost impossible that our judgments can be so correct or solid as they would have been, had our reason been mature from the moment of our birth, and had we always been guided by it alone.

It is true, however, that it is not customary to pull down all the houses of a town with the single design of rebuilding them differently, and thereby rendering the streets more handsome; but it often happens that a private individual takes down his own with the view of erecting it anew, and that people are even sometimes constrained to this when their houses are in danger of falling from age, or when the foundations are insecure. With this before me by way of example, I was persuaded that it would indeed be preposterous for a private individual to think of reforming a state by fundamentally changing it throughout, and overturning it in order to set it up amended; and the same I thought was true of any similar project for reforming the body of the sciences, or the order of teaching them established in the schools: but as for the opinions which up to that time I had embraced, I thought that I could not do better than resolve at once to sweep them wholly away, that I might afterwards be in a position to admit either others more correct, or even perhaps the same when they had undergone the scrutiny of reason. I firmly believed that in this way I should much better succeed in the conduct of my life, than if I built only upon old foundations, and leant upon principles which, in my youth, I had taken upon trust. For although I recognised various difficulties in this undertaking, these were not, however, without remedy, nor once to be compared with such as attend the slightest reformation in public affairs. Large bodies, if once overthrown, are with great difficulty set up again, or even kept erect when once seriously shaken, and the fall of such is always disastrous. Then if there are any imperfections in the constitutions of states (and that many such exist the diversity of constitutions is alone sufficient to assure us), custom has without doubt materially smoothed their inconveniences, and has even managed to steer altogether clear of, or insensibly corrected a number which sagacity could not have provided against with equal effect; and, in fine, the defects are almost always more tolerable than the change necessary for their removal; in the same manner that highways which wind among mountains, by being much frequented, become gradually so smooth and commodious, that it is much better to follow them than to seek a straighter path by climbing over the tops of rocks and descending to the bottoms of precipices.

Hence it is that I cannot in any degree approve of those restless and busy meddlers who, called neither by birth nor fortune to take part in the management of public affairs, are yet always projecting reforms; and if I thought that this track contained aught which might justify the suspicion that I was a victim of such folly, I would by no means permit its publication. I have never contemplated anything higher than the reformation of my own opinions, and basing them on a foundation wholly my own. And although my own satisfaction with my work has led me to present here a draft of it, I do not by any means therefore recommend to every one else to make a similar attempt. Those whom God has endowed with a larger measure of genius will entertain, perhaps, designs still more exalted; but for the many I am much afraid lest even the present undertaking be more than they can safely venture to imitate. The single design to strip one's self of all past beliefs is one that ought not to be taken by every one. The majority of men is composed of two classes, for neither of which would this be at all a befitting resolution: in the *first* place, of those who with more than a due confidence in their own powers, are precipitate in their judgments and want the patience requisite for orderly and circumspect thinking; whence it happens, that if men of this class once take the liberty to doubt of their accustomed opinions, and quit the beaten highway, they will never be able to thread the byway that would lead them by a shorter course, and will lose themselves and continue to wander for life; in the *second* place, of those who, possessed of sufficient sense or modesty to determine that there are others who excel them in the power of discriminating between truth and error, and by whom they may be instructed, ought rather to content themselves with the opinions of such than trust for more correct to their own reason.

For my own part, I should doubtless have belonged to the latter class, had I received instruction from but one master, or had I never known the diversities of opinion that from time immemorial have prevailed among men of the greatest learning. But I had become aware, even so early as during my college life, that no opinion, however absurd and incredible, can be imagined, which has not been maintained by some one of the philosophers; and afterwards in the course of my travels I remarked that all those whose opinions are decidedly repugnant to ours are not on that account barbarians and

savages, but on the contrary that many of these nations make
an equally good, if not a better, use of their reason than we
do. I took into account also the very different character which
a person brought up from infancy in France or Germany ex-
hibits, from that which, with the same mind originally, this
individual would have possessed had he lived always among
the Chinese or with savages, and the circumstance that in
dress itself the fashion which pleased us ten years ago, and
which may again, perhaps, be received into favour before ten
years have gone, appears to us at this moment extravagant
and ridiculous. I was thus led to infer that the ground of our
opinions is far more custom and example than any certain
knowledge. And, finally, although such be the ground of
our opinions, I remarked that a plurality of suffrages is no
guarantee of truth where it is at all of difficult discovery, as
in such cases it is much more likely that it will be found by
one than by many. I could, however, select from the crowd
no one whose opinions seemed worthy of preference, and thus
I found myself constrained, as it were, to use my own reason
in the conduct of my life.

But like one walking alone and in the dark, I resolved to
proceed so slowly and with such circumspection, that if I did
not advance far, I would at least guard against falling. I did
not even choose to dismiss summarily any of the opinions that
had crept into my belief without having been introduced by
reason, but first of all took sufficient time carefully to satisfy
myself of the general nature of the task I was setting myself,
and ascertain the true method by which to arrive at the knowledge of whatever lay within the compass of my powers.

Among the branches of philosophy, I had, at an earlier
period, given some attention to logic, and among those of the
mathematics to geometrical analysis and algebra,—three arts
or sciences which ought, as I conceived, to contribute something to my design. But, on examination, I found that, as for
logic, its syllogisms and the majority of its other precepts are
of avail rather in the communication of what we already know,
or even as the art of Lully, in speaking without judgment of
things of which we are ignorant, than in the investigation of
the unknown; and although this science contains indeed a

number of correct and very excellent precepts, there are, nevertheless, so many others, and these either injurious or superfluous, mingled with the former, that it is almost quite as difficult to effect a severance of the true from the false as it is to extract a Diana or a Minerva from a rough block of marble. Then as to the analysis of the ancients and the algebra of the moderns, besides that they embrace only matters highly abstract, and, to appearance, of no use, the former is so exclusively restricted to the consideration of figures, that it can exercise the understanding only on condition of greatly fatiguing the imagination; and, in the latter, there is so complete a subjection to certain rules and formulas, that there results an art full of confusion and obscurity calculated to embarrass, instead of a science fitted to cultivate the mind. By these considerations I was induced to seek some other method which would comprise the advantages of the three and be exempt from their defects. And as a multitude of laws often only hampers justice, so that a state is best governed when, with few laws, these are rigidly administered; in like manner, instead of the great number of precepts of which logic is composed, I believed that the four following would prove perfectly sufficient for me, provided I took the firm and unwavering resolution never in a single instance to fail in observing them.

The *first* was never to accept anything for true which I did not clearly know to be such; that is to say, carefully to avoid precipitancy and prejudice, and to comprise nothing more in my judgment than what was presented to my mind so clearly and distinctly as to exclude all ground of doubt.

The *second,* to divide each of the difficulties under examination into as many parts as possible, and as might be necessary for its adequate solution.

The *third,* to conduct my thoughts in such order that, by commencing with objects the simplest and easiest to know, I might ascend by little and little, and, as it were, step by step, to the knowledge of the more complex; assigning in thought a certain order even to those objects which in their own nature do not stand in a relation of antecedence and sequence.

And the *last,* in every case to make enumerations so complete and reviews so general, that I might be assured that nothing was omitted.

The long chains of simple and easy reasonings by means of which geometers are accustomed to reach the conclusions of their most difficult demonstrations, had led me to imagine that all things, to the knowledge of which man is competent, are mutually connected in the same way, and that there is nothing so far removed from us as to be beyond our reach, or so hidden that we cannot discover it, provided only we abstain from accepting the false for the true, and always preserve in our thoughts the order necessary for the deduction of one truth from another. And I had little difficulty in determining the objects with which it was necessary to commence, for I was already persuaded that it must be with the simplest and easiest to know, and, considering that of all those who have hitherto sought truth in the sciences, the mathematicians alone have been able to find any demonstrations, that is, any certain and evident reasons, I did not doubt but that such must have been the rule of their investigations. I resolved to commence, therefore, with the examination of the simplest objects, not anticipating, however, from this any other advantage than that to be found in accustoming my mind to the love and nourishment of truth, and to a distaste for all such reasonings as were unsound. But I had no intention on that account of attempting to master all the particular sciences commonly denominated mathematics: but observing that, however different their objects, they all agree in considering only the various relations or proportions subsisting among those objects, I thought it best for my purpose to consider these proportions in the most general form possible, without referring them to any objects in particular, except such as would most facilitate the knowledge of them, and without by any means restricting them to these, that afterwards I might thus be the better able to apply them to every other class of objects to which they are legitimately applicable. Perceiving further, that in order to understand these relations I should sometimes have to consider them one by one, and sometimes only to bear them in mind, or embrace them in the aggregate, I thought that, in order the better to consider them individually, I should view them as subsisting between straight lines, than which I could find no objects more simple, or capable of being more distinctly represented to my imagination and senses; and on the other hand, that in order to retain them in the memory, or embrace an aggregate of many, I should express them by certain characters the briefest possible. In this way I believed that I could borrow all that was best both in geometrical analysis and in algebra, and correct all the defects of the one by help of the other.

And, in point of fact, the accurate observance of these few precepts gave me, I take the liberty of saying, such ease in un-ravelling all the questions embraced in these two sciences, that in the two or three months I devoted to their examination, not only did I reach solutions of questions I had formerly deemed exceedingly difficult, but even as regards questions of the solution of which I continued ignorant, I was enabled, as it appeared to me, to determine the means whereby, and the extent to which, a solution was possible; results attributable to the circumstance that I commenced with the simplest and most general truths, and that thus each truth discovered was a rule available in the discovery of subsequent ones. Nor in this perhaps shall I appear too vain, if it be considered that, as the truth on any particular point is one, whoever appre-hends the truth, knows all that on that point can be known. The child, for example, who has been instructed in the ele-ments of arithmetic, and has made a particular addition, ac-cording to rule, may be assured that he has found, with respect to the sum of the numbers before him, all that in this instance is within the reach of human genius. Now, in conclusion, the method which teaches adherence to the true order, and an exact enumeration of all the conditions of the thing sought includes all that gives certitude to the rules of arithmetic.

But the chief ground of my satisfaction with this method, was the assurance I had of thereby exercising my reason in all matters, if not with absolute perfection, at least with the greatest attainable by me: besides, I was conscious that by its use my mind was becoming gradually habituated to clearer and more distinct conceptions of its objects; and I hoped also, from not having restricted this method to any particular matter, to apply it to the difficulties of the other sciences, with not less success than to those of algebra. I should not, however, on this account have ventured at once on the examination of all the difficulties of the sciences which presented themselves to me, for this would have been contrary to the order prescribed in the method, but observing that the knowledge of such is dependent on principles borrowed from philosophy, in which I found nothing certain, I thought it necessary first of all to endeavour to establish its principles. And because I observed, besides, that an inquiry of this kind was of all others of the greatest moment, and one in which precipitancy and anticipation in judgment were most to be dreaded, I thought that I ought not to approach it till I had reached a more mature age (being at that time but twenty-three), and had first of all employed much of my time in preparation for the work, as well by eradicating from my mind all the erroneous opinions I had up to that moment accepted, as by amassing variety of experience to afford materials for my reasonings, and by continually exercising myself in my chosen method with a view to increase skill in its application.

PART III

And, finally, as it is not enough, before commencing to rebuild the house in which we live, that it be pulled down, and materials and builders provided, or that we engage in the work ourselves, according to a plan which we have beforehand carefully drawn out, but as it is likewise necessary that we be furnished with some other house in which we may live commodiously during the operations, so that I might not remain irresolute in my actions, while my reason compelled me to suspend my judgment, and that I might not be prevented from living thenceforward in the greatest possible felicity, I formed a provisory code of morals, composed of three or four maxims, with which I am desirous to make you acquainted.

The *first* was to obey the laws and customs of my country, adhering firmly to the faith in which, by the grace of God, I had been educated from my childhood, and regulating my conduct in every other matter according to the most moderate opinions, and the farthest removed from extremes, which should happen to be adopted in practice with general consent of the most judicious of those among whom I might be living. For, as I had from that time begun to hold my own opinions for nought because I wished to subject them all to examination, I was convinced that I could not do better than follow in the meantime the opinions of the most judicious; and although there are some perhaps among the Persians and Chinese as judicious as among ourselves, expediency seemed to dictate that I should regulate my practice conformably to the opinions of those with whom I should have to live; and it appeared to me that, in order to ascertain the real opinions

of such, I ought rather to take cognisance of what they practised than of what they said, not only because, in the corrup-
tion of our manners, there are few disposed to speak exactly
as they believe, but also because very many are not aware of
what it is that they really believe; for, as the act of mind by
which a thing is believed is different from that by which we
know that we believe it, the one act is often found without
the other. Also, amid many opinions held in equal repute, I
chose always the most moderate, as much for the reason that
these are always the most convenient for practice, and probably the best (for all excess is generally vicious), as that, in the
event of my falling into error, I might be at less distance from
the truth than if, having chosen one of the extremes, it should
turn out to be the other which I ought to have adopted. And
I placed in the class of extremes especially all promises by
which somewhat of our freedom is abridged; not that I disap-
proved of the laws which, to provide against the instability
of men of feeble resolution, when what is sought to be accomplished is some good, permit engagements by vows and
contracts binding the parties to persevere in it, or even, for
the security of commerce, sanction similar engagements where
the purpose sought to be realised is indifferent: but because
I did not find anything on earth which was wholly superior to
change, and because, for myself in particular, I hoped gradually to perfect my judgments, and not to suffer them to de-
teriorate, I would have deemed it a grave sin against good
sense, if, for the reason that I approved of something at a
particular time, I therefore bound myself to hold it for good
at a subsequent time, when perhaps it had ceased to be so, or
I had ceased to esteem it such.

My *second* maxim was to be as firm and resolute in my
actions as I was able, and not to adhere less steadfastly to the
most doubtful opinions, when once adopted, than if they had
been highly certain; imitating in this the example of travellers
who, when they have lost their way in a forest, ought not to
wander from side to side, far less remain in one place, but
proceed constantly towards the same side in as straight a line
as possible, without changing their direction for slight reasons,
although perhaps it might be chance alone which at first de-

termined the selection; for in this way, if they do not exactly reach the point they desire, they will come at least in the end to some place that will probably be preferable to the middle of a forest. In the same way, since in action it frequently happens that no delay is permissible, it is very certain that, when it is not in our power to determine what is true, we ought to act according to what is most probable; and even although we should not remark a greater probability in one opinion than in another, we ought notwithstanding to choose one or the other, and afterwards consider it, in so far as it relates to practice, as no longer dubious, but manifestly true and certain, since the reason by which our choice has been determined is itself possessed of these qualities. This principle was sufficient thenceforward to rid me of all those repentings and pangs of remorse that usually disturb the consciences of such feeble and uncertain minds as, destitute of any clear and determinate principle of choice, allow themselves one day to adopt a course of action as the best, which they abandon the next, as the opposite.

My *third* maxim was to endeavour always to conquer myself rather than fortune, and change my desires rather than the order of the world, and in general, accustom myself to the persuasion that, except our own thoughts, there is nothing absolutely in our power; so that when we have done our best in respect of things external to us, all wherein we fail of success is to be held, as regards us, absolutely impossible: and this single principle seemed to me sufficient to prevent me from desiring for the future anything which I could not obtain, and thus render me contented; for since our will naturally seeks those objects alone which the understanding represents as in some way possible of attainment, it is plain, that if we consider all external goods as equally beyond our power, we shall no more regret the absence of such goods as seem due to our birth, when deprived of them without any fault of ours, than our not possessing the kingdoms of China or Mexico; and thus making, so to speak, a virtue of necessity, we shall no more desire health in disease, or freedom in imprisonment, than we now do bodies incorruptible as diamonds, or the wings of birds to fly with. But I confess there is need of prolonged discipline and frequently repeated meditation to accustom the mind to view all objects in this light; and I believe that in this chiefly consisted the secret of the power of such philosophers as in former times were enabled to rise superior to the influence of fortune, and, amid suffering and poverty, enjoy a happiness which their gods might have envied. For, occupied incessantly with the consideration of the limits prescribed to their power by nature, they became so entirely convinced that nothing was at their disposal except their own thoughts, that this conviction was of itself sufficient to prevent their entertaining any desire of other objects; and over their thoughts they acquired a sway so absolute, that they had some ground on this account for esteeming themselves more rich and more powerful, more free and more happy, than other men who, whatever be the favours heaped on them by nature and fortune, if destitute of this philosophy, can never command the realization of all their desires.

In fine, to conclude this code of morals, I thought of reviewing the different occupations of men in this life, with the view of making choice of the best. And, without wishing to offer any remarks on the employments of others, I may state that it was my conviction that I could not do better than continue in that in which I was engaged, viz., in devoting my whole life to the culture of my reason, and in making the greatest progress I was able in the knowledge of truth, on the principles of the method which I had prescribed to myself. This method, from the time I had begun to apply it, had been to me the source of satisfaction so intense as to lead me to believe that more perfect or more innocent could not be enjoyed in this life; and as by its means I daily discovered truths that appeared to me of some importance, and of which other men were generally ignorant, the gratification thence arising so occupied my mind that I was wholly indifferent to every other object. Besides, the three preceding maxims were founded singly on the design of continuing the work of self-instruction. For since God has endowed each of us with some light of reason by which to distinguish truth from error, I could not have believed that I ought for a single moment to rest satisfied with the opinions of another, unless I had resolved to exercise my own judgment in examining these whenever I should be duly qualified for the task. Nor could I have proceeded on such opinions without scruple, had I supposed that I should thereby forfeit any advantage for attaining still more accurate, should such exist. And, in fine, I could not have restrained my desires, nor remained satisfied, had I not followed a path in which I thought myself certain of attaining all the knowledge to the acquisition of which I was competent, as well as the largest amount of what is truly good which I could ever hope to secure. Inasmuch as we neither seek nor shun any object except in so far as our understanding represents it as good or bad, all that is necessary to right action is right judgment, and to the best action the most correct judgment,—that is, to the acquisition of all the virtues with all else that is truly valuable and within our reach; and the assurance of such an acquisition cannot fail to render us contented.

Having thus provided myself with these maxims, and having placed them in reserve along with the truths of faith, which have ever occupied the first place in my belief, I came to the conclusion that I might with freedom set about ridding myself of what remained of my opinions. And, inasmuch as I hoped to be better able successfully to accomplish this work by holding intercourse with mankind, than by remaining longer shut up in the retirement where these thoughts had occurred to me, I betook me again to travelling before the winter was well ended. And, during the nine subsequent years, I did nothing but roam from one place to another, desirous of being a spectator rather than an actor in the plays exhibited on the theatre of the world; and, as I made it my business in each matter to reflect particularly upon what might fairly be doubted and prove a source of error, I gradually rooted out from my mind all the errors which had hitherto crept into it. Not that in this I imitated the sceptics who doubt only that they may doubt, and seek nothing beyond uncertainty itself; for, on the contrary, my design was singly to find ground of assurance, and cast aside the loose earth and sand, that I might reach the rock or the clay. In this, as appears to me, I was successful enough; for, since I endeavoured to discover the falsehood or incertitude of the propositions I examined, not by feeble conjectures, but by clear and certain reasonings, I met with nothing so doubtful as not to yield some conclusion of adequate certainty, although this were merely the inference, that the matter in question contained nothing certain. And, just as in pulling down an old house, we usually reserve the ruins to contribute towards the erection, so, in destroying such of my opinions as I judged to be ill-founded, I made a variety of observations and acquired an amount of experience of which I availed myself in the establishment of more certain. And further, I continued to exercise myself in the method I had prescribed; for, besides taking care in general to conduct all my thoughts according to its rules, I reserved some hours from time to time which I expressly devoted to the employment of the method in the solution of mathematical difficulties, or even in the solution likewise of some questions belonging to other sciences, but which, by my having detached them from such principles of these sciences as were of inadequate certainty, were rendered almost mathematical: the truth of this will be manifest from the numerous examples contained in this volume.[1] And thus, without in appearance living otherwise than those who, with no other occupation than that of spending their lives agreeably and innocently, study to sever pleasure from vice, and who, that they may enjoy their leisure without ennui, have recourse to such pursuits as are honourable, I was nevertheless prosecuting my design, and making greater progress in the knowledge of truth, than I might, perhaps, have made had I been engaged in the perusal of books merely, or in holding converse with men of letters.

These nine years passed away, however, before I had come to any determinate judgment respecting the difficulties which form matter of dispute among the learned, or had commenced to seek the principles of any philosophy more certain than the vulgar. And the examples of many men of the highest genius, who had, in former times, engaged in this inquiry, but, as appeared to me, without success, led me to imagine it to be a work of so much difficulty, that I would not perhaps have

[1] The "Discourse on Method" was originally published along with the "Dioptrics," the "Meteorics," and the "Geometry."—*Tr.*

ventured on it so soon had I not heard it currently rumoured that I had already completed the inquiry. I know not what were the grounds of this opinion; and, if my conversation contributed in any measure to its rise, this must have happened rather from my having confessed my ignorance with greater freedom than those are accustomed to do who have studied a little, and expounded, perhaps, the reasons that led me to doubt of many of those things that by others are esteemed certain, than from my having boasted of any system of philosophy. But, as I am of a disposition that makes me unwilling to be esteemed different from what I really am, I thought it necessary to endeavour by all means to render myself worthy of the reputation accorded to me; and it is now exactly eight years since this desire constrained me to remove from all those places where interruption from any of my acquaintances was possible, and betake myself to this country,[2] in which the long duration of the war has led to the establishment of such discipline, that the armies maintained seem to be of use only in enabling the inhabitants to enjoy more securely the blessings of peace; and where, in the midst of a great crowd actively engaged in business, and more careful of their own affairs than curious about those of others, I have been enabled to live without being deprived of any of the conveniences to be had in the most populous cities, and yet as solitary and as retired as in the midst of the most remote deserts.

[2] Holland; to which country he withdrew in 1629.—*Tr.*

PART IV

I am in doubt as to the propriety of making my first meditations in the place above mentioned matter of discourse; for these are so metaphysical, and so uncommon, as not, perhaps, to be acceptable to every one. And yet, that it may be determined whether the foundations that I have laid are sufficiently secure, I find myself in a measure constrained to advert to them. I had long before remarked that, in relation to practice, it is sometimes necessary to adopt, as if above doubt, opinions which we discern to be highly uncertain, as has been already said; but as I then desired to give my attention solely to the search after truth, I thought that a procedure exactly the opposite was called for, and that I ought to reject as absolutely false all opinions in regard to which I could suppose the least ground for doubt, in order to ascertain whether after that there remained aught in my belief that was wholly indubitable. Accordingly, seeing that our senses sometimes deceive us, I was willing to suppose that there existed nothing really such as they presented to us; and because some men err in reasoning, and fall into paralogisms, even on the simplest matters of geometry, I, convinced that I was as open to error as any other, rejected as false all the reasonings I had hitherto taken for demonstrations; and finally, when I considered that the very same thoughts (presentations) which we experience when awake may also be experienced when we are asleep, while there is at that time not one of them true, I supposed that all the objects (presentations) that had ever entered into my mind when awake, had in them no more truth than the illusions of my dreams. But immediately upon this I observed that, whilst I thus wished to think that all was false, it was absolutely necessary that I, who thus thought, should be somewhat; and as I observed that this truth, *I think, hence I am,* was so certain and of such evidence, that no ground of doubt, however extravagant, could be alleged by the sceptics capable of shaking it, I concluded that I might, without scruple, accept it as the first principle of the philosophy of which I was in search.

In the next place, I attentively examined what I was, and as I observed that I could suppose that I had no body, and that there was no world nor any place in which I might be; but that I could not therefore suppose that I was not; and that, on the contrary, from the very circumstance that I thought to doubt of the truth of other things, it most clearly and certainly followed that I was; while, on the other hand, if I had only ceased to think, although all the other objects which I had ever imagined had been in reality existent, I would have had no reason to believe that I existed; I thence concluded that I was a substance whose whole essence or nature consists only in thinking, and which, that it may exist, has need of no place, nor is dependent on any material things; so that "I," that is to say, the mind by which I am what I am, is wholly distinct from the body, and is even more easily known than the latter, and is such, that although the latter were not, it would still continue to be all that it is.

After this I inquired in general into what is essential to the truth and certainty of a proposition; for since I had discovered one which I knew to be true, I thought that I must likewise be able to discover the ground of this certitude. And as I observed that in the words *I think, hence I am,* there is nothing at all which gives me assurance of their truth beyond this, that I see very clearly that in order to think it is necessary to exist, I concluded that I might take, as a general rule, the principle, that all the things which we very clearly and distinctly conceive are true, only observing, however, that there is some difficulty in rightly determining the objects which we distinctly conceive.

In the next place, from reflecting on the circumstance that I doubted, and that consequently my being was not wholly perfect (for I clearly saw that it was a greater perfection to know than to doubt), I was led to inquire whence I had learned to think of something more perfect than myself; and I clearly recognised that I must hold this notion from some nature which in reality was more perfect. As for the thoughts of many other objects external to me, as of the sky, the earth, light, heat, and a thousand more, I was less at a loss to know whence these came; for since I remarked in them nothing which seemed to render them superior to myself, I could believe that, if these were true, they were dependencies on my own nature, in so far as it possessed a certain perfection, and, if they were false, that I held them from nothing, that is to say, that they were in me because of a certain imperfection of my nature. But this could not be the case with the idea of a nature more perfect than myself; for to receive it from nothing was a thing manifestly impossible; and, because it is not less repugnant that the more perfect should be an effect of, and dependence on the less perfect, than that something should proceed from nothing, it was equally impossible that I could hold it from myself: accordingly, it but remained that it had been placed in me by a nature which was in reality more perfect than mine, and which even possessed within itself all the perfections of which I could form any idea; that is to say, in a single word, which was God. And to this I added that, since I knew some perfections which I did not possess, I was not the only being in existence (I will here, with your permission, freely use the terms of the schools); but, on the contrary, that there was of necessity some other more perfect Being upon whom I was dependent, and from whom I had received all that I possessed; for if I had existed alone, and independently of every other being, so as to have had from myself all the perfection, however little, which I actually possessed, I should have been able, for the same reason, to have had from myself the whole remainder of perfection, of the want of which I was conscious, and thus could of myself have become infinite, eternal, immutable, omniscient, all-powerful, and, in fine, have possessed all the perfections which I could recognise in God. For in order to know the nature of God (whose existence has been established by the

preceding reasonings), as far as my own nature permitted, I
had only to consider in reference to all the properties of which
I found in my mind some idea, whether their possession was
a mark of perfection; and I was assured that no one which
indicated any imperfection was in him, and that none of the
rest was awanting. Thus I perceived that doubt, inconstancy,
sadness, and such like, could not be found in God, since I
myself would have been happy to be free from them. Besides,
I had ideas of many sensible and corporeal things; for although
I might suppose that I was dreaming, and that all which I saw
or imagined was false, I could not, nevertheless, deny that the
ideas were in reality in my thoughts. But, because I had already very clearly recognised in myself that the intelligent nature is distinct from the corporeal, and as I observed that all
composition is an evidence of dependency, and that a state
of dependency is manifestly a state of imperfection, I therefore determined that it could not be a perfection in God to
be compounded of these two natures, and that consequently
he was not so compounded; but that if there were any bodies
in the world, or even any intelligences, or other natures that
were not wholly perfect, their existence depended on his power
in such a way that they could not subsist without him for a
single moment.

I was disposed straightway to search for other truths; and
when I had represented to myself the object of the geometers,
which I conceived to be a continuous body, or a space indefinitely extended in length, breadth, and height or depth, divisible into divers parts which admit of different figures and
sizes, and of being moved or transposed in all manner of ways
(for all this the geometers suppose to be in the object they
contemplate), I went over some of their simplest demonstrations. And, in the first place, I observed, that the great certitude which by common consent is accorded to these demonstrations, is founded solely upon this, that they are clearly
conceived in accordance with the rules I have already laid
down. In the next place, I perceived that there was nothing
at all in these demonstrations which could assure me of the
existence of their object: thus, for example, supposing a triangle to be given, I distinctly perceived that its three angles

were necessarily equal to two right angles, but I did not on that account perceive anything which could assure me that any triangle existed: while, on the contrary, recurring to the examination of the idea of a Perfect Being, I found that the existence of the Being was comprised in the idea in the same way that the equality of its three angles to two right angles is comprised in the idea of a triangle, or as in the idea of a sphere, the equidistance of all points on its surface from the centre, or even still more clearly; and that consequently it is at least as certain that God, who is this Perfect Being, is, or exists, as any demonstration of geometry can be.

But the reason which leads many to persuade themselves that there is a difficulty in knowing this truth, and even also in knowing what their mind really is, is that they never raise their thoughts above sensible objects, and are so accustomed to consider nothing except by way of imagination, which is a mode of thinking limited to material objects, that all that is not imaginable seems to them not intelligible. The truth of this is sufficiently manifest from the single circumstance, that the philosophers of the schools accept as a maxim that there is nothing in the understanding which was not previously in the senses, in which however it is certain that the ideas of God and of the soul have never been; and it appears to me that they who make use of their imagination to comprehend these ideas do exactly the same thing as if, in order to hear sounds or smell odours, they strove to avail themselves of their eyes; unless indeed that there is this difference, that the sense of sight does not afford us an inferior assurance to those of smell or hearing; in place of which, neither our imagination nor our senses can give us assurance of anything unless our understanding intervene.

Finally, if there be still persons who are not sufficiently persuaded of the existence of God and of the soul, by the reasons I have adduced, I am desirous that they should know that all the other propositions, of the truth of which they deem themselves perhaps more assured, as that we have a body, and that there exist stars and an earth, and such like, are less certain; for, although we have a moral assurance of these things, which is so strong that there is an appearance of extravagance in doubting of their existence, yet at the same time no one, unless his intellect is impaired, can deny, when the question relates to a metaphysical certitude, that there is sufficient reason to exclude entire assurance, in the observation that when asleep we can in the same way imagine ourselves possessed of another body and that we see other stars and another earth, when there is nothing of the kind. For how do we know that the thoughts which occur in dreaming are false rather than those other which we experience when awake, since the former are often not less vivid and distinct than the latter? And though men of the highest genius study this question as long as they please, I do not believe that they will be able to give any reason which can be sufficient to remove this doubt, unless they presuppose the existence of God. For, in the first place, even the principle which I have already taken as a rule, viz., that all the things which we clearly and distinctly conceive are true, is certain only because God is or exists and because he is a Perfect Being, and because all that we possess is derived from him: whence it follows that our ideas or notions, which to the extent of their clearness and distinctness are real, and proceed from God, must to that extent be true. Accordingly, whereas we not unfrequently have ideas or notions in which some falsity is contained, this can only be the case with such as are to some extent confused and obscure, and in this proceed from nothing (participate of negation), that is, exist in us thus confused because we are not wholly perfect. And it is evident that it is not less repugnant that falsity or imperfection, in so far as it is imperfection, should proceed from God, than that truth or perfection should proceed from nothing. But if we did not know that all which we possess of real and true proceeds from a Perfect and Infinite Being, however clear and distinct our ideas might be, we should have no ground on that account for the assurance that they possessed the perfection of being true.

But after the knowledge of God and of the soul has rendered us certain of this rule, we can easily understand that the truth of the thoughts we experience when awake, ought not in the slightest degree to be called in question on account of the illusions of our dreams. For if it happened that an individual, even when asleep, had some very distinct idea, as, for example, if a geometer should discover some new demonstration, the circumstance of his being asleep would not militate against its truth; and as for the most ordinary error of our dreams, which consists in their representing to us various objects in the same way as our external senses, this is not prejudicial, since it leads us very properly to suspect the truth of the ideas of sense; for we are not unfrequently deceived in the same manner when awake; as when persons in the jaundice see all objects yellow, or when the stars or bodies at a great distance appear to us much smaller than they are. For, in fine, whether awake or asleep, we ought never to allow ourselves to be persuaded of the truth of anything unless on the evidence of our reason. And it must be noted that I say of our *reason*, and not of our imagination or of our senses: thus, for example, although we very clearly see the sun, we ought not therefore to determine that it is only of the size which our sense of sight presents; and we may very distinctly imagine the head of a lion joined to the body of a goat, without being therefore shut up to the conclusion that a chimera exists; for it is not a dictate of reason that what we thus see or imagine is in reality existent; but it plainly tells us that all our ideas or notions contain in them some truth; for otherwise it could not be that God, who is wholly perfect and veracious, should have placed them in us. And because our reasonings are never so clear or so complete during sleep as when we are awake, although sometimes the acts of our imagination are then as lively and distinct, if not more so than in our waking moments, reason further dictates that, since all our thoughts cannot be true because of our partial imperfection, those possessing truth must infallibly be found in the experience of our waking moments rather than in that of our dreams.

PART V

I would here willingly have proceeded to exhibit the whole chain of truths which I deduced from these primary; but as with a view to this it would have been necessary now to treat of many questions in dispute among the learned, with whom I do not wish to be embroiled, I believe that it will be better for me to refrain from this exposition, and only mention in general what these truths are, that the more judicious may be able to determine whether a more special account of them would conduce to the public advantage. I have ever remained firm in my original resolution to suppose no other principle than that of which I have recently availed myself in demonstrating the existence of God and of the soul, and to accept as true nothing that did not appear to me more clear and certain than the demonstrations of the geometers had formerly appeared; and yet I venture to state that not only have I found means to satisfy myself in a short time on all the principal difficulties which are usually treated of in philosophy, but I have also observed certain laws established in nature by God in such a manner, and of which he has impressed on our minds such notions, that after we have reflected sufficiently upon these, we cannot doubt that they are accurately observed in all that exists or takes place in the world: and farther, by considering the concatenation of these laws, it appears to me that I have discovered many truths more useful and more important than all I had before learned, or even had expected to learn.

But because I have essayed to expound the chief of these discoveries in a treatise which certain considerations prevent

me from publishing, I cannot make the results known more
conveniently than by here giving a summary of the contents
of this treatise. It was my design to comprise in it all that, before I set myself to write it, I thought I knew of the nature
of material objects. But like the painters who, finding themselves unable to represent equally well on a plain surface all
the different faces of a solid body, select one of the chief, on
which alone they make the light fall, and throwing the rest
into the shade, allow them to appear only in so far as they can
be seen while looking at the principal one; so, fearing lest I
should not be able to comprise in my discourse all that was
in my mind, I resolved to expound singly, though at considerable length, my opinions regarding light; then to take the
opportunity of adding something on the sun and the fixed
stars, since light almost wholly proceeds from them; on the
heavens since they transmit it; on the planets, comets, and
earth, since they reflect it; and particularly on all the bodies
that are upon the earth, since they are either coloured, or
transparent, or luminous; and finally on man, since he is the
spectator of these objects. Further, to enable me to cast this
variety of subjects somewhat into the shade, and to express
my judgment regarding them with greater freedom, without
being necessitated to adopt or refute the opinions of the
learned, I resolved to leave all the people here to their disputes, and to speak only of what would happen in a new
world, if God were now to create somewhere in the imaginary
spaces matters sufficient to compose one, and were to agitate
variously and confusedly the different parts of this matter, so
that there resulted a chaos as disordered as the poets ever
feigned, and after that did nothing more than lend his ordinary concurrence to nature, and allow her to act in accordance
with the laws which he had established. On this supposition,
I, in the first place, described this matter, and essayed to represent it in such a manner that to my mind there can be nothing clearer and more intelligible, except what has been recently said regarding God and the soul; for I even expressly
supposed that it possessed none of those forms or qualities
which are so debated in the schools, nor in general anything
the knowledge of which is not so natural to our minds that

no one can so much as imagine himself ignorant of it. Besides, I have pointed out what are the laws of nature; and, with no other principle upon which to found my reasonings except the infinite perfection of God, I endeavoured to demonstrate all those about which there could be any room for doubt, and to prove that they are such, that even if God had created more worlds, there could have been none in which these laws were not observed. Thereafter, I showed how the greatest part of the matter of this chaos must, in accordance with these laws, dispose and arrange itself in such a way as to present the appearance of heavens; how in the meantime some of its parts must compose an earth and some planets and comets, and others a sun and fixed stars. And, making a digression at this stage on the subject of light, I expounded at considerable length what the nature of that light must be which is found in the sun and the stars, and how thence in an instant of time it traverses the immense spaces of the heavens, and how from the planets and comets it is reflected towards the earth. To this I likewise added much respecting the substance, the situation, the motions, and all the different qualities of these heavens and stars; so that I thought I had said enough respecting them to show that there is nothing observable in the heavens or stars of our system that must not, or at least may not appear precisely alike in those of the system which I described. I came next to speak of the earth in particular, and to show how, even though I had expressly supposed that God had given no weight to the matter of which it is composed, this should not prevent all its parts from tending exactly to its centre; how with water and air on its surface, the disposition of the heavens and heavenly bodies, more especially of the moon, must cause a flow and ebb, like in all its circumstances to that observed in our seas, as also a certain current both of water and air from east to west, such as is likewise observed between the tropics; how the mountains, seas, fountains, and rivers might naturally be formed in it, and the metals produced in the mines, and the plants grow in the fields; and in general, how all the bodies which are commonly denominated mixed or composite might be generated: and, among other things in the discoveries alluded to, inasmuch as besides the stars, I knew nothing except fire which produces light, I spared no pains to set forth all that pertains to its nature,—the manner of its production and support, and to explain how heat is sometimes found without light, and light without heat; to show how it can induce various colours upon different bodies and other diverse qualities; how it reduces some to a liquid state and hardens others; how it can consume almost all bodies, or convert them into ashes and smoke; and finally, how from these ashes, by the mere intensity of its action, it forms glass: for as this transmutation of ashes into glass appeared to me as wonderful as any other in nature, I took a special pleasure in describing it.

I was not, however, disposed, from these circumstances, to conclude that this world had been created in the manner I described; for it is much more likely that God made it at the first such as it was to be. But this is certain, and an opinion commonly received among theologians, that the action by which he now sustains it is the same with that by which he originally created it; so that even although he had from the beginning given it no other form than that of chaos, provided only he had established certain laws of nature, and had lent it his concurrence to enable it to act as it is wont to do, it may be believed, without discredit to the miracle of creation, that, in this way alone, things purely material might, in course of time, have become such as we observe them at present; and their nature is much more easily conceived when they are beheld coming in this manner gradually into existence, than when they are only considered as produced at once in a finished and perfect state.

From the description of inanimate bodies and plants, I passed to animals, and particularly to man. But since I had not as yet sufficient knowledge to enable me to treat of these in the same manner as of the rest, that is to say, by deducing effects from their causes, and by showing from what elements and in what manner nature must produce them, I remained satisfied with the supposition that God formed the body of man wholly like to one of ours, as well in the external shape of the members as in the internal conformation of the organs, of the same matter with that I had described, and at first placed in it no rational soul, nor any other principle, in room of the vegetative or sensitive soul, beyond kindling in the heart one of those fires without light, such as I had already described, and which I thought was not different from the heat in hay that has been heaped together before it is dry, or that which causes fermentation in new wines before they are run clear of the fruit. For, when I examined the kind of functions which might, as consequences of this supposition, exist in this body, I found precisely all those which may exist in us independently of all power of thinking, and consequently without being in any measure owing to the soul; in other words, to that part of us which is distinct from the body, and of which it has been said above that the nature distinctively consists in thinking,—functions in which the animals void of reason may be said wholly to resemble us; but among which I could not discover any of those that, as dependent on thought alone, belong to us as men, while, on the other hand, I did afterwards discover these as soon as I supposed God to have created a rational soul, and to have annexed it to this body in a particular manner which I described.

But, in order to show how I there handled this matter, I mean here to give the explication of the motion of the heart and arteries, which, as the first and most general motion observed in animals, will afford the means of readily determining what should be thought of all the rest. And that there may be less difficulty in understanding what I am about to say on this subject, I advise those who are not versed in anatomy, before they commence the perusal of these observations, to take the trouble of getting dissected in their presence the heart of some large animal possessed of lungs (for this is throughout sufficiently like the human), and to have shown to them its two ventricles or cavities: in the first place, that in the right side, with which correspond two very ample tubes, viz., the hollow vein (*vena cava*), which is the principal receptacle of the blood, and the trunk of the tree, as it were, of which all the other veins in the body are branches; and the arterial vein (*vena arteriosa*), inappropriately so denominated, since it is in truth only an artery, which, taking its rise in the heart, is divided, after passing out from it, into many branches which presently disperse themselves all over the lungs; in the second place, the cavity in the left side, with which correspond in the same manner two canals in size equal to or larger than the preceding, viz., the venous artery (*arteria venosa*), likewise inappropriately thus designated, because it is simply a vein which comes from the lungs, where it is divided into many branches, interlaced with those of the arterial vein, and those of the tube called the windpipe, through which the air we breathe enters; and the great artery which, issuing from the heart, sends its branches all over the body. I should wish also that such persons were carefully shown the eleven pellicles which, like so many small valves, open and shut the four orifices that are in these two cavities, viz., three at the entrance of the hollow vein, where they are disposed in such a manner as by no means to prevent the blood which it contains from flowing into the right ventricle of the heart, and yet exactly to prevent its flowing out; three at the entrance to the arterial vein, which, arranged in a manner exactly the opposite of the former, readily permit the blood contained in this cavity to pass into the lungs, but hinder that contained in the lungs from returning to this cavity; and, in like manner, two others at the mouth of the venous artery, which allow the blood from the lungs to flow into the left cavity of the heart, but preclude its return; and three at the mouth of the great artery, which suffer the blood to flow from the heart, but prevent its reflux. Nor do we need to seek any other reason for the number of these pellicles beyond this that the orifice of the venous artery being of an oval shape from the nature of its situation, can be adequately closed with two, whereas the others being round are more conveniently closed with three. Besides, I wish such persons to observe that the grand artery and the arterial vein are of much harder and firmer texture than the venous artery and the hollow vein; and that the two last expand before entering the heart, and there form, as it were, two pouches denominated the auricles of the heart, which are composed of a substance similar to that of the heart itself; and that there is always more warmth in the heart than in any other part of the body; and, finally, that this heat is capable of causing any drop of blood that passes into the cavities rapidly to expand and dilate, just as all liquors do when allowed to fall drop by drop into a highly heated vessel.

For, after these things, it is not necessary for me to say anything more with a view to explain the motion of the heart, except that when its cavities are not full of blood, into these the blood of necessity flows,—from the hollow vein into the right, and from the venous artery into the left; because these two vessels are always full of blood, and their orifices, which are turned towards the heart, cannot then be closed. But as soon as two drops of blood have thus passed, one into each of the cavities, these drops which cannot but be very large, because the orifices through which they pass are wide, and the vessels from which they come full of blood, are immediately rarefied, and dilated by the heat they meet with. In this way they cause the whole heart to expand, and at the same time press home and shut the five small valves that are at the entrances of the two vessels from which they flow, and thus prevent any more blood from coming down into the heart, and becoming more and more rarefied, they push open the six small valves that are in the orifices of the other two vessels, through which they pass out, causing in this way all the branches of the arterial vein and of the grand artery to expand almost simultaneously with the heart—which immediately thereafter begins to contract, as do also the arteries, because the blood that has entered them has cooled, and the six small valves close, and the five of the hollow vein and of the venous artery open anew and allow a passage to other two drops of blood, which cause the heart and the arteries again to expand as before. And, because the blood which thus enters into the heart passes through these two pouches called auricles, it thence happens that their motion is the contrary of that of the heart, and that when it expands they contract. But lest those who are ignorant of the force of mathematical demonstrations, and who are not accustomed to distinguish true reasons from mere verisimilitudes, should venture, without examination, to deny what has been said, I wish it to be considered that the motion which I have now explained follows as necessarily from the very arrangement of the parts, which may be observed in the heart by the eye alone, and from the heat which may be felt with the fingers, and from the nature of the blood as learned from experience, as does the motion of a clock from the power, the situation, and shape of its counterweights and wheels.

But if it be asked how it happens that the blood in the veins, flowing in this way continually into the heart, is not exhausted, and why the arteries do not become too full, since all the blood which passes through the heart flows into them, I need only mention in reply what has been written by a physician[1] of England, who has the honour of having broken the ice on this subject, and of having been the first to teach that there are many small passages at the extremities of the arteries, through which the blood received by them from the heart passes into the small branches of the veins, whence it again returns to the heart; so that its course amounts precisely to a perpetual circulation. Of this we have abundant proof in the ordinary experience of surgeons, who, by binding the arm with a tie of moderate straitness above the part where they open the vein, cause the blood to flow more copiously than it would have done without any ligature; whereas quite the contrary would happen were they to bind it below; that is, between the hand and the opening, or were to make the ligature above the opening very tight. For it is manifest that the tie, moderately straitened, while adequate to hinder the blood already in the arm from returning towards the heart by the veins, cannot on that account prevent new blood from coming forward through the arteries, because these are situated below the veins, and their coverings, from their greater consistency, are more difficult to compress; and also that the blood which comes from the heart tends to pass through them to the hand with greater force than it does to return from the hand to the heart through the veins. And since the latter current escapes from the arm by the opening made in one of the veins, there must of necessity be certain passages below the ligature, that is, towards the extremities of the arm through which it can come thither from the arteries. This

[1] Harvey—*Lat. Tr.*

physician likewise abundantly establishes what he has advanced respecting the motion of the blood, from the existence of certain pellicles, so disposed in various places along the course of the veins, in the manner of small valves, as not to permit the blood to pass from the middle of the body towards the extremities, but only to return from the extremities to the heart; and farther, from experience which shows that all the blood which is in the body may flow out of it in a very short time through a single artery that has been cut, even although this had been closely tied in the immediate neighbourhood of the heart, and cut between the heart and the ligature, so as to prevent the supposition that the blood flowing out of it could come from any other quarter than the heart.

But there are many other circumstances which evince that what I have alleged is the true cause of the motion of the blood: thus, in the first place, the difference that is observed between the blood which flows from the veins, and that from the arteries, can only arise from this, that being rarefied, and, as it were, distilled by passing through the heart, it is thinner, and more vivid, and warmer immediately after leaving the heart, in other words, when in the arteries, than it was a short time before passing into either, in other words, when it was in the veins; and if attention be given, it will be found that this difference is very marked only in the neighbourhood of the heart; and is not so evident in parts more remote from it. In the next place, the consistency of the coats of which the arterial vein and the great artery are composed, sufficiently shows that the blood is impelled against them with more force than against the veins. And why should the left cavity of the heart and the great artery be wider and larger than the right cavity and the arterial vein, were it not that the blood of the venous artery, having only been in the lungs after it has passed through the heart, is thinner, and rarefies more readily, and in a higher degree, than the blood which proceeds immediately from the hollow vein? And what can physicians conjecture from feeling the pulse unless they know that according as the blood changes its nature it can be rarefied by the warmth of the heart, in a higher or lower degree, and more or less quickly than before? And if it be inquired how this heat is communicated to the other members, must it not be admitted that this is effected by means of the blood, which, passing through the heart, is there heated anew, and thence diffused over all the body? Whence it happens, that if the blood be withdrawn from any part, the heat is likewise withdrawn by the same means; and although the heart were as hot as glowing iron, it would not be capable of warming the feet and hands as at present, unless it continually sent thither new blood. We likewise perceive from this, that the true use of respiration is to bring sufficient fresh air into the lungs, to cause the blood which flows into them from the right ventricle of the heart, where it has been rarefied and, as it were, changed into vapours, to become thick, and to convert it anew into blood, before it flows into the left cavity, without which process it would be unfit for the nourishment of the fire that is there. This receives confirmation from the circumstance, that it is observed of animals destitute of lungs that they have also but one cavity in the heart, and that in children who cannot use them while in the womb, there is a hole through which the blood flows from the hollow vein into the left cavity of the heart, and a tube through which it passes from the arterial vein into the grand artery without passing through the lung. In the next place, how could digestion be carried on in the stomach unless the heart communicated heat to it through the arteries, and along with this certain of the more fluid parts of the blood, which assist in the dissolution of the food that has been taken in? Is not also the operation which converts the juice of food into blood easily comprehended, when it is considered that it is distilled by passing and repassing through the heart perhaps more than one or two hundred times in a day? And what more need be adduced to explain nutrition, and the production of the different humours of the body, beyond saying, that the force with which the blood, in being rarefied, passes from the heart towards the extremities of the arteries, causes certain of its parts to remain in the members at which they arrive, and there occupy the place of some others expelled by them; and that according to the situation, shape, or smallness of the pores with which they meet, some rather than others flow into certain parts, in the same way that some sieves are observed to act, which, by being variously perforated, serve to separate different species of grain? And, in the last place, what above all is here worthy of observation, is the generation of the animal spirits, which are like a very subtle wind, or rather a very pure and vivid flame which, continually ascending in great abundance from the heart to the brain, thence penetrates through the nerves into the muscles, and gives motion to all the members; so that to account for other parts of the blood which, as most agitated and penetrating, are the fittest to compose these spirits, proceeding towards the brain, it is not necessary to suppose any other cause, than simply, that the arteries which carry them thither proceed from the heart in the most direct lines, and that, according to the rules of mechanics, which are the same with those of nature, when many objects tend at once to the same point where there is not sufficient room for all (as is the case with the parts of the blood which flow forth from the left cavity of the heart and tend towards the brain), the weaker and less agitated parts must necessarily be driven aside from that point by the stronger which alone in this way reach it.

I had expounded all these matters with sufficient minuteness in the treatise which I formerly thought of publishing. And after these, I had shown what must be the fabric of the nerves and muscles of the human body to give the animal spirits contained in it the power to move the members, as when we see heads shortly after they have been struck off still move and bite the earth, although no longer animated; what changes must take place in the brain to produce waking, sleep, and dreams; how light, sounds, odours, tastes, heat, and all the other qualities of external objects impress it with different ideas by means of the senses; how hunger, thirst, and the other internal affections can likewise impress upon it divers ideas; what must be understood by the common sense (sensus communis) in which these ideas are received, by the memory which retains them, by the fantasy which can change them in various ways, and out of them compose new ideas, and which, by the same means, distributing the animal spirits through the muscles, can cause the members of such a body to move in as many different ways, and in a manner as suited, whether to the objects that are presented to its senses or to its internal affections, as can take place in our own case apart from the guidance of the will. Nor will this appear at all strange to those who are acquainted with the variety of movements performed by the different automata, or moving machines fabricated by human industry, and that with help of but few pieces compared with the great multitude of bones, muscles, nerves, arteries, veins, and other parts that are found in the body of each animal. Such persons will look upon this body as a machine made by the hands of God, which is incomparably better arranged, and adequate to movements more admirable than is any machine of human invention. And here I specially stayed to show that, were there such machines exactly resembling in organs and outward form an ape or any other irrational animal, we could have no means of knowing that they were in any respect of a different nature from these animals; but if there were machines bearing the image of our bodies, and capable of imitating our actions as far as it is morally possible, there would still remain two most certain tests whereby to know that they were not therefore really men. Of these the first is that they could never use words or other signs arranged in such a manner as is competent to us in order to declare our thoughts to others: for we may easily conceive a machine to be so constructed that it emits vocables, and even that it emits some correspondent to the action upon it of external objects which cause a change in its organs; for example, if touched in a particular place it may demand what we wish to say to it; if in another it may cry out that it is hurt, and such like; but not that it should arrange them variously so as appositely to reply to what is said in its presence, as men of the lowest grade of intellect can do. The second test is, that although such machines might execute many things with equal or perhaps greater perfection than any of us, they would, without doubt, fail in certain others from which it could be discovered that they did not act from knowledge, but solely from the disposition of their organs: for while reason is an universal instrument that is alike available on every occasion, these organs, on the contrary, need a particular

arrangement for each particular action; whence it must be morally impossible that there should exist in any machine a diversity of organs sufficient to enable it to act in all the occurrences of life, in the way in which our reason enables us to
act. Again, by means of these two tests we may likewise know
the difference between men and brutes. For it is highly deserving of remark, that there are no men so dull and stupid,
not even idiots, as to be incapable of joining together different
words, and thereby constructing a declaration by which to
make their thoughts understood; and that on the other hand,
there is no other animal, however perfect or happily circum-
stanced, which can do the like. Nor does this inability arise
from want of organs: for we observe that magpies and parrots
can utter words like ourselves, and are yet unable to speak as
we do, that is, so as to show that they understand what they
say; in place of which men born deaf and dumb, and thus not
less, but rather more than the brutes, destitute of the organs
which others use in speaking, are in the habit of spontaneously inventing certain signs by which they discover their
thoughts to those who, being usually in their company, have
leisure to learn their language. And this proves not only that
the brutes have less reason than man, but that they have none
at all: for we see that very little is required to enable a person
to speak; and since a certain inequality of capacity is observable among animals of the same species, as well as among
men, and since some are more capable of being instructed
than others, it is incredible that the most perfect ape or parrot
of its species, should not in this be equal to the most stupid
infant of its kind, or at least to one that was crack-brained,
unless the soul of brutes were of a nature wholly different
from ours. And we ought not to confound speech with the
natural movements which indicate the passions, and can be
imitated by machines as well as manifested by animals; nor
must it be thought with certain of the ancients, that the brutes
speak, although we do not understand their language. For if
such were the case, since they are endowed with many organs
analogous to ours, they could as easily communicate their
thoughts to us as to their fellows. It is also very worthy of
remark, that, though there are many animals which manifest

more industry than we in certain of their actions, the same
animals are yet observed to show none at all in many others:
so that the circumstance that they do better than we does not
prove that they are endowed with mind, for it would thence
follow that they possessed greater reason than any of us, and
could surpass us in all things; on the contrary, it rather proves
that they are destitute of reason, and that it is nature which
acts in them according to the disposition of their organs: thus
it is seen, that a clock composed only of wheels and weights
can number the hours and measure time more exactly than we
with all our skill.

I had after this described the reasonable soul, and shown
that it could by no means be educed from the power of matter,
as the other things of which I had spoken, but that it must
be expressly created; and that it is not sufficient that it be
lodged in the human body exactly like a pilot in a ship, unless
perhaps to move its members, but that it is necessary for it
to be joined and united more closely to the body, in order
to have sensations and appetites similar to ours, and thus constitute a real man. I here entered, in conclusion, upon the
subject of the soul at considerable length, because it is of the
greatest moment: for after the error of those who deny the
existence of God, an error which I think I have already sufficiently refuted, there is none that is more powerful in leading
feeble minds astray from the straight path of virtue than the
supposition that the soul of the brutes is of the same nature
with our own; and consequently that after this life we have
nothing to hope for or fear, more than flies and ants; in place
of which, when we know how far they differ we much better
comprehend the reasons which establish that the soul is of a
nature wholly independent of the body, and that consequently
it is not liable to die with the latter; and, finally, because no
other causes are observed capable of destroying it, we are naturally led thence to judge that it is immortal.

PART VI

Three years have now elapsed since I finished the treatise containing all these matters; and I was beginning to revise it, with the view to put it into the hands of a printer, when I learned that persons to whom I greatly defer, and whose authority over my actions is hardly less influential than is my own reason over my thoughts, had condemned a certain doctrine in physics, published a short time previously by another individual,[1] to which I will not say that I adhered, but only that, previously to their censure, I had observed in it nothing which I could imagine to be prejudicial either to religion or to the state, and nothing therefore which would have prevented me from giving expression to it in writing, if reason had persuaded me of its truth; and this led me to fear lest among my own doctrines likewise some one might be found in which I had departed from the truth, notwithstanding the great care I have always taken not to accord belief to new opinions of which I had not the most certain demonstrations, and not to give expression to aught that might tend to the hurt of any one. This has been sufficient to make me alter my purpose of publishing them; for although the reasons by which I had been induced to take this resolution were very strong, yet my inclination, which has always been hostile to writing books, enabled me immediately to discover other considerations sufficient to excuse me for not undertaking the task. And these reasons, on one side and the other, are such, that not only is it in some measure my interest here to state them, but that of the public, perhaps, to know them.

[1] Galileo.—*Tr.*

I have never made much account of what has proceeded
from my own mind; and so long as I gathered no other advantage from the method I employ beyond satisfying myself
on some difficulties belonging to the speculative sciences, or
endeavouring to regulate my actions according to the principles it taught me, I never thought myself bound to publish
anything respecting it. For in what regards manners, every one
is so full of his own wisdom, that there might be found as
many reformers as heads, if any were allowed to take upon
themselves the task of mending them, except those whom God
has constituted the supreme rulers of his people, or to whom
he has given sufficient grace and zeal to be prophets; and although my speculations greatly pleased myself, I believed that
others had theirs, which perhaps pleased them still more. But
as soon as I had acquired some general notions respecting
physics, and beginning to make trial of them in various particular difficulties, had observed how far they can carry us,
and how much they differ from the principles that have been
employed up to the present time, I believed that I could not
keep them concealed without sinning grievously against the
law by which we are bound to promote, as far as in us lies, the
general good of mankind. For by them I perceived it to be
possible to arrive at knowledge highly useful in life; and in
room of the speculative philosophy usually taught in the
schools, to discover a practical, by means of which, knowing
the force and action of fire, water, air, the stars, the heavens,
and all the other bodies that surround us, as distinctly as we
know the various crafts of our artisans, we might also apply
them in the same way to all the uses to which they are
adapted, and thus render ourselves the lords and possessors of
nature. And this is a result to be desired, not only in order to
the invention of an infinity of arts, by which we might be
enabled to enjoy without any trouble the fruits of the earth,
and all its comforts, but also and especially for the preservation of health, which is without doubt, of all the blessings of
this life, the first and fundamental one; for the mind is so
intimately dependent upon the condition and relation of the
organs of the body, that if any means can ever be found to
render men wiser and more ingenious than hitherto, I believe

that it is in medicine they must be sought for. It is true that the science of medicine, as it now exists, contains few things whose utility is very remarkable: but without any wish to depreciate it, I am confident that there is no one, even among those whose profession it is, who does not admit that all at present known in it is almost nothing in comparison of what remains to be discovered; and that we could free ourselves from an infinity of maladies of body as well as of mind, and perhaps also even from the debility of age, if we had sufficiently ample knowledge of their causes, and of all the remedies provided for us by nature. But since I designed to employ my whole life in the search after so necessary a science, and since I had fallen in with a path which seems to me such, that if any one follow it he must inevitably reach the end desired, unless he be hindered either by the shortness of life or the want of experiments, I judged that there could be no more effectual provision against these two impediments than if I were faithfully to communicate to the public all the little I might myself have found, and incite men of superior genius to strive to proceed farther, by contributing, each according to his inclination and ability, to the experiments which it would be necessary to make, and also by informing the public of all they might discover, so that, by the last beginning where those before them had left off, and thus connecting the lives and labours of many, we might collectively proceed much farther than each by himself could do.

I remarked, moreover, with respect to experiments, that they become always more necessary the more one is advanced in knowledge; for, at the commencement, it is better to make use only of what is spontaneously presented to our senses, and of which we cannot remain ignorant, provided we bestow on it any reflection, however slight, than to concern ourselves about more uncommon and recondite phenomena: the reason of which is, that the more uncommon often only mislead us so long as the causes of the more ordinary are still unknown; and the circumstances upon which they depend are almost always so special and minute as to be highly difficult to detect. But in this I have adopted the following order: first, I have essayed to find in general the principles, or first causes of all

that is or can be in the world, without taking into consideration for this end anything but God himself who has created
it, and without educing them from any other source than from
certain germs of truths naturally existing in our minds. In
the second place, I examined what were the first and most
ordinary effects that could be deduced from these causes; and
it appears to me that, in this way, I have found heavens, stars,
an earth, and even on the earth, water, air, fire, minerals,
and some other things of this kind, which of all others are the
most common and simple, and hence the easiest to know.
Afterwards, when I wished to descend to the more particular,
so many diverse objects presented themselves to me, that I
believed it to be impossible for the human mind to distinguish
the forms or species of bodies that are upon the earth, from
an infinity of others which might have been, if it had pleased
God to place them there, or consequently to apply them to
our use, unless we rise to causes through their effects, and
avail ourselves of many particular experiments. Thereupon,
turning over in my mind all the objects that had ever been
presented to my senses, I freely venture to state that I have
never observed any which I could not satisfactorily explain
by the principles I had discovered. But it is necessary also to
confess that the power of nature is so ample and vast, and
these principles so simple and general, that I have hardly observed a single particular effect which I cannot at once recognise as capable of being deduced in many different modes
from the principles, and that my greatest difficulty usually is
to discover in which of these modes the effect is dependent
upon them; for out of this difficulty I cannot otherwise extri-
cate myself than by again seeking certain experiments, which
may be such that their result is not the same, if it is in the one
of these modes that we must explain it, as it would be if it
were to be explained in the other. As to what remains, I am
now in a position to discern, as I think, with sufficient clearness what course must be taken to make the majority of those
experiments which may conduce to this end: but I perceive
likewise that they are such and so numerous, that neither my
hands nor my income, though it were a thousand times larger
than it is, would be sufficient for them all; so that, according

as henceforward I shall have the means of making more or fewer experiments, I shall in the same proportion make greater or less progress in the knowledge of nature. This was what I had hoped to make known by the treatise I had written, and so clearly to exhibit the advantage that would thence accrue to the public, as to induce all who have the common good of man at heart, that is, all who are virtuous in truth, and not merely in appearance, or according to opinion, as well to communicate to me the experiments they had already made, as to assist me in those that remain to be made.

But since that time other reasons have occurred to me, by which I have been led to change my opinion, and to think that I ought indeed to go on committing to writing all the results which I deemed of any moment, as soon as I should have tested their truth, and to bestow the same care upon them as I would have done had it been my design to publish them. This course commended itself to me, as well because I thus afforded myself more ample inducement to examine them thoroughly, for doubtless that is always more narrowly scrutinised which we believe will be read by many, than that which is written merely for our private use (and frequently what has seemed to me true when I first conceived it, has appeared false when I have set about committing it to writing), as because I thus lost no opportunity of advancing the interests of the public, as far as in me lay, and since thus likewise, if my writings possess any value, those into whose hands they may fall after my death may be able to put them to what use they deem proper. But I resolved by no means to consent to their publication during my lifetime, lest either the oppositions or the controversies to which they might give rise, or even the reputation, such as it might be, which they would acquire for me, should be any occasion of my losing the time that I had set apart for my own improvement. For though it be true that every one is bound to promote to the extent of his ability the good of others, and that to be useful to no one is really to be worthless, yet it is likewise true that our cares ought to extend beyond the present; and it is good to omit doing what might perhaps bring some profit to the living, when we have in view the accomplishment of other ends that will be of much greater advantage to posterity. And in truth, I am quite willing it should be known that the little I have hitherto learned is almost nothing in comparison with that of which I am ignorant, and to the knowledge of which I do not despair of being able to attain; for it is much the same with those who gradually discover truth in the sciences, as with those who when growing rich find less difficulty in making great acquisitions, than they formerly experienced when poor in making acquisitions of much smaller amount. Or they may be compared to the commanders of armies, whose forces usually increase in proportion to their victories, and who need greater prudence to keep together the residue of their troops after a defeat than after a victory to take towns and provinces. For he truly engages in battle who endeavours to surmount all the difficulties and errors which prevent him from reaching the knowledge of truth, and he is overcome in fight who admits a false opinion touching a matter of any generality and importance, and he requires thereafter much more skill to recover his former position than to make great advances when once in possession of thoroughly ascertained principles. As for myself, if I have succeeded in discovering any truths in the sciences (and I trust that what is contained in this volume will show that I have found some), I can declare that they are but the consequences and results of five or six principal difficulties which I have surmounted, and my encounters with which I reckoned as battles in which victory declared for me. I will not hesitate even to avow my belief that nothing further is wanting to enable me fully to realise my designs than to gain two or three similar victories; and that I am not so far advanced in years but that, according to the ordinary course of nature, I may still have sufficient leisure for this end. But I conceive myself the more bound to husband the time that remains the greater my expectation of being able to employ it aright, and I should doubtless have much to rob me of it, were I to publish the principles of my physics: for although they are almost all so evident that to assent to them no more is needed than simply to understand them, and although there is not one of them of which I do not expect to be able to give demonstration, yet, as it is impossible that they can be in accordance with all the diverse opinions of others, I foresee that I should frequently be turned aside from my grand design, on occasion of the opposition which they would be sure to awaken.

It may be said, that these oppositions would be useful both in making me aware of my errors, and, if my speculations contain anything of value, in bringing others to a fuller understanding of it; and still farther, as many can see better than one, in leading others who are now beginning to avail themselves of my principles, to assist me in turn with their discoveries. But though I recognise my extreme liability to error, and scarce ever trust to the first thoughts which occur to me, yet the experience I have had of possible objections to my views prevents me from anticipating any profit from them. For I have already had frequent proof of the judgments, as well of those I esteemed friends, as of some others to whom I thought I was an object of indifference, and even of some whose malignity and envy would, I knew, determine them to endeavour to discover what partiality concealed from the eyes of my friends. But it has rarely happened that anything has been objected to me which I had myself altogether overlooked, unless it were something far removed from the subject: so that I have never met with a single critic of my opinions who did not appear to me either less rigorous or less equitable than myself. And further, I have never observed that any truth before unknown has been brought to light by the disputations that are practised in the schools; for while each strives for the victory, each is much more occupied in making the best of mere verisimilitude, than in weighing the reasons on both sides of the question; and those who have been long good advocates are not afterwards on that account the better judges.

As for the advantage that others would derive from the communication of my thoughts, it could not be very great; because I have not yet so far prosecuted them as that much does not remain to be added before they can be applied to practice. And I think I may say without vanity, that if there is any one who can carry them out that length, it must be myself rather than another: not that there may not be in the world many minds incomparably superior to mine, but because one cannot so well seize a thing and make it one's own, when it has been learned from another, as when one has himself discovered it. And so true is this of the present subject that, though I have often explained some of my opinions to persons of much acuteness, who, whilst I was speaking, appeared to understand them very distinctly, yet, when they repeated them, I have observed that they almost always changed them to such an extent that I could no longer acknowledge them as mine. I am glad, by the way, to take this opportunity of requesting posterity never to believe on hearsay that anything has proceeded from me which has not been published by myself; and I am not at all astonished at the extravagances attributed to those ancient philosophers whose own writings we do not possess; whose thoughts, however, I do not on that account suppose to have been really absurd, seeing they were among the ablest men of their times, but only that these have been falsely represented to us. It is observable, accordingly, that scarcely in a single instance has any one of their disciples surpassed them; and I am quite sure that the most devoted of the present followers of Aristotle would think themselves happy if they had as much knowledge of nature as he possessed, were it even under the condition that they should never afterwards attain to higher. In this respect they are like the ivy which never strives to rise above the tree that sustains it, and which frequently even returns downwards when it has reached the top; for it seems to me that they also sink, in other words, render themselves less wise than they would be if they gave up study, who, not contented with knowing all that is intelligibly explained in their author, desire in addition to find in him the solution of many difficulties of which he says not a word, and never perhaps so much as thought. Their fashion of philosophising, however, is well suited to persons whose abilities fall below mediocrity; for the obscurity of the distinctions and principles of which they make use enables them to speak of all things with as much confidence as if they really knew them, and to defend all that they say on any subject against the most subtle and skilful, without its being possible for any one to convict them of error. In this they seem to me to be like a blind man, who, in order to fight on equal terms with a person that sees, should have made him descend to the bottom of an intensely dark cave: and I may say that such persons have an interest in my refraining from publishing the principles of the philosophy of which I make use; for, since these are of a kind the simplest and most evident, I should, by publishing them, do much the same as if I were to throw open the windows, and allow the light of day to enter the cave into which the combatants had descended. But even superior men have no reason for any great anxiety to know these principles, for if what they desire is to be able to speak of all things, and to acquire a reputation for learning, they will gain their end more easily by remaining satisfied with the appearance of truth, which can be found without much difficulty in all sorts of matters, than by seeking the truth itself which unfolds itself but slowly and that only in some departments, while it obliges us, when we have to speak of others, freely to confess our ignorance. If, however, they prefer the knowledge of some few truths to the vanity of appearing ignorant of none, as such knowledge is undoubtedly much to be preferred, and, if they choose to follow a course similar to mine, they do not require for this that I should say anything more than I have already said in this discourse. For if they are capable of making greater advancement than I have made, they will much more be able of themselves to discover all that I believe myself to have found; since as I have never examined aught except in order, it is certain that what yet remains to be discovered is in itself more difficult and recondite, than that which I have already been enabled to find, and the gratification would be much less in learning it from me than in discovering it for themselves. Besides this, the habit which they will acquire, by seeking first what is easy, and then passing onward slowly and step by step to the more difficult, will benefit them more than all my instructions. Thus, in my own case, I am persuaded that if I had been taught from my youth all the truths of which I have since sought out demonstrations, and had thus learned them without labour, I should never, perhaps, have known any beyond these; at least, I should never have acquired the habit and the facility which I think I possess in always discovering new truths in proportion as I give myself to the search. And, in a single word, if there is any work in the world which cannot be so well finished by another as by him who has commenced it, it is that at which I labour.

It is true, indeed, as regards the experiments which may conduce to this end, that one man is not equal to the task of making them all; but yet he can advantageously avail himself, in this work, of no hands besides his own, unless those of artisans, or parties of the same kind, whom he could pay, and whom the hope of gain (a means of great efficacy) might stimulate to accuracy in the performance of what was prescribed to them. For as to those who, through curiosity or a desire of learning, of their own accord, perhaps, offer him their services, besides that in general their promises exceed their performance, and that they sketch out fine designs of which not one is ever realised, they will, without doubt, expect to be compensated for their trouble by the explication of some difficulties, or, at least, by compliments and useless speeches, in which he cannot spend any portion of his time without loss to himself. And as for the experiments that others have already made, even although these parties should be willing of themselves to communicate them to him (which is what those who esteem them secrets will never do), the experiments are, for the most part, accompanied with so many circumstances and superfluous elements, as to make it exceedingly difficult to disentangle the truth from its adjuncts; besides, he will find almost all of them so ill described, or even so false (because those who made them have wished to see in them only such facts as they deemed conformable to their principles), that, if in the entire number there should be some of a nature suited to his purpose, still their value could not compensate for the time what would be necessary to make the selection. So that if there existed any one whom we assuredly knew to be capable of making discoveries of the highest kind, and of the greatest possible utility to the public; and if all other men were therefore eager by all means to assist him in successfully prosecuting his designs, I do not see that they could do aught else for him beyond contributing to defray the expenses of the experiments that might be necessary; and for the rest, prevent his being deprived of his leisure by the unseasonable interruptions of any one. But besides that I neither have so high an opinion of myself as to be willing to make promise of anything extraordinary, nor feed on imaginations so vain as to fancy that the public must be much interested in my designs; I do not, on the other hand, own a soul so mean as to be capable of accepting from any one a favour of which it could be supposed that I was unworthy.

These considerations taken together were the reason why, for the last three years, I have been unwilling to publish the treatise I had on hand, and why I even resolved to give publicity during my life to no other that was so general, or by which the principles of my physics might be understood. But since then, two other reasons have come into operation that have determined me here to subjoin some particular specimens, and give the public some account of my doings and designs. Of these considerations, the first is, that if I failed to do so, many who were cognisant of my previous intention to publish some writings, might have imagined that the reasons which induced me to refrain from so doing, were less to my credit than they really are; for although I am not immoderately desirous of glory, or even, if I may venture so to say, although I am averse from it in so far as I deem it hostile to repose which I hold in greater account than aught else, yet, at the same time, I have never sought to conceal my actions as if they were crimes, nor made use of many precautions that I might remain unknown; and this partly because I should have thought such a course of conduct a wrong against myself, and partly because it would have occasioned me some sort of uneasiness which would again have been contrary to the perfect mental tranquillity which I court. And forasmuch as, while thus indifferent to the thought alike of fame or of forgetfulness, I have yet been unable to prevent myself from acquiring some sort of reputation, I have thought it incumbent on me to do my best to save myself at least from being ill-spoken of. The other reason that has determined me to commit to writing these specimens of philosophy is, that I am becoming daily more and more alive to the delay which my design of self-instruction suffers, for want of the infinity of experiments I require, and which it is impossible for me to make without the assistance of others: and, without flattering myself so much as to expect the public to take a large share in my interests, I am yet unwilling to be found so far wanting in the duty I owe to myself, as to give occasion to those who shall survive me to make it matter of reproach against me some day, that I might have left them many things in a much more perfect state than I have done, had I not too much neglected to make them aware of the ways in which they could have promoted the accomplishment of my designs.

And I thought that it was easy for me to select some matters which should neither be obnoxious to much controversy, nor should compel me to expound more of my principles than I desired, and which should yet be sufficient clearly to exhibit what I can or cannot accomplish in the sciences. Whether or not I have succeeded in this it is not for me to say; and I do not wish to forestall the judgments of others by speaking myself of my writings; but it will gratify me if they be examined, and, to afford the greater inducement to this, I request all who may have any objections to make to them, to take the trouble of forwarding these to my publisher, who will give me notice of them, that I may endeavour to subjoin at the same time my reply; and in this way readers seeing both at once will more easily determine where the truth lies; for I do not engage in any case to make prolix replies, but only with perfect frankness to avow my errors if I am convinced of them, or if I cannot perceive them, simply to state what I think is required for defence of the matters I have written, adding thereto no explication of any new matter that it may not be necessary to pass without end from one thing to another.

If some of the matters of which I have spoken in the beginning of the "Dioptrics" and "Meteorics" should offend at first sight, because I call them hypotheses and seem indifferent about giving proof of them, I request a patient and attentive reading of the whole, from which I hope those hesitating will derive satisfaction; for it appears to me that the reasonings are so mutually connected in these treatises, that, as the last are demonstrated by the first which are their causes, the first are in their turn demonstrated by the last which are their effects. Nor must it be imagined that I here commit the fallacy which the logicians call a circle; for since experience renders the majority of these effects most certain, the causes from which I deduce them do not serve so much to establish their reality as to explain their existence; but on the contrary, the reality of the causes is established by the reality of the effects. Nor have I called them hypotheses with any other end in view except that it may be known that I think I am able to deduce them from those first truths which I have already expounded; and yet that I have expressly determined not to do so, to prevent a certain class of minds from thence taking occasion to build some extravagant philosophy upon what they may take to be my principles, and my being blamed for it. I refer to those who imagine that they can master in a day all that another has taken twenty years to think out, as soon as he has spoken two or three words to them on the subject; or who are the more liable to error and the less capable of perceiving truth in very proportion as they are more subtle and lively. As to the opinions which are truly and wholly mine, I offer no apology for them as new,—persuaded as I am that if their reasons be well considered they will be found to be so simple and so conformed to common sense as to appear less extraordinary and less paradoxical than any others which can be held on the same subjects; nor do I even boast of being the earliest discoverer of any of them, but only of having adopted them, neither because they had nor because they had not been held by others, but solely because reason has convinced me of their truth.

Though artisans may not be able at once to execute the invention which is explained in the "Dioptrics," I do not think that any one on that account is entitled to condemn it; for since address and practice are required in order so to make and adjust the machines described by me as not to overlook the smallest particular, I should not be less astonished if they succeeded on the first attempt than if a person were in one day to become an accomplished performer on the guitar, by merely having excellent sheets of music set up before him. And if I write in French, which is the language of my country, in preference to Latin, which is that of my preceptors, it is because I expect that those who make use of their unprejudiced natural reason will be better judges of my opinions than those who give heed to the writings of the ancients only; and as for those who unite good sense with habits of study, whom alone I desire for judges, they will not, I feel assured, be so partial to Latin as to refuse to listen to my reasonings merely because I expound them in the vulgar tongue.

In conclusion, I am unwilling here to say anything very specific of the progress which I expect to make for the future in the sciences, or to bind myself to the public by any promise which I am not certain of being able to fulfil; but this only will I say, that I have resolved to devote what time I may still have to live to no other occupation than that of endeavouring to acquire some knowledge of Nature, which shall be of such a kind as to enable us therefrom to deduce rules in medicine of greater certainty than those at present in use; and that my inclination is so much opposed to all other pursuits, especially to such as cannot be useful to some without being hurtful to others, that if, by any circumstances, I had been constrained to engage in such, I do not believe that I should have been able to succeed. Of this I here make a public declaration, though well aware that it cannot serve to procure for me any consideration in the world, which, however, I do not in the least affect; and I shall always hold myself more obliged to those through whose favour I am permitted to enjoy my retirement without interruption than to any who might offer me the highest earthly preferments.

MEDITATIONS

ON

THE FIRST PHILOSOPHY

THE VERY SAGE AND ILLUSTRIOUS

THE

DEAN AND DOCTORS OF THE SACRED FACULTY OF THEOLOGY OF PARIS

GENTLEMEN,—The motive which impels me to present this treatise to you is so reasonable, and, when you shall learn its design, I am confident that you also will consider that there is ground so valid for your taking it under your protection, that I can in no way better recommend it to you than by briefly stating the end which I proposed to myself in it. I have always been of opinion that the two questions respecting God and the soul were the chief of those that ought to be determined by help of philosophy rather than of theology; for although to us, the faithful, it be sufficient to hold as matters of faith, that the human soul does not perish with the body, and that God exists, it yet assuredly seems impossible ever to persuade infidels of the reality of any religion, or almost even any moral virtue, unless, first of all, those two things be proved to them by natural reason. And since in this life there are frequently greater rewards held out to vice than to virtue, few would prefer the right to the useful, if they were restrained neither by the fear of God nor the expectation of another life; and although it is quite true that the existence of God is to be believed since it is taught in the sacred Scriptures, and that, on the other hand, the sacred Scriptures are to be believed because they come from God (for since faith is a gift of God, the same Being who bestows grace to enable us to believe other things, can likewise impart of it to enable us to believe his own existence), nevertheless, this cannot be submitted to infidels, who would consider that the reasoning proceeded in a circle. And, indeed, I have observed that you, with all the other theologians, not only affirmed the sufficiency of natural reason for the proof of the existence of God, but also, that it may be inferred from sacred Scripture, that the knowledge of God is much clearer than of many created things, and that it is really so easy of acquisition as to leave those who do not possess it blame-worthy. This is manifest from these words of the Book of Wisdom, chap. xiii., where it is said, *Howbeit they are not to be excused; for if their understanding was so great that they could discern the world and the creatures; why did they not rather find out the Lord thereof?* And in Romans, chap. i., it is said that they are *without excuse;* and again, in the same place, by these words,—*That which may be known of God is manifest in them*—we seem to be admonished that all which can be known of God may be made manifest by reasons obtained from no other source than the inspection of our own minds. I have, therefore, thought that it would not be un-becoming in me to inquire how and by what way, without going out of ourselves, God may be more easily and certainly known than the things of the world.

And as regards the soul, although many have judged that its nature could not be easily discovered, and some have even ventured to say that human reason led to the conclusion that it perished with the body, and that the contrary opinion could be held through faith alone; nevertheless, since the Lateran Council, held under Leo X. (in session viii.), condemns these, and expressly enjoins Christian philosophers to refute their arguments, and establish the truth according to their ability, I have ventured to attempt it in this work. Moreover, I am aware that most of the irreligious deny the existence of God, and the distinctness of the human soul from the body, for no other reason than because these points, as they allege, have never as yet been demonstrated. Now, although I am by no means of their opinion, but, on the contrary, hold that almost all the proofs which have been adduced on these questions by great men, possess, when rightly understood, the force of dem-onstrations, and that it is next to impossible to discover new, yet there is, I apprehend, no more useful service to be per-formed in philosophy, than if some one were, once for all, carefully to seek out the best of these reasons, and expound them so accurately and clearly that, for the future, it might be manifest to all that they are real demonstrations. And finally, since many persons were greatly desirous of this, who knew that I had cultivated a certain method of resolving all kinds of difficulties in the sciences, which is not indeed new (there being nothing older than truth), but of which they were aware I had made successful use in other instances, I judged it to be my duty to make trial of it also on the present matter.

Now the sum of what I have been able to accomplish on the subject is contained in this treatise. Not that I here essayed to collect all the diverse reasons which might be adduced as proofs on his subject, for this does not seem to be necessary, unless on matters where no one proof of adequate certainty is to be had; but I treated the first and chief alone in such a manner that I should venture now to propose them as demonstrations of the highest certainty and evidence. And I will also add that they are such as to lead me to think that there is no way open to the mind of man by which proofs superior to them can ever be discovered; for the importance of the subject, and the glory of God, to which all this relates, constrain me to speak here somewhat more freely of myself than I have been accustomed to do. Nevertheless, whatever certitude and evidence I may find in these demonstrations, I cannot therefore persuade myself that they are level to the comprehension of all. But just as in geometry there are many of the demonstrations of Archimedes, Apollonius, Pappus, and others, which, though received by all as evident even and certain (because indeed they manifestly contain nothing which, considered by itself, it is not very easy to understand, and no consequents that are inaccurately related to their antecedents), are nevertheless understood by a very limited number, because they are somewhat long, and demand the whole attention of the reader: so in the same way, although I consider the demonstrations of which I here make use, to be equal or even superior to the geometrical in certitude and evidence, I am afraid, nevertheless, that they will not be adequately understood by many, as well because they also are somewhat long and involved, as chiefly because they require the mind to be entirely free from prejudice, and able with ease to detach itself from the commerce of the senses. And, to speak the truth, the ability for metaphysical studies is less general than for those of geometry. And, besides, there is still this difference that, as in geometry, all are persuaded that nothing is usually advanced of which there is not a certain demonstration, those but partially versed in it err more frequently in assenting to what is false, from a desire of seeming to understand it, than in denying what is true. In philosophy, on the other hand, where it is believed that all is doubtful, few sincerely give themselves to the search after truth, and by far the greater number seek the reputation of bold thinkers by audaciously impugning such truths as are of the greatest moment.

Hence it is that, whatever force my reasonings may possess, yet because they belong to philosophy, I do not expect they will have much effect on the minds of men, unless you extend to them your patronage and approval. But since your faculty is held in so great esteem by all, and since the name of SORBONNE is of such authority, that not only in matters of faith, but even also in what regards human philosophy, has the judgment of no other society, after the sacred councils, received so great deference, it being the universal conviction that it is impossible elsewhere to find greater perspicacity and solidity, or greater wisdom and integrity in giving judgment, I doubt not, —if you but condescend to pay so much regard to this treatise as to be willing, in the first place, to correct it (for, mindful not only of my humanity, but chiefly also of my ignorance, I do not affirm that it is free from errors); in the second place, to supply what is wanting in it, to perfect what is incomplete, and to give more ample illustration where it is demanded, or at least to indicate these defects to myself that I may endeavour to remedy them; and, finally, when the reasonings contained in it, by which the existence of God and the distinction of the human soul from the body are established, shall have been brought to such degree of perspicuity as to be esteemed exact demonstrations, of which I am assured they admit, if you condescend to accord them the authority of your approbation, and render a public testimony of their truth and certainty,—I doubt not, I say, but that henceforward all

the errors which have ever been entertained on these questions will very soon be effaced from the minds of men. For
truth itself will readily lead the remainder of the ingenious
and the learned to subscribe to your judgment; and your authority will cause the atheists, who are in general sciolists
rather than ingenious or learned, to lay aside the spirit of
contradiction, and lead them, perhaps, to do battle in their
own persons for reasonings which they find considered demonstrations by all men of genius, lest they should seem not to
understand them; and, finally, the rest of mankind will readily
trust to so many testimonies, and there will no longer be any
one who will venture to doubt either the existence of God or
the real distinction of mind and body. It is for you, in your
singular wisdom, to judge of the importance of the establishment of such beliefs [who are cognisant of the disorders which
doubt of these truths produces].[1] But it would not here become me to commend at greater length the cause of God and
religion to you, who have always proved the strongest support
of the Catholic Church.

[1] The *square* brackets, here and throughout the Meditations, are
used to mark additions to the original of the revised French trans-
lation.

PREFACE TO THE READER

I have already slightly touched upon the questions respecting the existence of God and the nature of the human soul, in the *Discourse on the Method of rightly conducting the Reason and seeking truth in the Sciences*, published in French in the year 1637; not, however, with the design of there treating of them fully, but only, as it were, in passing, that I might learn from the judgments of my readers in what way I should afterwards handle them: for these questions appeared to me to be of such moment as to be worthy of being considered more than once, and the path which I follow in discussing them is so little trodden, and so remote from the ordinary route, that I thought it would not be expedient to illustrate it at greater length in French, and in a discourse that might be read by all, lest even the more feeble minds should believe that this path might be entered upon by them.

But, as in the discourse on Method, I had requested all who might find aught meriting censure in my writings, to do me the favour of pointing it out to me, I may state that no objections worthy of remark have been alleged against what I then said on these questions, except two, to which I will here briefly reply, before undertaking their more detailed discussion.

The first objection is that though, while the human mind reflects on itself, it does not perceive that it is any other than a thinking thing, it does not follow that its nature or essence consists only in its being a thing which thinks; so that the word *only* shall exclude all other things which might also perhaps be said to pertain to the nature of the mind.

To this objection I reply, that it was not my intention in that place to exclude these according to the order of truth in the matter (of which I did not then treat), but only according to the order of thought (perception); so that my meaning was, that I clearly apprehended nothing, so far as I was conscious, as belonging to my essence, except that I was a thinking thing, or a thing possessing in itself the faculty of thinking. But I will show hereafter how, from the consciousness that nothing besides thinking belongs to the essence of the mind, it follows that nothing else does in truth belong to it.

The second objection is that it does not follow, from my possessing the idea of a thing more perfect than I am, that the idea itself is more perfect than myself, and much less that what is represented by the idea exists.

But I reply that in the term *idea* there is here something equivocal; for it may be taken either materially for an act of the understanding, and in this sense it cannot be said to be more perfect than I, or objectively, for the thing represented by that act, which, although it be not supposed to exist out of my understanding, may, nevertheless, be more perfect than myself, by reason of its essence. But, in the sequel of this treatise I will show more amply how, from my possessing the idea of a thing more perfect than myself, it follows that this thing really exists.

Besides these two objections, I have seen, indeed, two treatises of sufficient length relating to the present matter. In these, however, my conclusions, much more than my premises were impugned, and that by arguments borrowed from the common-places of the atheists. But, as arguments of this sort can make no impression on the minds of those who shall rightly understand my reasonings, and as the judgments of many are so irrational and weak that they are persuaded rather by the opinions on a subject that are first presented to them, however false and opposed to reason they may be, than by a true and solid, but subsequently received, refutation of them, I am unwilling here to reply to these strictures from a dread of being, in the first instance, obliged to state them.

I will only say, in general, that all which the atheists commonly allege in favour of the non-existence of God arises continually from one or other of these two things, namely, either the ascription of human affections to Deity, or the undue attribution to our minds of so much vigour and wisdom that we may essay to determine and comprehend both what God can and ought to do; hence all that is alleged by them will occasion us no difficulty, provided only we keep in remembrance that our minds must be considered finite, while Deity is incomprehensible and infinite.

Now that I have once, in some measure, made proof of the opinions of men regarding my work, I again undertake to treat of God and the human soul, and at the same time to discuss the principles of the entire first philosophy, without, however, expecting any commendation from the crowd for my endeavours, or a wide circle of readers. On the contrary, I would advise none to read this work, unless such as are able and willing to meditate with me in earnest, to detach their minds from commerce with the senses, and likewise to deliver themselves from all prejudice; and individuals of this character are, I well know, remarkably rare. But with regard to those who, without caring to comprehend the order and connection of the reasonings, shall study only detached clauses for the purpose of small but noisy criticism, as is the custom with many, I may say that such persons will not profit greatly by the reading of this treatise; and although perhaps they may find opportunity for cavilling in several places, they will yet hardly start any pressing objections, or such as shall be deserving of reply.

But since, indeed, I do not promise to satisfy others on all these subjects at first sight, nor arrogate so much to myself as to believe that I have been able to foresee all that may be the source of difficulty to each one, I shall expound, first of all, in the *Meditations*, those considerations by which I feel persuaded that I have arrived at a certain and evident knowledge of truth, in order that I may ascertain whether the reasonings which have prevailed with myself will also be effectual in convincing others. I will then reply to the objections of some men, illustrious for their genius and learning, to whom these meditations were sent for criticism before they were committed to the press; for these objections are so numerous and varied that I venture to anticipate that nothing, at least nothing of any moment, will readily occur to any mind which has not been touched upon in them.

Hence it is that I earnestly entreat my readers not to come to any judgment on the questions raised in the meditations until they have taken care to read the whole of the objections, with the relative replies.

In the First Meditation I expound the grounds on which we may doubt in general of all things, and especially of material objects, so long, at least, as we have no other foundations for the sciences than those we have hitherto possessed. Now, although the utility of a doubt so general may not be manifest at first sight, it is nevertheless of the greatest, since it delivers us from all prejudice, and affords the easiest pathway by which the mind may withdraw itself from the senses; and, finally, makes it impossible for us to doubt wherever we afterwards discover truth.

In the Second, the mind which, in the exercise of the freedom peculiar to itself, supposes that no object is, of the existence of which it has even the slightest doubt, finds that, meanwhile, it must itself exist. And this point is likewise of the highest moment, for the mind is thus enabled easily to distinguish what pertains to itself, that is, to the intellectual nature, from what is to be referred to the body. But since some, perhaps, will expect, at this stage of our progress, a statement of the reasons which establish the doctrine of the immortality of the soul, I think it proper here to make such aware, that it was my aim to write nothing of which I could not give exact demonstration, and that I therefore felt myself obliged to adopt an order similar to that in use among the geometers, viz., to premise all upon which the proposition in question depends, before coming to any conclusion respecting it. Now, the first and chief pre-requisite for the knowledge of the immortality of the soul is our being able to form the clearest possible conception (*conceptus*—concept) of the soul

itself, and such as shall be absolutely distinct from all our notions of body; and how this is to be accomplished is there
shown. There is required, besides this, the assurance that all
objects which we clearly and distinctly think are true (really
exist) in that very mode in which we think them: and this
could not be established previously to the Fourth Meditation.
Farther, it is necessary, for the same purpose, that we possess
a distinct conception of corporeal nature, which is given partly
in the Second and partly in the Fifth and Sixth Meditations.
And, finally, on these grounds, we are necessitated to conclude, that all those objects which are clearly and distinctly
conceived to be diverse substances, as mind and body, are
substances really reciprocally distinct; and this inference is
made in the Sixth Meditation. The absolute distinction of mind
and body is, besides, confirmed in this Second Meditation, by
showing that we cannot conceive body unless as divisible;
while, on the other hand, mind cannot be conceived unless as
indivisible. For we are not able to conceive the half of a mind,
as we can of any body, however small, so that the natures
of these two substances are to be held, not only as diverse,
but even in some measure as contraries. I have not, however,
pursued this discussion further in the present treatise, as well
for the reason that these considerations are sufficient to show
that the destruction of the mind does not follow from the cor-
ruption of the body, and thus to afford to men the hope of a
future life, as also because the premises from which it is competent for us to infer the immortality of the soul, involve an
explication of the whole principles of physics: in order to establish, in the first place, that generally all substances, that is,
all things which can exist only in consequence of having been
created by God, are in their own nature incorruptible, and
can never cease to be, unless God himself, by refusing his
concurrence to them, reduce them to nothing; and, in the second place, that body, taken generally, is a substance, and
therefore can never perish, but that the human body, in as far
as it differs from other bodies, is constituted only by a certain
configuration of members, and by other accidents of this sort,
while the human mind is not made up of accidents, but is a
pure substance. For although all the accidents of the mind be

changed—although, for example, it think certain things, will others, and perceive others, the mind itself does not vary with these changes; while, on the contrary, the human body is no longer the same if a change take place in the form of any of its parts: from which it follows that the body may, indeed, without difficulty perish, but that the mind is in its own nature immortal.

In the Third Meditation, I have unfolded at sufficient length, as appears to me, my chief argument for the existence of God. But yet, since I was there desirous to avoid the use of comparisons taken from material objects, that I might withdraw, as far as possible, the minds of my readers from the senses, numerous obscurities perhaps remain, which, however, will, I trust, be afterwards entirely removed in the replies to the objections: thus, among other things, it may be difficult to understand how the idea of a being absolutely perfect, which is found in our minds, possesses so much objective reality [*i.e.*, participates by representation in so many degrees of being and perfection] that it must be held to arise from a course absolutely perfect. This is illustrated in the replies by the comparison of a highly perfect machine, the idea of which exists in the mind of some workmen; for as the objective (*i.e.*, representative) perfection of this idea must have some cause, viz., either the science of the workman, or of some other person from whom he has received the idea, in the same way the idea of God, which is found in us, demands God himself for its cause.

In the Fourth, it is shown that all which we clearly and distinctly perceive (apprehend) is true; and, at the same time, is explained wherein consists the nature of error; points that require to be known as well for confirming the preceding truths, as for the better understanding of those that are to follow. But, meanwhile, it must be observed, that I do not at all there treat of Sin, that is, of error committed in the pursuit of good and evil, but of that sort alone which arises in the determination of the true and the false. Nor do I refer to matters of faith, or to the conduct of life, but only to what regards speculative truths, and such as are known by means of the natural light alone.

In the Fifth, besides the illustration of corporeal nature, taken generically, a new demonstration is given of the existence of God, not free, perhaps, any more than the former, from certain difficulties, but of these the solution will be found in the replies to the objections. I further show in what sense it is true that the certitude of geometrical demonstrations themselves is dependent on the knowledge of God.

Finally, in the Sixth, the act of the understanding (*intellectio*) is distinguished from that of the imagination (*imaginatio*); the marks of this distinction are described; the human mind is shown to be really distinct from the body, and, nevertheless, to be so closely conjoined therewith, as together to form, as it were, a unity. The whole of the errors which arise from the senses are brought under review, while the means of avoiding them are pointed out; and, finally, all the grounds are adduced from which the existence of material objects may be inferred; not, however, because I deemed them of great utility in establishing what they prove, viz., that there is in reality a world, that men are possessed of bodies, and the like, the truth of which no one of sound mind ever seriously doubted; but because, from a close consideration of them, it is perceived that they are neither so strong nor clear as the reasonings which conduct us to the knowledge of our mind and of God; so that the latter are, of all which come under human knowledge, the most certain and manifest—a conclusion which it was my single aim in these Meditations to establish; on which account I here omit mention of the various other questions which, in the course of the discussion, I had occasion likewise to consider.

MEDITATIONS ON

THE FIRST PHILOSOPHY

IN WHICH

THE EXISTENCE OF GOD, AND THE REAL DISTINCTION

OF MIND AND BODY, ARE DEMONSTRATED

MEDITATION I

OF THE THINGS OF WHICH WE MAY DOUBT

Several years have now elapsed since I first became aware that I had accepted, even from my youth, many false opinions for true, and that consequently what I afterwards based on such principles was highly doubtful; and from that time I was convinced of the necessity of undertaking once in my life to rid myself of all the opinions I had adopted, and of commencing anew the work of building from the foundation, if I desired to establish a firm and abiding superstructure in the sciences. But as this enterprise appeared to me to be one of great magnitude, I waited until I had attained an age so mature as to leave me no hope that at any stage of life more advanced I should be better able to execute my design. On this account, I have delayed so long that I should henceforth consider I was doing wrong were I still to consume in deliberation any of the time that now remains for action. Today, then, since I have opportunely freed my mind from all cares [and am happily disturbed by no passions], and since I am in the secure possession of leisure in a peaceable retirement, I will at length apply myself earnestly and freely to the general overthrow of all my former opinions. But, to this end, it will not be necessary for me to show that the whole of these are false—a point, perhaps, which I shall never reach; but as even now my reason convinces me that I ought not the less carefully to withhold belief from what is not entirely certain and indubitable, than from what is manifestly false, it will be sufficient to justify the rejection of the whole if I shall find in each some ground for doubt. Nor for this purpose will it be necessary even to deal with each belief individually, which would be truly an endless labour; but, as the removal from below of the foundation necessarily involves the downfall of the whole edifice, I will at once approach the criticism of the principles on which all my former beliefs rested.

All that I have, up to this moment, accepted as possessed of the highest truth and certainty, I received either from or through the senses. I observed, however, that these sometimes misled us; and it is the part of prudence not to place absolute confidence in that by which we have even once been deceived.

But it may be said, perhaps, that, although the senses occasionally mislead us respecting minute objects, and such as are so far removed from us as to be beyond the reach of close observation, there are yet many other of their informations (presentations), of the truth of which it is manifestly impossible to doubt; as for example, that I am in this place, seated by the fire, clothed in a winter dressing-gown, that I hold in my hands this piece of paper, with other intimations of the same nature. But how could I deny that I possess these hands and this body, and withal escape being classed with persons in a state of insanity, whose brains are so disordered and clouded by dark bilious vapours as to cause them pertinaciously to assert that they are monarchs when they are in the greatest poverty; or clothed [in gold] and purple when destitute of any covering; or that their head is made of clay, their body of glass, or that they are gourds? I should certainly be not less insane than they, were I to regulate my procedure according to examples so extravagant.

Though this be true, I must nevertheless here consider that I am a man, and that, consequently, I am in the habit of sleeping, and representing to myself in dreams those same things, or even sometimes others less probable, which the insane think are presented to them in their waking moments. How often have I dreamt that I was in these familiar circumstances—that I was dressed, and occupied this place by the fire, when I was lying undressed in bed? At the present moment, however, I certainly look upon this paper with eyes

wide awake; the head which I now move is not asleep; I extend this hand consciously and with express purpose, and I
perceive it; the occurrences in sleep are not so distinct as all
this. But I cannot forget that, at other times, I have been deceived in sleep by similar illusions; and, attentively considering those cases, I perceive so clearly that there exist no certain
marks by which the state of waking can ever be distinguished
from sleep, that I feel greatly astonished; and in amazement
I almost persuade myself that I am now dreaming.

Let us suppose, then, that we are dreaming, and that all
these particulars—namely, the opening of the eyes, the motion
of the head, the forth-putting of the hands—are merely illusions; and even that we really possess neither an entire body
nor hands such as we see. Nevertheless, it must be admitted
at least that the objects which appear to us in sleep are, as it
were, painted representations which could not have been
formed unless in the likeness of realities; and, therefore, that
those general objects, at all events—namely, eyes, a head,
hands, and an entire body—are not simply imaginary, but
really existent. For, in truth, painters themselves, even when
they study to represent sirens and satyrs by forms the most
fantastic and extraordinary, cannot bestow upon them natures
absolutely new, but can only make a certain medley of the
members of different animals; or if they chance to imagine
something so novel that nothing at all similar has ever been
seen before, and such as is, therefore, purely fictitious and
absolutely false, it is at least certain that the colours of which
this is composed are real.

And on the same principle, although these general objects,
viz. [a body], eyes, a head, hands, and the like, be imaginary,
we are nevertheless absolutely necessitated to admit the reality
at least of some other objects still more simple and universal
than these, of which, just as of certain real colours, all those
images of things, whether true and real, or false and fantastic,
that are found in our consciousness (*cogitatio*), are formed.

To this class of objects seem to belong corporeal nature in
general and its extension; the figure of extended things, their
quantity or magnitude, and their number, as also the place
in, and the time during, which they exist, and other things of

the same sort. We will not, therefore, perhaps reason illegiti-
mately if we conclude from this that physics, astronomy,
medicine, and all the other sciences that have for their end
the consideration of composite objects, are indeed of a doubtful character; but that arithmetic, geometry, and the other
sciences of the same class, which regard merely the simplest
and most general objects, and scarcely inquire whether or not
these are really existent, contain somewhat that is certain and
indubitable: for whether I am awake or dreaming, it remains
true that two and three make five, and that a square has but
four sides; nor does it seem possible that truths so apparent
can ever fall under a suspicion of falsity [or incertitude].

Nevertheless, the belief that there is a God who is all-
powerful, and who created me, such as I am, has for a long
time obtained steady possession of my mind. How, then, do
I know that he has not arranged that there should be neither
earth, nor sky, nor any extended thing, nor figure, nor magnitude, nor place, providing at the same time, however, for
[the rise in me of the perceptions of all these objects, and] the
persuasion that these do not exist otherwise than as I perceive
them? And further, as I sometimes think that others are in
error respecting matters of which they believe themselves to
possess a perfect knowledge, how do I know that I am not
also deceived each time I add together two and three, or number the sides of a square, or form some judgment still more
simple, if more simple indeed can be imagined? But perhaps
Deity has not been willing that I should be thus deceived, for
he is said to be supremely good. If, however, it were repugnant to the goodness of Deity to have created me subject to
constant deception, it would seem likewise to be contrary to
his goodness to allow me to be occasionally deceived; and yet
it is clear that this is permitted. Some, indeed, might perhaps
be found who would be disposed rather to deny the existence
of a being so powerful than to believe that there is nothing
certain. But let us for the present refrain from opposing this
opinion, and grant that all which is here said of a Deity is
fabulous: nevertheless, in whatever way it be supposed that
I reached the state in which I exist, whether by fate, or
chance, or by an endless series of antecedents and consequents,

or by any other means, it is clear (since to be deceived and to err is a certain defect) that the probability of my being so imperfect as to be the constant victim of deception, will be increased exactly in proportion as the power possessed by the cause, to which they assign my origin, is lessened. To these reasonings I have assuredly nothing to reply, but am constrained at last to avow that there is nothing at all that I formerly believed to be true of which it is impossible to doubt, and that not through thoughtlessness or levity, but from cogent and maturely considered reasons; so that henceforward, if I desire to discover anything certain, I ought not the less carefully to refrain from assenting to those same opinions than to what might be shown to be manifestly false.

But it is not sufficient to have made these observations; care must be taken likewise to keep them in remembrance. For those old and customary opinions perpetually recur—long and familiar usage giving them the right of occupying my mind, even almost against my will, and subduing my belief; nor will I lose the habit of deferring to them and confiding in them so long as I shall consider them to be what in truth they are, viz., opinions to some extent doubtful, as I have already shown, but still highly probable, and such as it is much more reasonable to believe than deny. It is for this reason I am persuaded that I shall not be doing wrong, if, taking an opposite judgment of deliberate design, I become my own deceiver, by supposing, for a time, that all those opinions are entirely false and imaginary, until at length, having thus balanced my old by my new prejudices, my judgment shall no longer be turned aside by perverted usage from the path that may conduct to the perception of truth. For I am assured that, meanwhile, there will arise neither peril nor error from this course, and that I cannot for the present yield too much to distrust, since the end I now seek is not action but knowledge.

I will suppose, then, not that Deity, who is sovereignly good and the fountain of truth, but that some malignant demon, who is at once exceedingly potent and deceitful, has employed all his artifice to deceive me; I will suppose that the sky, the air, the earth, colours, figures, sounds, and all external things, are nothing better than the illusions of dreams, by means of which this being has laid snares for my credulity; I will consider myself as without hands, eyes, flesh, blood, or any of the senses, and as falsely believing that I am possessed of these; I will continue resolutely fixed in this belief, and if indeed by this means it be not in my power to arrive at the knowledge of truth, I shall at least do what is in my power, viz. [suspend my judgment], and guard with settled purpose against giving my assent to what is false, and being imposed upon by this deceiver, whatever be his power and artifice.

But this undertaking is arduous, and a certain indolence insensibly leads me back to my ordinary course of life; and just as the captive, who, perchance, was enjoying in his dreams an imaginary liberty, when he begins to suspect that it is but a vision, dreads awakening, and conspires with the agreeable illusions that the deception may be prolonged; so I, of my own accord, fall back into the train of my former beliefs, and fear to arouse myself from my slumber, lest the time of laborious wakefulness that would succeed this quiet rest, in place of bringing any light of day, should prove inadequate to dispel the darkness that will arise from the difficulties that have now been raised.

MEDITATION II

OF THE NATURE OF THE HUMAN MIND; AND THAT IT

IS MORE EASILY KNOWN THAN THE BODY

The Meditation of yesterday has filled my mind with so many doubts, that it is no longer in my power to forget them. Nor do I see, meanwhile, any principle on which they can be resolved; and, just as if I had fallen all of a sudden into very deep water, I am so greatly disconcerted as to be made unable either to plant my feet firmly on the bottom or sustain myself by swimming on the surface. I will, nevertheless, make an effort, and try anew the same path on which I had entered yesterday, that is, proceed by casting aside all that admits of the slightest doubt, not less than if I had discovered it to be absolutely false; and I will continue always in this track until I shall find something that is certain, or at least, if I can do nothing more, until I shall know with certainty that there is nothing certain. Archimedes, that he might transport the entire globe from the place it occupied to another, demanded only a point that was firm and immovable; so also, I shall be entitled to entertain the highest expectations, if I am fortunate enough to discover only one thing that is certain and indubitable.

I suppose, accordingly, that all the things which I see are false (fictitious); I believe that none of those objects which my fallacious memory represents ever existed; I suppose that I possess no senses; I believe that body, figure, extension, motion, and place are merely fictions of my mind. What is there, then, that can be esteemed true? Perhaps this only, that there is absolutely nothing certain.

But how do I know that there is not something different altogether from the objects I have now enumerated, of which it is impossible to entertain the slightest doubt? Is there not a God, or some being, by whatever name I may designate him, who causes these thoughts to arise in my mind? But why suppose such a being, for it may be I myself am capable of producing them? Am I, then, at least not something? But I before denied that I possessed senses or a body; I hesitate, however, for what follows from that? Am I so dependent on the body and the senses that without these I cannot exist? But I had the persuasion that there was absolutely nothing in the world, that there was no sky and no earth, neither minds nor bodies; was I not, therefore, at the same time, persuaded that I did not exist? Far from it; I assuredly existed, since I was persuaded. But there is I know not what being, who is possessed at once of the highest power and the deepest cunning, who is constantly employing all his ingenuity in deceiving me. Doubtless, then, I exist, since I am deceived; and, let him deceive me as he may, he can never bring it about that I am nothing, so long as I shall be conscious that I am something. So that it must, in fine, be maintained, all things being maturely and carefully considered, that this proposition (*pronunciatum*) I am, I exist, is necessarily true each time it is expressed by me, or conceived in my mind.

But I do not yet know with sufficient clearness what I am, though assured that I am; and hence, in the next place, I must take care, lest perchance I inconsiderately substitute some other object in room of what is properly myself, and thus wander from truth, even in that knowledge (cognition) which I hold to be of all others the most certain and evident. For this reason, I will now consider anew what I formerly believed myself to be, before I entered on the present train of thought; and of my previous opinion I will retrench all that can in the least be invalidated by the grounds of doubt I have adduced, in order that there may at length remain nothing but what is certain and indubitable. What then did I formerly think I was? Undoubtedly I judged that I was a man. But what is a man? Shall I say a rational animal? Assuredly not; for it would be necessary forthwith to inquire into what is meant by animal, and what by rational, and thus, from a single question, I should insensibly glide into others, and these more difficult than the first; nor do I now possess enough of leisure to warrant me in wasting my time amid subtleties of this sort. I prefer here to attend to the thoughts that sprung up of themselves in my mind, and were inspired by my own nature alone, when I applied myself to the consideration of what I was. In the first place, then, I thought that I possessed a countenance, hands, arms, and all the fabric of members that appears in a corpse, and which I called by the name of body. It further occurred to me that I was nourished, that I walked, perceived, and thought, and all those actions I referred to the soul; but what the soul itself was I either did not stay to consider, or, if I did, I imagined that it was something extremely rare and subtile, like wind, or flame, or ether, spread through my grosser parts. As regarded the body, I did not even doubt of its nature, but thought I distinctly knew it, and if I had wished to describe it according to the notions I then entertained, I should have explained myself in this manner: By body I understand all that can be terminated by a certain figure; that can be comprised in a certain place, and so fill a certain space as therefrom to exclude every other body; that can be perceived either by touch, sight, hearing, taste, or smell; that can be moved in different ways, not indeed of itself, but by something foreign to it by which it is touched [and from which it receives the impression]; for the power of self-motion, as likewise that of perceiving and thinking, I held as by no means pertaining to the nature of body; on the contrary, I was somewhat astonished to find such faculties existing in some bodies.

But [as to myself, what can I now say that I am], since I suppose there exists an extremely powerful, and, if I may so speak, malignant being, whose whole endeavours are directed towards deceiving me? Can I affirm that I possess any one of all those attributes of which I have lately spoken as belonging to the nature of body? After attentively considering them in my own mind, I find none of them that can properly be said to belong to myself. To recount them were idle and tedious. Let us pass, then, to the attributes of the soul. The first mentioned were the powers of nutrition and walking; but, if it be true that I have no body, it is true likewise that I am capable neither of walking nor of being nourished. Perception is another attribute of the soul; but perception too is impossible without the body: besides, I have frequently, during sleep, believed that I perceived objects which I afterwards observed I did not in reality perceive. Thinking is another attribute of the soul; and here I discover what properly belongs to myself. This alone is inseparable from me. I am—I exist: this is certain; but how often? As often as I think; for perhaps it would even happen, if I should wholly cease to think, that I should at the same time altogether cease to be. I now admit nothing that is not necessarily true: I am therefore, precisely speaking, only a thinking thing, that is, a mind (*mens sive animus*), understanding, or reason,—terms whose signification was before unknown to me. I am, however, a real thing, and really existent; but what thing? The answer was, a thinking thing. The question now arises, am I aught besides? I will stimulate my imagination with a view to discover whether I am not still something more than a thinking being. Now it is plain I am not the assemblage of members called the human body; I am not a thin and penetrating air diffused through all these members, or wind, or flame, or vapour, or breath, or any of all the things I can imagine; for I supposed that all these were not, and, without changing the supposition, I find that I still feel assured of my existence.

But it is true, perhaps, that those very things which I suppose to be non-existent, because they are unknown to me, are not in truth different from myself whom I know. This is a point I cannot determine, and do not now enter into any dispute regarding it. I can only judge of things that are known to me: I am conscious that I exist, and I who know that I exist inquire into what I am. It is, however, perfectly certain that the knowledge of my existence, thus precisely taken, is not dependent on things, the existence of which is as yet unknown to me: and consequently it is not dependent on any of the things I can feign in imagination. Moreover, the phrase itself, I frame an image (*effingo*), reminds me of my error; for I should in truth frame one if I were to imagine myself to be anything, since to imagine is nothing more than to contemplate the figure or image of a corporeal thing; but I already know that I exist, and that it is possible at the same time that all those images, and in general all that relates to the nature of body, are merely dreams [or chimeras]. From this I discover that it is not more reasonable to say, I will excite my imagination that I may know more distinctly what I am, than to express myself as follows: I am now awake, and perceive something real; but because my perception is not sufficiently clear, I will of express purpose go to sleep that my dreams may represent to me the object of my perception with more truth and clearness. And, therefore, I know that nothing of all that I can embrace in imagination belongs to the knowledge which I have of myself, and that there is need to recall with the utmost care the mind from this mode of thinking, that it may be able to know its own nature with perfect distinctness.

But what, then, am I? A thinking thing, it has been said. But what is a thinking thing? It is a thing that doubts, understands [conceives], affirms, denies, wills, refuses, that imagines also, and perceives. Assuredly it is not little, if all these properties belong to my nature. But why should they not belong to it? Am I not that very being who now doubts of almost everything; who, for all that, understands and conceives certain things, who affirms one alone as true, and denies the others; who desires to know more of them, and does not wish to be deceived; who imagines many things, sometimes even despite his will; and is likewise percipient of many, as if through the medium of the senses. Is there nothing of all this as true as that I am, even although I should be always dreaming, and although he who gave me being employed all his ingenuity to deceive me? Is there also any one of these attributes that can be properly distinguished from my thought, or that can be said to be separate from myself? For it is of itself so evident that it is I who doubt, I who understand, and I who desire, that it is here unnecessary to add anything by way of rendering it more clear. And I am as certainly the same being who imagines; for, although it may be (as I before supposed) that nothing I imagine is true, still the power of imagination does not cease really to exist in me and to form part of my thoughts. In fine, I am the same being who perceives, that is, who apprehends certain objects as by the organs of sense, since, in truth, I see light, hear a noise, and feel heat. But it will be said that these presentations are false, and that I am dreaming. Let it be so. At all events it is certain that I seem to see light, hear a noise, and feel heat; this cannot be false, and this is what in me is properly called perceiving (*sentire*), which is nothing else than thinking. From this I begin to know what I am with somewhat greater clearness and distinctness than heretofore.

But, nevertheless, it still seems to me, and I cannot help believing, that corporeal things, whose images are formed by thought [which fall under the senses], and are examined by the same, are known with much greater distinctness than that I know not what part of myself which is not imaginable; although, in truth, it may seem strange to say that I know and comprehend with greater distinctness things whose existence appears to me doubtful, that are unknown, and do not belong to me, than others of whose reality I am persuaded, that are known to me, and appertain to my proper nature; in a word, than myself. But I see clearly what is the state of the case. My mind is apt to wander, and will not yet submit to be restrained within the limits of truth. Let us therefore leave the mind to itself once more, and, according to it every kind of liberty [permit it to consider the objects that appear to it from without], in order that, having afterwards withdrawn it from these gently and opportunely [and fixed it on the consideration of its being and the properties it finds in itself], it may then be the more easily controlled.

Let us now accordingly consider the objects that are commonly thought to be [the most easily, and likewise] the most distinctly known, viz., the bodies we touch and see; not, indeed, bodies in general, for these general notions are usually somewhat more confused, but one body in particular. Take, for example, this piece of wax; it is quite fresh, having been but recently taken from the beehive; it has not yet lost the sweetness of the honey it contained; it still retains somewhat of the odour of the flowers from which it was gathered; its colour, figure, size, are apparent (to the sight); it is hard, cold, easily handled; and sounds when struck upon with the finger. In fine, all that contributes to make a body as distinctly known as possible, is found in the one before us. But, while I am speaking, let it be placed near the fire—what remained of the taste exhales, the smell evaporates, the colour changes, its figure is destroyed, its size increases, it becomes liquid, it grows hot, it can hardly be handled, and, although struck upon, it emits no sound. Does the same wax still remain after this change? It must be admitted that it does remain; no one doubts it, or judges otherwise. What, then, was it I knew with so much distinctness in the piece of wax? Assuredly, it could be nothing of all that I observed by means of the senses, since all the things that fell under taste, smell, sight, touch, and hearing are changed, and yet the same wax remains. It was perhaps what I now think, viz., that this wax was neither the sweetness of honey, the pleasant odour of flowers, the whiteness, the figure, nor the sound, but only a body that a little before appeared to me conspicuous under these forms, and which is now perceived under others. But, to speak precisely, what is it that I imagine when I think of it in this way? Let it be attentively considered, and, retrenching all that does not belong to the wax, let us see what remains. There certainly remains nothing, except something extended, flexible, and movable. But what is meant by flexible and movable? Is it not that I imagine that the piece of wax, being round, is capable of becoming square, or of passing from a square into a triangular figure? Assuredly such is not the case, because I conceive that it admits of an infinity of similar changes; and I am, moreover, unable to compass this infinity by imagination, and consequently this conception which I have of the wax is not the product of the faculty of imagination. But what now is this extension? Is it not also unknown? for it becomes greater when the wax is melted, greater when it is boiled, and greater still when the heat increases; and I should not conceive [clearly and] according to truth, the wax as it is, if I did not suppose that the piece we are considering admitted even of a wider variety of extension than I ever imagined. I must, therefore, admit that I cannot even comprehend by imagination what the piece of wax is, and that it is the mind alone (*mens*, Lat.;

entendement, F.) which perceives it. I speak of one piece in particular; for, as to wax in general, this is still more evident. But what is the piece of wax that can be perceived only by the [understanding of] mind? It is certainly the same which I see, touch, imagine; and, in fine, it is the same which, from the beginning, I believed it to be. But (and this it is of moment to observe) the perception of it is neither an act of sight, of touch, nor of imagination, and never was either of these, though it might formerly seem so, but is simply an intuition (*inspectio*) of the mind, which may be imperfect and confused, as it formerly was, or very clear and distinct, as it is at present, according as the attention is more or less directed to the elements which it contains, and of which it is composed.

But, meanwhile, I feel greatly astonished when I observe [the weakness of my mind, and] its proneness to error. For although, without at all giving expression to what I think, I consider all this in my own mind, words yet occasionally impede my progress, and I am almost led into error by the terms of ordinary language. We say, for example, that we see the same wax when it is before us, and not that we judge it to be the same from its retaining the same colour and figure: whence I should forthwith be disposed to conclude that the wax is known by the act of sight, and not by the intuition of the mind alone, were it not for the analogous instance of human beings passing on in the street below, as observed from a window. In this case I do not fail to say that I see the men themselves, just as I say that I see the wax; and yet what do I see from the window beyond hats and cloaks that might cover artificial machines, whose motions might be determined by springs? But I judge that there are human beings from these appearances, and thus I comprehend, by the faculty of judgment alone which is in the mind, what I believed I saw with my eyes.

The man who makes it his aim to rise to knowledge superior to the common, ought to be ashamed to seek occasions of doubting from the vulgar forms of speech: instead, therefore, of doing this, I shall proceed with the matter in hand, and inquire whether I had a clearer and more perfect perception of the piece of wax when I first saw it, and when I thought I knew it by means of the external sense itself, or, at all events, by the common sense (*sensus communis*), as it is called, that is, by the imaginative faculty; or whether I rather apprehend it more clearly at present, after having examined with greater care, both what it is, and in what way it can be known. It would certainly be ridiculous to entertain any doubt on this point. For what, in that first perception, was there distinct? What did I perceive which any animal might not have perceived? But when I distinguish the wax from its exterior forms, and when, as if I had stripped it of its vestments, I consider it quite naked, it is certain, although some error may still be found in my judgment, that I cannot, nevertheless, thus apprehend it without possessing a human mind.

But, finally, what shall I say of the mind itself, that is, of myself? for as yet I do not admit that I am anything but mind. What, then! I who seem to possess so distinct an apprehension of the piece of wax,—do I not know myself, both with greater truth and certitude, and also much more distinctly and clearly? For if I judge that the wax exists because I see it, it assuredly follows, much more evidently, that I myself am or exist, for the same reason: for it is possible that what I see may not in truth be wax, and that I do not even possess eyes with which to see anything; but it cannot be that when I see, or, which comes to the same thing, when I think I see, I myself who think am nothing. So likewise, if I judge that the wax exists because I touch it, it will still also follow that I am; and if I determine that my imagination, or any other cause, whatever it be, persuades me of the existence of the wax, I will still draw the same conclusion. And what is here remarked of the piece of wax is applicable to all the other things that are external to me. And further, if the [notion or] perception of wax appeared to me more precise and distinct, after that not only sight and touch, but many other causes besides, rendered it manifest to my apprehension, with how much greater distinctness must I now know myself, since all the reasons that contribute to the knowledge of the nature of wax, or of any body whatever, manifest still better the nature of my mind? And there are besides so many other things in the mind itself that contribute to the illustration of its nature, that those dependent on the body, to which I have here referred, scarcely merit to be taken into account.

But, in conclusion, I find I have insensibly reverted to the point I desired; for, since it is now manifest to me that bodies themselves are not properly perceived by the senses nor by the faculty of imagination, but by the intellect alone; and since they are not perceived because they are seen and touched, but only because they are understood [or rightly comprehended by thought], I readily discover that there is nothing more easily or clearly apprehended than my own mind. But because it is difficult to rid one's self so promptly of an opinion to which one has been long accustomed, it will be desirable to tarry for some time at this stage, that, by long continued meditation, I may more deeply impress upon my memory this new knowledge.

MEDITATION III

OF GOD: THAT HE EXISTS

I will now close my eyes, I will stop my ears, I will turn away my senses from their objects, I will even efface from my consciousness all the images of corporeal things; or at least, because this can hardly be accomplished, I will consider them as empty and false; and thus, holding converse only with myself, and closely examining my nature, I will endeavour to obtain by degrees a more intimate and familiar knowledge of myself. I am a thinking (conscious) thing, that is, a being who doubts, affirms, denies, knows a few objects, and is ignorant of many,—[who loves, hates], wills, refuses,—who imagines likewise, and perceives; for, as I before remarked, although the things which I perceive or imagine are perhaps nothing at all apart from me [and in themselves], I am nevertheless assured that those modes of consciousness which I call perceptions and imaginations, in as far only as they are modes of consciousness, exist in me. And in the little I have said I think I have summed up all that I really know, or at least all that up to this time I was aware I knew. Now, as I am endeavouring to extend my knowledge more widely, I will use circumspection, and consider with care whether I can still discover in myself anything further which I have not yet hitherto observed. I am certain that I am a thinking thing; but do I not therefore likewise know what is required to render me certain of a truth? In this first knowledge, doubtless, there is nothing that gives me assurance of its truth except the clear and distinct perception of what I affirm, which would not indeed be sufficient to give me the assurance that what I say is true, if it could ever happen that anything I thus clearly and distinctly perceived should prove false; and accordingly it seems to me that I may now take as a general rule, that all that is very clearly and distinctly apprehended (conceived) is true.

Nevertheless I before received and admitted many things as wholly certain and manifest, which yet I afterwards found to be doubtful. What, then, were those? They were the earth, the sky, the stars, and all the other objects which I was in the habit of perceiving by the senses. But what was it that I clearly [and distinctly] perceived in them? Nothing more than that the ideas and the thoughts of those objects were presented to my mind. And even now I do not deny that these ideas are found in my mind. But there was yet another thing which I affirmed, and which, from having been accustomed to believe it, I thought I clearly perceived, although, in truth, I did not perceive it at all; I mean the existence of objects external to me, from which those ideas proceeded, and to which they had a perfect resemblance; and it was here I was mistaken, or if I judged correctly, this assuredly was not to be traced to any knowledge I possessed (the force of my perception, Lat.).

But when I considered any matter in arithmetic and geometry, that was very simple and easy, as, for example, that two and three added together make five, and things of this sort, did I not view them with at least sufficient clearness to warrant me in affirming their truth? Indeed, if I afterwards judged that we ought to doubt of these things, it was for no other reason than because it occurred to me that a God might perhaps have given me such a nature as that I should be deceived, even respecting the matters that appeared to me the most evidently true. But as often as this preconceived opinion of the sovereign power of a God presents itself to my mind, I am constrained to admit that it is easy for him, if he wishes it, to cause me to err, even in matters where I think I possess the highest evidence; and, on the other hand, as often as I direct my attention to things which I think I apprehend with great clearness I am so persuaded of their truth that I naturally break out into expressions such as these: Deceive me who may, no one will yet ever be able to bring it about that I am not, so long as I shall be conscious that I am, or at any future time cause it to be true that I have never been, it being now true that I am, or make two and three more or less than five, in supposing which, and other like absurdities, I discover a manifest contradiction.

And in truth, as I have no ground for believing that Deity is deceitful, and as, indeed, I have not even considered the reasons by which the existence of a Deity of any kind is established, the ground of doubt that rests only on this supposition is very slight, and, so to speak, metaphysical. But, that I may be able wholly to remove it, I must inquire whether there is a God, as soon as an opportunity of doing so shall present itself; and if I find that there is a God, I must examine likewise whether he can be a deceiver; for, without the knowledge of these two truths, I do not see that I can ever be certain of anything. And that I may be enabled to examine this without interrupting the order of meditation I have proposed to myself [which is, to pass by degrees from the notions that I shall find first in my mind to those I shall afterwards discover in it], it is necessary at this stage to divide all my thoughts into certain classes, and to consider in which of these classes truth and error are, strictly speaking, to be found.

Of my thoughts some are, as it were, images of things and to these alone properly belongs the name *idea;* as when I think [represent to my mind] a man, a chimera, the sky, an angel, or God. Others, again, have certain other forms; as when I will, fear, affirm, or deny, I always, indeed, apprehend something as the object of my thought, but I also embrace in thought something more than the representation of the object; and of this class of thoughts some are called volitions or affections, and others judgments.

Now, with respect to ideas, if these are considered only in themselves, and are not referred to any object beyond them, they cannot, properly speaking, be false; for whether I imagine a goat or a chimera, it is not less true that I imagine the one than the other. Nor need we fear that falsity may exist in the will or affections; for, although I may desire objects that are wrong, and even that never existed, it is still true that I desire them. There thus only remain our judgments, in which we must take diligent heed that we be not deceived. But the chief and most ordinary error that arises in them consists in judging that the ideas which are in us are like or conformed to the things that are external to us; for assuredly, if we but considered the ideas themselves as certain modes of our thought (consciousness), without referring them to anything beyond, they would hardly afford any occasion of error.

But, among these ideas, some appear to me to be innate, others adventitious, and others to be made by myself (factitious); for, as I have the power of conceiving what is called a thing, or a truth, or a thought, it seems to me that I hold this power from no other source than my own nature; but if I now hear a noise, if I see the sun, or if I feel heat, I have all along judged that these sensations proceeded from certain objects existing out of myself; and, in fine, it appears to me that sirens, hippogryphs, and the like, are inventions of my own mind. But I may even perhaps come to be of opinion that all my ideas are of the class which I call adventitious, or that they are all innate, or that they are all factitious, for I have not yet clearly discovered their true origin; and what I have here principally to do is to consider, with reference to those that appear to come from certain objects without me, what grounds there are for thinking them like these objects.

The first of these grounds is that it seems to me I am so taught by nature; and the second that I am conscious that those ideas are not dependent on my will, and therefore not on myself, for they are frequently presented to me against my will,—as at present, whether I will or not, I feel heat; and I am thus persuaded that this sensation or idea (*sensum vel ideam*) of heat is produced in me by something different from myself, viz., by the heat of the fire by which I sit. And it is very reasonable to suppose that this object impresses me with its own likeness rather than any other thing.

But I must consider whether these reasons are sufficiently strong and convincing. When I speak of being taught by nature in this matter, I understand by the word nature only a certain spontaneous impetus that impels me to believe in a resemblance between ideas and their objects, and not a natural light that affords a knowledge of its truth. But these two things are widely different; for what the natural light shows to be true can be in no degree doubtful, as, for example, that I am because I doubt, and other truths of the like kind: inasmuch as I possess no other faculty whereby to distinguish truth from error, which can teach me the falsity of what the natural light declares to be true, and which is equally trustworthy; but with respect to [seemingly] natural impulses, I have observed, when the question related to the choice of right or wrong in action, that they frequently led me to take the worse part; nor do I see that I have any better ground for following them in what relates to truth and error. Then, with respect to the other reason, which is that because these ideas do not depend on my will, they must arise from objects existing without me, I do not find it more convincing than the former; for, just as those natural impulses, of which I have lately spoken, are found in me, notwithstanding that they are not always in harmony with my will, so likewise it may be that I possess some power not sufficiently known to myself capable of producing ideas without the aid of external objects, and, indeed, it has always hitherto appeared to me that they are formed during sleep, by some power of this nature, without the aid of aught external. And, in fine, although I should grant that they proceeded from those objects, it is not a necessary consequence that they must be like them. On the contrary, I have observed, in a number of instances, that there was a great difference between the object and its idea. Thus, for example, I find in my mind two wholly diverse ideas of the sun; the one, by which it appears to me extremely small, draws its origin from the senses, and should be placed in the class of adventitious ideas; the other, by which it seems to be many times larger than the whole earth, is taken up on astronomical grounds, that is, elicited from certain notions born with me, or is framed by myself in some other manner. These two ideas cannot certainly both resemble the same sun; and reason teaches me that the one which seems to have immediately emanated from it is the most unlike. And these things sufficiently prove that hitherto it has not been from a certain and deliberate judgment, but only from a sort of blind impulse, that I believed in the existence of certain things different from myself, which, by the organs of sense, or by whatever other means it might be, conveyed their ideas or images into my mind [and impressed it with their likenesses].

But there is still another way of inquiring whether, of the objects whose ideas are in my mind, there are any that exist out of me. If ideas are taken in so far only as they are certain modes of consciousness, I do not remark any difference or inequality among them, and all seem, in the same manner, to proceed from myself; but, considering them as images, of which one represents one thing and another a different, it is evident that a great diversity obtains among them. For, without doubt, those that represent substances are something more, and contain in themselves, so to speak, more objective reality [that is, participate by representation in higher degrees of being or perfection] than those that represent only modes or accidents; and again, the idea by which I conceive a God [sovereign], eternal, infinite [immutable], all-knowing, all-powerful, and the creator of all things that are out of himself, —this, I say, has certainly in it more objective reality than those ideas by which finite substances are represented.

Now, it is manifest by the natural light that there must at least be as much reality in the efficient and total cause as in its effect; for whence can the effect draw its reality if not from its cause? and how could the cause communicate to it this reality unless it possessed it in itself? And hence it follows, not only that what is cannot be produced by what is not, but likewise that the more perfect,—in other words, that which contains in itself more reality,—cannot be the effect of the less perfect: and this is not only evidently true of those effects, whose reality is actual or formal, but likewise of ideas, whose reality is only considered as objective. Thus, for example, the stone that is not yet in existence, not only cannot now commence to be, unless it be produced by that which possesses in itself, formally or eminently, all that enters into its composition [in other words, by that which contains in itself the same properties that are in the stone, or others superior to them]; and heat can only be produced in a subject that was before devoid of it, by a cause that is of an order [degree or kind] at least as perfect as heat; and so of the others. But further, even the idea of the heat, or of the stone, cannot exist in me unless it be put there by a cause that contains, at least, as much reality as I conceive existent in the heat or in the stone: for, although that cause may not transmit into my idea anything of its actual or formal reality, we ought not on this account to imagine that it is less real; but we ought to consider that [as every idea is a work of the mind], its nature is such as of itself to demand no other formal reality than that which it borrows from our consciousness, of which it is but a mode [that is, a manner or way of thinking]. But in order that an idea may contain this objective reality rather than that, it must doubtless derive it from some cause in which is found at least as much formal reality as the idea contains an objective; for, if we suppose that there is found in an idea anything which was not in its cause, it must of course derive this from nothing. But, however imperfect may be the mode of existence by which a thing is objectively [or by representation] in the understanding by its idea, we certainly cannot, for all that, allege that this mode of existence is nothing, nor, consequently, that the idea owes its origin to nothing. Nor must it be imagined that, since the reality which is considered in these ideas is only objective, the same reality need not be formally (actually) in the causes of these ideas, but only objectively; for, just as the mode of existing objectively belongs to ideas by their peculiar nature, so likewise the mode of existing formally appertains to the causes of these ideas (at least to the first and principal), by their peculiar nature. And although an idea may give rise to another idea, this regress cannot, nevertheless, be infinite; we must in the end reach a first idea, the cause of which is, as it were, the archetype in which all the reality [or perfection] that is found objectively [or by representation] in these ideas is contained formally [and in act]. I am thus clearly taught by the natural light that ideas exist in me as pictures or images, which may in truth readily fall short of the perfection of the objects from which they are taken, but can never contain anything greater or more perfect.

And in proportion to the time and care with which I examine all those matters, the conviction of their truth brightens and becomes distinct. But, to sum up, what conclusion shall I draw from it all? It is this;—if the objective reality [or perfection] of any one of my ideas be such as clearly to convince me, that this same reality exists in me neither formally nor eminently, and if, as follows from this, I myself cannot be the cause of it, it is a necessary consequence that I am not alone in the world, but that there is besides myself some other being who exists as the cause of that idea; while, on the contrary, if no such idea be found in my mind, I shall have no sufficient ground of assurance of the existence of any other being besides myself, for, after a most careful search, I have, up to this moment, been unable to discover any other ground.

But, among these my ideas, besides that which represents myself, respecting which there can be here no difficulty, there is one that represents a God; others that represent corporeal and inanimate things; others angels; others animals; and, finally, there are some that represent men like myself. But with respect to the ideas that represent other men, or animals, or angels, I can easily suppose that they were formed by the mingling and composition of the other ideas which I have of myself, of corporeal things, and of God, although there were, apart from myself, neither men, animals, nor angels. And with regard to the ideas of corporeal objects, I never discovered in them anything so great or excellent which I myself did not appear capable of originating; for, by considering these ideas closely and scrutinising them individually, in the same way that I yesterday examined the idea of wax, I find that there is but little in them that is clearly and distinctly perceived. As belonging to the class of things that are clearly apprehended, I recognise the following, viz., magnitude or extension in length, breadth, and depth; figure, which results from the termination of extension; situation, which bodies of diverse figures preserve with reference to each other; and motion or the change of situation; to which may be added substance, duration, and number. But with regard to light, colours, sounds, odours, tastes, heat, cold and the other tactile qualities, they are thought with so much obscurity and confusion, that I cannot determine even whether they are true or false; in other words, whether or not the ideas I have of these qualities are in truth the ideas of real objects. For although I before remarked that it is only in judgments that formal falsity, or falsity properly so called, can be met with, there may nevertheless be found in ideas a certain material falsity, which arises when they represent what is nothing as if it were something. Thus, for example, the ideas I have of cold and heat are so far from being clear and distinct, that I am unable from them to discover whether cold is only the privation of heat, or heat the privation of cold; or whether they are or are not real qualities: and since, ideas being as it were images, there can be none that does not seem to us to represent some object, the idea which represents cold as something real and positive will not improperly be called false, if it be correct to say that cold is nothing but a privation of heat; and so in other cases. To ideas of this kind, indeed, it is not necessary that I should assign any author besides myself: for if they are false, that is, represent objects that are unreal, the natural light teaches me that they proceed from nothing; in other words, that they are in me only because something is wanting to the perfection of my nature; but if these ideas are true, yet because they exhibit to me so little reality that I cannot even distinguish the object represented from non-being, I do not see why I should not be the author of them.

With reference to those ideas of corporeal things that are clear and distinct, there are some which, as appears to me, might have been taken from the idea I have of myself, as those of substance, duration, number, and the like. For when I think that a stone is a substance, or a thing capable of existing of itself, and that I am likewise a substance, although I conceive that I am a thinking and non-extended thing, and that the stone, on the contrary, is extended and unconscious, there being thus the greatest diversity between the two concepts,—yet these two ideas seem to have this in common that they both represent substances. In the same way, when I think of myself as now existing, and recollect besides that I existed some time ago, and when I am conscious of various thoughts whose number I know, I then acquire the ideas of duration and number, which I can afterwards transfer to as many objects as I please. With respect to the other qualities that go to make up the ideas of corporeal objects, viz., extension, figure, situation, and motion, it is true that they are not formally in me, since I am merely a thinking being; but because they are only certain modes of substance, and because I myself am a substance, it seems possible that they may be contained in me eminently.

There only remains, therefore, the idea of God, in which I must consider whether there is anything that cannot be supposed to originate with myself. By the name God, I understand a substance infinite [eternal, immutable], independent, all-knowing, all-powerful, and by which I myself, and every other thing that exists, if any such there be, were created. But these properties are so great and excellent, that the more attentively I consider them the less I feel persuaded that the idea I have of them owes its origin to myself alone. And thus it is absolutely necessary to conclude, from all that I have before said, that God exists: for though the idea of substance be in my mind owing to this, that I myself am a substance, I should not, however, have the idea of an infinite substance, seeing I am a finite being, unless it were given me by some substance in reality infinite.

And I must not imagine that I do not apprehend the infinite by a true idea, but only by the negation of the finite, in the same way that I comprehend repose and darkness by the negation of motion and light: since, on the contrary, I clearly perceive that there is more reality in the infinite substance than in the finite, and therefore that in some way I possess the perception (notion) of the infinite before that of the finite, that is, the perception of God before that of myself, for how could I know that I doubt, desire, or that something is wanting to me, and that I am not wholly perfect, if I possessed no idea of a being more perfect than myself, by comparison of which I knew the deficiencies of my nature?

And it cannot be said that this idea of God is perhaps materially false, and consequently that it may have arisen from nothing [in other words, that it may exist in me from my imperfection], as I before said of the ideas of heat and cold, and the like: for, on the contrary, as this idea is very clear and distinct, and contains in itself more objective reality than any other, there can be no one of itself more true, or less open to the suspicion of falsity.

The idea, I say, of a being supremely perfect, and infinite, is in the highest degree true; for although, perhaps, we may imagine that such a being does not exist, we cannot, nevertheless, suppose that his idea represents nothing real, as I have already said of the idea of cold. It is likewise clear and distinct in the highest degree, since whatever the mind clearly and distinctly conceives as real or true, and as implying any perfection, is contained entire in this idea. And this is true, nevertheless, although I do not comprehend the infinite, and although there may be in God an infinity of things that I cannot comprehend, nor perhaps even compass by thought in any way; for it is of the nature of the infinite that it should not be comprehended by the finite; and it is enough that I rightly understand this, and judge that all which I clearly perceive, and in which I know there is some perfection, and perhaps also an infinity of properties of which I am ignorant, are formally or eminently in God, in order that the idea I have of him may become the most true, clear, and distinct of all the ideas in my mind.

But perhaps I am something more than I suppose myself to be, and it may be that all those perfections which I attribute to God, in some way exist potentially in me, although they do not yet show themselves, and are not reduced to act. Indeed, I am already conscious that my knowledge is being increased [and perfected] by degrees; and I see nothing to prevent it from thus gradually increasing to infinity, nor any reason why, after such increase and perfection, I should not be able thereby to acquire all the other perfections of the Divine nature; nor, in fine, why the power I possess of acquiring those perfections, if it really now exist in me, should not be sufficient to produce the ideas of them. Yet, on looking more closely into the matter, I discover that this cannot be; for, in the first place, although it were true that my knowledge daily acquired new degrees of perfection, and although there were potentially in my nature much that was not as yet actually in it, still all these excellences make not the slightest approach to the idea I have of the Deity, in whom there is no perfection merely potentially [but all actually] existent; for it is even an unmistakable token of imperfection in my knowledge, that it is augmented by degrees. Further, although my knowledge increase more and more, nevertheless I am not, therefore, induced to think that it will ever be actually infinite, since it can never reach that point beyond which it shall be incapable of further increase. But I conceived God as actually infinite, so that nothing can be added to his perfection. And, in fine, I readily perceive that the objective being of an idea cannot be produced by a being that is merely potentially existent, which, properly speaking, is nothing, but only by a being existing formally or actually.

And, truly, I see nothing in all that I have now said which it is not easy for any one, who shall carefully consider it, to discern by the natural light; but when I allow my attention in some degree to relax, the vision of my mind being obscured, and, as it were, blinded by the images of sensible objects, I do not readily remember the reason why the idea of a being more perfect than myself, must of necessity have proceeded from a being in reality more perfect. On this account I am here desirous to inquire further, whether I, who possess this idea of God, could exist supposing there were no God. And I ask, from whom could I, in that case, derive my existence? Perhaps from myself, or from my parents, or from some other causes less perfect than God; for anything more perfect, or even equal to God, cannot be thought or imagined. But if I [were independent of every other existence, and] were myself the author of my being, I should doubt of nothing, I should desire nothing, and, in fine, no perfection would be awanting to me; for I should have bestowed upon myself every perfection of which I possess the idea, and I should thus be God. And it must not be imagined that what is now wanting to me is perhaps of more difficult acquisition than that of which I am already possessed; for, on the contrary, it is quite manifest that it was a matter of much higher difficulty that I, a thinking being, should arise from nothing, than it would be for me to acquire the knowledge of many things of which I am ignorant, and which are merely the accidents of a thinking substance; and certainly, if I possessed of myself the greater perfection of which I have now spoken [in other words, if I were the author of my own existence], I would not at least have denied to myself things that may be more easily obtained [as that infinite variety of knowledge of which I am at present destitute]. I could not, indeed, have denied to myself any property which I perceive is contained in the idea of God, because there is none of these that seems to me to be more difficult to make or acquire; and if there were any that should happen to be more difficult to acquire, they would certainly appear so to me (supposing that I myself were the source of the other things I possess), because I should discover in them a limit to my power. And though I were to suppose that I always was as I now am, I should not, on this ground, escape the force of these reasonings, since it would not follow, even on this supposition, that no author of my existence needed to be sought after. For the whole time of my life may be divided into an infinity of parts, each of which is in no way dependent on any other; and, accordingly, because I was in existence a short time ago, it does not follow that I must now exist, unless in this moment some cause create me anew, as it were,—that is, conserve me. In truth, it is perfectly clear and evident to all who will attentively consider the nature of duration that the conservation of a substance, in each moment of its dura-tion, requires the same power and act that would be necessary to create it, supposing it were not yet in existence; so that it is manifestly a dictate of the natural light that conservation and creation differ merely in respect of our mode of thinking [and not in reality]. All that is here required, therefore, is that I interrogate myself to discover whether I possess any power by means of which I can bring it about that I, who now am, shall exist a moment afterwards: for, since I am merely a thinking thing (or since, at least, the precise question, in the meantime, is only of that part of myself), if such a power resided in me, I should, without doubt, be conscious of it; but I am conscious of no such power, and thereby I manifestly know that I am dependent upon some being different from myself.

But perhaps the being upon whom I am dependent is not God, and I have been produced either by my parents, or by some causes less perfect than Deity. This cannot be: for, as I before said, it is perfectly evident that there must at least be as much reality in the cause as in its effect; and accordingly, since I am a thinking thing, and possess in myself an idea of God, whatever in the end be the cause of my existence, it must of necessity be admitted that it is likewise a thinking being, and that it possesses in itself the idea and all the perfections I attribute to Deity. Then it may again be inquired whether this cause owes its origin and existence to itself, or to some other cause. For if it be self-existent, it follows, from what I have before laid down, that this cause is God; for, since it possesses the perfection of self-existence, it must likewise, without doubt, have the power of actually possessing every perfection of which it has the idea,—in other words, all the perfections I conceive to belong to God. But if it owe its existence to another cause than itself, we demand again, for a similar reason, whether this second cause exists of itself or through some other, until, from stage to stage, we at length arrive at an ultimate cause, which will be God. And it is quite manifest that in this matter there can be no infinite regress of causes, seeing that the question raised respects not so much the cause which once produced me, as that by which I am at this present moment conserved.

Nor can it be supposed that several causes concerned in my production, and that from one I received the idea of one of the perfections I attribute to Deity, and from another the idea of some other, and thus that all those perfections are indeed found somewhere in the universe, but do not all exist together in a single being who is God; for, on the contrary, the unity, the simplicity or inseparability of all the properties of Deity, is one of the chief perfections I conceive him to possess; and the idea of this unity of all the perfections of Deity could certainly not be put into my mind by any cause from which I did not likewise receive the ideas of all the other perfections; for no power could enable me to embrace them in an inseparable unity, without at the same time giving me the knowledge of what they were [and of their existence in a particular mode].

Finally, with regard to my parents [from whom it appears I sprung], although all that I believed respecting them be true, it does not, nevertheless, follow that I am conserved by them, or even that I was produced by them, in so far as I am a thinking being. All that, at the most, they contributed to my origin was the giving of certain dispositions (modifications) to the matter in which I have hitherto judged that I or my mind, which is what alone I now consider to be myself, is enclosed; and thus there can here be no difficulty with respect to them, and it is absolutely necessary to conclude from this alone that I am, and possess the idea of a being absolutely perfect, that is, of God, that his existence is most clearly demonstrated.

There remains only the inquiry as to the way in which I received this idea from God; for I have not drawn it from the senses, nor is it even presented to me unexpectedly, as is usual with the ideas of sensible objects, when these are presented or appear to be presented to the external organs of the senses; it is not even a pure production or fiction of my mind, for it is not in my power to take from or add to it; and consequently there but remains the alternative that it is innate, in the same way as is the idea of myself. And, in truth, it is not to be wondered at that God, at my creation, implanted this idea in me, that it might serve, as it were, for the mark of the workman impressed on his work; and it is not also necessary that the mark should be something different from the work itself; but considering only that God is my creator, it is highly probable that he in some way fashioned me after his own image and likeness, and that I perceive this likeness, in which is contained the idea of God, by the same faculty by which I apprehend myself,—in other words, when I make myself the object of reflection, I not only find that I am an incomplete [imperfect] and dependent being, and one who unceasingly aspires after something better and greater than he is; but, at the same time, I am assured likewise that he upon whom I am dependent possesses in himself all the goods after which I aspire [and the ideas of which I find in my mind], and that not merely indefinitely and potentially, but infinitely and actually, and that he is thus God. And the whole force of the argument of which I have here availed myself to establish the existence of God, consists in this, that I perceive I could not possibly be of such a nature as I am, and yet have in my mind the idea of a God, if God did not in reality exist,—this same God, I say, whose idea is in my mind—that is, a being who possesses all those lofty perfections, of which the mind may have some slight conception, without, however, being able fully to comprehend them,—and who is wholly superior to all defect [and has nothing that marks imperfection]: whence it is sufficiently manifest that he cannot be a deceiver, since it is a dictate of the natural light that all fraud and deception spring from some defect.

But before I examine this with more attention, and pass on to the consideration of other truths that may be evolved out of it, I think it proper to remain here for some time in the contemplation of God himself—that I may ponder at leisure his marvellous attributes—and behold, admire, and adore the beauty of this light so unspeakably great, as far, at least, as the strength of my mind, which is to some degree dazzled by the sight, will permit. For just as we learn by faith that the supreme felicity of another life consists in the contemplation of the Divine majesty alone, so even now we learn from experience that a like meditation, though incomparably less perfect, is the source of the highest satisfaction of which we are susceptible in this life.

MEDITATION IV

OF TRUTH AND ERROR

I have been habituated these bygone days to detach my mind from the senses, and I have accurately observed that there is exceedingly little which is known with certainty respecting corporeal objects,—that we know much more of the human mind, and still more of God himself. I am thus able now without difficulty to abstract my mind from the contemplation of [sensible or] imaginable objects, and apply it to those which, as disengaged from all matter, are purely intelligible. And certainly the idea I have of the human mind in so far as it is a thinking thing, and not extended in length, breadth, and depth, and participating in none of the properties of body, is incomparably more distinct than the idea of any corporeal object; and when I consider that I doubt, in other words, that I am an incomplete and dependent being, the idea of a complete and independent being, that is to say of God, occurs to my mind with so much clearness and distinctness,—and from the fact alone that this idea is found in me, or that I who possess it exist, the conclusions that God exists, and that my own existence, each moment of its continuance, is absolutely dependent upon him, are so manifest, —as to lead me to believe it impossible that the human mind can know anything with more clearness and certitude. And now I seem to discover a path that will conduct us from the contemplation of the true God, in whom are contained all the treasures of science and wisdom, to the knowledge of the other things in the universe.

For, in the first place, I discover that it is impossible for him ever to deceive me, for in all fraud and deceit there is a certain imperfection: and although it may seem that the ability to deceive is a mark of subtlety or power, yet the will testifies without doubt of malice and weakness; and such, accordingly, can be found in God. In the next place, I am conscious that I possess a certain faculty of judging [or discerning truth from error], which I doubtless received from God, along with whatever else is mine; and since it is impossible that he should will to deceive me, it is likewise certain that he has not given me a faculty that will ever lead me into error, provided I use it aright.

And there would remain no doubt on this head, did it not seem to follow from this, that I can never therefore be deceived; for if all I possess be from God, and if he planted in me no faculty that is deceitful, it seems to follow that I can never fall into error. Accordingly, it is true that when I think only of God (when I look upon myself as coming from God, Fr.), and turn wholly to him, I discover [in myself] no cause of error or falsity: but immediately thereafter, recurring to myself, experience assures me that I am nevertheless subject to innumerable errors. When I come to inquire into the cause of these, I observe that there is not only present to my consciousness a real and positive idea of God, or of a being supremely perfect, but also, so to speak, a certain negative idea of nothing,—in other words, of that which is at an infinite distance from every sort of perfection, and that I am, as it were, a mean between God and nothing, or placed in such a way between absolute existence and non-existence, that there is in truth nothing in me to lead me into error, in so far as an absolute being is my creator; but that, on the other hand, as I thus likewise participate in some degree of nothing or of non-being, in other words, as I am not myself the supreme Being, and as I am wanting in many perfections, it is not surprising I should fall into error. And I hence discern that error, so far as error is not something real, which depends for its existence on God, but is simply defect; and therefore that, in order to fall into it, it is not necessary God should have given me a faculty expressly for this end, but that my being deceived arises from the circumstance that the power which God has given me of discerning truth from error is not infinite.

Nevertheless this is not yet quite satisfactory; for error is not a pure negation [in other words, it is not the simple deficiency or want of some knowledge which is not due], but the privation or want of some knowledge which it would seem I ought to possess. But, on considering the nature of God, it seems impossible that he should have planted in his creature any faculty not perfect in its kind, that is, wanting in some perfection due to it: for if it be true, that in proportion to the skill of the maker the perfection of his work is greater, what thing can have been produced by the supreme Creator of the universe that is not absolutely perfect in all its parts? And assuredly there is no doubt that God could have created me such as that I should never be deceived; it is certain, likewise, that he always wills what is best: is it better, then, that I should be capable of being deceived than that I should not?

Considering this more attentively, the first thing that occurs to me is the reflection that I must not be surprised if I am not always capable of comprehending the reasons why God acts as he does; nor must I doubt of his existence because I find, perhaps, that there are several other things, besides the present respecting which I understand neither why nor how they were created by him; for, knowing already that my nature is extremely weak and limited, and that the nature of God, on the other hand, is immense, incomprehensible, and infinite, I have no longer any difficulty in discerning that there is an infinity of things in his power whose causes transcend the grasp of my mind: and this consideration alone is sufficient to convince me, that the whole class of final causes is of no avail in physical [or natural] things; for it appears to me that I cannot, without exposing myself to the charge of temerity, seek to discover the [impenetrable] ends of Deity.

It further occurs to me that we must not consider only one creature apart from the others, if we wish to determine the perfection of the works of Deity, but generally all his creatures together; for the same object that might perhaps, with some show of reason, be deemed highly imperfect if it were alone in the world, may for all that be the most perfect possible, considered as forming part of the whole universe: and although, as it was my purpose to doubt of everything, I only as yet know with certainty my own existence and that of God, nevertheless, after having remarked the infinite power of Deity, I cannot deny that he may have produced many other objects, or at least that he is able to produce them, so that I may occupy a place in the relation of a part to the great whole of his creatures.

Whereupon, regarding myself more closely, and considering what my errors are (which alone testify to the existence of imperfection in me), I observe that these depend on the concurrence of two causes, viz., the faculty of cognition which I possess, and that of election or the power of free choice,—in other words, the understanding and the will. For by the understanding alone, I [neither affirm nor deny anything, but] merely apprehend (*percipio*) the ideas regarding which I may form a judgment; nor is any error, properly so called, found in it thus accurately taken. And although there are perhaps innumerable objects in the world of which I have no idea in my understanding, it cannot, on that account, be said that I am deprived of those ideas [as of something that is due to my nature], but simply that I do not possess them, because, in truth, there is no ground to prove that Deity ought to have endowed me with a larger faculty of cognition than he has actually bestowed upon me; and however skilful a workman I suppose him to be, I have no reason, on that account, to think that it was obligatory on him to give to each of his works all the perfections he is able to bestow upon some. Nor, moreover, can I complain that God has not given me freedom of choice, or a will sufficiently ample and perfect, since, in truth, I am conscious of will so ample and extended as to be superior to all limits. And what appears to me here to be highly remarkable is that, of all the other properties I possess, there is none so great and perfect as that I do not clearly discern it could be still greater and more perfect. For, to take an example, if I consider the faculty of understanding which I possess, I find that it is of very small extent, and greatly limited, and at the same time I form the idea of another faculty of the same nature, much more ample and even infinite; and seeing that I can frame the idea of it, I discover, from this circumstance alone, that it pertains to the nature of God. In the same way, if I examine the faculty of memory or imagination, or any other faculty I possess, I find none that is not small and circumscribed, and in God immense [and infinite]. It is the faculty of will only, or freedom of choice, which I experience to be so great that I am unable to conceive the idea of another that shall be more ample and extended; so that it is chiefly my will which leads me to discern that I bear a certain image and similitude of Deity. For although the faculty of will is incomparably greater in God than in myself, as well in respect of the knowledge and power that are conjoined with it, and that render it stronger and more efficacious, as in respect of the object, since in him it extends to a greater number of things, it does not, nevertheless, appear to me greater, considered in itself formally and precisely: for the power of will consists only in this, that we are able to do or not to do the same thing (that is, to affirm or deny, to pursue or shun it), or rather in this alone, that in affirming or denying, pursuing or shunning, what is proposed to us by the understanding, we so act that we are not conscious of being determined to a particular action by any external force. For, to the possession of freedom, it is not necessary that I be alike indifferent towards each of two contraries; but, on the contrary, the more I am inclined towards the one, whether because I clearly know that in it there is the reason of truth and goodness, or because God thus internally disposes my thought, the more freely do I choose and embrace it; and assuredly divine grace and natural knowledge, very far from diminishing liberty, rather augment and fortify it. But the indifference of which I am conscious when I am not impelled to one side rather than to another for want of a reason, is the lowest grade of liberty, and manifests defect or negation of knowledge rather than perfection, of will; for if I always clearly knew what was true and good, I should never have any difficulty in determining what judgment I ought to come to, and what choice I ought to make, and I should thus be entirely free without ever being indifferent.

From all this I discover, however, that neither the power of willing, which I have received from God, is of itself the source of my errors, for it is exceedingly ample and perfect in its kind; nor even the power of understanding, for as I conceive no object unless by means of the faculty that God bestowed upon me, all that I conceive is doubtless rightly conceived by me, and it is impossible for me to be deceived in it.

Whence, then, spring my errors? They arise from this cause alone, that I do not restrain the will, which is of much wider range than the understanding, within the same limits, but extend it even to things I do not understand, and as the will is of itself indifferent to such, it readily falls into error and sin by choosing the false in room of the true, and evil instead of good.

For example, when I lately considered whether aught really existed in the world, and found that because I considered this question, it very manifestly followed that I myself existed, I could not but judge that what I so clearly conceived was true, not that I was forced to this judgment by any external cause, but simply because great clearness of the understanding was succeeded by strong inclination in the will; and I believed this the more freely and spontaneously in proportion as I was less indifferent with respect to it. But now I not only know that I exist, in so far as I am a thinking being, but there is likewise presented to my mind a certain idea of corporeal nature; hence I am in doubt as to whether the thinking nature which is in me, or rather which I myself am, is different from that corporeal nature, or whether both are merely one and the same thing, and I here suppose that I am as yet ignorant of any reason that would determine me to adopt the one belief in preference to the other: whence it happens that it is a matter of perfect indifference to me which of the two suppositions I affirm or deny, or whether I form any judgment at all in the matter.

This indifference, moreover, extends not only to things of which the understanding has no knowledge at all, but in general also to all those which it does not discover with perfect clearness at the moment the will is deliberating upon them; for, however probable the conjectures may be that dispose me to form a judgment in a particular matter, the simple knowledge that these are merely conjectures, and not certain and indubitable reasons, is sufficient to lead me to form one that is directly the opposite. Of this I lately had abundant experience, when I laid aside as false all that I had before held for true, on the single ground that I could in some degree doubt of it. But if I abstain from judging of a thing when I do not conceive it with sufficient clearness and distinctness, it is plain that I act rightly, and am not deceived; but if I resolve to deny or affirm, I then do not make a right use of my free will; and if I affirm what is false, it is evident that I am deceived: moreover, even although I judge according to truth, I stumble upon it by chance, and do not therefore escape the imputation of a wrong use of my freedom; for it is a dictate of the natural light, that the knowledge of the understanding ought always to precede the determination of the will.

And it is this wrong use of freedom of the will in which is found the privation that constitutes the form of error. Privation, I say, is found in the act, in so far as it proceeds from myself, but it does not exist in the faculty which I received from God, nor even in the act, in so far as it depends on him; for I have assuredly no reason to complain that God has not given me a greater power of intelligence or more perfect natural light than he has actually bestowed, since it is of the nature of a finite understanding not to comprehend many things, and of the nature of a created understanding to be finite; on the contrary, I have every reason to render thanks to God, who owed me nothing, for having given me all the perfections I possess, and I should be far from thinking that he has unjustly deprived me of, or kept back, the other perfections which he has not bestowed upon me.

I have no reason, moreover, to complain because he has given me a will more ample than my understanding, since, as the will consists only of a single element, and that indivisible, it would appear that this faculty is of such a nature that nothing could be taken from it [without destroying it]; and certainly, the more extensive it is, the more cause I have to thank the goodness of him who bestowed it upon me.

And, finally, I ought not also to complain that God concurs with me in forming the acts of this will, or the judgments in which I am deceived, because those acts are wholly true and good, in so far as they depend on God; and the ability to form them is a higher degree of perfection in my nature than the want of it would be. With regard to privation, in which alone consists the formal reason of error and sin, this does not require the concurrence of Deity, because it is not a thing [or existence], and if it be referred to God as to its cause, it ought not to be called privation, but negation [according to the signification of these words in the schools]. For in truth it is no imperfection in Deity that he has accorded to me the power of giving or withholding my assent from certain things of which he has not put a clear and distinct knowledge in my understanding; but it is doubtless an imperfection in me that I do not use my freedom aright, and readily give my judgment on matters which I only obscurely and confusedly conceive.

I perceive, nevertheless, that it was easy for Deity so to have constituted me as that I should never be deceived, although I still remained free and possessed of a limited knowledge, viz., by implanting in my understanding a clear and distinct knowledge of all the objects respecting which I should ever have to deliberate; or simply by so deeply engraving on my memory the resolution to judge of nothing without previously possessing a clear and distinct conception of it, that I should never forget it. And I easily understand that, in so far as I consider myself as a single whole, without reference to any other being in the universe, I should have been much more perfect than I now am, had Deity created me superior to error; but I cannot therefore deny that it is not somehow a greater perfection in the universe, that certain of its parts are not exempt from defect, as others are, than if they were all perfectly alike.

And I have no right to complain because God, who placed me in the world, was not willing that I should sustain that character which of all others is the chief and most perfect; I have even good reason to remain satisfied on the ground that, if he has not given me the perfection of being superior to error by the first means I have pointed out above, which depends on a clear and evident knowledge of all the matters regarding which I can deliberate, he has at least left in my power the other means, which is, firmly to retain the resolution never to judge where the truth is not clearly known to me: for, although

I am conscious of the weakness of not being able to keep my mind continually fixed on the same thought, I can neverthe-less, by attentive and oft-repeated meditation, impress it so strongly on my memory that I shall never fail to recollect it as often as I require it, and I can acquire in this way the habitude of not erring; and since it is in being superior to error that the highest and chief perfection of man consists, I deem that I have not gained little by this day's meditation, in having discovered the source of error and falsity.

And certainly this can be no other than what I have now explained: for as often as I so restrain my will within the limits of my knowledge, that it forms no judgment except regarding objects which are clearly and distinctly represented to it by the understanding, I can never be deceived; because every clear and distinct conception is doubtless something, and as such cannot owe its origin to nothing, but must of necessity have God for its author—God, I say, who, as supremely per-fect, cannot, without a contradiction, be the cause of any er-ror; and consequently it is necessary to conclude that every such conception [or judgment] is true. Nor have I merely learned to-day what I must avoid to escape error, but also what I must do to arrive at the knowledge of truth; for I will assuredly reach truth if I only fix my attention sufficiently on all the things I conceive perfectly, and separate these from others which I conceive more confusedly and obscurely: to which for the future I shall give diligent heed.

MEDITATION V

OF THE ESSENCE OF MATERIAL THINGS; AND, AGAIN,

OF GOD: THAT HE EXISTS

Several other questions remain for consideration respecting the attributes of God and my own nature or mind. I will, however, on some other occasion perhaps resume the investigation of these. Meanwhile, as I have discovered what must be done, and what avoided to arrive at the knowledge of truth, what I have chiefly to do is to essay to emerge from the state of doubt in which I have for some time been, and to discover whether anything can be known with certainty regarding material objects. But before considering whether such objects as I conceive exist without me, I must examine their ideas in so far as these are to be found in my consciousness, and discover which of them are distinct and which confused.

In the first place, I distinctly imagine that quantity which the philosophers commonly call continuous, or the extension in length, breadth, and depth that is in this quantity, or rather in the object to which it is attributed. Further, I can enumerate in it many diverse parts, and attribute to each of these all sorts of sizes, figures, situations, and local motions; and, in fine, I can assign to each of these motions all degrees of duration. And I not only distinctly know these things when I thus consider them in general; but besides, by a little attention, I discover innumerable particulars respecting figures, numbers, motion, and the like, which are so evidently true, and so accordant with my nature, that when I now discover them I do not so much appear to learn anything new, as to call to remembrance what I before knew, or for the first time to remark what was before in my mind, but to which I had not hitherto directed my attention. And what I here find of most importance is, that I discover in my mind innumerable ideas of certain objects, which cannot be esteemed pure negations, although perhaps they possess no reality beyond my thought, and which are not framed by me though it may be in my power to think, or not to think them, but possess true and immutable natures of their own. As, for example, when I imagine a triangle, although there is not perhaps and never was in any place in the universe apart from my thought one such figure, it remains true nevertheless that this figure possesses a certain determinate nature, form, or essence, which is immutable and eternal, and not framed by me, nor in any degree dependent on my thought; as appears from the circumstance, that diverse properties of the triangle may be demonstrated, viz., that its three angles are equal to two right, that its greatest side is subtended by its greatest angle, and the like, which, whether I will or not, I now clearly discern to belong to it, although before I did not at all think of them, when, for the first time, I imagined a triangle, and which accordingly cannot be said to have been invented by me. Nor is it a valid objection to allege, that perhaps this idea of a triangle came into my mind by the medium of the senses, through my having seen bodies of a triangular figure; for I am able to form in thought an innumerable variety of figures with regard to which it cannot be supposed that they were ever objects of sense, and I can nevertheless demonstrate diverse properties of their nature no less than of the triangle, all of which are assuredly true since I clearly conceive them; and they are therefore something, and not mere negations; for it is highly evident that all that is true is something [truth being identical with existence]; and I have already fully shown the truth of the principle, that whatever is clearly and distinctly known is true. And although this had not been demonstrated, yet the nature of my mind is such as to compel me to assent to what I clearly conceive while I so conceive it; and I recollect that even when I still strongly adhered to the objects of sense, I reckoned among the number of the most certain truths those I clearly conceived relating to figures, numbers, and other matters that pertain to arithmetic and geometry, and in general to the pure mathematics.

But now if because I can draw from my thought the idea of an object, it follows that all I clearly and distinctly apprehend to pertain to this object, does in truth belong to it, may I not from this derive an argument for the existence of God? It is certain that I no less find the idea of a God in my consciousness, that is, the idea of a being supremely perfect, than that of any figure or number whatever: and I know with not less clearness and distinctness that an [actual and] eternal existence pertains to his nature than that all which is demonstrable of any figure or number really belongs to the nature of that figure or number; and, therefore, although all the conclusions of the preceding Meditations were false, the existence of God would pass with me for a truth at least as certain as I ever judged any truth of mathematics to be, although indeed such a doctrine may at first sight appear to contain more sophistry than truth. For, as I have been accustomed in every other matter to distinguish between existence and essence, I easily believe that the existence can be separated from the essence of God, and that thus God may be conceived as not actually existing. But, nevertheless, when I think of it more attentively, it appears that the existence can no more be separated from the essence of God than the idea of a mountain from that of a valley, or the equality of its three angles to two right angles, from the essence of a [rectilineal] triangle; so that it is not less impossible to conceive a God, that is, a being supremely perfect, to whom existence is awanting, or who is devoid of a certain perfection, than to conceive a mountain without a valley.

But though, in truth, I cannot conceive a God unless as existing, any more than I can a mountain without a valley, yet, just as it does not follow that there is any mountain in the world merely because I conceive a mountain with a valley, so likewise, though I conceive God as existing, it does not seem to follow on that account that God exists; for my thought imposes no necessity on things; and as I may imagine a winged horse, though there be none such, so I could perhaps attribute existence to God, though no God existed. But the cases are not analogous, and a fallacy lurks under the semblance of this objection: for because I cannot conceive a mountain without a valley, it does not follow that there is any mountain or valley in existence, but simply that the mountain or valley, whether they do or do not exist, are inseparable from each other; whereas, on the other hand, because I cannot conceive God unless as existing, it follows that existence is inseparable from him, and therefore that he really exists: not that this is brought about by my thought, or that it imposes any necessity on things, but, on the contrary, the necessity which lies in the thing itself, that is, the necessity of the existence of God, determines me to think in this way, for it is not in my power to conceive a God without existence, that is a being supremely perfect, and yet devoid of an absolute perfection, as I am free to imagine a horse with or without wings.

Nor must it be alleged here as an objection, that it is in truth necessary to admit that God exists, after having supposed him to possess all perfections, since existence is one of them, but that my original supposition was not necessary; just as it is not necessary to think that all quadrilateral figures can be inscribed in the circle, since, if I supposed this, I should be constrained to admit that the rhombus, being a figure of four sides, can be therein inscribed, which, however, is manifestly false. This objection is, I say, incompetent; for although it may not be necessary that I shall at any time entertain the notion of Deity, yet each time I happen to think of a first and sovereign being, and to draw, so to speak, the idea of him from the store-house of the mind, I am necessitated to attribute to him all kinds of perfections, though I may not then enumerate them all, nor think of each of them in particular. And this necessity is sufficient, as soon as I discover that existence is a perfection, to cause me to infer the existence of this first and sovereign being; just as it is not necessary that I should ever imagine any triangle, but whenever I am desirous of considering a rectilineal figure composed of only three angles, it is absolutely necessary to attribute those properties to it from which it is correctly inferred that its three angles are not greater than two right angles, although perhaps I may not then advert to this relation in particular. But when I consider what figures are capable of being inscribed in the circle, it is by no means necessary to hold that all quadrilateral figures are of this number; on the contrary, I cannot even imagine such to be the case, so long as I shall be unwilling to accept in thought aught that I do not clearly and distinctly conceive: and consequently there is a vast difference between false suppositions, as is the one in question, and the true ideas that were born with me, the first and chief of which is the idea of God. For indeed I discern on many grounds that this idea is not factitious, depending simply on my thought, but that it is the representation of a true and immutable nature: in the first place, because I can conceive no other being, except God, to whose essence existence [necessarily] pertains; in the second, because it is impossible to conceive two or more gods of this kind; and it being supposed that one such God exists, I clearly see that he must have existed from all eternity, and will exist to all eternity; and finally, because I apprehend many other properties in God, none of which I can either diminish or change.

But, indeed, whatever mode of probation I in the end adopt, it always returns to this, that it is only the things I clearly and distinctly conceive which have the power of completely persuading me. And although, of the objects I conceive in this manner, some, indeed, are obvious to every one, while others are only discovered after close and careful investigation; nevertheless, after they are once discovered, the latter are not esteemed less certain than the former. Thus, for example, to take the case of a right-angled triangle, although it is not so manifest at first that the square of the base is equal to the squares of the other two sides, as that the base is opposite to the greatest angle; nevertheless, after it is once apprehended, we are as firmly persuaded of the truth of the former as of the latter. And, with respect to God, if I were not preoccupied by prejudices, and my thoughts beset on all sides by the continual presence of the images of sensible objects, I should know nothing sooner or more easily than the fact of his being. For is there any truth more clear than the existence of a Supreme Being, or of God, seeing it is to his essence alone that [necessary and eternal] existence pertains?

And although the right conception of this truth has cost me much close thinking, nevertheless at present I feel not only as assured of it as of what I deem most certain, but I remark further that the certitude of all other truths is so absolutely dependent on it, that without this knowledge it is impossible ever to know anything perfectly.

For although I am of such a nature as to be unable, while I possess a very clear and distinct apprehension of a matter, to resist the conviction of its truth, yet because my constitution is also such as to incapacitate me from keeping my mind continually fixed on the same object, and as I frequently recollect a past judgment without at the same time being able to recall the grounds of it, it may happen meanwhile that other reasons are presented to me which would readily cause me to change my opinion, if I did not know that God existed; and thus I should possess no true and certain knowledge, but merely vague and vacillating opinions. Thus, for example, when I consider the nature of the [rectilineal] triangle, it most clearly appears to me, who have been instructed in the principles of geometry, that its three angles are equal to two right angles, and I find it impossible to believe otherwise, while I apply my mind to the demonstration; but as soon as I cease from attending to the process of proof, although I still remember that I had a clear comprehension of it, yet I may readily come to doubt of the truth demonstrated, if I do not know that there is a God: for I may persuade myself that I have been so constituted by nature as to be sometimes deceived, even in matters which I think I apprehend with the greatest evidence and certitude, especially when I recollect that I frequently considered many things to be true and certain which other reasons afterwards constrained me to reckon as wholly false.

But after I have discovered that God exists, seeing I also at the same time observed that all things depend on him, and that he is no deceiver, and thence inferred that all which I clearly and distinctly perceive is of necessity true: although I no longer attend to the grounds of a judgment, no opposite reason can be alleged sufficient to lead me to doubt of its truth, provided only I remember that I once possessed a clear and distinct comprehension of it. My knowledge of it thus becomes true and certain. And this same knowledge extends likewise to whatever I remember to have formerly demonstrated, as the truths of geometry and the like: for what can be alleged against them to lead me to doubt of them? Will it be that my nature is such that I may be frequently deceived? But I already know that I cannot be deceived in judgments of the grounds of which I possess a clear knowledge. Will it be that I formerly deemed things to be true and certain which I afterwards discovered to be false? But I had no clear and distinct knowledge of any of those things, and, being as yet ignorant of the rule by which I am assured of the truth of a judgment, I was led to give my assent to them on grounds which I afterwards discovered were less strong than at the time I imagined them to be. What further objection, then, is there? Will it be said that perhaps I am dreaming (an objection I lately myself raised), or that all the thoughts of which I am now conscious have no more truth than the reveries of my dreams? But although, in truth, I should be dreaming, the rule still holds that all which is clearly presented to my intellect is indisputably true.

And thus I very clearly see that the certitude and truth of all science depends on the knowledge alone of the true God, insomuch that, before I knew him, I could have no perfect knowledge of any other thing. And now that I know him, I possess the means of acquiring a perfect knowledge respecting innumerable matters, as well relative to God himself and other intellectual objects as to corporeal nature, in so far as it is the object of pure mathematics [which do not consider whether it exists or not].

MEDITATION VI

OF THE EXISTENCE OF MATERIAL THINGS, AND OF THE REAL

DISTINCTION BETWEEN THE MIND AND BODY OF MAN

There now only remains the inquiry as to whether material things exist. With regard to this question, I at least know with certainty that such things may exist, in as far as they constitute the object of the pure mathematics, since, regarding them in this aspect, I can conceive them clearly and distinctly. For there can be no doubt that God possesses the power of producing all the objects I am able distinctly to conceive, and I never considered anything impossible to him, unless when I experienced a contradiction in the attempt to conceive it aright. Further, the faculty of imagination which I possess, and of which I am conscious that I make use when I apply myself to the consideration of material things, is sufficient to persuade me of their existence: for, when I attentively consider what imagination is, I find that it is simply a certain application of the cognitive faculty (*facultas cognoscitiva*) to a body which is immediately present to it, and which therefore exists.

And to render this quite clear, I remark, in the first place, the difference that subsists between imagination and pure intellection [or conception]. For example, when I imagine a triangle I not only conceive (*intelligo*) that it is a figure comprehended by three lines, but at the same time also I look upon (*intueor*) these three lines as present by the power and internal application of my mind (*acie mentis*), and this is what I call imagining. But if I desire to think of a chiliagon, I indeed rightly conceive that it is a figure composed of a thousand sides, as easily as I conceive that a triangle is a figure composed of only three sides; but I cannot imagine the thousand sides of a chiliagon as I do the three sides of a triangle, nor, so to speak, view them as present [with the eyes of my mind]. And although, in accordance with the habit I have of always imagining something when I think of corporeal things, it may happen that, in conceiving a chiliagon, I confusedly represent some figure to myself, yet it is quite evident that this is not a chiliagon, since it in no wise differs from that which I would represent to myself, if I were to think of a myriogon, or any other figure of many sides; nor would this representation be of any use in discovering and unfolding the properties that constitute the difference between a chiliagon and other polygons. But if the question turns on a pentagon, it is quite true that I can conceive its figure, as well as that of a chiliagon, without the aid of imagination; but I can likewise imagine it by applying the attention of my mind to its five sides, and at the same time to the area which they contain. Thus I observe that a special effort of mind is necessary to the act of imagination, which is not required to conceiving or understanding (*ad intelligendum*); and this special exertion of mind clearly shows the difference between imagination and pure intellection (*imaginatio et intellectio pura*). I remark, besides, that this power of imagination which I possess, in as far as it differs from the power of conceiving, is in no way necessary to my [nature or] essence, that is, to the essence of my mind; for although I did not possess it, I should still remain the same that I now am, from which it seems we may conclude that it depends on something different from the mind. And I easily understand that, if some body exists, with which my mind is so conjoined and united as to be able, as it were, to consider it when it chooses, it may thus imagine corporeal objects; so that this mode of thinking differs from pure intellection only in this respect, that the mind in conceiving turns in some way upon itself, and considers some one of the ideas it possesses within itself; but in imagining it turns towards the body, and contemplates in it some object conformed to the idea which it either of itself conceived or apprehended by sense. I easily understand, I say, that imagination may be thus formed, if it is true that there are bodies; and because I find no other obvious mode of explaining it, I thence, with probability, conjecture that they exist, but only with probability; and although I carefully examine all things, nevertheless I do not find that, from the distinct idea of corporeal nature I have in my imagination, I can necessarily infer the existence of any body.

But I am accustomed to imagine many other objects besides that corporeal nature which is the object of the pure mathematics, as, for example, colours, sounds, tastes, pain, and the like, although with less distinctness; and, inasmuch as I perceive these objects much better by the senses, through the medium of which and of memory, they seem to have reached the imagination, I believe that, in order the more advantageously to examine them, it is proper I should at the same time examine what sense-perception is, and inquire whether from those ideas that are apprehended by this mode of thinking (consciousness), I cannot obtain a certain proof of the existence of corporeal objects.

And, in the first place, I will recall to my mind the things I have hitherto held as true, because perceived by the senses, and the foundations upon which my belief in their truth rested; I will, in the second place, examine the reasons that afterwards constrained me to doubt of them; and, finally, I will consider what of them I ought now to believe.

Firstly, then, I perceived that I had a head, hands, feet, and other members composing that body which I considered as part, or perhaps even as the whole, of myself. I perceived further, that that body was placed among many others, by which it was capable of being affected in diverse ways, both beneficial and hurtful; and what was beneficial I remarked by a certain sensation of pleasure, and what was hurtful by a sensation of pain. And, besides this pleasure and pain, I was likewise conscious of hunger, thirst, and other appetites, as well as certain corporeal inclinations towards joy, sadness, anger, and similar passions. And, out of myself, besides the extension, figure, and motions of bodies, I likewise perceived in them hardness, heat, and the other tactile qualities, and, in addition, light, colours, odours, tastes, and sounds, the variety of which gave me the means of distinguishing the sky, the earth, the sea, and generally all the other bodies, from one another. And certainly, considering the ideas of all these qualities, which were presented to my mind, and which alone I properly and immediately perceived, it was not without reason that I thought I perceived certain objects wholly different from my thought, namely, bodies from which those ideas proceeded; for I was conscious that the ideas were presented to me without my consent being required, so that I could not perceive any object, however desirous I might be, unless it were present to the organ of sense; and it was wholly out of my power not to perceive it when it was thus present. And because the ideas I perceived by the senses were much more lively and clear, and even, in their own way, more distinct than any of those I could of myself frame by meditation, or which I found impressed on my memory, it seemed that they could not have proceeded from myself, and must therefore have been caused in me by some other objects: and as of those objects I had no knowledge beyond what the ideas themselves gave me, nothing was so likely to occur to my mind as the supposition that the objects were similar to the ideas which they caused. And because I recollected also that I had formerly trusted to the senses, rather than to reason, and that the ideas which I myself formed were not so clear as those I perceived by sense, and that they were even for the most part composed of parts of the latter, I was readily persuaded that I had no idea in my intellect which had not formerly passed through the senses. Nor was I altogether wrong in likewise believing that that body which, by a special right, I called my own, pertained to me more properly and strictly than any of the others; for in truth, I could never be separated from it as from other bodies: I felt in it and on account of it all my appetites and affections, and in fine I was affected in its parts by pain and the titillation of pleasure, and not in the parts of the other bodies that were separated from it. But when I inquired into the reason why, from this I know not what sensation of pain, sadness of mind should follow, and why from the sensation of pleasure joy should arise, or why this indescribable twitching of the stomach, which I call hunger, should put me in mind of taking food, and the parchedness of the throat of drink, and so in other cases, I was unable to give any explanation, unless that I was so taught by nature; for there is assuredly no affinity, at least none that I am able to comprehend, between this irritation of the stomach and the desire of food, any more than between the perception of an object that causes pain and the consciousness of sadness which springs from the perception. And in the same way it seemed to me that all the other judgments I had formed regarding the objects of sense, were dictates of nature; because I remarked that those judgments were formed in me, before I had leisure to weigh and consider the reasons that might constrain me to form them.

But, afterwards, a wide experience by degrees sapped the faith I had reposed in my senses; for I frequently observed that towers, which at a distance seemed round, appeared square when more closely viewed, and that colossal figures, raised on the summits of these towers, looked like small statues, when viewed from the bottom of them; and, in other instances without number, I also discovered error in judgments founded on the external senses; and not only in those founded on the external, but even in those that rested on the internal senses; for is there aught more internal than pain? and yet I have sometimes been informed by parties whose arm or leg had been amputated, that they still occasionally seemed to feel pain in that part of the body which they had lost,—a circumstance that led me to think that I could not be quite certain even that any one of my members was affected when I felt pain in it. And to these grounds of doubt I shortly afterwards also added two others of very wide generality: the first of them was that I believed I never perceived anything when awake which I could not occasionally think I also perceived when asleep, and as I do not believe that the ideas I seem to perceive in my sleep proceed from objects external to me, I did not any more observe any ground for believing this of such as I seem to perceive when awake; the second was that since I was as yet ignorant of the author of my being, or at least supposed myself to be so, I saw nothing to prevent my having been so constituted by nature as that I should be deceived even in matters that appeared to me to possess the greatest truth. And, with respect to the grounds on which I had before been persuaded of the existence of sensible objects, I had no great difficulty in finding suitable answers to them; for as nature seemed to incline me to many things from which reason made me averse, I thought that I ought not to confide much in its teachings. And although the perceptions of the senses were not dependent on my will, I did not think that I ought on that ground to conclude that they proceeded from things different from myself, since perhaps there might be found in me some faculty, though hitherto unknown to me, which produced them.

But now that I begin to know myself better, and to discover more clearly the author of my being, I do not, indeed, think that I ought rashly to admit all which the senses seem to teach, nor, on the other hand, is it my conviction that I ought to doubt in general of their teachings.

And, firstly, because I know that all which I clearly and distinctly conceive can be produced by God exactly as I conceive it, it is sufficient that I am able clearly and distinctly to conceive one thing apart from another, in order to be certain that the one is different from the other, seeing they may at least be made to exist separately, by the omnipotence of God; and it matters not by what power this separation is made, in order to be compelled to judge them different; and, therefore, merely because I know with certitude that I exist, and because, in the meantime, I do not observe that aught necessarily belongs to my nature or essence beyond my being a thinking thing, I rightly conclude that my essence consists only in my being a thinking thing [or a substance whose whole essence or nature is merely thinking]. And although I may, or rather, as I will shortly say, although I certainly do possess a body with which I am very closely conjoined; nevertheless, because, on the one hand, I have a clear and distinct idea of myself, in as far as I am only a thinking and unextended thing, and as, on the other hand, I possess a distinct idea of body, in as far as it is only an extended and unthinking thing, it is certain that I [that is, my mind, by which I am what I am] is entirely and truly distinct from my body, and may exist without it.

Moreover, I find in myself diverse faculties of thinking that have each their special mode: for example, I find I possess the faculties of imagining and perceiving, without which I can indeed clearly and distinctly conceive myself as entire, but I cannot reciprocally conceive them without conceiving myself, that is to say, without an intelligent substance in which they reside, for [in the notion we have of them, or to use the terms of the schools] in their formal concept, they comprise some sort of intellection; whence I perceive that they are distinct from myself as modes are from things. I remark likewise certain other faculties, as the power of changing place, of assuming diverse figures, and the like, that cannot be conceived and cannot therefore exist, any more than the preceding, apart from a substance in which they inhere. It is very evident, however, that these faculties, if they really exist, must belong to some corporeal or extended substance, since in their clear and distinct concept there is contained some sort of extension, but no intellection at all. Farther, I cannot doubt but that there is in me a certain passive faculty of perception, that is, of receiving and taking knowledge of the ideas of sensible things; but this would be useless to me, if there did not also exist in me, or in some other thing, another active faculty capable of forming and producing those ideas. But this active faculty cannot be in me [in as far as I am but a thinking thing], seeing that it does not presuppose thought, and also that those ideas are frequently produced in my mind without my contributing to it in any way, and even frequently contrary to my will. This faculty must therefore exist in some substance different from me, in which all the objective reality of the ideas that are produced by this faculty is contained formally or eminently, as I before remarked: and this substance is either a body, that is to say, a corporeal nature in which is contained formally [and in effect] all that is objectively [and by representation] in those ideas; or it is God himself, or some other creature, of a rank superior to body, in which the same is contained eminently. But as God is no deceiver, it is manifest that he does not of himself and immediately communicate those ideas to me, nor even by the intervention of any creature in which their objective reality is not formally, but only eminently, contained. For as he has given me no faculty whereby I can discover this to be the case, but, on the contrary, a very strong inclination to believe that those ideas arise from corporeal objects, I do not see how he could be vindicated from the charge of deceit, if in truth they proceeded from any other source, or were produced by other causes than corporeal things: and accordingly it must be concluded, that corporeal objects exist. Nevertheless they are not perhaps exactly such as we perceive by the senses, for their comprehension by the senses is, in many instances, very obscure and confused; but it is at least necessary to admit that all which I clearly and distinctly conceive as in them, that is, generally speaking, all that is comprehended in the object of speculative geometry, really exists external to me.

But with respect to other things which are either only particular, as, for example, that the sun is of such a size and figure, etc., or are conceived with less clearness and distinctness, as light, sound, pain, and the like, although they are highly dubious and uncertain, nevertheless on the ground alone that God is no deceiver, and that consequently he has permitted no falsity in my opinions which he has not likewise given me a faculty of correcting, I think I may with safety conclude that I possess in myself the means of arriving at the truth. And, in the first place, it cannot be doubted that in each of the dictates of nature there is some truth: for by nature, considered in general, I now understand nothing more than God himself, or the order and disposition established by God in created things; and by my nature in particular I understand the assemblage of all that God has given me.

But there is nothing which that nature teaches me more expressly [or more sensibly] than that I have a body which is ill affected when I feel pain, and stands in need of food and drink when I experience the sensations of hunger and thirst, etc. And therefore I ought not to doubt but that there is some truth in these informations.

Nature likewise teaches me by these sensations of pain, hunger, thirst, etc., that I am not only lodged in my body as a pilot in a vessel, but that I am besides so intimately conjoined, and as it were intermixed with it, that my mind and body compose a certain unity. For if this were not the case, I should not feel pain when my body is hurt, seeing I am merely a thinking thing, but should perceive the wound by the understanding alone, just as a pilot perceives by sight when any part of his vessel is damaged; and when my body has need of food or drink, I should have a clear knowledge of this, and not be made aware of it by the confused sensations of hunger and thirst: for, in truth, all these sensations of hunger, thirst, pain, etc., are nothing more than certain confused modes of thinking, arising from the union and apparent fusion of mind and body.

Besides this, nature teaches me that my own body is surrounded by many other bodies, some of which I have to seek after, and others to shun. And indeed, as I perceive different sorts of colours, sounds, odours, tastes, heat, hardness, etc., I safely conclude that there are in the bodies from which the diverse perceptions of the senses proceed, certain varieties corresponding to them, although, perhaps, not in reality like them; and since, among these diverse perceptions of the senses, some are agreeable, and others disagreeable, there can be no doubt that my body, or rather my entire self, in as far as I am composed of body and mind, may be variously affected, both beneficially and hurtfully, by surrounding bodies.

But there are many other beliefs which, though seemingly the teaching of nature, are not in reality so, but which obtained a place in my mind through a habit of judging inconsiderately of things. It may thus easily happen that such judgments shall contain error: thus, for example, the opinion I have that all space in which there is nothing to affect [or make an impression on] my senses is void; that in a hot body there is something in every respect similar to the idea of heat in my mind; that in a white or green body there is the same whiteness or greenness which I perceive; that in a bitter or sweet body there is the same taste, and so in other instances; that the stars, towers, and all distant bodies, are of the same size and figure as they appear to our eyes, etc. But that I may avoid everything like indistinctness of conception, I must accurately define what I properly understand by being taught by nature. For nature is here taken in a narrower sense than when it signifies the sum of all the things which God has given me; seeing that in that meaning the notion comprehends much that belongs only to the mind [to which I am not here to be understood as referring when I use the term nature]; as, for example, the notion I have of the truth, that what is done cannot be undone, and all the other truths I discern by the natural light [without the aid of the body]; and seeing that it comprehends likewise much besides that belongs only to body, and is not here any more contained under the name nature, as the quality of heaviness, and the like, of which I do not speak,—the term being reserved exclusively to designate the things which God has given to me as a being composed of mind and body. But nature, taking the term in the sense explained, teaches me to shun what causes in me the sensation of pain, and to pursue what affords me the sensation of pleasure, and other things of this sort; but I do not discover that it teaches me, in addition to this, from these diverse perceptions of the senses, to draw any conclusions respecting external objects without a previous [careful and mature] consideration of them by the mind: for it is, as appears to me, the office of the mind alone, and not of the composite whole of mind and body, to discern the truth in those matters. Thus, although the impression a star makes on my eye is not larger than that from the flame of a candle, I do not, nevertheless, experience any real or positive impulse determining me to believe that the star is not greater than the flame; the true account of the matter being merely that I have so judged from my youth without any rational ground. And, though on approaching the fire I feel heat, and even pain on approaching it too closely, I have, however, from this no ground for holding that something resembling the heat I feel is in the fire, any more than that there is something similar to the pain; all that I have ground for believing is, that there is something in it, whatever it may be, which excites in me those sensations of heat or pain. So also, although there are spaces in which I find nothing to excite and affect my senses, I must not therefore conclude that those spaces contain in them no body; for I see that in this, as in many other similar matters, I have been accustomed to pervert the order of nature, because these perceptions of the senses, although given me by nature merely to signify to my mind what things are beneficial and hurtful to the composite whole of which it is a part, and being sufficiently clear and distinct for that purpose, are nevertheless used by me as infallible rules by which to determine immediately the essence of the bodies that exist out of me, of which they can of course afford me only the most obscure and confused knowledge.

But I have already sufficiently considered how it happens that, notwithstanding the supreme goodness of God, there is falsity in my judgments. A difficulty, however, here presents itself, respecting the things which I am taught by nature must be pursued or avoided, and also respecting the internal sensations in which I seem to have occasionally detected error [and thus to be directly deceived by nature]: thus, for example, I may be so deceived by the agreeable taste of some viand with which poison has been mixed, as to be induced to take the poison. In this case, however, nature may be excused, for it simply leads me to desire the viand for its agreeable taste, and not the poison, which is unknown to it; and thus we can infer nothing from this circumstance beyond that our nature is not omniscient; at which there is assuredly no ground for surprise, since, man being of a finite nature, his knowledge must likewise be of limited perfection. But we also not unfrequently err in that to which we are directly impelled by nature, as is the case with invalids who desire drink or food that would be hurtful to them. It will here, perhaps, be alleged that the reason why such persons are deceived is that their nature is corrupted; but this leaves the difficulty untouched, for a sick man is not less really the creature of God than a man who is in full health; and therefore it is as repugnant to the goodness of God that the nature of the former should be deceitful as it is for that of the latter to be so. And, as a clock, composed of wheels and counter-weights, observes not the less accurately all the laws of nature when it is ill made, and points out the hours incorrectly, than when it satisfies the desire of the maker in every respect; so likewise if the body of man be considered as a kind of machine, so made up and composed of bones, nerves, muscles, veins, blood, and skin, that although there were in it no mind, it would still exhibit the same motions which it at present manifests involuntarily, and therefore without the aid of the mind [and simply by the dispositions of its organs], I easily discern that it would also be as natural for such a body, supposing it dropsical, for example, to experience the parchedness of the throat that is usually accompanied in the mind by the sensation of thirst, and to be disposed by this parchedness to move its nerves and its other parts in the way required for drinking, and thus increase its malady and do itself harm, as it is natural for it, when it is not indisposed to be stimulated to drink for its good by a similar cause; and although looking to the use for which a clock was destined by its maker, I may say that it is deflected from its proper nature when it incorrectly indicates the hours, and on the same principle, considering the machine of the human body as having been formed by God for the sake of the motions which it usually manifests, although I may likewise have ground for thinking that it does not follow the order of its nature when the throat is parched and drink does not tend to its preservation, nevertheless I yet plainly discern that this latter acceptation of the term nature is very different from the other; for this is nothing more than a certain denomination, depending entirely on my thought, and hence called extrinsic, by which I compare a sick man and an imperfectly constructed clock with the idea I have of a man in good health and a well-made clock; while by the other acceptation of nature is understood something which is truly found in things, and therefore possessed of some truth.

But certainly, although in respect of a dropsical body, it is only by way of exterior denomination that we say its nature is corrupted, when, without requiring drink, the throat is parched; yet, in respect of the composite whole, that is, of the mind in its union with the body, it is not a pure denomination, but really an error of nature, for it to feel thirst when drink would be hurtful to it: and, accordingly, it still remains to be considered why it is that the goodness of God does not prevent the nature of man thus taken from being fallacious.

To commence this examination accordingly, I here remark, in the first place, that there is a vast difference between mind and body, in respect that body, from its nature, is always divisible, and that mind is entirely indivisible. For in truth, when I consider the mind, that is, when I consider myself in so far only as I am a thinking thing, I can distinguish in myself no parts, but I very clearly discern that I am somewhat absolutely one and entire; and although the whole mind seems to be united to the whole body, yet, when a foot, an arm, or any other part is cut off, I am conscious that nothing has been taken from my mind; nor can the faculties of willing, perceiving, conceiving, etc., properly be called its parts, for it is the same mind that is exercised [all entire] in willing, in perceiving, and in conceiving, etc. But quite the opposite holds in corporeal or extended things; for I cannot imagine any one of them [how small soever it may be], which I cannot easily sunder in thought, and which, therefore, I do not know to be divisible. This would be sufficient to teach me that the mind or soul of man is entirely different from the body, if I had not already been apprised of it on other grounds.

I remark, in the next place, that the mind does not immediately receive the impression from all the parts of the body, but only from the brain, or perhaps even from one small part of it, viz., that in which the common sense (*sensus communis*) is said to be, which as often as it is affected in the same way, gives rise to the same perception in the mind, although meanwhile the other parts of the body may be diversely disposed, as is proved by innumerable experiments, which it is unnecessary here to enumerate.

I remark, besides, that the nature of body is such that none of its parts can be moved by another part a little removed from the other, which cannot likewise be moved in the same way by any one of the parts that lie between those two, although the most remote part does not act at all. As, for example, in the cord A, B, C, D [which is in tension], if its last part D be pulled, the first part A will not be moved in a different way than it would be were one of the intermediate parts B or C to be pulled, and the last part D meanwhile to remain fixed. And in the same way, when I feel pain in the foot, the science of physics teaches me that this sensation is experienced by means of the nerves dispersed over the foot, which, extending like cords from it to the brain, when they are contracted in the foot, contract at the same time the inmost parts of the brain in which they have their origin, and excite in these parts a certain motion appointed by nature to cause in the mind a sensation of pain, as if existing in the foot: but as these nerves must pass through the tibia, the leg, the loins, the back, and neck, in order to reach the brain, it may happen that although their extremities in the foot are not affected, but only certain of their parts that pass through the loins or neck, the same movements, nevertheless, are excited in the brain by this motion as would have been caused there by a hurt received in the foot, and hence the mind will necessarily feel pain in the foot, just as if it had been hurt; and the same is true of all the other perceptions of our senses.

I remark, finally, that as each of the movements that are made in the part of the brain by which the mind is immediately affected, impresses it with but a single sensation, the most likely supposition in the circumstances is, that this movement causes the mind to experience, among all the sensations which it is capable of impressing upon it, that one which is the best fitted, and generally the most useful for the preservation of the human body when it is in full health. But experience shows us that all the perceptions which nature has given us are of such a kind as I have mentioned; and accordingly, there is nothing found in them that does not manifest the power and goodness of God. Thus, for example, when the nerves of the foot are violently or more than usually shaken, the motion passing through the medulla of the spine to the innermost parts of the brain affords a sign to the mind on which it experiences a sensation, viz., of pain, as if it were in the foot, by which the mind is admonished and excited to do its utmost to remove the cause of it as dangerous and hurtful to the foot. It is true that God could have so constituted the nature of man as that the same motion in the brain would have informed the mind of something altogether different: the motion might, for example, have been the occasion on which the mind became conscious of itself, in so far as it is in the brain, or in so far as it is in some place intermediate between the foot and the brain, or, finally, the occasion on which it perceived some other object quite different, whatever that might be; but nothing of all this would have so well contributed to the preservation of the body as that which the mind actually feels. In the same way, when we stand in need of drink, there arises from this want a certain parchedness in the throat that moves its nerves, and by means of them the internal parts of the brain, and this movement affects the mind with the sensation of thirst, because there is nothing on that occasion which is more useful for us than to be made aware that we have need of drink for the preservation of our health; and so in other instances.

Whence it is quite manifest, that notwithstanding the sovereign goodness of God, the nature of man, in so far as it is composed of mind and body, cannot but be sometimes fallacious. For, if there is any cause which excites, not in the foot, but in some one of the parts of the nerves that stretch from the foot to the brain, or even in the brain itself, the same movement that is ordinarily created when the foot is ill affected, pain will be felt, as it were, in the foot, and the sense will thus be naturally deceived; for as the same movement in the brain can but impress the mind with the same sensation, and as this sensation is much more frequently excited by a cause which hurts the foot than by one acting in a different quarter, it is reasonable that it should lead the mind to feel pain in the foot rather than in any other part of the body. And if it sometimes happens that the parchedness of the throat does not arise, as is usual, from drink being necessary for the health of the body, but from quite the opposite cause, as is the case with the dropsical; yet it is much better that it should be deceitful in that instance, than if, on the contrary, it were continually fallacious when the body is well-disposed; and the same holds true in other cases.

And certainly this consideration is of great service, not only in enabling me to recognise the errors to which my nature is liable, but likewise in rendering it more easy to avoid or correct them: for, knowing that all my senses more usually indicate to me what is true than what is false, in matters relating to the advantage of the body, and being able almost always to make use of more than a single sense in examining the same object, and besides this, being able to use my memory in connecting present with past knowledge, and my understanding which has already discovered all the causes of my errors, I ought no longer to fear that falsity may be met with in what is daily presented to me by the senses. And I ought to reject all the doubts of those bygone days as hyperbolical and ridiculous, especially the general uncertainty respecting sleep, which I could not distinguish from the waking state: for I now find a very marked difference between the two states, in respect that our memory can never connect our dreams with each other and with the course of life, in the way it is in the habit of doing with events that occur when we are awake. And, in truth, if some one, when I am awake, appeared to me all of a sudden and as suddenly disappeared, as do the images I see in sleep, so that I could not observe either whence he came or whither he went, I should not without reason esteem it either a spectre or phantom formed in my brain, rather than a real man. But when I perceive objects with regard to which I can distinctly determine both the place whence they come, and that in which they are, and the time at which they appear to me, and when, without interruption, I can connect the perception I have of them with the whole of the other parts of my life, I am perfectly sure that what I thus perceive occurs while I am awake and not during sleep. And I ought not in the least degree to doubt of the truth of those presentations, if, after having called together all my senses, my memory, and my understanding for the purpose of examining them, no deliverance is given by any one of these faculties which is repugnant to that of any other: for since God is no deceiver, it necessarily follows that I am not herein deceived. But because the necessities of action frequently oblige us to come to a determination before we have had leisure for so careful an examination, it must be confessed that the life of man is frequently obnoxious to error with respect to individual objects; and we must, in conclusion, acknowledge the weakness of our nature.

BENEDICT DE SPINOZA

THE ETHICS

[Ethica Ordine Geometrico Demonstrata]

THE ETHICS

PART I CONCERNING GOD

DEFINITIONS

I. By that which is *self-caused*, I mean that of which the essence involves existence, or that of which the nature is only conceivable as existent.

II. A thing is called *finite after its kind*, when it can be limited by another thing of the same nature; for instance, a body is called finite because we always conceive another greater body. So, also, a thought is limited by another thought, but a body is not limited by thought, nor a thought by body.

III. By *substance*, I mean that which is in itself, and is conceived through itself: in other words, that of which a conception can be formed independently of any other conception.

IV. By *attribute*, I mean that which the intellect perceives as constituting the essence of substance.

V. By *mode*, I mean the modifications[1] of substance, or that which exists in, and is conceived through, something other than itself.

VI. By *God*, I mean a being absolutely infinite—that is, a substance consisting in infinite attributes, of which each expresses eternal and infinite essentiality.

Explanation.—I say absolutely infinite, not infinite after its kind: for, of a thing infinite only after its kind, infinite attributes may be denied; but that which is absolutely infinite, contains in its essence whatever expresses reality, and involves no negation.

VII. That thing is called free, which exists solely by the

---

[1] *"Affectiones."*

necessity of its own nature, and of which the action is determined by itself alone. On the other hand, that thing is necessary, or rather constrained, which is determined by something external to itself to a fixed and definite method of existence or action.

VIII. By *eternity*, I mean existence itself, in so far as it is conceived necessarily to follow solely from the definition of that which is eternal.

Explanation.—Existence of this kind is conceived as an eternal truth, like the essence of a thing, and, therefore, cannot be explained by means of continuance or time, though continuance may be conceived without a beginning or end.

AXIOMS

I. Everything which exists, exists either in itself or in something else.

II. That which cannot be conceived through anything else must be conceived through itself.

III. From a given definite cause an effect necessarily follows; and, on the other hand, if no definite cause be granted, it is impossible that an effect can follow.

IV. The knowledge of an effect depends on and involves the knowledge of a cause.

V. Things which have nothing in common cannot be understood, the one by means of the other; the conception of one does not involve the conception of the other.

VI. A true idea must correspond with its ideate or object.

VII. If a thing can be conceived as non-existing, its essence does not involve existence.

PROPOSITIONS

PROP. I. *Substance is by nature prior to its modifications.*
Proof.—This is clear from Deff. iii. and v.

PROP. II. *Two substances, whose attributes are different, have nothing in common.*
Proof.—Also evident from Def. iii. For each must exist in itself, and be conceived through itself; in other words, the

conception of one does not imply the conception of the other.

PROP. III. *Things which have nothing in common cannot be one the cause of the other.*

Proof.—If they have nothing in common, it follows that one cannot be apprehended by means of the other (Ax. v.), and, therefore, one cannot be the cause of the other (Ax. iv.). *Q.E.D.*

PROP. IV. *Two or more distinct things are distinguished one from the other either by the difference of the attributes of the substances, or by the difference of their modifications.*

Proof.—Everything which exists, exists either in itself or in something else (Ax. i.),—that is (by Deff. iii. and v.), nothing is granted in addition to the understanding, except substance and its modifications. Nothing is, therefore, given besides the understanding, by which several things may be distinguished one from the other, except the substances, or, in other words (see Ax. iv.), their attributes and modifications. *Q.E.D.*

PROP. V. *There cannot exist in the universe two or more substances having the same nature or attribute.*

Proof.—If several distinct substances be granted, they must be distinguished one from the other, either by the difference of their attributes, or by the difference of their modifications (Prop. iv.). If only by the difference of their attributes, it will be granted that there cannot be more than one with an identical attribute. If by the difference of their modifications—as substance is naturally prior to its modifications (Prop. i.),—it follows that setting the modifications aside, and considering substance in itself, that is truly, (Deff. iii. and vi.), there cannot be conceived one substance different from another,—that is (by Prop. iv.), there cannot be granted several substances, but one substance only. *Q.E.D.*

PROP. VI. *One substance cannot be produced by another substance.*

Proof.—It is impossible that there should be in the universe two substances with an identical attribute, *i.e.* which have anything common to them both (Prop. ii.), and, therefore (Prop. iii.), one cannot be the cause of another, neither can one be produced by the other. *Q.E.D.*

Corollary.—Hence it follows that a substance cannot be produced by anything external to itself. For in the universe nothing is granted, save substances and their modifications (as appears from Ax. i. and Deff. iii. and v.). Now (by the last Prop.) substance cannot be produced by another substance, therefore it cannot be produced by anything external to itself. *Q.E.D.* This is shown still more readily by the absurdity of the contradictory. For, if substance be produced by an external cause, the knowledge of it would depend on the knowledge of its cause (Ax. iv.), and (by Def. iii.) it would itself not be substance.

PROP. VII. *Existence belongs to the nature of substance.*

Proof.—Substance cannot be produced by anything external (Corollary, Prop. vi.), it must, therefore, be its own cause—that is, its essence necessarily involves existence, or existence belongs to its nature.

PROP. VIII. *Every substance is necessarily infinite.*

Proof.—There can only be one substance with an identical attribute, and existence follows from its nature (Prop. vii.); its nature, therefore, involves existence, either as finite or infinite. It does not exist as finite, for (by Def. ii.) it would then be limited by something else of the same kind, which would also necessarily exist (Prop. vii.); and there would be two substances with an identical attribute, which is absurd (Prop. v.). It therefore exists as infinite. *Q.E.D.*

Note I.—As finite existence involves a partial negation, and infinite existence is the absolute affirmation of the given nature, it follows (solely from Prop. vii.) that every substance is necessarily infinite.

Note II.—No doubt it will be difficult for those who think about things loosely, and have not been accustomed to know them by their primary causes, to comprehend the demonstration of Prop. vii.: for such persons make no distinction between the modifications of substances and the substances themselves, and are ignorant of the manner in which things are produced; hence they attribute to substances the beginning which they observe in natural objects. Those who are ignorant of true causes, make complete confusion—think that trees might talk just as well as men—that men might be formed from stones as well as from seed; and imagine that any form might be changed into any other. So, also, those who confuse the two natures, divine and human, readily attribute human passions to the deity, especially so long as they do not know how passions originate in the mind. But, if people would consider the nature of substance, they would have no doubt about the truth of Prop. vii. In fact, this proposition would be a universal axiom, and accounted a truism. For, by substance, would be understood that which is in itself, and is conceived through itself—that is, something of which the conception requires not the conception of anything else; whereas modifications exist in something external to themselves, and a conception of them is formed by means of a conception of the thing in which they exist. Therefore, we may have true ideas of non-existent modifications; for, although they may have no *actual* existence apart from the conceiving intellect, yet their essence is so involved in something external to themselves that they may through it be conceived. Whereas the only truth substances can have, external to the intellect, must consist in their existence, because they are conceived through themselves. Therefore, for a person to say that he has a clear and distinct—that is, a true—idea of a substance, but that he is not sure whether such substance exists, would be the same as if he said that he had a true idea, but was not sure whether or not it was false (a little consideration will make this plain); or if anyone affirmed that substance is created, it would be the same as saying that a false idea was true—in short, the height of absurdity. It must, then, necessarily be admitted that the existence of substance as its essence is an eternal truth. And we can hence conclude by another process of reasoning—that there is but one such substance. I think that this may profitably be done at once; and, in order to proceed regularly with the demonstration, we must premise:—

1. The true definition of a thing neither involves nor expresses anything beyond the nature of the thing defined. From this it follows that—

2. No definition implies or expresses a certain number of individuals, inasmuch as it expresses nothing beyond the nature of the thing defined. For instance, the definition of a

triangle expresses nothing beyond the actual nature of a triangle: it does not imply any fixed number of triangles.

3. There is necessarily for each individual existent thing a cause why it should exist.

4. This cause of existence must either be contained in the nature and definition of the thing defined, or must be postulated apart from such definition.

It therefore follows that, if a given number of individual things exist in nature, there must be some cause for the existence of exactly that number, neither more nor less. For example, if twenty men exist in the universe (for simplicity's sake, I will suppose them existing simultaneously, and to have had no predecessors), and we want to account for the existence of these twenty men, it will not be enough to show the cause of human existence in general; we must also show why there are exactly twenty men, neither more nor less: for a cause must be assigned for the existence of each individual. Now this cause cannot be contained in the actual nature of man, for the true definition of man does not involve any consideration of the number twenty. Consequently, the cause for the existence of these twenty men, and, consequently, of each of them, must necessarily be sought externally to each individual. Hence we may lay down the absolute rule, that everything which may consist of several individuals must have an external cause. And, as it has been shown already that existence appertains to the nature of substance, existence must necessarily be included in its definition; and from its definition alone existence must be deducible. But from its definition (as we have shown, Notes 2, 3), we cannot infer the existence of several substances; therefore it follows that there is only one substance of the same nature. *Q.E.D.*

PROP. IX. *The more reality or being a thing has, the greater the number of its attributes* (Def. iv.).

PROP. X. *Each particular attribute of the one substance must be conceived through itself.*

Proof.—An attribute is that which the intellect perceives of substance, as constituting its essence (Def. iv.), and, therefore, must be conceived through itself (Def. iii.). *Q.E.D.*

Note.—It is thus evident that, though two attributes are,

in fact, conceived as distinct—that is, one without the help of the other—yet we cannot, therefore, conclude that they constitute two entities, or two different substances. For it is the nature of substance that each of its attributes is conceived through itself, inasmuch as all the attributes it has have always existed simultaneously in it, and none could be produced by any other; but each expresses the reality or being of substance. It is, then, far from an absurdity to ascribe several attributes to one substance: for nothing in nature is more clear than that each and every entity must be conceived under some attribute, and that its reality or being is in proportion to the number of its attributes expressing necessity or eternity and infinity. Consequently it is abundantly clear, that an absolutely infinite being must necessarily be defined as consisting in infinite attributes, each of which expresses a certain eternal and infinite essence.

If anyone now ask, by what sign shall he be able to distinguish different substances, let him read the following propositions, which show that there is but one substance in the universe, and that it is absolutely infinite, wherefore such a sign would be sought for in vain.

PROP. XI. *God, or substance, consisting of infinite attributes, of which each expresses eternal and infinite essentiality, necessarily exists.*

Proof.—If this be denied, conceive, if possible, that God does not exist: then his essence does not involve existence. But this (by Prop. vii.) is absurd. Therefore God necessarily exists.

Another proof.—Of everything whatsoever a cause or reason must be assigned, either for its existence, or for its non-existence—*e.g.* if a triangle exist, a reason or cause must be granted for its existence; if, on the contrary, it does not exist, a cause must also be granted, which prevents it from existing, or annuls its existence. This reason or cause must either be contained in the nature of the thing in question, or be external to it. For instance, the reason for the non-existence of a square circle is indicated in its nature, namely, because it would involve a contradiction. On the other hand, the existence of substance follows also solely from its nature, inasmuch as its nature involves existence. (See Prop. vii.)

But the reason for the existence of a triangle or a circle does not follow from the nature of those figures, but from the order of universal nature in extension. From the latter it must follow, either that a triangle necessarily exists, or that it is impossible that it should exist. So much is self-evident. It follows therefrom that a thing necessarily exists, if no cause or reason be granted which prevents its existence.

If, then, no cause or reason can be given, which prevents the existence of God, or which destroys his existence, we must certainly conclude that he necessarily does exist. If such a reason or cause should be given, it must either be drawn from the very nature of God, or be external to him—that is, drawn from another substance of another nature. For if it were of the same nature, God, by that very fact, would be admitted to exist. But substance of another nature could have nothing in common with God (by Prop. ii.), and therefore would be unable either to cause or to destroy his existence.

As, then, a reason or cause which would annul the divine existence cannot be drawn from anything external to the divine nature, such cause must perforce, if God does not exist, be drawn from God's own nature, which would involve a contradiction. To make such an affirmation about a being absolutely infinite and supremely perfect, is absurd; therefore, neither in the nature of God, nor externally to his nature, can a cause or reason be assigned which would annul his existence. Therefore, God necessarily exists. *Q.E.D.*

Another proof.—The potentiality of non-existence is a negation of power, and contrariwise the potentiality of existence is a power, as is obvious. If, then, that which necessarily exists is nothing but finite beings, such finite beings are more powerful than a being absolutely infinite, which is obviously absurd; therefore, either nothing exists, or else a being absolutely infinite necessarily exists also. Now we exist either in ourselves, or in something else which necessarily exists (see Ax. i. and Prop. vii.). Therefore a being absolutely infinite—in other words, God (Def. vi.)—necessarily exists. *Q.E.D.*

Note.—In this last proof, I have purposely shown God's ex-

istence *à posteriori*, so that the proof might be more easily
followed, not because, from the same premises, God's existence does not follow *à priori*. For, as the potentiality of existence is a power, it follows that, in proportion as reality increases in the nature of a thing, so also will it increase its
strength for existence. Therefore a being absolutely infinite,
such as God, has from himself an absolutely infinite power
of existence, and hence he does absolutely exist. Perhaps there
will be many who will be unable to see the force of this proof,
inasmuch as they are accustomed only to consider those things
which flow from external causes. Of such things, they see that
those which quickly come to pass—that is, quickly come into
existence—quickly also disappear; whereas they regard as more
difficult of accomplishment—that is, not so easily brought into
existence—those things which they conceive as more compli-
cated.

However, to do away with this misconception, I need not
here show the measure of truth in the proverb, "What comes
quickly, goes quickly," nor discuss whether, from the point of
view of universal nature, all things are equally easy, or otherwise: I need only remark, that I am not here speaking of
things, which come to pass through causes external to themselves, but only of substances which (by Prop. vi.) cannot be
produced by any external cause. Things which are produced
by external causes, whether they consist of many parts or few,
owe whatsoever perfection or reality they possess solely to the
efficacy of their external cause, and therefore their existence
arises solely from the perfection of their external cause, not
from their own. Contrariwise, whatsoever perfection is possessed by substance is due to no external cause; wherefore the
existence of substance must arise solely from its own nature,
which is nothing else but its essence. Thus, the perfection of
a thing does not annul its existence, but, on the contrary, asserts it. Imperfection, on the other hand, does annul it; therefore we cannot be more certain of the existence of anything,
than of the existence of a being absolutely infinite or perfect
—that is, of God. For inasmuch as his essence excludes all imperfection, and involves absolute perfection, all cause for
doubt concerning his existence is done away, and the utmost

certainty on the question is given. This, I think, will be evident to every moderately attentive reader.

PROP. XII. *No attribute of substance can be conceived from which it would follow that substance can be divided.*

Proof.—The parts into which substance as thus conceived would be divided, either will retain the nature of substance, or they will not. If the former, then (by Prop. viii.) each part will necessarily be infinite, and (by Prop. vi.) self-caused, and (by Prop. v.) will perforce consist of a different attribute, so that, in that case, several substances could be formed out of one substance, which (by Prop. vi.) is absurd. Moreover, the parts (by Prop. ii.) would have nothing in common with their whole, and the whole (by Def. iv. and Prop. x.) could both exist and be conceived without its parts, which everyone will admit to be absurd. If we adopt the second alternative—namely, that the parts will not retain the nature of substance—then, if the whole substance were divided into equal parts, it would lose the nature of substance, and would cease to exist, which (by Prop. vii.) is absurd.

PROP. XIII. *Substance absolutely infinite is indivisible.*

Proof.—If it could be divided, the parts into which it was divided would either retain the nature of absolutely infinite substance, or they would not. If the former, we should have several substances of the same nature, which (by Prop. v.) is absurd. If the latter, then (by Prop. vii.) substance absolutely infinite could cease to exist, which (by Prop. xi.) is also absurd.

Corollary.—It follows, that no substance, and consequently no extended substance, in so far as it is substance, is divisible.

Note.—The indivisibility of substance may be more easily understood as follows. The nature of substance can only be conceived as infinite, and by a part of substance, nothing else can be understood than finite substance, which (by Prop. viii.) involves a manifest contradiction.

PROP. XIV. *Besides God no substance can be granted or conceived.*

Proof.—As God is a being absolutely infinite, of whom no attribute that expresses the essence of substance can be denied (by Def. vi.), and he necessarily exists (by Prop. xi.); if any substance besides God were granted, it would have to be explained by some attribute of God, and thus two substances with the same attribute would exist, which (by Prop. v.) is absurd; therefore, besides God no substance can be granted, or, consequently, be conceived. If it could be conceived, it would necessarily have to be conceived as existent; but this (by the first part of this proof) is absurd. Therefore, besides God no substance can be granted or conceived. *Q.E.D.*

Corollary I.—Clearly, therefore: 1. God is one, that is (by Def. vi.) only one substance can be granted in the universe, and that substance is absolutely infinite, as we have already indicated (in the note to Prop. x.).

Corollary II.—It follows: 2. That extension and thought are either attributes of God or (by Ax. i.) accidents (*affectiones*) of the attributes of God.

PROP. XV. *Whatsoever is, is in God, and without God nothing can be, or be conceived.*

Proof.—Besides God, no substance is granted or can be conceived (by Prop. xiv.), that is (by Def. iii.) nothing which is in itself and is conceived through itself. But modes (by Def. v.) can neither be, nor be conceived without substance; wherefore they can only be in the divine nature, and can only through it be conceived. But substances and modes form the sum total of existence (by Ax. i.), therefore, without God nothing can be, or be conceived. *Q.E.D.*

Note.—Some assert that God, like a man, consists of body and mind, and is susceptible of passions. How far such persons have strayed from the truth is sufficiently evident from what has been said. But these I pass over. For all who have in anywise reflected on the divine nature deny that God has a body. Of this they find excellent proof in the fact that we understand by body a definite quantity, so long, so broad, so deep, bounded by a certain shape, and it is the height of absurdity to predicate such a thing of God, a being absolutely infinite. But meanwhile by the other reasons with which they try to prove their point, they show that they think corporeal or extended substance wholly apart from the divine nature, and say it was created by God. Wherefrom the divine nature can have been created, they are wholly ignorant; thus they clearly show, that they do not know the meaning of their own words. I myself have proved sufficiently clearly, at any rate in my own judgment (Coroll. Prop. vi., and Note 2, Prop. viii.), that no substance can be produced or created by anything other than itself. Further, I showed (in Prop. xiv.), that besides God no substance can be granted or conceived. Hence we drew the conclusion that extended substance is one of the infinite attributes of God. However, in order to explain more fully, I will refute the arguments of my adversaries, which all start from the following points:—

Extended substance, in so far as it is substance, consists, as they think, in parts, wherefore they deny that it can be infinite, or, consequently, that it can appertain to God. This they illustrate with many examples, of which I will take one or two. If extended substance, they say, is infinite, let it be conceived to be divided into two parts; each part will then be either finite or infinite. If the former, then infinite substance is composed of two finite parts, which is absurd. If the latter, then one infinite will be twice as large as another infinite, which is also absurd.

Further, if an infinite line be measured out in foot lengths, it will consist of an infinite number of such parts; it would equally consist of an infinite number of parts, if each part measured only an inch: therefore, one infinity would be twelve times as great as the other.

Lastly, if from a single point there be conceived to be drawn two diverging lines which at first are at a definite distance apart, but are produced to infinity, it is certain that the distance between the two lines will be continually increased, until at length it changes from definite to indefinable. As these absurdities follow, it is said, from considering quantity as infinite, the conclusion is drawn, that extended substance must necessarily be finite, and, consequently, cannot appertain to the nature of God.

The second argument is also drawn from God's supreme perfection. God, it is said, inasmuch as he is a supremely perfect being, cannot be passive; but extended substance, in so far as it is divisible, is passive. It follows, therefore, that extended substance does not appertain to the essence of God.

Such are the arguments I find on the subject in writers,

who by them try to prove that extended substance is unworthy
of the divine nature, and cannot possibly appertain thereto.
However, I think an attentive reader will see that I have already answered their propositions; for all their arguments are
founded on the hypothesis that extended substance is composed of parts, and such a hypothesis I have shown (Prop.
xii., and Coroll. Prop. xiii.) to be absurd. Moreover, anyone
who reflects will see that all these absurdities (if absurdities
they be, which I am not now discussing), from which it is
sought to extract the conclusion that extended substance is
finite, do not at all follow from the notion of an infinite quantity, but merely from the notion that an infinite quantity is
measurable, and composed of finite parts: therefore, the only
fair conclusion to be drawn is that infinite quantity is not
measurable, and cannot be composed of finite parts. This is
exactly what we have already proved (in Prop. xii.). Wherefore the weapon which they aimed at us has in reality recoiled
upon themselves. If, from this absurdity of theirs, they persist
in drawing the conclusion that extended substance must be
finite, they will in good sooth be acting like a man who asserts
that circles have the properties of squares, and, finding himself thereby landed in absurdities, proceeds to deny that circles
have any centre, from which all lines drawn to the circumference are equal. For, taking extended substance, which can
only be conceived as infinite, one, and indivisible (Props. viii.,
v., xii.) they assert, in order to prove that it is finite, that it
is composed of finite parts, and that it can be multiplied and
divided.

So, also, others, after asserting that a line is composed of
points, can produce many arguments to prove that a line cannot be infinitely divided. Assuredly it is not less absurd to
assert that extended substance is made up of bodies or parts,
than it would be to assert that a solid is made up of surfaces,
a surface of lines, and a line of points. This must be admitted
by all who know clear reason to be infallible, and most of all
by those who deny the possibility of a vacuum. For if extended
substance could be so divided that its parts were really separate, why should not one part admit of being destroyed, the
others remaining joined together as before? And why should

all be so fitted into one another as to leave no vacuum? Surely in the case of things, which are really distinct one from the other, one can exist without the other, and can remain in its original condition. As, then, there does not exist a vacuum in nature (of which anon), but all parts are bound to come together to prevent it, it follows from this also that the parts cannot be really distinguished, and that extended substance in so far as it is substance cannot be divided.

If anyone asks me the further question, Why are we naturally so prone to divide quantity? I answer, that quantity is conceived by us in two ways; in the abstract and superficially, as we imagine it; or as substance, as we conceive it solely by the intellect. If, then, we regard quantity as it is represented in our imagination, which we often and more easily do, we shall find that it is finite, divisible, and compounded of parts; but if we regard it as it is represented in our intellect, and conceive it as substance, which it is very difficult to do, we shall then, as I have sufficiently proved, find that it is infinite, one, and indivisible. This will be plain enough to all, who make a distinction between the intellect and the imagination, especially if it be remembered, that matter is everywhere the same, that its parts are not distinguishable, except in so far as we conceive matter as diversely modified, whence its parts are distinguished, not really, but modally. For instance, water, in so far as it is water, we conceive to be divided, and its parts to be separated one from the other; but not in so far as it is extended substance; from this point of view it is neither separated nor divisible. Further, water, in so far as it is water, is produced and corrupted; but, in so far as it is substance, it is neither produced nor corrupted.

I think I have now answered the second argument; it is, in fact, founded on the same assumption as the first—namely, that matter, in so far as it is substance, is divisible, and composed of parts. Even if it were so, I do not know why it should be considered unworthy of the divine nature, inasmuch as besides God (by Prop. xiv.) no substance can be granted, wherefrom it could receive its modifications. All things, I repeat, are in God, and all things which come to pass, come to pass solely through the laws of the infinite nature of God, and follow (as I will shortly show) from the necessity of his essence. Wherefore it can in nowise be said, that God is passive in respect to anything other than himself, or that extended substance is unworthy of the divine nature, even if it be supposed divisible, so long as it is granted to be infinite and eternal. But enough of this for the present.

PROP. XVI. *From the necessity of the divine nature must follow an infinite number of things in infinite ways—that is, all things which can fall within the sphere of infinite intellect.*

Proof.—This proposition will be clear to everyone, who remembers that from the given definition of any thing the intellect infers several properties, which really necessarily follow therefrom (that is, from the actual essence of the thing defined); and it infers more properties in proportion as the definition of the thing expresses more reality, that is, in proportion as the essence of the thing defined involves more reality. Now, as the divine nature has absolutely infinite attributes (by Def. vi.), of which each expresses infinite essence after its kind, it follows that from the necessity of its nature an infinite number of things (that is, everything which can fall within the sphere of an infinite intellect) must necessarily follow. *Q.E.D.*

Corollary I.—Hence it follows, that God is the efficient cause of all that can fall within the sphere of an infinite intellect.

Corollary II.—It also follows that God is a cause in himself, and not through an accident of his nature.

Corollary III.—It follows, thirdly, that God is the absolutely first cause.

PROP. XVII. *God acts solely by the laws of his own nature, and is not constrained by anyone.*

Proof.—We have just shown (in Prop. xvi.), that solely from the necessity of the divine nature, or, what is the same thing, solely from the laws of his nature, an infinite number of things absolutely follow in an infinite number of ways; and we proved (in Prop. xv.), that without God nothing can be nor be conceived; but that all things are in God. Wherefore nothing can exist outside himself, whereby he can be conditioned or constrained to act. Wherefore God acts solely by the laws of his own nature, and is not constrained by anyone. *Q.E.D.*

Corollary I.—It follows: 1. That there can be no cause which, either extrinsically or intrinsically, besides the perfection of his own nature, moves God to act.

Corollary II.—It follows: 2. That God is the sole free cause. For God alone exists by the sole necessity of his nature (by Prop xi. and Prop. xiv., Coroll. i.), and acts by the sole necessity of his nature, wherefore God is (by Def. vii.) the sole free cause. *Q.E.D.*

Note.—Others think that God is a free cause, because he can, as they think, bring it about, that those things which we have said follow from his nature—that is, which are in his power, should not come to pass, or should not be produced by him. But this is the same as if they said, that God could bring it about, that it should not follow from the nature of a triangle, that its three interior angles should not be equal to two right angles; or that from a given cause no effect should follow, which is absurd.

Moreover, I will show below, without the aid of this proposition, that neither intellect nor will appertain to God's nature. I know that there are many who think that they can show, that supreme intellect and free will do appertain to God's nature; for they say they know of nothing more perfect, which they can attribute to God, than that which is the highest perfection in ourselves. Further, although they conceive God as actually supremely intelligent, they yet do not believe, that he can bring into existence everything which he actually understands, for they think that they would thus destroy God's power. If, they contend, God had created everything which is in his intellect, he would not be able to create anything more, and this, they think, would clash with God's omnipotence; therefore, they prefer to assert that God is indifferent to all things, and that he creates nothing except that which he has decided, by some absolute exercise of will, to create. However, I think I have shown sufficiently clearly (by Prop. xvi.), that from God's supreme power, or infinite nature, an infinite number of things—that is, all things have necessarily flowed forth in an infinite number of ways, or always follow from the same necessity; in the same way as from the nature of a triangle it follows from eternity and for eternity, that its three interior angles are equal to two right angles. Wherefore the omnipotence of God has been displayed from all eternity, and will for all eternity remain in the same state of activity. This manner of treating the question attributes to God an omnipotence, in my opinion, far more perfect. For, otherwise, we are compelled to confess that God understands an infinite number of creatable things, which he will never be able to create, for, if he created all that he understands, he would, according to this showing, exhaust his omnipotence, and render himself imperfect. Wherefore, in order to establish that God is perfect, we should be reduced to establishing at the same time, that he cannot bring to pass everything over which his power extends; this seems to be a hypothesis most absurd, and most repugnant to God's omnipotence.

Further (to say a word here concerning the intellect and the will which we attribute to God), if intellect and will appertain to the eternal essence of God, we must take these words in some significations quite different from those they usually bear. For intellect and will, which should constitute the essence of God, would perforce be as far apart as the poles from the human intellect and will, in fact, would have nothing in common with them but the name; there would be about as much correspondence between the two as there is between the Dog, the heavenly constellation, and a dog, an animal that barks. This I will prove as follows. If intellect belongs to the divine nature, it cannot be in nature, as ours is generally thought to be, posterior to, or simultaneous with the things understood, inasmuch as God is prior to all things by reason of his causality (Prop. xvi., Coroll. i.). On the contrary, the truth and formal essence of things is as it is, because it exists by representation as such in the intellect of God. Wherefore the intellect of God, in so far as it is conceived to constitute God's essence, is, in reality, the cause of things, both of their essence and of their existence. This seems to have been recognized by those who have asserted, that God's intellect, God's will, and God's power, are one and the same. As, therefore, God's intellect is the sole cause of things, namely, both of their essence and existence, it must necessarily differ from them in respect to its essence, and in respect to its existence.

For a cause differs from a thing it causes, precisely in the quality which the latter gains from the former.

For example, a man is the cause of another man's existence, but not of his essence (for the latter is an eternal truth), and, therefore, the two men may be entirely similar in essence, but must be different in existence; and hence if the existence of one of them cease, the existence of the other will not necessarily cease also; but if the essence of one could be destroyed, and be made false, the essence of the other would be destroyed also. Wherefore, a thing which is the cause both of the essence and of the existence of a given effect, must differ from such effect both in respect to its essence, and also in respect to its existence. Now the intellect of God is the cause of both the essence and the existence of our intellect; therefore, the intellect of God in so far as it is conceived to constitute the divine essence, differs from our intellect both in respect to essence and in respect to existence, nor can it in anywise agree therewith save in name, as we said before. The reasoning would be identical in the case of the will, as anyone can easily see.

PROP. XVIII. *God is the indwelling and not the transient cause of all things.*

Proof.—All things which are, are in God, and must be conceived through God (by Prop. xv.), therefore (by Prop. xvi., Coroll. i.) God is the cause of those things which are in him. This is our first point. Further, besides God there can be no substance (by Prop. xiv.), that is nothing in itself external to God. This is our second point. God, therefore, is the indwelling and not the transient cause of all things. Q.E.D.

PROP. XIX. *God, and all the attributes of God, are eternal.*

Proof.—God (by Def. vi.) is substance, which (by Prop. xi.) necessarily exists, that is (by Prop. vii.) existence appertains to its nature, or (what is the same thing) follows from its definition; therefore, God is eternal (by Def. viii.). Further, by the attributes of God we must understand that which (by Def. iv.) expresses the essence of the divine substance—in other words, that which appertains to substance: that, I say, should be involved in the attributes of substance. Now eternity appertains to the nature of substance (as I have already shown in Prop. vii.); therefore, eternity must appertain to each of the attributes, and thus all are eternal. *Q.E.D.*

Note.—This proposition is also evident from the manner in which (in Prop. xi.) I demonstrated the existence of God; it is evident, I repeat, from that proof, that the existence of God, like his essence, is an eternal truth. Further (in Prop. xix. of my "Principles of the Cartesian Philosophy"), I have proved the eternity of God, in another manner, which I need not here repeat.

PROP. XX. *The existence of God and his essence are one and the same.*

Proof.—God (by the last Prop.) and all his attributes are eternal, that is (by Def. viii.) each of his attributes expresses existence. Therefore the same attributes of God which explain his eternal essence, explain at the same time his eternal existence—in other words, that which constitutes God's essence constitutes at the same time his existence. Wherefore God's existence and God's essence are one and the same. *Q.E.D.*

Coroll. I.—Hence it follows that God's existence, like His essence, is an eternal truth.

Coroll. II.—Secondly, it follows that God, and all the attributes of God, are unchangeable. For if they could be changed in respect to existence, they must also be able to be changed in respect to essence—that is, obviously, be changed from true to false, which is absurd.

PROP. XXI. *All things which follow from the absolute nature of any attribute of God must always exist and be infinite, or, in other words, are eternal and infinite through the said attribute.*

Proof.—Conceive, if it be possible (supposing the proposition to be denied), that something in some attribute of God can follow from the absolute nature of the said attribute, and that at the same time it is finite, and has a conditioned existence or duration; for instance, the idea of God expressed in the attribute thought. Now thought, in so far as it is supposed to be an attribute of God, is necessarily (by Prop. xi.) in its nature infinite. But, in so far as it possesses the idea of God, it is supposed finite. It cannot, however, be conceived as finite, unless it be limited by thought (by Def. ii.); but it is not limited by thought itself, in so far as it has constituted the idea of God (for so far it is supposed to be finite); therefore, it is limited by thought, in so far as it has not constituted the idea of God, which nevertheless (by Prop. xi.) must necessarily exist.

We have now granted, therefore, thought not constituting the idea of God, and, accordingly, the idea of God does not naturally follow from its nature in so far as it is absolute thought (for it is conceived as constituting, and also as not constituting, the idea of God), which is against our hypothesis. Wherefore, if the idea of God expressed in the attribute thought, or, indeed, anything else in any attribute of God (for we may take any example, as the proof is of universal application) follows from the necessity of the absolute nature of the said attribute, the said thing must necessarily be infinite, which was our first point.

Furthermore, a thing which thus follows from the necessity of the nature of any attribute cannot have a limited duration. For if it can, suppose a thing, which follows from the necessity of the nature of some attribute, to exist in some attribute of God, for instance, the idea of God expressed in the attribute thought, and let it be supposed at some time not to have existed, or to be about not to exist.

Now thought being an attribute of God, must necessarily exist unchanged (by Prop. xi., and Prop. xx., Coroll. ii.); and beyond the limits of the duration of the idea of God (supposing the latter at some time not to have existed, or not to be going to exist) thought would perforce have existed without the idea of God, which is contrary to our hypothesis, for we supposed that, thought being given, the idea of God necessarily flowed therefrom. Therefore the idea of God expressed in thought, or anything which necessarily follows from the absolute nature of some attribute of God, cannot have a limited duration, but through the said attribute is eternal, which is our second point. Bear in mind that the same proposition may be affirmed of anything, which in any attribute necessarily follows from God's absolute nature.

PROP. XXII. *Whatsoever follows from any attribute of God, in so far as it is modified by a modification, which exists neces-*

sarily and as infinite, through the said attribute, must also exist necessarily and as infinite.

Proof.—The proof of this proposition is similar to that of the preceding one.

PROP. XXIII. *Every mode which exists both necessarily and as infinite must necessarily follow either from the absolute nature of some attribute of God, or from an attribute modified by a modification which exists necessarily and as infinite.*

Proof.—A mode exists in something else, through which it must be conceived (Def. v.), that is (Prop. xv.), it exists solely in God, and solely through God can be conceived. If therefore a mode is conceived as necessarily existing and infinite, it must necessarily be inferred or perceived through some attribute of God, in so far as such attribute is conceived as expressing the infinity and necessity of existence, in other words (Def. viii.) eternity; that is, in so far as it is considered absolutely. A mode, therefore, which necessarily exists as infinite, must follow from the absolute nature of some attribute of God, either immediately (Prop. xxi.) or through the means of some modification, which follows from the absolute nature of the said attribute; that is (by Prop. xxii.), which exists necessarily and as infinite.

PROP. XXIV. *The essence of things produced by God does not involve existence.*

Proof.—This proposition is evident from Def. i. For that of which the nature (considered in itself) involves existence is self-caused, and exists by the sole necessity of its own nature.

Corollary.—Hence it follows that God is not only the cause of things coming into existence, but also of their continuing in existence, that is, in scholastic phraseology, God is cause of the being of things (*essendi rerum*). For whether things exist, or do not exist, whenever we contemplate their essence, we see that it involves neither existence nor duration; consequently, it cannot be the cause of either the one or the other. God must be the sole cause, inasmuch as to him alone does existence appertain. (Prop. xiv. Coroll. i.) *Q.E.D.*

PROP. XXV. *God is the efficient cause not only of the existence of things, but also of their essence.*

Proof.—If this be denied, then God is not the cause of the essence of things; and therefore the essence of things can (by Ax. iv.) be conceived without God. This (by Prop. xv.) is absurd. Therefore, God is the cause of the essence of things. Q.E.D.

Note.—This proposition follows more clearly from Prop. xvi. For it is evident thereby that, given the divine nature, the essence of things must be inferred from it, no less than their existence—in a word, God must be called the cause of all things, in the same sense as he is called the cause of himself. This will be made still clearer by the following corollary.

Corollary.—Individual things are nothing but modifications of the attributes of God, or modes by which the attributes of God are expressed in a fixed and definite manner. The proof appears from Prop. xv. and Def. v.

PROP. XXVI. *A thing which is conditioned to act in a particular manner has necessarily been thus conditioned by God; and that which has not been conditioned by God cannot condition itself to act.*

Proof.—That by which things are said to be conditioned to act in a particular manner is necessarily something positive (this is obvious); therefore both of its essence and of its existence God by the necessity of his nature is the efficient cause (Props. xxv. and xvi.); this is our first point. Our second point is plainly to be inferred therefrom. For if a thing, which has not been conditioned by God, could condition itself, the first part of our proof would be false, and this, as we have shown, is absurd.

PROP. XXVII. *A thing, which has been conditioned by God to act in a particular way, cannot render itself unconditioned.*

Proof.—This proposition is evident from the third axiom.

PROP. XXVIII.—*Every individual thing, or everything which is finite and has a conditioned existence, cannot exist or be conditioned to act, unless it be conditioned for existence and action by a cause other than itself, which also is finite and has a conditioned existence; and likewise this cause cannot in its turn exist or be conditioned to act, unless it be conditioned for existence and action by another cause, which also is finite and has a conditioned existence, and so on to infinity.*

Proof.—Whatsoever is conditioned to exist and act, has been thus conditioned by God (by Prop. xxvi. and Prop. xxiv., Coroll.)

But that which is finite, and has a conditioned existence, cannot be produced by the absolute nature of any attribute of God; for whatsoever follows from the absolute nature of any attribute of God is infinite and eternal (by Prop. xxi.). It must, therefore, follow from some attribute of God, in so far as the said attribute is considered as in some way modified; for substance and modes make up the sum total of existence (by Ax. i. and Deff. iii., v.), while modes are merely modifications of the attributes of God. But from God, or from any of his attributes, in so far as the latter is modified by a modification infinite and eternal, a conditioned thing cannot follow. Wherefore it must follow from, or be conditioned for, existence and action by God or one of his attributes, in so far as the latter are modified by some modification which is finite, and has a conditioned existence. This is our first point. Again, this cause or this modification (for the reason by which we established the first part of this proof) must in its turn be conditioned by another cause, which also is finite, and has a conditioned existence, and, again, this last by another (for the same reason); and so on (for the same reason) to infinity. Q.E.D.

Note.—As certain things must be produced immediately by God, namely those things which necessarily follow from his absolute nature, through the means of these primary attributes, which, nevertheless, can neither exist nor be conceived without God, it follows:—1. That God is absolutely the proximate cause of those things immediately produced by him. I say absolutely, not after his kind, as is usually stated. For the effects of God cannot either exist or be conceived without a cause (Prop. xv. and Prop. xxiv., Coroll.). 2. That God cannot properly be styled the remote cause of individual things, except for the sake of distinguishing these from what he immediately produces, or rather from what follows from his absolute nature. For, by a remote cause, we understand a cause which is in no way conjoined to the effect. But all things which are, are in God, and so depend on God, that without him they can neither be nor be conceived.

PROP. XXIX. *Nothing in the universe is contingent, but all things are conditioned to exist and operate in a particular manner by the necessity of the divine nature.*

Proof.—Whatsoever is, is in God (Prop. xv.). But God cannot be called a thing contingent. For (by Prop. xi.) he exists necessarily, and not contingently. Further, the modes of the divine nature follow therefrom necessarily, and not contingently (Prop. xvi.); and they thus follow, whether we consider the divine nature absolutely, or whether we consider it as in any way conditioned to act (Prop. xxvii.). Further, God is not only the cause of these modes, in so far as they simply exist (by Prop. xxiv., Coroll.), but also in so far as they are considered as conditioned for operating in a particular manner (Prop. xxvi.). If they be not conditioned by God (Prop. xxvi.), it is impossible, and not contingent, that they should condition themselves; contrariwise, if they be conditioned by God, it is impossible, and not contingent, that they should render themselves unconditioned. Wherefore all things are conditioned by the necessity of the divine nature, not only to exist, but also to exist and operate in a particular manner, and there is nothing that is contingent. *Q.E.D.*

Note.—Before going any further, I wish here to explain, what we should understand by nature viewed as active (*natura naturans*), and nature viewed as passive (*natura naturata*). I say to explain, or rather call attention to it, for I think that, from what has been said, it is sufficiently clear, that by nature viewed as active we should understand that which is in itself, and is conceived through itself, or those attributes of substance, which express eternal and infinite essence, in other words (Prop. xiv., Coroll. i., and Prop. xvii., Coroll. ii.) God, in so far as he is considered as a free cause.

By nature viewed as passive I understand all that which follows from the necessity of the nature of God, or of any of the attributes of God, that is, all the modes of the attributes of God, in so far as they are considered as things which are in God, and which without God cannot exist or be conceived.

PROP. XXX. *Intellect, in function finite, or in function infinite, must comprehend the attributes of God and the modifications of God, and nothing else.*

Proof.—A true idea must agree with its object (Ax. vi.); in other words (obviously), that which is contained in the intellect in representation must necessarily be granted in nature. But in nature (by Prop. xiv., Coroll. i.) there is no substance save God, nor any modifications save those (Prop. xv.) which are in God, and cannot without God either be or be conceived. Therefore the intellect, in function finite, or in function infinite, must comprehend the attributes of God and the modifications of God, and nothing else. *Q.E.D.*

Prop. XXXI. *The intellect in function, whether finite or infinite, as will, desire, love, &c., should be referred to passive nature and not to active nature.*

Proof.—By the intellect we do not (obviously) mean absolute thought, but only a certain mode of thinking, differing from other modes, such as love, desire, &c., and therefore (Def. v.) requiring to be conceived through absolute thought. It must (by Prop. xv. and Def. vi.), through some attribute of God which expresses the eternal and infinite essence of thought, be so conceived, that without such attribute it could neither be nor be conceived. It must therefore be referred to nature passive rather than to nature active, as must also the other modes of thinking. *Q.E.D.*

Note.—I do not here, by speaking of intellect in function, admit that there is such a thing as intellect in potentiality: but, wishing to avoid all confusion, I desire to speak only of what is most clearly perceived by us, namely, of the very act of understanding, than which nothing is more clearly perceived. For we cannot perceive anything without adding to our knowledge of the act of understanding.

Prop. XXXII. *Will cannot be called a free cause, but only a necessary cause.*

Proof.—Will is only a particular mode of thinking, like intellect; therefore (by Prop. xxviii.) no volition can exist, nor be conditioned to act, unless it be conditioned by some cause other than itself, which cause is conditioned by a third cause, and so on to infinity. But if will be supposed infinite, it must also be conditioned to exist and act by God, not by virtue of his being substance absolutely infinite, but by virtue of his possessing an attribute which expresses the infinite and eternal essence of thought (by Prop. xxiii.). Thus, however it be conceived, whether as finite or infinite, it requires a cause by which it should be conditioned to exist and act. Thus (Def. vii.) it cannot be called a free cause, but only a necessary or constrained cause. *Q.E.D.*

Coroll. I.—Hence it follows, first, that God does not act according to freedom of the will.

Coroll. II.—It follows, secondly, that will and intellect stand in the same relation to the nature of God as do motion, and rest, and absolutely all natural phenomena, which must be conditioned by God (Prop. xxix.) to exist and act in a particular manner. For will, like the rest, stands in need of a cause, by which it is conditioned to exist and act in a particular manner. And although, when will or intellect be granted, an infinite number of results may follow, yet God cannot on that account be said to act from freedom of the will, any more than the infinite number of results from motion and rest would justify us in saying that motion and rest act by free will. Wherefore will no more appertains to God than does anything else in nature, but stands in the same relation to him as motion, rest, and the like, which we have shown to follow from the necessity of the divine nature, and to be conditioned by it to exist and act in a particular manner.

PROP. XXXIII. *Things could not have been brought into being by God in any manner or in any order different from that which has in fact obtained.*

Proof.—All things necessarily follow from the nature of God (Prop. xvi.), and by the nature of God are conditioned to exist and act in a particular way (Prop. xxix.). If things, therefore, could have been of a different nature, or have been conditioned to act in a different way, so that the order of nature would have been different, God's nature would also have been able to be different from what it now is; and therefore (by Prop. xi.) that different nature also would have perforce existed, and consequently there would have been able to be two or more Gods. This (by Prop. xiv., Coroll. i.) is absurd. Therefore things could not have been brought into being by God in any other manner, &c. *Q.E.D.*

Note I.—As I have thus shown, more clearly than the sun

at noonday, that there is nothing to justify us in calling things contingent, I wish to explain briefly what meaning we shall attach to the word contingent; but I will first explain the words necessary and impossible.

A thing is called necessary either in respect to its essence or in respect to its cause; for the existence of a thing necessarily follows, either from its essence and definition, or from a given efficient cause. For similar reasons a thing is said to be impossible; namely, inasmuch as its essence or definition involves a contradiction, or because no external cause is granted, which is conditioned to produce such an effect; but a thing can in no respect be called contingent, save in relation to the imperfection of our knowledge.

A thing of which we do not know whether the essence does or does not involve a contradiction, or of which, knowing that it does not involve a contradiction, we are still in doubt concerning the existence, because the order of causes escapes us, —such a thing, I say, cannot appear to us either necessary or impossible. Wherefore we call it contingent or possible.

Note II.—It clearly follows from what we have said, that things have been brought into being by God in the highest perfection, inasmuch as they have necessarily followed from a most perfect nature. Nor does this prove any imperfection in God, for it has compelled us to affirm his perfection. From its contrary proposition, we should clearly gather (as I have just shown), that God is not supremely perfect, for if things had been brought into being in any other way, we should have to assign to God a nature different from that, which we are bound to attribute to him from the consideration of an absolutely perfect being.

I do not doubt, that many will scout this idea as absurd, and will refuse to give their minds up to contemplating it, simply because they are accustomed to assign to God a freedom very different from that which we (Def. vii.) have deduced. They assign to him, in short, absolute free will. However, I am also convinced that if such persons reflect on the matter, and duly weigh in their minds our series of propositions, they will reject such freedom as they now attribute to God, not only as nugatory, but also as a great impediment to organized knowledge. There is no need for me to repeat what I said in the note to Prop. xvii. But, for the sake of my opponents, I will show further, that although it be granted that will appertains to the essence of God, it nevertheless follows from his perfection, that things could not have been by him created other than they are, or in a different order; this is easily proved, if we reflect on what our opponents themselves concede, namely, that it depends solely on the decree and will of God, that each thing is what it is. If it were otherwise, God would not be the cause of all things. Further, that all the decrees of God have been ratified from all eternity by God himself. If it were otherwise, God would be convicted of imperfection or change. But in eternity there is no such thing as when, before, or after; hence it follows solely from the perfection of God, that God never can decree, or never could have decreed anything but what is; that God did not exist before his decrees, and would not exist without them. But, it is said, supposing that God had made a different universe, or had ordained other decrees from all eternity concerning nature and her order, we could not therefore conclude any imperfection in God. But persons who say this must admit that God can change his decrees. For if God had ordained any decrees concerning nature and her order, different from those which he has ordained—in other words, if he had willed and conceived something different concerning nature—he would perforce have had a different intellect from that which he has, and also a different will. But if it were allowable to assign to God a different intellect and a different will, without any change in his essence or his perfection, what would there be to prevent him changing the decrees which he has made concerning created things, and nevertheless remaining perfect? For his intellect and will concerning things created and their order are the same, in respect to his essence and perfection, however they be conceived.

Further, all the philosophers whom I have read admit that God's intellect is entirely actual, and not at all potential; as they also admit that God's intellect, and God's will, and God's essence are identical, it follows that, if God had had a different actual intellect and a different will, his essence would also have been different; and thus, as I concluded at first, if things had been brought into being by God in a different way from that which has obtained, God's intellect and will, that is (as is admitted) his essence would perforce have been different, which is absurd.

As these things could not have been brought into being by God in any but the actual way and order which has obtained; and as the truth of this proposition follows from the supreme perfection of God; we can have no sound reason for persuading ourselves to believe that God did not wish to create all the things which were in his intellect, and to create them in the same perfection as he had understood them.

But, it will be said, there is in things no perfection nor imperfection; that which is in them, and which causes them to be called perfect or imperfect, good or bad, depends solely on the will of God. If God had so willed, he might have brought it about that what is now perfection should be extreme imperfection, and *vice versâ*. What is such an assertion, but an open declaration that God, who necessarily understands that which he wishes, might bring it about by his will, that he should understand things differently from the way in which he does understand them? This (as we have just shown) is the height of absurdity. Wherefore, I may turn the argument against its employers, as follows:—All things depend on the power of God. In order that things should be different from what they are, God's will would necessarily have to be different. But God's will cannot be different (as we have just most clearly demonstrated) from God's perfection. Therefore neither can things be different. I confess, that the theory which subjects all things to the will of an indifferent deity, and asserts that they are all dependent on his fiat, is less far from the truth than the theory of those, who maintain that God acts in all things with a view of promoting what is good. For these latter persons seem to set up something beyond God, which does not depend on God, but which God in acting looks to as an exemplar, or which he aims at as a definite goal. This is only another name for subjecting God to the dominion of destiny, an utter absurdity in respect to God, whom we have shown to be the first and only free cause of the essence of all things and also of their existence. I need, therefore, spend no time in refuting such wild theories.

PROP. XXXIV. *God's power is identical with his essence.*

Proof.—From the sole necessity of the essence of God it follows that God is the cause of himself (Prop. xi.) and of all things (Prop. xvi. and Coroll. ii). Wherefore the power of God, by which he and all things are and act, is identical with his essence. *Q.E.D.*

PROP. XXXV. *Whatsoever we conceive to be in the power of God, necessarily exists.*

Proof.—Whatsoever is in God's power, must (by the last Prop.) be comprehended in his essence in such a manner, that it necessarily follows therefrom, and therefore necessarily exists. *Q.E.D.*

PROP. XXXVI. *There is no cause from whose nature some effect does not follow.*

Proof.—Whatsoever exists expresses God's nature or essence in a given conditioned manner (by Prop. xxv., Coroll.); that is (by Prop. xxxiv.), whatsoever exists, expresses in a given conditioned manner God's power, which is the cause of all things, therefore an effect must (by Prop. xvi.) necessarily follow. *Q.E.D.*

APPENDIX.—In the foregoing I have explained the nature and properties of God. I have shown that he necessarily exists, that he is one: that he is, and acts solely by the necessity of his own nature; that he is the free cause of all things, and how he is so; that all things are in God, and so depend on him, that without him they could neither exist nor be conceived; lastly, that all things are predetermined by God, not through his free will or absolute fiat, but from the very nature of God or infinite power. I have further, where occasion offered, taken care to remove the prejudices, which might impede the comprehension of my demonstrations. Yet there still remain misconceptions not a few, which might and may prove very grave hindrances to the understanding of the concatenation of things, as I have explained it above. I have therefore thought it worth while to bring these misconceptions before the bar of reason.

All such opinions spring from the notion commonly entertained, that all things in nature act as men themselves act,
namely, with an end in view. It is accepted as certain, that
God himself directs all things to a definite goal (for it is said
that God made all things for man, and man that he might
worship him). I will, therefore, consider this opinion, asking
first, why it obtains general credence, and why all men are
naturally so prone to adopt it? secondly, I will point out its
falsity; and, lastly, I will show how it has given rise to prejudices about good and bad, right and wrong, praise and blame,
order and confusion, beauty and ugliness, and the like. However, this is not the place to deduce these misconceptions from
the nature of the human mind: it will be sufficient here, if I
assume as a starting point, what ought to be universally admitted, namely, that all men are born ignorant of the causes
of things, that all have the desire to seek for what is useful
to them, and that they are conscious of such desire. Herefrom
it follows, first, that men think themselves free inasmuch as
they are conscious of their volitions and desires, and never
even dream, in their ignorance, of the causes which have disposed them so to wish and desire. Secondly, that men do all
things for an end, namely, for that which is useful to them,
and which they seek. Thus it comes to pass that they only
look for a knowledge of the final causes of events, and when
these are learned, they are content, as having no cause for
further doubt. If they cannot learn such causes from external
sources, they are compelled to turn to considering themselves,
and reflecting what end would have induced them personally
to bring about the given event, and thus they necessarily judge
other natures by their own. Further, as they find in themselves
and outside themselves many means which assist them not a
little in their search for what is useful, for instance, eyes for
seeing, teeth for chewing, herbs and animals for yielding food,
the sun for giving light, the sea for breeding fish, &c., they
come to look on the whole of nature as a means for obtaining
such conveniences. Now as they are aware, that they found
these conveniences and did not make them, they think they
have cause for believing, that some other being has made them
for their use. As they look upon things as means, they cannot

believe them to be self-created; but, judging from the means which they are accustomed to prepare for themselves, they are bound to believe in some ruler or rulers of the universe endowed with human freedom, who have arranged and adapted everything for human use. They are bound to estimate the nature of such rulers (having no information on the subject) in accordance with their own nature, and therefore they assert that the gods ordained everything for the use of man, in order to bind man to themselves and obtain from him the highest honour. Hence also it follows, that everyone thought out for himself, according to his abilities, a different way of worshipping God, so that God might love him more than his fellows, and direct the whole course of nature for the satisfaction of his blind cupidity and insatiable avarice. Thus the prejudice developed into superstition, and took deep root in the human mind; and for this reason everyone strove most zealously to understand and explain the final causes of things; but in their endeavour to show that nature does nothing in vain, *i.e.*, nothing which is useless to man, they only seem to have demonstrated that nature, the gods, and men are all mad together. Consider, I pray you, the result: among the many helps of nature they were bound to find some hindrances, such as storms, earthquakes, diseases, &c.: so they declared that such things happen, because the gods are angry at some wrong done them by men, or at some fault committed in their worship. Experience day by day protested and showed by infinite examples, that good and evil fortunes fall to the lot of pious and impious alike; still they would not abandon their inveterate prejudice, for it was more easy for them to class such contradictions among other unknown things of whose use they were ignorant, and thus to retain their actual and innate condition of ignorance, than to destroy the whole fabric of their reasoning and start afresh. They therefore laid down as an axiom, that God's judgments far transcend human understanding. Such a doctrine might well have sufficed to conceal the truth from the human race for all eternity, if mathematics had not furnished another standard of verity in considering solely the essence and properties of figures without regard to their final causes. There are other reasons (which I need not mention here) besides mathematics, which might have caused men's minds to be directed to these general prejudices, and have led them to the knowledge of the truth.

I have now sufficiently explained my first point. There is no need to show at length, that nature has no particular goal in view, and that final causes are mere human figments. This, I think, is already evident enough, both from the causes and foundations on which I have shown such prejudice to be based, and also from Prop. xvi., and the Corollary of Prop. xxxii., and, in fact, all those propositions in which I have shown, that everything in nature proceeds from a sort of necessity, and with the utmost perfection. However, I will add a few remarks, in order to overthrow this doctrine of a final cause utterly. That which is really a cause it considers as an effect, and *vice versâ:* it makes that which is by nature first to be last, and that which is highest and most perfect to be most imperfect. Passing over the questions of cause and priority as self-evident, it is plain from Props. xxi., xxii., xxiii. that that effect is most perfect which is produced immediately by God; the effect which requires for its production several intermediate causes is, in that respect, more imperfect. But if those things which were made immediately by God were made to enable him to attain his end, then the things which come after, for the sake of which the first were made, are necessarily the most excellent of all.

Further, this doctrine does away with the perfection of God: for, if God acts for an object, he necessarily desires something which he lacks. Certainly, theologians and metaphysicians draw a distinction between the object of want and the object of assimilation; still they confess that God made all things for the sake of himself, not for the sake of creation. They are unable to point to anything prior to creation, except God himself, as an object for which God should act, and are therefore driven to admit (as they clearly must), that God lacked those things for whose attainment he created means, and further that he desired them.

We must not omit to notice that the followers of this doctrine, anxious to display their talent in assigning final causes, have imported a new method of argument in proof of their theory—namely, a reduction, not to the impossible, but to ignorance; thus showing that they have no other method of exhibiting their doctrine. For example, if a stone falls from a roof on to someone's head, and kills him, they will demonstrate by their new method, that the stone fell in order to kill the man; for, if it had not by God's will fallen with that object, how could so many circumstances (and there are often many concurrent circumstances) have all happened together by chance? Perhaps you will answer that the event is due to the facts that the wind was blowing, and the man was walking that way. "But why," they will insist, "was the wind blowing, and why was the man at that very time walking that way?" If you again answer, that the wind had then sprung up because the sea had begun to be agitated the day before, the weather being previously calm, and that the man had been invited by a friend, they will again insist: "But why was the sea agitated, and why was the man invited at that time?" So they will pursue their questions from cause to cause, till at last you take refuge in the will of God—in other words, the sanctuary of ignorance. So, again, when they survey the frame of the human body, they are amazed; and being ignorant of the causes of so great a work of art, conclude that it has been fashioned, not mechanically, but by divine and supernatural skill, and has been so put together that one part shall not hurt another.

Hence anyone who seeks for the true causes of miracles, and strives to understand natural phenomena as an intelligent being, and not to gaze at them like a fool, is set down and denounced as an impious heretic by those, whom the masses adore as the interpreters of nature and the gods. Such persons know that, with the removal of ignorance, the wonder which forms their only available means for proving and preserving their authority would vanish also. But I now quit this subject, and pass on to my third point.

After men persuaded themselves, that everything which is created is created for their sake, they were bound to consider as the chief quality in everything that which is most useful to themselves, and to account those things the best of all which have the most beneficial effect on mankind. Further, they were bound to form abstract notions for the explanation of the nature of things, such as *goodness, badness, order, confusion, warmth, cold, beauty, deformity,* and so on; and from the belief that they are free agents arose the further notions *praise* and *blame, sin* and *merit.*

I will speak of these latter hereafter, when I treat of human nature; the former I will briefly explain here.

Everything which conduces to health and the worship of God they have called *good,* everything which hinders these objects they have styled *bad;* and inasmuch as those who do not understand the nature of things do not verify phenomena in any way, but merely imagine them after a fashion, and mistake their imagination for understanding, such persons firmly believe that there is an *order* in things, being really ignorant both of things and their own nature. When phenomena are of such a kind, that the impression they make on our senses requires little effort of imagination, and can consequently be easily remembered, we say that they are *well-ordered;* if the contrary, that they are *ill-ordered* or *confused.* Further, as things which are easily imagined are more pleasing to us, men prefer order to confusion—as though there were any order in nature, except in relation to our imagination— and say that God has created all things in order; thus, without knowing it, attributing imagination to God, unless, indeed, they would have it that God foresaw human imagination, and arranged everything, so that it should be most easily imagined. If this be their theory, they would not, perhaps, be daunted by the fact that we find an infinite number of phenomena, far surpassing our imagination, and very many others which confound its weakness. But enough has been said on this subject. The other abstract notions are nothing but modes of imagining, in which the imagination is differently affected, though they are considered by the ignorant as the chief attributes of things, inasmuch as they believe that everything was created for the sake of themselves; and, according as they are affected by it, style it good or bad, healthy or rotten and corrupt. For instance, if the motion which objects we see communicate to our nerves be conducive to health, the objects causing it are styled *beautiful;* if a contrary motion be excited, they are styled *ugly.*

Things which are perceived through our sense of smell are styled fragrant or fetid; if through our taste, sweet or bitter, full-flavoured or insipid; if through our touch, hard or soft, rough or smooth, &c.

Whatsoever affects our ears is said to give rise to noise, sound, or harmony. In this last case, there are men lunatic enough to believe, that even God himself takes pleasure in harmony; and philosophers are not lacking who have persuaded themselves, that the motion of the heavenly bodies gives rise to harmony—all of which instances sufficiently show that everyone judges of things according to the state of his brain, or rather mistakes for things the forms of his imagination. We need no longer wonder that there have arisen all the controversies we have witnessed, and finally scepticism: for, although human bodies in many respects agree, yet in very many others they differ; so that what seems good to one seems bad to another; what seems well ordered to one seems confused to another; what is pleasing to one displeases another, and so on. I need not further enumerate, because this is not the place to treat the subject at length, and also because the fact is sufficiently well known. It is commonly said: "So many men, so many minds; everyone is wise in his own way; brains differ as completely as palates." All of which proverbs show, that men judge of things according to their mental disposition, and rather imagine than understand: for, if they understood phenomena, they would, as mathematics attest, be convinced, if not attracted, by what I have urged.

We have now perceived, that all the explanations commonly given of nature are mere modes of imagining, and do not indicate the true nature of anything, but only the constitution of the imagination; and, although they have names, as though they were entities, existing externally to the imagination, I call them entities imaginary rather than real; and, therefore, all arguments against us drawn from such abstractions are easily rebutted.

Many argue in this way. If all things follow from a necessity of the absolutely perfect nature of God, why are there so many imperfections in nature? such, for instance, as things corrupt to the point of putridity, loathsome deformity, confusion, evil, sin, &c. But these reasoners are, as I have said, easily confuted, for the perfection of things is to be reckoned only from their own nature and power; things are not more or less perfect, according as they delight or offend human senses, or according as they are serviceable or repugnant to mankind. To those who ask why God did not so create all men, that they should be governed only by reason, I give no answer but this: because matter was not lacking to him for the creation of every degree of perfection from highest to lowest; or, more strictly, because the laws of his nature are so vast, as to suffice for the production of everything conceivable by an infinite intelligence, as I have shown in Prop. xvi.

Such are the misconceptions I have undertaken to note; if there are any more of the same sort, everyone may easily dissipate them for himself with the aid of a little reflection.

PART II

OF THE NATURE AND ORIGIN OF THE MIND

PREFACE

I now pass on to explaining the results, which must necessarily follow from the essence of God, or of the eternal and infinite being; not, indeed, all of them (for we proved in Part. i., Prop. xvi., that an infinite number must follow in an infinite number of ways), but only those which are able to lead us, as it were by the hand, to the knowledge of the human mind and its highest blessedness.

DEFINITIONS

I. By *body* I mean a mode which expresses in a certain determinate manner the essence of God, in so far as he is considered as an extended thing. (See Pt. i., Prop. xxv. Coroll.)

II. I consider as belonging to the essence of a thing that, which being given, the thing is necessarily given also, and, which being removed, the thing is necessarily removed also; in other words, that without which the thing, and which itself without the thing, can neither be nor be conceived.

III. By *idea*, I mean the mental conception which is formed by the mind as a thinking thing.

Explanation.—I say *conception* rather than perception, because the word perception seems to imply that the mind is passive in respect to the object; whereas conception seems to express an activity of the mind.

IV. By *an adequate idea*, I mean an idea which, in so far

as it is considered in itself, without relation to the object, has all the properties or intrinsic marks of a true idea.

Explanation.—I say *intrinsic,* in order to exclude that mark which is extrinsic, namely, the agreement between the idea and its object (*ideatum*).

V. *Duration* is the indefinite continuance of existing.

Explanation.—I say *indefinite,* because it cannot be determined through the existence itself of the existing thing, or by its efficient cause, which necessarily gives the existence of the thing, but does not take it away.

VI. *Reality* and *perfection* I use as synonymous terms.

VII. By *particular things,* I mean things which are finite and have a conditioned existence; but if several individual things concur in one action, so as to be all simultaneously the effect of one cause, I consider them all, so far, as one particular thing.

AXIOMS

I. The essence of man does not involve necessary existence, that is, it may, in the order of nature, come to pass that this or that man does or does not exist.

II. Man thinks.

III. Modes of thinking, such as love, desire, or any other of the passions, do not take place, unless there be in the same individual an idea of the thing loved, desired, &c. But the idea can exist without the presence of any other mode of thinking.

IV. We perceive that a certain body is affected in many ways.

V. We feel and perceive no particular things, save bodies and modes of thought.

N.B. *The postulates are given after the conclusion of* Prop. xiii.

PROPOSITIONS

PROP. I. *Thought is an attribute of God, or God is a thinking thing.*

Proof.—Particular thoughts, or this or that thought, are modes which, in a certain conditioned manner, express the nature of God (Pt. i., Prop. xxv., Coroll.). God therefore possesses the attribute (Pt. i., Def. iv.) of which the concept is involved in all particular thoughts, which latter are conceived thereby. Thought, therefore, is one of the infinite attributes of God, which express God's eternal and infinite essence (Pt. i., Def. vi.). In other words, God is a thinking thing. Q.E.D.

Note.—This proposition is also evident from the fact, that we are able to conceive an infinite thinking being. For, in proportion as a thinking being is conceived as thinking more thoughts, so is it conceived as containing more reality or perfection. Therefore a being, which can think an infinite number of things in an infinite number of ways, is, necessarily, in respect of thinking, infinite. As, therefore, from the consideration of thought alone we conceive an infinite being, thought is necessarily (Pt. i., Deff. iv. and vi.) one of the infinite attributes of God, as we were desirous of showing.

PROP. II. *Extension is an attribute of God, or God is an extended thing.*

Proof.—The proof of this proposition is similar to that of the last.

PROP. III. *In God there is necessarily the idea not only of his essence, but also of all things which necessarily follow from his essence.*

Proof.—God (by the first Prop. of this Part) can think an infinite number of things in infinite ways, or (what is the same thing, by Prop. xvi., Part i.) can form the idea of his essence, and of all things which necessarily follow therefrom. Now all that is in the power of God necessarily is. (Pt. i., Prop. xxxv.) Therefore, such an idea as we are considering necessarily is, and in God alone. Q.E.D. (Part i., Prop. xv.)

Note.—The multitude understand by the power of God the free will of God, and the right over all things that exist, which latter are accordingly generally considered as contingent. For it is said that God has the power to destroy all things, and to reduce them to nothing. Further, the power of God is very often likened to the power of kings. But this doctrine we have refuted (Pt. i., Prop. xxxii., Corolls. i. and ii.), and we have shown (Part i., Prop. xvi.) that God acts by the same necessity, as that by which he understands himself; in other words, as it follows from the necessity of the divine

nature (as all admit), that God understands himself, so also
does it follow by the same necessity, that God performs infinite acts in infinite ways. We further showed (Part i., Prop.
xxxiv.), that God's power is identical with God's essence in
action; therefore it is as impossible for us to conceive God as
not acting, as to conceive him as non-existent. If we might
pursue the subject further, I could point out, that the power
which is commonly attributed to God is not only human (as
showing that God is conceived by the multitude as a man, or
in the likeness of a man), but involves a negation of power.
However, I am unwilling to go over the same ground so often.
I would only beg the reader again and again, to turn over
frequently in his mind what I have said in Part i. from Prop.
xvi. to the end. No one will be able to follow my meaning,
unless he is scrupulously careful not to confound the power
of God with the human power and right of kings.

PROP. IV. *The idea of God, from which an infinite number
of things follow in infinite ways, can only be one.*

Proof.—Infinite intellect comprehends nothing save the attributes of God and his modifications (Part i., Prop. xxx.).
Now God is one (Part i., Prop. xiv., Coroll. i.). Therefore the
idea of God, wherefrom an infinite number of things follow
in infinite ways, can only be one. *Q.E.D.*

PROP. V. *The actual being of ideas owns God as its cause,
only in so far as he is considered as a thinking thing, not in
so far as he is unfolded in any other attribute; that is, the ideas
both of the attributes of God and of particular things do not
own as their efficient cause their objects, or the things
perceived, but God himself in so far as he is a thinking thing.*

Proof.—This proposition is evident from Prop. iii. of this
Part. We there drew the conclusion, that God can form the
idea of his essence, and of all things which follow necessarily
therefrom, solely because he is a thinking thing, and not because he is the object of his own idea. Wherefore the actual
being of ideas owns for cause God, in so far as he is a thinking
thing. It may be differently proved as follows; the actual being of ideas is (obviously) a mode of thought, that is (Part i.,
Prop. xxv., Coroll.) a mode which expresses in a certain manner the nature of God, in so far as he is a thinking thing, and

therefore (Part i., Prop. x.) involves the conception of no other attribute of God, and consequently (by Part i., Ax. iv.) is not the effect of any attribute save thought. Therefore the actual being of ideas owns God as its cause, in so far as he is considered as a thinking thing, &c. *Q.E.D.*

PROP. VI. *The modes of any given attribute are caused by God, in so far as he is considered through the attribute of which they are modes, and not in so far as he is considered through any other attribute.*

Proof.—Each attribute is conceived through itself, without any other (Part i., Prop. x.); wherefore the modes of each attribute involve the conception of that attribute, but not of any other. Thus (Part i., Ax. iv.) they are caused by God, only in so far as he is considered through the attribute whose modes they are, and not in so far as he is considered through any other. *Q.E.D.*

Corollary.—Hence the actual being of things, which are not modes of thought, does not follow from the divine nature, because that nature has prior knowledge of the things. Things represented in ideas follow, and are derived from their particular attribute, in the same manner, and with the same necessity as ideas follow (according to what we have shown) from the attribute of thought.

PROP. VII. *The order and connection of ideas is the same as the order and connection of things.*

Proof.—This proposition is evident from Part i., Ax. iv. For the idea of everything that is caused depends on a knowledge of the cause, whereof it is an effect.

Corollary.—Hence God's power of thinking is equal to his realized power of action—that is, whatsoever follows from the infinite nature of God in the world of extension (*formaliter*), follows without exception in the same order and connection from the idea of God in the world of thought (*objective*).

Note.—Before going any further, I wish to recall to mind what has been pointed out above—namely, that whatsoever can be perceived by the infinite intellect as constituting the essence of substance, belongs altogether only to one substance: consequently, substance thinking and substance extended are one and the same substance, comprehended now through one attribute, now through the other. So, also, a mode of extension and the idea of that mode are one and the same thing, though expressed in two ways. This truth seems to have been dimly recognized by those Jews who maintained that God, God's intellect, and the things understood by God are identical. For instance, a circle existing in nature, and the idea of a circle existing, which is also in God, are one and the same thing displayed through different attributes. Thus, whether we conceive nature under the attribute of extension, or under the attribute of thought, or under any other attribute, we shall find the same order, or one and the same chain of causes—that is, the same things following in either case.

I said that God is the cause of an idea—for instance, of the idea of a circle,—in so far as he is a thinking thing; and of a circle, in so far as he is an extended thing, simply because the actual being of the idea of a circle can only be perceived as a proximate cause through another mode of thinking, and that again through another, and so on to infinity; so that, so long as we consider things as modes of thinking, we must explain the order of the whole of nature, or the whole chain of causes, through the attribute of thought only. And, in so far as we consider things as modes of extension, we must explain the order of the whole of nature through the attribute of extension only; and so on, in the case of other attributes. Wherefore of things as they are in themselves God is really the cause, inasmuch as he consists of infinite attributes. I cannot for the present explain my meaning more clearly.

PROP. VIII. *The ideas of particular things, or of modes, that do not exist, must be comprehended in the infinite idea of God, in the same way as the formal essences of particular things or modes are contained in the attributes of God.*

Proof.—This proposition is evident from the last; it is understood more clearly from the preceding note.

Corollary.—Hence, so long as particular things do not exist, except in so far as they are comprehended in the attributes of God, their representations in thought or ideas do not exist, except in so far as the infinite idea of God exists; and when particular things are said to exist, not only in so far as they are involved in the attributes of God, but also in so far as they are said to continue, their ideas will also involve existence, through which they are said to continue.

Note.—If anyone desires an example to throw more light on this question, I shall, I fear, not be able to give him any, which adequately explains the thing of which I here speak, inasmuch as it is unique; however, I will endeavour to illustrate it as far as possible. The nature of a circle is such that if any number of straight lines intersect within it, the rectangles formed by their segments will be equal to one another; thus, infinite equal rectangles are contained in a circle. Yet none of these rectangles can be said to exist, except in so far as the circle exists; nor can the idea of any of these rectangles be said to exist, except in so far as they are comprehended in the idea of the circle. Let us grant that, from this infinite number of rectangles, two only exist. The ideas of these two not only exist, in so far as they are contained in the idea of the circle, but also as they involve the existence of those rectangles; wherefore they are distinguished from the remaining ideas of the remaining rectangles.

PROP. IX. *The idea of an individual thing actually existing is caused by God, not in so far as he is infinite, but in so far as he is considered as affected by another idea of a thing actually existing, of which he is the cause, in so far as he is affected by a third idea, and so on to infinity.*

Proof.—The idea of an individual thing actually existing is an individual mode of thinking, and is distinct from other modes (by the Corollary and Note to Prop. viii. of this part); thus (by Prop. vi. of this part) it is caused by God, in so far only as he is a thinking thing. But not (by Prop. xxviii. of Part i.) in so far as he is a thing thinking absolutely, only in so far as he is considered as affected by another mode of thinking; and he is the cause of this latter, as being affected by a third, and so on to infinity. Now, the order and connection of ideas is (by Prop. vii. of this book) the same as the order and connection of causes. Therefore of a given individual idea another individual idea, or God, in so far as he is considered as modified by that idea, is the cause; and of this second idea God is the cause, in so far as he is affected by another idea, and so on to infinity. *Q.E.D.*

Corollary.—Whatsoever takes place in the individual object of any idea, the knowledge thereof is in God, in so far only as he has the idea of the object.

Proof.—Whatsoever takes place in the object of any idea, its idea is in God (by Prop. iii. of this part), not in so far as he is infinite, but in so far as he is considered as affected by another idea of an individual thing (by the last Prop.); but (by Prop. vii. of this part) the order and connection of ideas is the same as the order and connection of things. The knowledge, therefore, of that which takes place in any individual object will be in God, in so far only as he has the idea of that object. *Q.E.D.*

Prop. X. *The being of substance does not appertain to the essence of man—in other words, substance does not constitute the actual being[1] of man.*

Proof.—The being of substance involves necessary existence (Part i., Prop. vii.). If, therefore, the being of substance appertains to the essence of man, substance being granted, man would necessarily be granted also (II. Def. ii.), and, consequently, man would necessarily exist, which is absurd (II. Ax. i.). Therefore, &c. *Q.E.D.*

Note.—This proposition may also be proved from I. v., in which it is shown that there cannot be two substances of the same nature; for as there may be many men, the being of substance is not that which constitutes the actual being of man. Again, the proposition is evident from the other properties of substance—namely, that substance is in its nature infinite, immutable, indivisible, &c., as anyone may see for himself.

Corollary.—Hence it follows, that the essence of man is constituted by certain modifications of the attributes of God. For (by the last Prop.) the being of substance does not belong to the essence of man. That essence therefore (by I. xv.) is something which is in God, and which without God can neither be nor be conceived, whether it be a modification (I. xxv. Coroll.), or a mode which expresses God's nature in a certain conditioned manner.

[1] *"Forma."*

Note.—Everyone must surely admit, that nothing can be or be conceived without God. All men agree that God is the one and only cause of all things, both of their essence and of their existence; that is, God is not only the cause of things in respect to their being made (*secundum fieri*), but also in respect to their being (*secundum esse*).

At the same time many assert, that that, without which a thing cannot be nor be conceived, belongs to the essence of that thing; wherefore they believe that either the nature of God appertains to the essence of created things, or else that created things can be or be conceived without God; or else, as is more probably the case, they hold inconsistent doctrines. I think the cause for such confusion is mainly, that they do not keep to the proper order of philosophic thinking. The nature of God, which should be reflected on first, inasmuch as it is prior both in the order of knowledge and the order of nature, they have taken to be last in the order of knowledge, and have put into the first place what they call the objects of sensation; hence, while they are considering natural phenomena, they give no attention at all to the divine nature, and, when afterwards they apply their mind to the study of the divine nature, they are quite unable to bear in mind the first hypotheses, with which they have overlaid the knowledge of natural phenomena, inasmuch as such hypotheses are no help towards understanding the divine nature. So that it is hardly to be wondered at, that these persons contradict themselves freely.

However, I pass over this point. My intention here was only to give a reason for not saying, that that, without which a thing cannot be or be conceived, belongs to the essence of that thing: individual things cannot be or be conceived without God, yet God does not appertain to their essence. I said that "I considered as belonging to the essence of a thing that, which being given, the thing is necessarily given also, and which being removed, the thing is necessarily removed also; or that without which the thing, and which itself without the thing can neither be nor be conceived." (II. Def. ii.)

PROP. XI. *The first element, which constitutes the actual*

being of the human mind, is the idea of some particular thing actually existing.

Proof.—The essence of man (by the Coroll. of the last Prop.) is constituted by certain modes of the attributes of God, namely (by II. Ax. ii.), by the modes of thinking, of all which (by II. Ax. iii.) the idea is prior in nature, and, when the idea is given, the other modes (namely, those of which the idea is prior in nature) must be in the same individual (by the same Axiom). Therefore an idea is the first element constituting the human mind. But not the idea of a non-existent thing, for then (II. viii. Coroll.) the idea itself cannot be said to exist; it must therefore be the idea of something actually existing. But not of an infinite thing. For an infinite thing (I. xxi., xxii.), must always necessarily exist; this would (by II. Ax. i.) involve an absurdity. Therefore the first element, which constitutes the actual being of the human mind, is the idea of something actually existing. *Q.E.D.*

Corollary.—Hence it follows, that the human mind is part of the infinite intellect of God; thus when we say, that the human mind perceives this or that, we make the assertion, that God has this or that idea, not in so far as he is infinite, but in so far as he is displayed through the nature of the human mind, or in so far as he constitutes the essence of the human mind; and when we say that God has this or that idea, not only in so far as he constitutes the essence of the human mind, but also in so far as he, simultaneously with the human mind, has the further idea of another thing, we assert that the human mind perceives a thing in part or inadequately.

Note.—Here, I doubt not, readers will come to a stand, and will call to mind many things which will cause them to hesitate; I therefore beg them to accompany me slowly, step by step, and not to pronounce on my statements, till they have read to the end.

PROP. XII. *Whatsoever comes to pass in the object of the idea, which constitutes the human mind, must be perceived by the human mind, or there will necessarily be an idea in the human mind of the said occurrence. That is, if the object of the idea constituting the human mind be a body, nothing can take place in that body without being perceived by the mind.*

Proof.—Whatsoever comes to pass in the object of any idea, the knowledge thereof is necessarily in God (II. ix. Coroll.), in so far as he is considered as affected by the idea of the said object, that is (II. xi.), in so far as he constitutes the mind of anything. Therefore, whatsoever takes place in the object constituting the idea of the human mind, the knowledge thereof is necessarily in God, in so far as he constitutes the nature of the human mind; that is (by II. xi. Coroll.) the knowledge of the said thing will necessarily be in the mind, in other words the mind perceives it.

Note.—This proposition is also evident, and is more clearly to be understood from II. vii., which see.

PROP. XIII. *The object of the idea constituting the human mind is the body, in other words a certain mode of extension which actually exists, and nothing else.*

Proof.—If indeed the body were not the object of the human mind, the ideas of the modifications of the body would not be in God (II. ix. Coroll.) in virtue of his constituting our mind, but in virtue of his constituting the mind of something else; that is (II. xi. Coroll.) the ideas of the modifications of the body would not be in our mind: now (by II. Ax. iv.) we do possess the ideas of the modifications of the body. Therefore the object of the idea constituting the human mind is the body, and the body as it actually exists (II. xi.). Further, if there were any other object of the idea constituting the mind besides body, then, as nothing can exist from which some effect does not follow (I. xxxvi.) there would necessarily have to be in our mind an idea, which would be the effect of that other object (II. xi.); but (II. Ax. v.) there is no such idea. Wherefore the object of our mind is the body as it exists, and nothing else. *Q.E.D.*

Note.—We thus comprehend, not only that the human mind is united to the body, but also the nature of the union between mind and body. However, no one will be able to grasp this adequately or distinctly, unless he first has adequate knowledge of the nature of our body. The propositions we have advanced hitherto have been entirely general, applying not more to men than to other individual things, all of which, though in different degrees, are animated.[2] For of everything there is necessarily an idea in God, of which God is the cause, in the same way as there is an idea of the human body; thus whatever we have asserted of the idea of the human body must necessarily also be asserted of the idea of everything else. Still, on the other hand, we cannot deny that ideas, like objects, differ one from the other, one being more excellent than another and containing more reality, just as the object of one idea is more excellent than the object of another idea, and contains more reality.

Wherefore, in order to determine, wherein the human mind differs from other things, and wherein it surpasses them, it is necessary for us to know the nature of its object, that is, of the human body. What this nature is, I am not able here to explain, nor is it necessary for the proof of what I advance, that I should do so. I will only say generally, that in proportion as any given body is more fitted than others for doing many actions or receiving many impressions at once, so also is the mind, of which it is the object, more fitted than others for forming many simultaneous perceptions; and the more the actions of one body depend on itself alone, and the fewer other bodies concur with it in action, the more fitted is the mind of which it is the object for distinct comprehension. We may thus recognize the superiority of one mind over others, and may further see the cause, why we have only a very confused knowledge of our body, and also many kindred questions, which I will, in the following propositions, deduce from what has been advanced. Wherefore I have thought it worth while to explain and prove more strictly my present statements. In order to do so, I must premise a few propositions concerning the nature of bodies.

Axiom I. All bodies are either in motion or at rest.

Axiom II. Every body is moved sometimes more slowly, sometimes more quickly.

Lemma I. *Bodies are distinguished from one another in respect of motion and rest, quickness and slowness, and not in respect of substance.*

Proof.—The first part of this proposition is, I take it, self-

2 *"Animata."*

evident. That bodies are not distinguished in respect of substance, is plain both from I. v. and I. viii. It is brought out still more clearly from I. xv., note.

LEMMA II. *All bodies agree in certain respects.*

Proof.—All bodies agree in the fact, that they involve the conception of one and the same attribute (II., Def. i.). Further, in the fact that they may be moved less or more quickly, and may be absolutely in motion or at rest.

LEMMA III. *A body in motion or at rest must be determined to motion or rest by another body, which other body has been determined to motion or rest by a third body, and that third again by a fourth, and so on to infinity.*

Proof.—Bodies are individual things (II., Def. i.), which (Lemma I.) are distinguished one from the other in respect to motion and rest; thus (I. xxviii.) each must necessarily be determined to motion or rest by another individual thing, namely (II. vi.), by another body, which other body is also (Ax. i.) in motion or at rest. And this body again can only have been set in motion or caused to rest by being determined by a third body to motion or rest. This third body again by a fourth, and so on to infinity. *Q.E.D.*

Corollary.—Hence it follows, that a body in motion keeps in motion, until it is determined to a state of rest by some other body; and a body at rest remains so, until it is determined to a state of motion by some other body. This is indeed self-evident. For when I suppose, for instance, that a given body, A, is at rest, and do not take into consideration other bodies in motion, I cannot affirm anything concerning the body A, except that it is at rest. If it afterwards comes to pass that A is in motion, this cannot have resulted from its having been at rest, for no other consequence could have been involved than its remaining at rest. If, on the other hand, A be given in motion, we shall, so long as we only consider A, be unable to affirm anything concerning it, except that it is in motion. If A is subsequently found to be at rest, this rest cannot be the result of A's previous motion, for such motion can only have led to continued motion; the state of rest therefore must have resulted from something, which was not in A, namely, from an external cause determining A to a state of rest.

Axiom I.—All modes, wherein one body is affected by another body, follow simultaneously from the nature of the body affected and the body affecting; so that one and the same body may be moved in different modes, according to the difference in the nature of the bodies moving it; on the other hand, different bodies may be moved in different modes by one and the same body.

Axiom II.—When a body in motion impinges on another body at rest, which it is unable to move, it recoils, in order to continue its motion, and the angle made by the line of motion in the recoil and the plane of the body at rest, whereon the moving body has impinged, will be equal to the angle formed by the line of motion of incidence and the same plane.

So far we have been speaking only of the most simple bodies, which are only distinguished one from the other by motion and rest, quickness and slowness. We now pass on to compound bodies.

Definition.—When any given bodies of the same or different magnitude are compelled by other bodies to remain in contact, or if they be moved at the same or different rates of speed, so that their mutual movements should preserve among themselves a certain fixed relation, we say that such bodies are in union, and that together they compose one body or individual, which is distinguished from other bodies by this fact of union.

Axiom III.—In proportion as the parts of an individual, or a compound body, are in contact over a greater or less superficies, they will with greater or less difficulty admit of being moved from their position; consequently the individual will, with greater or less difficulty, be brought to assume another form. Those bodies, whose parts are in contact over large superficies, are called *hard;* those, whose parts are in contact over small superficies, are called *soft;* those, whose parts are in motion among one another, are called *fluid.*

LEMMA IV. *If from a body or individual, compounded of several bodies, certain bodies be separated, and if, at the same time, an equal number of other bodies of the same nature take their place, the individual will preserve its nature as before, without any change in its actuality (forma).*

Proof.—Bodies (Lemma i.) are not distinguished in respect of substance: that which constitutes the actuality (*formam*) of an individual consists (by the last Def.) in a union of bodies; but this union, although there is a continual change of bodies, will (by our hypothesis) be maintained; the individual, therefore, will retain its nature as before, both in respect of substance and in respect of mode. *Q.E.D.*

LEMMA V. *If the parts composing an individual become greater or less, but in such proportion, that they all preserve the same mutual relations of motion and rest, the individual will still preserve its original nature, and its actuality will not be changed.*

Proof.—The same as for the last Lemma.

LEMMA VI. *If certain bodies composing an individual be compelled to change the motion, which they have in one direction, for motion in another direction, but in such a manner, that they be able to continue their motions and their mutual communication in the same relations as before, the individual will retain its own nature without any change of its actuality.*

Proof.—This proposition is self-evident, for the individual is supposed to retain all that, which, in its definition, we spoke of as its actual being.

LEMMA VII. *Furthermore, the individual thus composed preserves its nature, whether it be, as a whole, in motion or at rest, whether it be moved in this or that direction; so long as each part retains its motion, and preserves its communication with other parts as before.*

Proof.—This proposition is evident from the definition of an individual prefixed to Lemma iv.

Note.—We thus see, how a composite individual may be affected in many different ways, and preserve its nature notwithstanding. Thus far we have conceived an individual as composed of bodies only distinguished one from the other in respect of motion and rest, speed and slowness; that is, of bodies of the most simple character. If, however, we now conceive another individual composed of several individuals of diverse natures, we shall find that the number of ways in which it can be affected, without losing its nature, will be greatly multiplied. Each of its parts would consist of several bodies, and therefore (by Lemma vi.) each part would admit, without change to its nature, of quicker or slower motion, and would consequently be able to transmit its motions more quickly or more slowly to the remaining parts. If we further conceive a third kind of individuals composed of individuals of this second kind, we shall find that they may be affected in a still greater number of ways without changing their actuality. We may easily proceed thus to infinity, and conceive the whole of nature as one individual, whose parts, that is, all bodies, vary in infinite ways, without any change in the individual as a whole. I should feel bound to explain and demonstrate this point at more length, if I were writing a special treatise on body. But I have already said that such is not my object, I have only touched on the question, because it enables me to prove easily that which I have in view.

POSTULATES

I. The human body is composed of a number of individual parts, of diverse nature, each one of which is in itself extremely complex.

II. Of the individual parts composing the human body some are fluid, some soft, some hard.

III. The individual parts composing the human body, and consequently the human body itself, are affected in a variety of ways by external bodies.

IV. The human body stands in need for its preservation of a number of other bodies, by which it is continually, so to speak, regenerated.

V. When the fluid part of the human body is determined by an external body to impinge often on another soft part, it changes the surface of the latter, and, as it were, leaves the impression thereupon of the external body which impels it.

VI. The human body can move external bodies, and arrange them in a variety of ways.

PROP. XIV. *The human mind is capable of perceiving a great number of things, and is so in proportion as its body is capable of receiving a great number of impressions.*

Proof.—The human body (by Post. iii. and vi.) is affected

in very many ways by external bodies, and is capable in very many ways of affecting external bodies. But (II. xii.) the human mind must perceive all that takes place in the human body; the human mind is, therefore, capable of perceiving a great number of things, and is so in proportion, &c. *Q.E.D.*

PROP. XV. *The idea, which constitutes the actual being of the human mind, is not simple, but compounded of a great number of ideas.*

Proof.—The idea constituting the actual being of the human mind is the idea of the body (II. xiii.), which (Post. i.) is composed of a great number of complex individual parts. But there is necessarily in God the idea of each individual part whereof the body is composed (II. viii. Coroll.); therefore (II. vii.), the idea of the human body is composed of these numerous ideas of its component parts. *Q.E.D.*

PROP. XVI. *The idea of every mode, in which the human body is affected by external bodies, must involve the nature of the human body, and also the nature of the external body.*

Proof.—All the modes, in which any given body is affected, follow from the nature of the body affected, and also from the nature of the affecting body (by Ax. i., after the Coroll. of Lemma iii.), wherefore their idea also necessarily (by I. Ax. iv.) involves the nature of both bodies; therefore, the idea of every mode, in which the human body is affected by external bodies, involves the nature of the human body and of the external body. *Q.E.D.*

Corollary I.—Hence it follows, first, that the human mind perceives the nature of a variety of bodies, together with the nature of its own.

Corollary II.—It follows, secondly, that the ideas, which we have of external bodies, indicate rather the constitution of our own body than the nature of external bodies. I have amply illustrated this in the Appendix to Part I.

PROP. XVII. *If the human body is affected in a manner which involves the nature of any external body, the human mind will regard the said external body as actually existing, or as present to itself, until the human body be affected in such a way, as to exclude the existence or the presence of the said external body.*

Proof.—This proposition is self-evident, for so long as the human body continues to be thus affected, so long will the human mind (II. xii.) regard this modification of the body—that is (by the last Prop.), it will have the idea of the mode as actually existing, and this idea involves the nature of the external body. In other words, it will have the idea which does not exclude, but postulates the existence or presence of the nature of the external body; therefore the mind (by II. xvi., Coroll. i.) will regard the external body as actually existing, until it is affected, &c. *Q.E.D.*

Corollary.—The mind is able to regard as present external bodies, by which the human body has once been affected, even though they be no longer in existence or present.

Proof.—When external bodies determine the fluid parts of the human body, so that they often impinge on the softer parts, they change the surface of the last named (Post. v.); hence (Ax. ii., after Coroll. of Lemma iii.) they are refracted therefrom in a different manner from that which they followed before such change; and, further, when afterwards they impinge on the new surfaces by their own spontaneous movement, they will be refracted in the same manner, as though they had been impelled towards those surfaces by external bodies; consequently, they will, while they continue to be thus refracted, affect the human body in the same manner, whereof the mind (II. xii.) will again take cognizance—that is (II. xvii.), the mind will again regard the external body as present, and will do so, as often as the fluid parts of the human body impinge on the aforesaid surfaces by their own spontaneous motion. Wherefore, although the external bodies, by which the human body has once been affected, be no longer in existence, the mind will nevertheless regard them as present, as often as this action of the body is repeated. *Q.E.D.*

Note.—We thus see how it comes about, as is often the case, that we regard as present things which are not. It is possible that the same result may be brought about by other causes; but I think it suffices for me here to have indicated one possible explanation, just as well as if I had pointed out the true cause. Indeed, I do not think I am very far from the truth, for all my assumptions are based on postulates, which rest, almost without exception, on experience, that cannot be controverted by those who have shown, as we have, that the human body, as we feel it, exists (Coroll. after II. xiii.). Furthermore (II. vii. Coroll., II. xvi. Coroll. ii.), we clearly understand what is the difference between the idea, say, of Peter, which constitutes the essence of Peter's mind, and the idea of the said Peter, which is in another man, say, Paul. The former directly answers to the essence of Peter's own body, and only implies existence so long as Peter exists; the latter indicates rather the disposition of Paul's body than the nature of Peter, and, therefore, while this disposition of Paul's body lasts, Paul's mind will regard Peter as present to itself, even though he no longer exists. Further, to retain the usual phraseology, the modifications of the human body, of which the ideas represent external bodies as present to us, we will call the images of things, though they do not recall the figure of things. When the mind regards bodies in this fashion, we say that it imagines. I will here draw attention to the fact, in order to indicate where error lies, that the imaginations of the mind, looked at in themselves, do not contain error. The mind does not err in the mere act of imagining, but only in so far as it is regarded as being without the idea, which excludes the existence of such things as it imagines to be present to it. If the mind, while imagining non-existent things as present to it, is at the same time conscious that they do not really exist, this power of imagination must be set down to the efficacy of its nature, and not to a fault, especially if this faculty of imagination depend solely on its own nature—that is (I. Def. vii.), if this faculty of imagination be free.

PROP. XVIII. *If the human body has once been affected by two or more bodies at the same time, when the mind afterwards imagines any of them, it will straightway remember the others also.*

Proof.—The mind (II. xvii. Coroll.) imagines any given body, because the human body is affected and disposed by the impressions from an external body, in the same manner as it is affected when certain of its parts are acted on by the said external body; but (by our hypothesis) the body was then so disposed, that the mind imagined two bodies at once;

therefore, it will also in the second case imagine two bodies at once, and the mind, when it imagines one, will straightway remember the other. *Q.E.D.*

Note.—We now clearly see what *Memory* is. It is simply a certain association of ideas involving the nature of things outside the human body, which association arises in the mind according to the order and association of the modifications (*affectiones*) of the human body. I say, first, it is an association of those ideas only, which involve the nature of things outside the human body: not of ideas which answer to the nature of the said things: ideas of the modifications of the human body are, strictly speaking (II. xvi.), those which involve the nature both of the human body and of external bodies. I say, secondly, that this association arises according to the order and association of the modifications of the human body, in order to distinguish it from that association of ideas, which arises from the order of the intellect, whereby the mind perceives things through their primary causes, and which is in all men the same. And hence we can further clearly understand, why the mind from the thought of one thing, should straightway arrive at the thought of another thing, which has no similarity with the first; for instance, from the thought of the word *pomum* (an apple), a Roman would straightway arrive at the thought of the fruit apple, which has no similitude with the articulate sound in question, nor anything in common with it, except that the body of the man has often been affected by these two things; that is, that the man has often heard the word *pomum*, while he was looking at the fruit; similarly every man will go on from one thought to another, according as his habit has ordered the images of things in his body. For a soldier, for instance, when he sees the tracks of a horse in sand, will at once pass from the thought of a horse to the thought of a horseman, and thence to the thought of war, &c.; while a countryman will proceed from the thought of a horse to the thought of a plough, a field, &c. Thus every man will follow this or that train of thought, according as he has been in the habit of conjoining and associating the mental images of things in this or that manner.

Prop. XIX. *The human mind has no knowledge of the body,*

and does not know it to exist, save through the ideas of the modifications whereby the body is affected.

Proof.—The human mind is the very idea or knowledge of the human body (II. xiii.), which (II. ix.) is in God, in so far as he is regarded as affected by another idea of a particular thing actually existing: or, inasmuch as (Post. iv.) the human body stands in need of very many bodies whereby it is, as it were, continually regenerated; and the order and connection of ideas is the same as the order and connection of causes (II. vii.); this idea will therefore be in God, in so far as he is regarded as affected by the ideas of very many particular things. Thus God has the idea of the human body, or knows the human body, in so far as he is affected by very many other ideas, and not in so far as he constitutes the nature of the human mind; that is (by II. xi. Coroll.), the human mind does not know the human body. But the ideas of the modifications of body are in God, in so far as he constitutes the nature of the human mind, or the human mind perceives those modifications (II. xii.), and consequently (II. xvi.) the human body itself, and as actually existing; therefore the mind perceives thus far only the human body. *Q.E.D.*

PROP. XX. *The idea or knowledge of the human mind is also in God, following in God in the same manner, and being referred to God in the same manner, as the idea or knowledge of the human body.*

Proof.—Thought is an attribute of God (II. i.); therefore (II. iii.) there must necessarily be in God the idea both of thought itself and of all its modifications, consequently also of the human mind (II. xi.). Further, this idea or knowledge of the mind does not follow from God, in so far as he is infinite, but in so far as he is affected by another idea of an individual thing (II. ix.). But (II. vii.) the order and connection of ideas is the same as the order and connection of causes; therefore this idea or knowledge of the mind is in God and is referred to God, in the same manner as the idea or knowledge of the body. *Q.E.D.*

PROP. XXI. *This idea of the mind is united to the mind in the same way as the mind is united to the body.*

Proof.—That the mind is united to the body we have shown

from the fact, that the body is the object of the mind (II. xii. and xiii.); and so for the same reason the idea of the mind must be united with its object, that is, with the mind in the same manner as the mind is united to the body. *Q.E.D.*

Note.—This proposition is comprehended much more clearly from what we said in the note to II. vii. We there showed that the idea of body and body, that is, mind and body (II. xiii.), are one and the same individual conceived now under the attribute of thought, now under the attribute of extension; wherefore the idea of the mind and the mind itself are one and the same thing, which is conceived under one and the same attribute, namely, thought. The idea of the mind, I repeat, and the mind itself are in God by the same necessity and follow from him from the same power of thinking. Strictly speaking, the idea of the mind, that is, the idea of an idea, is nothing but the distinctive quality (*forma*) of the idea in so far as it is conceived as a mode of thought without reference to the object; if a man knows anything, he, by that very fact, knows that he knows it, and at the same time knows that he knows that he knows it, and so on to infinity. But I will treat of this hereafter.

PROP. XXII. *The human mind perceives not only the modifications of the body, but also the ideas of such modifications.*

Proof.—The ideas of the ideas of modifications follow in God in the same manner, and are referred to God in the same manner, as the ideas of the said modifications. This is proved in the same way as II. xx. But the ideas of the modifications of the body are in the human mind (II. xii.), that is, in God, in so far as he constitutes the essence of the human mind; therefore the ideas of these ideas will be in God, in so far as he has the knowledge or idea of the human mind, that is (II. xxi.), they will be in the human mind itself, which therefore perceives not only the modifications of the body, but also the ideas of such modifications. *Q.E.D.*

PROP. XXIII. *The mind does not know itself, except in so far as it perceives the ideas of the modifications of the body.*

Proof.—The idea or knowledge of the mind (II. xx.) follows in God in the same manner, and is referred to God in the same manner, as the idea or knowledge of the body. But since

(II. xix.) the human mind does not know the human body itself, that is (II. xi. Coroll.), since the knowledge of the human body is not referred to God, in so far as he constitutes the nature of the human mind; therefore, neither is the knowledge of the mind referred to God, in so far as he constitutes the essence of the human mind; therefore (by the same Coroll. II. xi.), the human mind thus far has no knowledge of itself. Further the ideas of the modifications, whereby the body is affected, involve the nature of the human body itself (II. xvi.), that is (II. xiii.), they agree with the nature of the mind; wherefore the knowledge of these ideas necessarily involves knowledge of the mind; but (by the last Prop.) the knowledge of these ideas is in the human mind itself; wherefore the human mind thus far only has knowledge of itself. *Q.E.D.*

Prop. XXIV.—*The human mind does not involve an adequate knowledge of the parts composing the human body.*

Proof.—The parts composing the human body do not belong to the essence of that body, except in so far as they communicate their motions to one another in a certain fixed relation (Def. after Lemma iii.), not in so far as they can be regarded as individuals without relation to the human body. The parts of the human body are highly complex individuals (Post. i.), whose parts (Lemma iv.) can be separated from the human body without in any way destroying the nature and distinctive quality of the latter, and they can communicate their motions (Ax. i., after Lemma iii.) to other bodies in another relation; therefore (II. iii.) the idea or knowledge of each part will be in God, inasmuch (II. ix.) as he is regarded as affected by another idea of a particular thing, which particular thing is prior in the order of nature to the aforesaid part (II. vii.). We may affirm the same thing of each part of each individual composing the human body; therefore, the knowledge of each part composing the human body is in God, in so far as he is affected by very many ideas of things, and not in so far as he has the idea of the human body only, in other words, the idea which constitutes the nature of the human mind (II. xiii.); therefore (II. xi. Coroll.), the human mind does not involve an adequate knowledge of the human body. *Q.E.D.*

PROP. XXV. *The idea of each modification of the human body does not involve an adequate knowledge of the external body.*

Proof.—We have shown that the idea of a modification of the human body involves the nature of an external body, in so far as that external body conditions the human body in a given manner. But, in so far as the external body is an individual, which has no reference to the human body, the knowledge or idea thereof is in God (II. ix.), in so far as God is regarded as affected by the idea of a further thing, which (II. vii.) is naturally prior to the said external body. Wherefore an adequate knowledge of the external body is not in God, in so far as he has the idea of the modification of the human body; in other words, the idea of the modification of the human body does not involve an adequate knowledge of the external body. *Q.E.D.*

PROP. XXVI. *The human mind does not perceive any external body as actually existing, except through the ideas of the modifications of its own body.*

Proof.—If the human body is in no way affected by a given external body, then (II. vii.) neither is the idea of the human body, in other words, the human mind, affected in any way by the idea of the existence of the said external body, nor does it in any manner perceive its existence. But, in so far as the human body is affected in any way by a given external body, thus far (II. xvi. and Coroll.) it perceives that external body. *Q.E.D.*

Corollary.—In so far as the human mind imagines an external body, it has not an adequate knowledge thereof.

Proof.—When the human mind regards external bodies through the ideas of the modifications of its own body, we say that it imagines (see II. xvii. note); now the mind can only imagine external bodies as actually existing. Therefore (by II. xxv.), in so far as the mind imagines external bodies, it has not an adequate knowledge of them. *Q.E.D.*

PROP. XXVII. *The idea of each modification of the human body does not involve an adequate knowledge of the human body itself.*

Proof.—Every idea of a modification of the human body involves the nature of the human body, in so far as the human body is regarded as affected in a given manner (II. xvi.). But, inasmuch as the human body is an individual which may be affected in many other ways, the idea of the said modification, &c. *Q.E.D.*

PROP. XXVIII. *The ideas of the modifications of the human body, in so far as they have reference only to the human mind, are not clear and distinct, but confused.*

Proof.—The ideas of the modifications of the human body involve the nature both of the human body and of external bodies (II. xvi.); they must involve the nature not only of the human body but also of its parts; for the modifications are modes (Post. iii.), whereby the parts of the human body, and, consequently, the human body as a whole are affected. But (by II. xxiv., xxv.) the adequate knowledge of external bodies, as also of the parts composing the human body, is not in God, in so far as he is regarded as affected by the human mind, but in so far as he is regarded as affected by other ideas. These ideas of modifications, in so far as they are referred to the human mind alone, are as consequences without premisses, in other words, confused ideas. *Q.E.D.*

Note.—The idea which constitutes the nature of the human mind is, in the same manner, proved not to be, when considered in itself alone, clear and distinct; as also is the case with the idea of the human mind, and the ideas of the ideas of the modifications of the human body, in so far as they are referred to the mind only, as everyone may easily see.

PROP. XXIX. *The idea of the idea of each modification of the human body does not involve an adequate knowledge of the human mind.*

Proof.—The idea of a modification of the human body (II. xxvii.) does not involve an adequate knowledge of the said body, in other words, does not adequately express its nature; that is (II. xiii.) it does not agree with the nature of the mind adequately; therefore (I. Ax. vi.) the idea of this idea does not adequately express the nature of the human mind, or does not involve an adequate knowledge thereof.

Corollary.—Hence it follows that the human mind, when it perceives things after the common order of nature, has not

an adequate but only a confused and fragmentary knowledge
of itself, of its own body, and of external bodies. For the mind
does not know itself, except in so far as it perceives the ideas
of the modifications of body (II. xxiii.). It only perceives its
own body (II. xix.) through the ideas of the modifications,
and only perceives external bodies through the same means;
thus, in so far as it has such ideas of modification, it has not
an adequate knowledge of itself (II. xxix.), nor of its own body
(II. xxvii.), nor of external bodies (II. xxv.), but only a fragmentary and confused knowledge thereof (II. xxviii. and
note). *Q.E.D.*

Note.—I say expressly, that the mind has not an adequate
but only a confused knowledge of itself, its own body, and of
external bodies, whenever it perceives things after the common order of nature; that is, whenever it is determined from
without, namely, by the fortuitous play of circumstance, to
regard this or that; not at such times as it is determined from
within, that is, by the fact of regarding several things at once,
to understand their points of agreement, difference, and con-
trast. Whenever it is determined in anywise from within, it
regards things clearly and distinctly, as I will show below.

PROP. XXX. *We can only have a very inadequate knowledge
of the duration of our body.*

Proof.—The duration of our body does not depend on its
essence (II. Ax. i.), nor on the absolute nature of God (I.
xxi.). But (I. xxviii.) it is conditioned to exist and operate by
causes, which in their turn are conditioned to exist and operate
in a fixed and definite relation by other causes, these last again
being conditioned by others, and so on to infinity. The duration of our body therefore depends on the common order of
nature, or the constitution of things. Now, however a thing
may be constituted, the adequate knowledge of that thing is
in God, in so far as he has the ideas of all things, and not in
so far as he has the idea of the human body only. (II. ix.
Coroll.) Wherefore the knowledge of the duration of our body
is in God very inadequate, in so far as he is only regarded as
constituting the nature of the human mind; that is (II. xi.
Coroll.), this knowledge is very inadequate in our mind.
Q.E.D.

Prop. XXXI. *We can only have a very inadequate knowl-edge of the duration of particular things external to ourselves.*

Proof.—Every particular thing, like the human body, must be conditioned by another particular thing to exist and operate in a fixed and definite relation; this other particular thing must likewise be conditioned by a third, and so on to infinity. (I. xxviii.) As we have shown in the foregoing proposition, from this common property of particular things, we have only a very inadequate knowledge of the duration of our body; we must draw a similar conclusion with regard to the duration of particular things, namely, that we can only have a very inade-quate knowledge of the duration thereof. *Q.E.D.*

Corollary.—Hence it follows that all particular things are contingent and perishable. For we can have no adequate idea of their duration (by the last Prop.), and this is what we must understand by the contingency and perishableness of things. (I. xxxiii., note i.) For (I. xxix.), except in this sense, nothing is contingent.

Prop. XXXII. *All ideas, in so far as they are referred to God, are true.*

Proof.—All ideas which are in God agree in every respect with their objects (II. vii. Coroll.), therefore (I. Ax. vi.) they are all true. *Q.E.D.*

Prop. XXXIII. *There is nothing positive in ideas, which causes them to be called false.*

Proof.—If this be denied, conceive, if possible, a positive mode of thinking, which should constitute the distinctive quality of falsehood. Such a mode of thinking cannot be in God (II. xxxii.); external to God it cannot be or be conceived (I. xv.). Therefore there is nothing positive in ideas which causes them to be called false. *Q.E.D.*

Prop. XXXIV. *Every idea, which in us is absolute or ade-quate and perfect, is true.*

Proof.—When we say that an idea in us is adequate and perfect, we say, in other words (II. xi. Coroll.), that the idea is adequate and perfect in God, in so far as he constitutes the essence of our mind; consequently (II. xxxii.), we say that such an idea is true. *Q.E.D.*

Prop. XXXV. *Falsity consists in the privation of knowl-*

edge, which inadequate, fragmentary, or confused ideas involve.

Proof.—There is nothing positive in ideas, which causes them to be called false (II. xxxiii.); but falsity cannot consist in simple privation (for minds, not bodies, are said to err and to be mistaken), neither can it consist in absolute ignorance, for ignorance and error are not identical; wherefore it consists in the privation of knowledge, which inadequate, fragmentary, or confused ideas involve. *Q.E.D.*

Note.—In the note to II. xvii. I explained how error consists in the privation of knowledge, but in order to throw more light on the subject I will give an example. For instance, men are mistaken in thinking themselves free; their opinion is made up of consciousness of their own actions, and ignorance of the causes by which they are conditioned. Their idea of freedom, therefore, is simply their ignorance of any cause for their actions. As for their saying that human actions depend on the will, this is a mere phrase without any idea to correspond thereto. What the will is, and how it moves the body, they none of them know; those who boast of such knowledge, and feign dwellings and habitations for the soul, are wont to provoke either laughter or disgust. So, again, when we look at the sun, we imagine that it is distant from us about two hundred feet; this error does not lie solely in this fancy, but in the fact that, while we thus imagine, we do not know the sun's true distance or the cause of the fancy. For although we afterwards learn, that the sun is distant from us more than six hundred of the earth's diameters, we none the less shall fancy it to be near; for we do not imagine the sun as near us, because we are ignorant of its true distance, but because the modification of our body involves the essence of the sun, in so far as our said body is affected thereby.

PROP. XXXVI. *Inadequate or confused ideas follow by the same necessity, as adequate or clear and distinct ideas.*

Proof.—All ideas are in God (I. xv.), and in so far as they are referred to God are true (II. xxxii.) and (II. vii. Coroll.) adequate; therefore there are no ideas confused or inadequate, except in respect to a particular mind (cf. II. xxiv. and xxviii.);

therefore all ideas, whether adequate or inadequate, follow by the same necessity (II. vi.). *Q.E.D.*

PROP. XXXVII. *That which is common to all (cf. Lemma II. above), and which is equally in a part and in the whole, does not constitute the essence of any particular thing.*

Proof.—If this be denied, conceive, if possible, that it constitutes the essence of some particular thing; for instance, the essence of B. Then (II. Def. ii.) it cannot without B either exist or be conceived; but this is against our hypothesis. Therefore it does not appertain to B's essence, nor does it constitute the essence of any particular thing. *Q.E.D.*

PROP. XXXVIII. *Those things, which are common to all, and which are equally in a part and in the whole, cannot be conceived except adequately.*

Proof.—Let A be something, which is common to all bodies, and which is equally present in the part of any given body and in the whole. I say A cannot be conceived except adequately. For the idea thereof in God will necessarily be adequate (II. vii. Coroll.), both in so far as God has the idea of the human body, and also in so far as he has the idea of the modifications of the human body, which (II. xvi., xxv., xxvii.) involve in part the nature of the human body and the nature of external bodies; that is (II. xii., xiii.), the idea in God will necessarily be adequate, both in so far as he constitutes the human mind, and in so far as he has the ideas, which are in the human mind. Therefore the mind (II. xi. Coroll.) necessarily perceives A adequately, and has this adequate perception, both in so far as it perceives itself, and in so far as it perceives its own or any external body, nor can A be conceived in any other manner. *Q.E.D.*

Corollary.—Hence it follows that there are certain ideas or notions common to all men; for (by Lemma ii.) all bodies agree in certain respects, which (by the foregoing Prop.) must be adequately or clearly and distinctly perceived by all.

PROP. XXXIX. *That, which is common to and a property of the human body and such other bodies as are wont to affect the human body, and which is present equally in each part of either, or in the whole, will be represented by an adequate idea in the mind.*

Proof.—If A be that, which is common to and a property of the human body and external bodies, and equally present in the human body and in the said external bodies, in each part of each external body and in the whole, there will be an adequate idea of A in God (II. vii. Coroll.), both in so far as he has the idea of the human body, and in so far as he has the ideas of the given external bodies. Let it now be granted, that the human body is affected by an external body through that, which it has in common therewith, namely, A; the idea of this modification will involve the property A (II. xvi.), and therefore (II. vii. Coroll.) the idea of this modification, in so far as it involves the property A, will be adequate in God, in so far as God is affected by the idea of the human body; that is (II. xiii.), in so far as he constitutes the nature of the human mind; therefore (II. xi. Coroll.) this idea is also adequate in the human mind. *Q.E.D.*

Corollary.—Hence it follows that the mind is fitted to perceive adequately more things, in proportion as its body has more in common with other bodies.

PROP. XL. *Whatsoever ideas in the mind follow from ideas which are therein adequate are also themselves adequate.*

Proof.—This proposition is self-evident. For when we say that an idea in the human mind follows from ideas which are therein adequate, we say, in other words (II. xi. Coroll.), that an idea is in the divine intellect, whereof God is the cause, not in so far as he is infinite, nor in so far as he is affected by the ideas of very many particular things, but only in so far as he constitutes the essence of the human mind.

Note I.—I have thus set forth the cause of those notions, which are common to all men, and which form the basis of our ratiocination. But there are other causes of certain axioms or notions, which it would be to the purpose to set forth by this method of ours; for it would thus appear what notions are more useful than others, and what notions have scarcely any use at all. Furthermore, we should see what notions are common to all men, and what notions are only clear and distinct to those who are unshackled by prejudice, and we should detect those which are ill-founded. Again we should discern whence the notions called *secondary* derived their origin, and consequently the axioms on which they are founded, and other points of interest connected with these questions. But I have decided to pass over the subject here, partly because I have set it aside for another treatise, partly because I am afraid of wearying the reader by too great prolixity. Nevertheless, in order not to omit anything necessary to be known, I will briefly set down the causes, whence are derived the terms styled *transcendental*, such as Being, Thing, Something. These terms arose from the fact, that the human body, being limited, is only capable of distinctly forming a certain number of images (what an image is I explained in II. xvii. note) within itself at the same time; if this number be exceeded, the images will begin to be confused; if this number of images, which the body is capable of forming distinctly within itself, be largely exceeded, all will become entirely confused one with another. This being so, it is evident (from II. Prop. xvii. Coroll. and xviii.) that the human mind can distinctly imagine as many things simultaneously, as its body can form images simultaneously. When the images become quite confused in the body, the mind also imagines all bodies confusedly without any distinction, and will comprehend them, as it were, under one attribute, namely, under the attribute of Being, Thing, &c. The same conclusion can be drawn from the fact that images are not always equally vivid, and from other analogous causes, which there is no need to explain here; for the purpose which we have in view it is sufficient for us to consider one only. All may be reduced to this, that these terms represent ideas in the highest degree confused. From similar causes arise those notions, which we call *general*, such as man, horse, dog, &c. They arise, to wit, from the fact that so many images, for instance, of men, are formed simultaneously in the human mind, that the powers of imagination break down, not indeed utterly, but to the extent of the mind losing count of small differences between individuals (*e.g.* colour, size, &c.) and their definite number, and only distinctly imagining that, in which all the individuals, in so far as the body is affected by them, agree; for that is the point, in which each of the said individuals chiefly affected the body; this the mind expresses by the name man, and this it predicates of an infinite number of particular individuals. For, as we have said, it is unable to imagine the definite number of individuals. We must, however, bear in mind, that these general notions are not formed by all men in the same way, but vary in each individual according as the point varies, whereby the body has been most often affected and which the mind most easily imagines or remembers. For instance, those who have most often regarded with admiration the stature of man, will by the name of man understand an animal of erect stature; those who have been accustomed to regard some other attribute, will form a different general image of man, for instance, that man is a laughing animal, a two-footed animal without feathers, a rational animal, and thus, in other cases, everyone will form general images of things according to the habit of his body.

It is thus not to be wondered at, that among philosophers, who seek to explain things in nature merely by the images formed of them, so many controversies should have arisen.

Note II.—From all that has been said above it is clear, that we, in many cases, perceive and form our general notions:—
(1.) From particular things represented to our intellect fragmentarily, confusedly, and without order through our senses (II. xxix. Coroll.); I have settled to call such perceptions by the name of knowledge from the mere suggestions of experience.[3] (2.) From symbols, *e.g.*, from the fact of having read or heard certain words we remember things and form certain ideas concerning them, similar to those through which we imagine things (II. xviii. note). I shall call both these ways of regarding things *knowledge of the first kind, opinion,* or *imagination.* (3.) From the fact that we have notions common to all men, and adequate ideas of the properties of things (II. xxxviii. Coroll., xxxix. and Coroll. and xl.); this I call *reason* and *knowledge of the second kind.* Besides these two kinds of knowledge, there is, as I will hereafter show, a third kind of knowledge, which we will call intuition. This kind of knowledge proceeds from an adequate idea of the absolute essence of certain attributes of God to the adequate knowledge of the essence of things. I will illustrate all three kinds of knowledge

[3] A Baconian phrase. Nov. Org. Aph. 100. [Pollock, p. 126, *n.*]

by a single example. Three numbers are given for finding a fourth, which shall be to the third as the second is to the first. Tradesmen without hesitation multiply the second by the third, and divide the product by the first; either because they have not forgotten the rule which they received from a master without any proof, or because they have often made trial of it with simple numbers, or by virtue of the proof of the nineteenth proposition of the seventh book of Euclid, namely, in virtue of the general property of proportionals.

But with very simple numbers there is no need of this. For instance, one, two, three, being given, everyone can see that the fourth proportional is six; and this is much clearer, because we infer the fourth number from an intuitive grasping of the ratio, which the first bears to the second.

PROP. XLI. *Knowledge of the first kind is the only source of falsity, knowledge of the second and third kinds is necessarily true.*

Proof.—To knowledge of the first kind we have (in the foregoing note) assigned all those ideas, which are inadequate and confused; therefore this kind of knowledge is the only source of falsity (II. xxxv.). Furthermore, we assigned to the second and third kinds of knowledge those ideas which are adequate; therefore these kinds are necessarily true (II. xxxiv.). *Q.E.D.*

PROP. XLII. *Knowledge of the second and third kinds, not knowledge of the first kind, teaches us to distinguish the true from the false.*

Proof.—This proposition is self-evident. He, who knows how to distinguish between true and false, must have an adequate idea of true and false. That is (II. xl., note ii.), he must know the true and the false by the second or third kind of knowledge.

PROP. XLIII. *He who has a true idea, simultaneously knows that he has a true idea, and cannot doubt of the truth of the thing perceived.*

Proof.—A true idea in us is an idea which is adequate in God, in so far as he is displayed through the nature of the human mind (II. xi. Coroll.). Let us suppose that there is in God, in so far as he is displayed through the human mind, an adequate idea, A. The idea of this idea must also necessarily

be in God, and be referred to him in the same way as the idea
A (by II. xx., whereof the proof is of universal application).
But the idea A is supposed to be referred to God, in so far as
he is displayed through the human mind; therefore, the idea
of the idea A must be referred to God in the same manner;
that is (by II. xi. Coroll.), the adequate idea of the idea A
will be in the mind, which has the adequate idea A; therefore
he, who has an adequate idea or knows a thing truly (II.
xxxiv.), must at the same time have an adequate idea or true
knowledge of his knowledge; that is, obviously, he must be
assured. *Q.E.D.*

Note.—I explained in the note to II. xxi. what is meant by
the idea of an idea; but we may remark that the foregoing
proposition is in itself sufficiently plain. No one, who has a
true idea, is ignorant that a true idea involves the highest
certainty. For to have a true idea is only another expression
for knowing a thing perfectly, or as well as possible. No one,
indeed, can doubt of this, unless he thinks that an idea is
something lifeless, like a picture on a panel, and not a mode
of thinking—namely, the very act of understanding. And who,
I ask, can know that he understands anything, unless he do
first understand it? In other words, who can know that he is
sure of a thing, unless he be first sure of that thing? Further,
what can there be more clear, and more certain, than a true
idea as a standard of truth? Even as light displays both itself
and darkness, so is truth a standard both of itself and of falsity.

I think I have thus sufficiently answered these questions—
namely, if a true idea is distinguished from a false idea, only
in so far as it is said to agree with its object, a true idea has no
more reality or perfection than a false idea (since the two are
only distinguished by an extrinsic mark); consequently, neither will a man who has true ideas have any advantage over
him who has only false ideas. Further, how comes it that men
have false ideas? Lastly, how can anyone be sure, that he has
ideas which agree with their objects? These questions, I repeat,
I have, in my opinion, sufficiently answered. The difference
between a true idea and a false idea is plain: from what was
said in II. xxxv., the former is related to the latter as being is
to not-being. The causes of falsity I have set forth very clearly

in II. xix. and II. xxxv. with the note. From what is there stated, the difference between a man who has true ideas, and a man who has only false ideas, is made apparent. As for the last question—as to how a man can be sure that he has ideas that agree with their objects, I have just pointed out, with abundant clearness, that his knowledge arises from the simple fact, that he has an idea which corresponds with its object— in other words, that truth is its own standard. We may add that our mind, in so far as it perceives things truly, is part of the infinite intellect of God (II. xi. Coroll.); therefore, the clear and distinct ideas of the mind are as necessarily true as the ideas of God.

Prop. XLIV. *It is not in the nature of reason to regard things as contingent, but as necessary.*

Proof.—It is in the nature of reason to perceive things truly (II. xli.), namely (I. Ax. vi.), as they are in themselves—that is (I. xxix.), not as contingent, but as necessary. *Q.E.D.*

Corollary I.—Hence it follows, that it is only through our imagination that we consider things, whether in respect to the future or the past, as contingent.

Note.—How this way of looking at things arises, I will briefly explain. We have shown above (II. xvii. and Coroll.) that the mind always regards things as present to itself, even though they be not in existence, until some causes arise which exclude their existence and presence. Further (II. xviii.), we showed that, if the human body has once been affected by two external bodies simultaneously, the mind, when it afterwards imagines one of the said external bodies, will straightway remember the other—that is, it will regard both as present to itself, unless there arise causes which exclude their existence and presence. Further, no one doubts that we imagine time, from the fact that we imagine bodies to be moved some more slowly than others, some more quickly, some at equal speed. Thus, let us suppose that a child yesterday saw Peter for the first time in the morning, Paul at noon, and Simon in the evening; then, that to-day he again sees Peter in the morning. It is evident, from II. Prop. xviii., that, as soon as he sees the morning light, he will imagine that the sun will traverse the same parts of the sky, as it did when he saw it on the preceding day; in other words, he will imagine a complete day, and, together with his imagination of the morning, he will imagine Peter; with noon, he will imagine Paul; and with evening, he will imagine Simon —that is, he will imagine the existence of Paul and Simon in relation to a future time; on the other hand, if he sees Simon in the evening, he will refer Peter and Paul to a past time, by imagining them simultaneously with the imagination of a past time. If it should at any time happen, that on some other evening the child should see James instead of Simon, he will, on the following morning, associate with his imagination of evening sometimes Simon, sometimes James, not both together: for the child is supposed to have seen, at evening, one or other of them, not both together. His imagination will therefore waver; and, with the imagination of future evenings, he will associate first one, then the other—that is, he will imagine them in the future, neither of them as certain, but both as contingent. This wavering of the imagination will be the same, if the imagination be concerned with things which we thus contemplate, standing in relation to time past or time present: consequently, we may imagine things as contingent, whether they be referred to time present, past, or future.

Corollary II.—It is in the nature of reason to perceive things under a certain form of eternity (*sub quâdam æternitatis specie*).

Proof.—It is in the nature of reason to regard things, not as contingent, but as necessary (II. xliv.). Reason perceives this necessity of things (II. xli.) truly—that is (I. Ax. vi.), as it is in itself. But (I. xvi.) this necessity of things is the very necessity of the eternal nature of God; therefore, it is in the nature of reason to regard things under this form of eternity. We may add that the bases of reason are the notions (II. xxxviii.), which answer to things common to all, and which (II. xxxvii.) do not answer to the essence of any particular thing: which must therefore be conceived without any relation to time, under a certain form of eternity.

PROP. XLV. *Every idea of every body, or of every particular thing actually existing, necessarily involves the eternal and infinite essence of God.*

Proof.—The idea of a particular thing actually existing necessarily involves both the existence and the essence of the said thing (II. viii.). Now particular things cannot be conceived without God (I. xv.); but, inasmuch as (II. vi.) they have God for their cause, in so far as he is regarded under the attribute of which the things in question are modes, their ideas must necessarily involve (I. Ax. iv.) the conception of the attribute of those ideas—that is (I. vi.), the eternal and infinite essence of God. *Q.E.D.*

Note.—By existence I do not here mean duration—that is, existence in so far as it is conceived abstractedly, and as a certain form of quantity. I am speaking of the very nature of existence, which is assigned to particular things, because they follow in infinite numbers and in infinite ways from the eternal necessity of God's nature (I. xvi.). I am speaking, I repeat, of the very existence of particular things, in so far as they are in God. For although each particular thing be conditioned by another particular thing to exist in a given way, yet the force whereby each particular thing perseveres in existing follows from the eternal necessity of God's nature (cf. I. xxiv. Coroll.).

PROP. XLVI. *The knowledge of the eternal and infinite essence of God, which every idea involves, is adequate and perfect.*

Proof.—The proof of the last proposition is universal; and whether a thing be considered as a part or a whole, the idea thereof, whether of the whole or of a part (by the last Prop.), will involve God's eternal and infinite essence. Wherefore, that, which gives knowledge of the eternal and infinite essence of God, is common to all, and is equally in the part and in the whole; therefore (II. xxxviii.) this knowledge will be adequate. *Q.E.D.*

PROP. XLVII. *The human mind has an adequate knowledge of the eternal and infinite essence of God.*

Proof.—The human mind has ideas (II. xxii.), from which (II. xxiii.) it perceives itself and its own body (II. xix.) and external bodies (II. xvi. Coroll. I. and II. xvii.) as actually existing; therefore (II. xlv. xlvi.) it has an adequate knowledge of the eternal and infinite essence of God. *Q.E.D.*

Note.—Hence we see, that the infinite essence and the eternity of God are known to all. Now as all things are in God, and are conceived through God, we can from this knowledge infer many things, which we may adequately know, and we may form that third kind of knowledge of which we spoke in the note to II. xl., and of the excellence and use of which we shall have occasion to speak in Part V. Men have not so clear a knowledge of God as they have of general notions, because they are unable to imagine God as they do bodies, and also because they have associated the name God with images of things that they are in the habit of seeing, as indeed they can hardly avoid doing, being, as they are, men, and continually affected by external bodies. Many errors, in truth, can be traced to this head, namely, that we do not apply names to things rightly. For instance, when a man says that the lines drawn from the centre of a circle to its circumference are not equal, he then, at all events, assuredly attaches a meaning to the word circle different from that assigned by mathematicians. So again, when men make mistakes in calculation, they have one set of figures in their mind, and another on the paper. If we could see into their minds, they do not make a mistake; they seem to do so, because we think, that they have the same numbers in their mind as they have on the paper. If this were not so, we should not believe them to be in error, any more than I thought that a man was in error, whom I lately heard exclaiming that his entrance hall had flown into a neighbour's hen, for his meaning seemed to me sufficiently clear. Very many controversies have arisen from the fact, that men do not rightly explain their meaning, or do not rightly interpret the meaning of others. For, as a matter of fact, as they flatly contradict themselves, they assume now one side, now another, of the argument, so as to oppose the opinions, which they consider mistaken and absurd in their opponents.

PROP. XLVIII. *In the mind there is no absolute or free will; but the mind is determined to wish this or that by a cause, which has also been determined by another cause, and this last by another cause, and so on to infinity.*

Proof.—The mind is a fixed and definite mode of thought (II. xi.), therefore it cannot be the free cause of its actions (I. xvii. Coroll. ii.); in other words, it cannot have an absolute faculty of positive or negative volition; but (by I. xxviii.) it must be determined by a cause, which has also been determined by another cause, and this last by another, &c. *Q.E.D.*

Note.—In the same way it is proved, that there is in the mind no absolute faculty of understanding, desiring, loving, &c. Whence it follows, that these and similar faculties are either entirely fictitious, or are merely abstract or general terms, such as we are accustomed to put together from particular things. Thus the intellect and the will stand in the same relation to this or that idea, or this or that volition, as "lapidity" to this or that stone, or as "man" to Peter and Paul. The cause which leads men to consider themselves free has been set forth in the Appendix to Part I. But, before I proceed further, I would here remark that, by the will to affirm and decide, I mean the faculty, not the desire. I mean, I repeat, the faculty, whereby the mind affirms or denies what is true or false, not the desire, wherewith the mind wishes for or turns away from any given thing. After we have proved, that these faculties of ours are general notions, which cannot be distinguished from the particular instances on which they are based, we must inquire whether volitions themselves are anything besides the ideas of things. We must inquire, I say, whether there is in the mind any affirmation or negation beyond that, which the idea, in so far as it is an idea, involves. On which subject see the following proposition, and II. Def. iii., lest the idea of pictures should suggest itself. For by ideas I do not mean images such as are formed at the back of the eye, or in the midst of the brain, but the conceptions of thought.

PROP. XLIX. *There is in the mind no volition or affirmation and negation, save that which an idea, inasmuch as it is an idea, involves.*

Proof.—There is in the mind no absolute faculty of positive or negative volition, but only particular volitions, namely, this or that affirmation, and this or that negation. Now let us conceive a particular volition, namely, the mode of thinking whereby the mind affirms, that the three interior angles of a triangle are equal to two right angles. This affirmation involves the conception or idea of a triangle, that is, without the idea of a triangle it cannot be conceived. It is the same thing to say, that the concept A must involve the concept B, as it is to say, that A cannot be conceived without B. Further, this affirmation cannot be made (II. Ax. iii.) without the idea of a triangle. Therefore, this affirmation can neither be nor be conceived, without the idea of a triangle. Again, this idea of a triangle must involve this same affirmation, namely, that its three interior angles are equal to two right angles. Wherefore, and *vice versâ*, this idea of a triangle can neither be nor be conceived without this affirmation, therefore, this affirmation belongs to the essence of the idea of a triangle, and is nothing besides. What we have said of this volition (inasmuch as we have selected it at random) may be said of any other volition, namely, that it is nothing but an idea. *Q.E.D.*

Corollary.—Will and understanding are one and the same.

Proof.—Will and understanding are nothing beyond the individual volitions and ideas (II. xlviii. and note). But a particular volition and a particular idea are one and the same (by the foregoing Prop.); therefore, will and understanding are one and the same. *Q.E.D.*

Note.—We have thus removed the cause which is commonly assigned for error. For we have shown above, that falsity consists solely in the privation of knowledge involved in ideas which are fragmentary and confused. Wherefore, a false idea, inasmuch as it is false, does not involve certainty. When we say, then, that a man acquiesces in what is false, and that he has no doubts on the subject, we do not say that he is certain, but only that he does not doubt, or that he acquiesces in what is false, inasmuch as there are no reasons, which should cause his imagination to waver (see II. xliv. note). Thus, although the man be assumed to acquiesce in what is false, we shall never say that he is certain. For by certainty we mean something positive (II. xliii. and note), not merely the absence of doubt.

However, in order that the foregoing proposition may be fully explained, I will draw attention to a few additional points, and I will furthermore answer the objections which may be advanced against our doctrine. Lastly, in order to remove every scruple, I have thought it worth while to point out some of the advantages, which follow therefrom. I say "some," for they will be better appreciated from what we shall set forth in the fifth part.

I begin, then, with the first point, and warn my readers to make an accurate distinction between an idea, or conception of the mind, and the images of things which we imagine. It is further necessary that they should distinguish between idea and words, whereby we signify things. These three—namely, images, words, and ideas—are by many persons either entirely confused together, or not distinguished with sufficient accuracy or care, and hence people are generally in ignorance, how absolutely necessary is a knowledge of this doctrine of the will, both for philosophic purposes and for the wise ordering of life. Those who think that ideas consist in images which are formed in us by contact with external bodies, persuade themselves that the ideas of those things, whereof we can form no mental picture, are not ideas, but only figments, which we invent by the free decree of our will; they thus regard ideas as though they were inanimate pictures on a panel, and, filled with this misconception, do not see that an idea, inasmuch as it is an idea, involves an affirmation or negation. Again, those who confuse words with ideas, or with the affirmation which an idea involves, think that they can wish something contrary to what they feel, affirm, or deny. This misconception will easily be laid aside by one, who reflects on the nature of knowledge, and seeing that it in no wise involves the conception of extension, will therefore clearly understand, that an idea (being a mode of thinking) does not consist in the image of anything, nor in words. The essence of words and images is put together by bodily motions, which in no wise involve the conception of thought.

These few words on this subject will suffice: I will therefore pass on to consider the objections, which may be raised against our doctrine. Of these, the first is advanced by those, who think that the will has a wider scope than the understanding, and that therefore it is different therefrom. The reason for their holding the belief, that the will has wider scope than the understanding, is that they assert, that they have no need of an increase in their faculty of assent, that is of affirmation or negation, in order to assent to an infinity of things which we do not perceive, but that they have need of an increase in their faculty of understanding. The will is thus distinguished from the intellect, the latter being finite and the former infinite. Secondly, it may be objected that experience seems to teach us especially clearly, that we are able to suspend our judgment before assenting to things which we perceive; this is confirmed by the fact that no one is said to be deceived, in so far as he perceives anything, but only in so far as he assents or dissents.

For instance, he who feigns a winged horse, does not therefore admit that a winged horse exists; that is, he is not deceived, unless he admits in addition that a winged horse does exist. Nothing therefore seems to be taught more clearly by experience, than that the will or faculty of assent is free and different from the faculty of understanding. Thirdly, it may be objected that one affirmation does not apparently contain more reality than another; in other words, that we do not seem to need for affirming, that what is true is true, any greater power than for affirming, that what is false is true. We have, however, seen that one idea has more reality or perfection than another, for as objects are some more excellent than others, so also are the ideas of them some more excellent than others; this also seems to point to a difference between the understanding and the will. Fourthly, it may be objected, if man does not act from free will, what will happen if the incentives to action are equally balanced, as in the case of Buridan's ass? Will he perish of hunger and thirst? If I say that he would, I shall seem to have in my thoughts an ass or the statue of a man rather than an actual man. If I say that he would not, he would then determine his own action, and would consequently possess the faculty of going and doing whatever he liked. Other objections might also be raised, but, as I am not bound to put in evidence everything that anyone may dream, I will only set myself to the task of refuting those I have mentioned, and that as briefly as possible.

To the *first* objection I answer, that I admit that the will has a wider scope than the understanding, if by the understanding be meant only clear and distinct ideas; but I deny that the will has a wider scope than the perceptions, and the faculty of forming conceptions; nor do I see why the faculty of volition should be called infinite, any more than the faculty of feeling: for, as we are able by the same faculty of volition to affirm an infinite number of things (one after the other, for we cannot affirm an infinite number simultaneously), so also can we, by the same faculty of feeling, feel or perceive (in succession) an infinite number of bodies. If it be said that there is an infinite number of things which we cannot perceive, I answer, that we cannot attain to such things by any thinking, nor, consequently, by any faculty of volition. But, it may still be urged, if God wished to bring it about that we should perceive them, he would be obliged to endow us with a greater faculty of perception, but not a greater faculty of volition than we have already. This is the same as to say that, if God wished to bring it about that we should understand an infinite number of other entities, it would be necessary for him to give us a greater understanding, but not a more universal idea of entity than that which we have already, in order to grasp such infinite entities. We have shown that will is a universal entity or idea, whereby we explain all particular volitions—in other words, that which is common to all such volitions.

As, then, our opponents maintain that this idea, common or universal to all volitions, is a faculty, it is little to be wondered at that they assert, that such a faculty extends itself into the infinite, beyond the limits of the understanding: for what is universal is predicated alike of one, of many, and of an infinite number of individuals.

To the *second* objection I reply by denying, that we have a free power of suspending our judgment: for, when we say that anyone suspends his judgment, we merely mean that he sees, that he does not perceive the matter in question adequately. Suspension of judgment is, therefore, strictly speaking, a perception, and not free will. In order to illustrate the point, let us suppose a boy imagining a horse, and perceiving

nothing else. Inasmuch as this imagination involves the
existence of the horse (II. xvii. Coroll.), and the boy does not
perceive anything which would exclude the existence of the
horse, he will necessarily regard the horse as present: he will
not be able to doubt of its existence, although he be not certain thereof. We have daily experience of such a state of
things in dreams; and I do not suppose that there is anyone,
who would maintain that, while he is dreaming, he has the
free power of suspending his judgment concerning the things
in his dream, and bringing it about that he should not dream
those things, which he dreams that he sees; yet it happens,
notwithstanding, that even in dreams we suspend our judgment, namely, when we dream that we are dreaming.

Further, I grant that no one can be deceived, so far as
actual perception extends—that is, I grant that the mind's
imaginations, regarded in themselves, do not involve error (II.
xvii., note); but I deny, that a man does not, in the act of
perception, make any affirmation. For what is the perception
of a winged horse, save affirming that a horse has wings?
If the mind could perceive nothing else but the winged horse,
it would regard the same as present to itself: it would have
no reasons for doubting its existence, nor any faculty of dis-
sent, unless the imagination of a winged horse be joined to an
idea which precludes the existence of the said horse, or unless
the mind perceives that the idea which it possesses of a
winged horse is inadequate, in which case it will either necessarily deny the existence of such a horse, or will necessarily
be in doubt on the subject.

I think that I have anticipated my answer to the *third*
objection, namely, that the will is something universal which
is predicated of all ideas, and that it only signifies that which
is common to all ideas, namely, an affirmation, whose adequate essence must, therefore, in so far as it is thus conceived
in the abstract, be in every idea, and be, in this respect alone,
the same in all, not in so far as it is considered as constituting
the idea's essence: for, in this respect, particular affirmations
differ one from the other, as much as do ideas. For instance,
the affirmation which involves the idea of a circle, differs

from that which involves the idea of a triangle, as much as the idea of a circle differs from the idea of a triangle.

Further, I absolutely deny, that we are in need of an equal power of thinking, to affirm that that which is true is true, and to affirm that that which is false is true. These two affirmations, if we regard the mind, are in the same relation to one another as being and not-being; for there is nothing positive in ideas, which constitutes the actual reality of falsehood (II. xxxv. note, and xlvii. note).

We must therefore conclude, that we are easily deceived, when we confuse universals with singulars, and the entities of reason and abstractions with realities. As for the *fourth* objection, I am quite ready to admit, that a man placed in the equilibrium described (namely, as perceiving nothing but hunger and thirst, a certain food and a certain drink, each equally distant from him) would die of hunger and thirst. If I am asked, whether such an one should not rather be considered an ass than a man; I answer, that I do not know, neither do I know how a man should be considered, who hangs himself, or how we should consider children, fools, madmen, &c.

It remains to point out the advantages of a knowledge of this doctrine as bearing on conduct, and this may be easily gathered from what has been said. The doctrine is good,

1. inasmuch as it teaches us to act solely according to the decree of God, and to be partakers in the Divine nature, and so much the more, as we perform more perfect actions and more and more understand God. Such a doctrine not only completely tranquillizes our spirit, but also shows us where our highest happiness or blessedness is, namely, solely in the knowledge of God, whereby we are led to act only as love and piety shall bid us. We may thus clearly understand, how far astray from a true estimate of virtue are those who expect to be decorated by God with high rewards for their virtue, and their best actions, as for having endured the direst slavery; as if virtue and the service of God were not in itself happiness and perfect freedom.

2. inasmuch as it teaches us, how we ought to conduct ourselves with respect to the gifts of fortune, or matters which

are not in our own power, and do not follow from our nature. For it shows us, that we should await and endure fortune's smiles or frowns with an equal mind, seeing that all things follow from the eternal decree of God by the same necessity, as it follows from the essence of a triangle, that the three angles are equal to two right angles.

3. This doctrine raises social life, inasmuch as it teaches us to hate no man, neither to despise, to deride, to envy, or to be angry with any. Further, as it tells us that each should be content with his own, and helpful to his neighbour, not from any womanish pity, favour, or superstition, but solely by the guidance of reason, according as the time and occasion demand, as I will show in Part III.

4. Lastly, this doctrine confers no small advantage on the commonwealth; for it teaches how citizens should be governed and led, not so as to become slaves, but so that they may freely do whatsoever things are best.

I have thus fulfilled the promise made at the beginning of this note, and I thus bring the second part of my treatise to a close. I think I have therein explained the nature and properties of the human mind at sufficient length, and, considering the difficulty of the subject, with sufficient clearness. I have laid a foundation, whereon may be raised many excellent conclusions of the highest utility and most necessary to be known, as will, in what follows, be partly made plain.

PART III ON THE ORIGIN AND
NATURE OF THE EMOTIONS

Most writers on the emotions and on human conduct seem to be treating rather of matters outside nature than of natural phenomena following nature's general laws. They appear to conceive man to be situated in nature as a kingdom within a kingdom: for they believe that he disturbs rather than follows nature's order, that he has absolute control over his actions, and that he is determined solely by himself. They attribute human infirmities and fickleness, not to the power of nature in general, but to some mysterious flaw in the nature of man, which accordingly they bemoan, deride, despise, or, as usually happens, abuse: he, who succeeds in hitting off the weakness of the human mind more eloquently or more acutely than his fellows, is looked upon as a seer. Still there has been no lack of very excellent men (to whose toil and industry I confess myself much indebted), who have written many noteworthy things concerning the right way of life, and have given much sage advice to mankind. But no one, so far as I know, has defined the nature and strength of the emotions, and the power of the mind against them for their restraint.

I do not forget, that the illustrious Descartes, though he believed, that the mind has absolute power over its actions, strove to explain human emotions by their primary causes, and, at the same time, to point out a way, by which the mind might attain to absolute dominion over them. However, in my opinion, he accomplishes nothing beyond a display of the acuteness of his own great intellect, as I will show in the proper place. For the present I wish to revert to those, who would rather abuse or deride human emotions than understand them. Such persons will, doubtless think it strange that I should attempt to treat of human vice and folly geometrically, and should wish to set forth with rigid reasoning those matters which they cry out against as repugnant to reason, frivolous, absurd, and dreadful. However, such is my plan. Nothing comes to pass in nature, which can be set down to a flaw therein; for nature is always the same, and everywhere one and the same in her efficacy and power of action; that is, nature's laws and ordinances, whereby all things come to pass and change from one form to another, are everywhere and always the same; so that there should be one and the same method of understanding the nature of all things whatsoever, namely, through nature's universal laws and rules. Thus the passions of hatred, anger, envy, and so on, considered in themselves, follow from this same necessity and efficacy of nature; they answer to certain definite causes, through which they are understood, and possess certain properties as worthy of being known as the properties of anything else, whereof the contemplation in itself affords us delight. I shall, therefore, treat of the nature and strength of the emotions according to the same method, as I employed heretofore in my investigations concerning God and the mind. I shall consider human actions and desires in exactly the same manner, as though I were concerned with lines, planes, and solids.

DEFINITIONS

I. By an *adequate* cause, I mean a cause through which its effect can be clearly and distinctly perceived. By an *inadequate* or partial cause, I mean a cause through which, by itself, its effect cannot be understood.

II. I say that we *act* when anything takes place, either within us or externally to us, whereof we are the adequate cause; that is (by the foregoing definition) when through our nature something takes place within us or externally to us, which can through our nature alone be clearly and distinctly understood. On the other hand, I say that we are passive as regards something when that something takes place within us, or follows from our nature externally, we being only the partial cause.

III. By *emotion* I mean the modifications of the body, whereby the active power of the said body is increased or diminished, aided or constrained, and also the ideas of such modifications.

N.B. If we can be the adequate cause of any of these modifications, I then call the emotion an activity, otherwise I call it a passion, or state wherein the mind is passive.

POSTULATES

I. The human body can be affected in many ways, whereby its power of activity is increased or diminished, and also in other ways which do not render its power of activity either greater or less.

N.B. This postulate or axiom rests on Postulate i. and Lemmas v. and vii., which see after II. xiii.

II. The human body can undergo many changes, and, nevertheless, retain the impressions or traces of objects (cf. II. Post. v.), and, consequently, the same images of things (see note II. xvii.).

PROP. I. *Our mind is in certain cases active, and in certain cases passive. In so far as it has adequate ideas, it is necessarily active, and in so far as it has inadequate ideas, it is necessarily passive.*

Proof.—In every human mind there are some adequate ideas, and some ideas that are fragmentary and confused (II. xl. note). Those ideas which are adequate in the mind are adequate also in God, inasmuch as he constitutes the essence of the mind (II. xl. Coroll.), and those which are inadequate in the mind are likewise (by the same Coroll.) adequate in God, not inasmuch as he contains in himself the essence of the given mind alone, but as he, at the same time, contains the minds of other things. Again, from any given idea some effect must necessarily follow (I. xxxvi.); of this effect God is the adequate cause (III. Def. i.), not inasmuch as he is infinite, but inasmuch as he is conceived as affected by the given idea (II. ix.). But of that effect whereof God is the cause, inasmuch as he is affected by an idea which is adequate in a given mind, of that effect, I repeat, the mind in question is the adequate cause (II. xi. Coroll.). Therefore our mind, in so far as it has adequate ideas (III. Def. ii.), is in certain cases necessarily active; this was our first point. Again, whatsoever necessarily follows from the idea which is adequate in God, not by virtue of his possessing in himself the mind of one man only, but by virtue of his containing, together with the mind of that one man, the minds of other things also, of such an effect (II. xi. Coroll.) the mind of the given man is not an adequate, but only a partial cause; thus (III. Def. ii.) the mind, inasmuch as it has inadequate ideas, is in certain cases necessarily passive; this was our second point. Therefore our mind, &c. *Q.E.D.*

Corollary.—Hence it follows that the mind is more or less liable to be acted upon, in proportion as it possesses inadequate ideas, and, contrariwise, is more or less active in proportion as it possesses adequate ideas.

Prop. II. *Body cannot determine mind to think, neither can mind determine body to motion or rest or any state different from these, if such there be.*

Proof.—All modes of thinking have for their cause God, by virtue of his being a thinking thing, and not by virtue of his being displayed under any other attribute (II. vi.). That, therefore, which determines the mind to thought is a mode of thought, and not a mode of extension; that is (II. Def. i.), it is not body. This was our first point. Again, the motion and rest of a body must arise from another body, which has also been determined to a state of motion or rest by a third body, and absolutely everything which takes place in a body must spring from God, in so far as he is regarded as affected by some mode of extension, and not by some mode of thought (II. vi.); that is, it cannot spring from the mind, which is a mode of thought. This was our second point. Therefore body cannot determine mind, &c. *Q.E.D.*

Note.—This is made more clear by what was said in the note to II. vii., namely, that mind and body are one and the same thing, conceived first under the attribute of thought, secondly, under the attribute of extension. Thus it follows that the order or concatenation of things is identical, whether nature be conceived under the one attribute or the other; consequently the order of states of activity and passivity in our body is simultaneous in nature with the order of states of activity and passivity in the mind. The same conclusion is evident from the manner in which we proved II. xii.

Nevertheless, though such is the case, and though there be no further room for doubt, I can scarcely believe, until the fact is proved by experience, that men can be induced to consider the question calmly and fairly, so firmly are they convinced that it is merely at the bidding of the mind, that the body is set in motion or at rest, or performs a variety of actions depending solely on the mind's will or the exercise of thought. However, no one has hitherto laid down the limits to the powers of the body, that is, no one has as yet been taught by experience what the body can accomplish solely by the laws of nature, in so far as she is regarded as extension. No one hitherto has gained such an accurate knowledge of the bodily mechanism, that he can explain all its functions; nor need I call attention to the fact that many actions are observed in the lower animals, which far transcend human sagacity, and that somnambulists do many things in their sleep, which they would not venture to do when awake: these instances are enough to show, that the body can by the sole laws of its nature do many things which the mind wonders at.

Again, no one knows how or by what means the mind moves the body, nor how many various degrees of motion it can impart to the body, nor how quickly it can move it. Thus, when men say that this or that physical action has its origin in the mind, which latter has dominion over the body, they are using words without meaning, or are confessing in specious phraseology that they are ignorant of the cause of the said action, and do not wonder at it.

But, they will say, whether we know or do not know the means whereby the mind acts on the body, we have, at any rate, experience of the fact that unless the human mind is in a fit state to think, the body remains inert. Moreover, we have experience, that the mind alone can determine whether we speak or are silent, and a variety of similar states which, accordingly, we say depend on the mind's decree. But, as to the first point, I ask such objectors, whether experience does not also teach, that if the body be inactive the mind is simultaneously unfitted for thinking? For when the body is at rest in sleep, the mind simultaneously is in a state of torpor also, and has no power of thinking, such as it possesses when the body is awake. Again, I think everyone's experience will confirm the statement, that the mind is not at all times equally fit for thinking on a given subject, but according as the body is more or less fitted for being stimulated by the image of this or that object, so also is the mind more or less fitted for contemplating the said object.

But, it will be urged, it is impossible that solely from the laws of nature considered as extended substance, we should be able to deduce the causes of buildings, pictures, and things of that kind, which are produced only by human art; nor would the human body, unless it were determined and led by the mind, be capable of building a single temple. However, I have just pointed out that the objectors cannot fix the limits of the body's power, or say what can be concluded from a consideration of its sole nature, whereas they have experience of many things being accomplished solely by the laws of nature, which they would never have believed possible except under the direction of mind: such are the actions performed by somnambulists while asleep, and wondered at by their performers when awake. I would further call attention to the mechanism of the human body, which far surpasses in complexity all that has been put together by human art, not to repeat what I have already shown, namely, that from nature, under whatever attribute she be considered, infinite results follow. As for the second objection, I submit that the world would be much happier, if men were as fully able to keep silence as they are to speak. Experience abundantly shows that men can govern anything more easily than their tongues, and restrain anything more easily than their appetites; whence it comes about that many believe, that we are only free in respect to objects which we moderately desire, because our desire for such can easily be controlled by the thought of something else frequently remembered, but that we are by no means free in respect to what we seek with violent emotion, for our desire cannot then be allayed with the remembrance of anything else. However, unless such persons had proved by experience that we do many things which we afterwards repent of, and again that we often, when assailed by contrary emotions, see the better and follow the worse, there would be nothing to prevent their believing that we are free in all things. Thus an infant believes that of its own free will it desires milk, an angry child believes that it freely desires vengeance, a timid child believes that it freely desires to run away; further, a drunken man believes that he utters from the free decision of his mind words which, when he is sober, he would willingly have withheld: thus, too, a delirious man, a garrulous woman, a child, and others of like complexion, believe that they speak from the free decision of their mind, when they are in reality unable to restrain their impulse to talk. Experience teaches us no less clearly than reason, that men believe themselves to be free, simply because they are conscious of their actions, and unconscious of the causes whereby those actions are determined; and, further, it is plain that the dictates of the mind are but another name for the appetites, and therefore vary according to the varying state of the body. Everyone shapes his actions according to his emotion, those who are assailed by conflicting emotions know not what they wish; those who are not attacked by any emotion are readily swayed this way or that. All these considerations clearly show that a mental decision and a bodily appetite, or determined state, are simultaneous, or rather are one and the same thing, which we call decision, when it is regarded under and explained through the attribute of thought, and a conditioned state, when it is regarded under the attribute of extension, and deduced from the laws of motion and rest. This will appear yet more plainly in the sequel. For the present I wish to call attention to another point, namely, that we cannot act by the decision of the mind, unless we have a remembrance of having done so. For instance, we cannot say a word without remembering that we have done so. Again, it is not within the free power of the mind to remember or forget a thing at will. Therefore the freedom of the mind must in any case be limited to the power of uttering or not uttering something which it remembers. But when we dream that we speak, we believe that we speak from a free decision of the mind, yet we do not speak, or, if we do, it is by a spontaneous motion of the body. Again, we dream that we are concealing something, and we seem to act from the same decision of the mind as that, whereby we keep silence when awake concerning something we know. Lastly, we dream that from the free decision of our mind we do something, which we should not dare to do when awake.

Now I should like to know whether there be in the mind two sorts of decisions, one sort illusive, and the other sort free? If our folly does not carry us so far as this, we must necessarily admit, that the decision of the mind, which is believed to be free, is not distinguishable from the imagination or memory, and is nothing more than the affirmation, which an idea, by virtue of being an idea, necessarily involves (II. xlix.). Wherefore these decisions of the mind arise in the mind by the same necessity, as the ideas of things actually existing. Therefore those who believe, that they speak or keep silence or act in any way from the free decision of their mind, do but dream with their eyes open.

PROP. III. *The activities of the mind arise solely from adequate ideas; the passive states of the mind depend solely on inadequate ideas.*

Proof.—The first element, which constitutes the essence of the mind, is nothing else but the idea of the actually existent body (II. xi. and xiii.), which (II. xv.) is compounded of many other ideas, whereof some are adequate and some inadequate (II. xxix. Coroll., II. xxxviii. Coroll.). Whatsoever therefore follows from the nature of mind, and has mind for its proximate cause, through which it must be understood, must necessarily follow either from an adequate or from an inadequate idea. But in so far as the mind (III. i.) has inadequate ideas, it is necessarily passive: wherefore the activities of the mind follow solely from adequate ideas, and accordingly the mind is only passive in so far as it has in-adequate ideas. *Q.E.D.*

Note.—Thus we see, that passive states are not attributed to the mind, except in so far as it contains something involving negation, or in so far as it is regarded as a part of nature, which cannot be clearly and distinctly perceived through it-self without other parts: I could thus show, that passive states are attributed to individual things in the same way that they are attributed to the mind, and that they cannot otherwise be perceived, but my purpose is solely to treat of the human mind.

PROP. IV. *Nothing can be destroyed, except by a cause external to itself.*

Proof.—This proposition is self-evident, for the definition of anything affirms the essence of that thing, but does not nega-tive it; in other words, it postulates the essence of the thing, but does not take it away. So long therefore as we regard only the thing itself, without taking into account external causes, we shall not be able to find in it anything which could destroy it. *Q.E.D.*

PROP. V. *Things are naturally contrary, that is, cannot exist in the same object, in so far as one is capable of destroying the other.*

Proof.—If they could agree together or co-exist in the same object, there would then be in the said object something which could destroy it; but this, by the foregoing proposi-tion, is absurd, therefore things, &c. *Q.E.D.*

PROP. VI. *Everything, in so far as it is in itself, endeavours to persist in its own being.*

Proof.—Individual things are modes whereby the attributes of God are expressed in a given determinate manner (I. xxv. Coroll.); that is (I. xxxiv.), they are things which express in a given determinate manner the power of God, whereby God is and acts; now no thing contains in itself anything whereby it can be destroyed, or which can take away its existence (III. iv.); but contrariwise it is opposed to all that could take away its existence (III. v.). Therefore, in so far as it can, and in so far as it is in itself, it endeavours to persist in its own being. *Q.E.D.*

PROP. VII. *The endeavour, wherewith everything endeavours to persist in its own being, is nothing else but the actual essence of the thing in question.*

Proof.—From the given essence of any thing certain consequences necessarily follow (I. xxxvi.), nor have things any power save such as necessarily follows from their nature as determined (I. xxix.); wherefore the power of any given thing, or the endeavour whereby, either alone or with other things, it acts, or endeavours to act, that is (III. vi.), the power or endeavour, wherewith it endeavours to persist in its own being, is nothing else but the given or actual essence of the thing in question. *Q.E.D.*

PROP. VIII. *The endeavour, whereby a thing endeavours to persist in its being, involves no finite time, but an indefinite time.*

Proof.—If it involved a limited time, which should determine the duration of the thing, it would then follow solely from that power whereby the thing exists, that the thing could not exist beyond the limits of that time, but that it must be destroyed; but this (III. iv.) is absurd. Wherefore the endeavour wherewith a thing exists involves no definite time; but, contrariwise, since (III. iv.) it will by the same power whereby it already exists always continue to exist, unless it be destroyed by some external cause, this endeavour involves an indefinite time.

PROP. IX. *The mind, both in so far as it has clear and distinct ideas, and also in so far as it has confused ideas, endeavours to persist in its being for an indefinite period, and of this endeavour it is conscious.*

Proof.—The essence of the mind is constituted by adequate and inadequate ideas (III. iii.), therefore (III. vii.), both in so far as it possesses the former, and in so far as it possesses the latter, it endeavours to persist in its own being, and that for an indefinite time (III. viii.). Now as the mind (II. xxiii.) is necessarily conscious of itself through the ideas of the modifications of the body, the mind is therefore (III. vii.) conscious of its own endeavour.

Note.—This endeavour, when referred solely to the mind, is called *will,* when referred to the mind and body in conjunction it is called *appetite;* it is, in fact, nothing else but man's essence, from the nature of which necessarily follow all those results which tend to its preservation; and which man has thus been determined to perform.

Further, between appetite and desire there is no difference, except that the term desire is generally applied to men, in so far as they are conscious of their appetite, and may accordingly be thus defined: *Desire is appetite with consciousness thereof.* It is thus plain from what has been said, that in no case do we strive for, wish for, long for, or desire anything, because we deem it to be good, but on the other hand we deem a thing to be good, because we strive for it, wish for it, long for it, or desire it.

PROP. X. *An idea which excludes the existence of our body, cannot be postulated in our mind, but is contrary thereto.*

Proof.—Whatsoever can destroy our body, cannot be postulated therein (III. v.). Therefore neither can the idea of such a thing occur in God, in so far as he has the idea of our body (II. ix. Coroll.); that is (II. xi. xiii.), the idea of that thing cannot be postulated as in our mind, but contrariwise, since (II. xi. xiii.) the first element, that constitutes the essence of the mind, is the idea of the human body as actually existing, it follows that the first and chief endeavour of our mind is the endeavour to affirm the existence of our body: thus, an idea, which negatives the existence of our body, is contrary to our mind, &c. *Q.E.D.*

PROP. XI. *Whatsoever increases or diminishes, helps or hinders the power of activity in our body, the idea thereof increases or diminishes, helps or hinders the power of thought in our mind.*

Proof.—This proposition is evident from II. vii. or from II. xiv.

Note.—Thus we see, that the mind can undergo many changes, and can pass sometimes to a state of greater perfection, sometimes to a state of lesser perfection. These passive states of transition explain to us the emotions of pleasure and pain. By *pleasure* therefore in the following propositions I shall signify *a passive state wherein the mind passes to a greater perfection.* By *pain* I shall signify *a passive state wherein the mind passes to a lesser perfection.* Further, the emotion of pleasure in reference to the body and mind together I shall call *stimulation* (*titillatio*) or *merriment* (*hilaritas*), the emotion of pain in the same relation I shall call *suffering* or *melancholy*. But we must bear in mind, that stimulation and suffering are attributed to man, when one part of his nature is more affected than the rest, merriment and melancholy, when all parts are alike affected. What I mean by desire I have explained in the note to Prop. ix. of this part; beyond these three I recognize no other primary emotion; I will show as I proceed, that all other emotions arise from these three. But, before I go further, I should like here to explain at greater length Prop. x. of this part, in order that we may clearly understand how one idea is contrary to another. In the note to II. xvii. we showed that the idea, which constitutes the essence of mind, involves the existence of body, so long as the body itself exists. Again, it follows from what we pointed out in the Coroll. to II. viii., that the present existence of our mind depends solely on the fact, that the mind involves the actual existence of the body. Lastly, we showed (II. xvii. xviii. and note) that the power of the mind, whereby it imagines and remembers things, also depends on the fact, that it involves the actual existence of the body. Whence it follows, that the present existence of the mind and its power of imagining are removed, as soon as the mind ceases to affirm the present existence of the body. Now the cause, why the mind ceases to affirm this existence of the body, cannot be the mind itself (III. iv.), nor again the fact that the body ceases to exist. For (by II. vi.) the cause, why the mind affirms the existence of the body, is not that the body began to exist; therefore, for the same reason, it does not cease to affirm the existence of the body, because the body ceases to exist; but (II. xvii.) this result follows from another idea, which excludes the present existence of our body and, consequently, of our mind, and which is therefore contrary to the idea constituting the essence of our mind.

PROP. XII. *The mind, as far as it can, endeavours to conceive those things, which increase or help the power of activity in the body.*

Proof.—So long as the human body is affected in a mode, which involves the nature of any external body, the human mind will regard that external body as present (II. xvii.), and consequently (II. vii.), so long as the human mind regards an external body as present, that is (II. xvii. note), conceives it, the human body is affected in a mode, which involves the nature of the said external body; thus so long as the mind conceives things, which increase or help the power of activity in our body, the body is affected in modes which increase or help its power of activity (III. Post. i.); consequently (III. xi.) the mind's power of thinking is for that period increased or helped. Thus (III. vi. ix.) the mind, as far as it can, endeavours to imagine such things. *Q.E.D.*

PROP. XIII. *When the mind conceives things which diminish or hinder the body's power of activity, it endeavours, as far as possible, to remember things which exclude the existence of the first-named things.*

Proof.—So long as the mind conceives anything of the kind alluded to, the power of the mind and body is diminished or constrained (cf. III. xii. Proof); nevertheless it will continue to conceive it, until the mind conceives something else, which excludes the present existence thereof (II. xvii.); that is (as I have just shown), the power of the mind and of the body is diminished, or constrained, until the mind conceives something else, which excludes the existence of the former thing conceived: therefore the mind (III. ix.), as far as it can, will endeavour to conceive or remember the latter. *Q.E.D.*

Corollary.—Hence it follows, that the mind shrinks from conceiving those things, which diminish or constrain the power of itself and of the body.

Note.—From what has been said we may clearly understand the nature of Love and Hate. *Love* is nothing else but *pleasure accompanied by the idea of an external cause: Hate* is nothing else but *pain accompanied by the idea of an external cause.* We further see, that he who loves necessarily endeavours to have, and to keep present to him, the object of his love; while he who hates endeavours to remove and destroy the object of his hatred. But I will treat of these matters at more length hereafter.

PROP. XIV. *If the mind has once been affected by two emotions at the same time, it will, whenever it is afterwards affected by one of the two, be also affected by the other.*

Proof.—If the human body has once been affected by two bodies at once, whenever afterwards the mind conceives one of them, it will straightway remember the other also (II. xviii.). But the mind's conceptions indicate rather the emotions of our body than the nature of external bodies (II. xvi. Coroll. ii.); therefore, if the body, and consequently the mind (III. Def. iii.) has been once affected by two emotions at the same time, it will, whenever it is afterwards affected by one of the two, be also affected by the other.

PROP. XV. *Anything can, accidentally, be the cause of pleasure, pain, or desire.*

Proof.—Let it be granted that the mind is simultaneously affected by two emotions, of which one neither increases nor diminishes its power of activity, and the other does either increase or diminish the said power (III. Post. i.). From the foregoing proposition it is evident that, whenever the mind is afterwards affected by the former, through its true cause, which (by hypothesis) neither increases nor diminishes its power of action, it will be at the same time affected by the latter, which does increase or diminish its power of activity, that is (III. xi. note) it will be affected with pleasure or pain. Thus the former of the two emotions will, not through itself, but accidentally, be the cause of pleasure or pain. In the same way also it can be easily shown, that a thing may be accidentally the cause of desire. *Q.E.D.*

Corollary.—Simply from the fact that we have regarded a thing with the emotion of pleasure or pain, though that thing be not the efficient cause of the emotion, we can either love or hate it.

Proof.—For from this fact alone it arises (III. xiv.), that the mind afterwards conceiving the said thing is affected with the emotion of pleasure or pain, that is (III. xi. note), according as the power of the mind and body may be increased or diminished, &c.; and consequently (III. xii.), according as the mind may desire or shrink from the conception of it (III. xiii.

Coroll.), in other words (III. xiii. note), according as it may love or hate the same. *Q.E.D.*

Note.—Hence we understand how it may happen, that we love or hate a thing without any cause for our emotion being known to us; merely, as the phrase is, from *sympathy* or *antipathy*. We should refer to the same category those objects, which affect us pleasurably or painfully, simply because they resemble other objects which affect us in the same way. This I will show in the next Prop. I am aware that certain authors, who were the first to introduce these terms "sympathy" and "antipathy," wished to signify thereby some occult qualities in things; nevertheless I think we may be permitted to use the same terms to indicate known or manifest qualities.

PROP. XVI. *Simply from the fact that we conceive that a given object has some point of resemblance with another object which is wont to affect the mind pleasurably or painfully, although the point of resemblance be not the efficient cause of the said emotions, we shall still regard the first-named object with love or hate.*

Proof.—The point of resemblance was in the object (by hypothesis), when we regarded it with pleasure or pain, thus (III. xiv.), when the mind is affected by the image thereof, it will straightway be affected by one or the other emotion, and consequently the thing, which we perceive to have the same point of resemblance, will be accidentally (III. xv.) a cause of pleasure or pain. Thus (by the foregoing Corollary), although the point in which the two objects resemble one another be not the efficient cause of the emotion, we shall still regard the first-named object with love or hate. *Q.E.D.*

PROP. XVII. *If we conceive that a thing which is wont to affect us painfully has any point of resemblance with another thing which is wont to affect us with an equally strong emotion of pleasure, we shall hate the first-named thing, and at the same time we shall love it.*

Proof.—The given thing is (by hypothesis) in itself a cause of pain, and (III. xiii. note), in so far as we imagine it with this emotion, we shall hate it: further, inasmuch as we conceive that it has some point of resemblance to something else, which is wont to affect us with an equally strong emotion of pleasure, we shall with an equally strong impulse of pleasure love it (III. xvi.); thus we shall both hate and love the same thing. *Q.E.D.*

Note.—This disposition of the mind, which arises from two contrary emotions, is called *vacillation;* it stands to the emotions in the same relation as doubt does to the imagination (II. xliv. note); vacillation and doubt do not differ one from the other, except as greater differs from less. But we must bear in mind that I have deduced this vacillation from causes, which give rise through themselves to one of the emotions, and to the other accidentally. I have done this, in order that they might be more easily deduced from what went before; but I do not deny that vacillation of the disposition generally arises from an object, which is the efficient cause of both emotions. The human body is composed (II. Post. i.) of a variety of individual parts of different nature, and may therefore (Ax. i. after Lemma iii. after II. xiii.) be affected in a variety of different ways by one and the same body; and contrariwise, as one and the same thing can be affected in many ways, it can also in many different ways affect one and the same part of the body. Hence we can easily conceive, that one and the same object may be the cause of many and conflicting emotions.

PROP. XVIII. *A man is as much affected pleasurably or painfully by the image of a thing past or future as by the image of a thing present.*

Proof.—So long as a man is affected by the image of anything, he will regard that thing as present, even though it be non-existent (II. xvii. and Coroll.), he will not conceive it as past or future, except in so far as its image is joined to the image of time past or future (II. xliv. note). Wherefore the image of a thing, regarded in itself alone, is identical, whether it be referred to time past, time future, or time present; that is (II. xvi. Coroll.), the disposition or emotion of the body is identical, whether the image be of a thing past, future, or present. Thus the emotion of pleasure or pain is the same, whether the image be of a thing past or future. *Q.E.D.*

Note I.—I call a thing past or future, according as we either have been or shall be affected thereby. For instance, according

as we have seen it, or are about to see it, according as it has
recreated us, or will recreate us, according as it has harmed
us, or will harm us. For, as we thus conceive it, we affirm its
existence; that is, the body is affected by no emotion which
excludes the existence of the thing, and therefore (II. xvii.)
the body is affected by the image of the thing, in the same
way as if the thing were actually present. However, as it generally happens that those, who have had many experiences,
vacillate, so long as they regard a thing as future or past, and
are usually in doubt about its issue (II. xliv. note); it follows
that the emotions which arise from similar images of things
are not so constant, but are generally disturbed by the images
of other things, until men become assured of the issue.

Note II.—From what has just been said, we understand what
is meant by the terms Hope, Fear, Confidence, Despair, Joy,
and Disappointment.[1] *Hope is nothing else but an inconstant
pleasure, arising from the image of something future or past,
whereof we do not yet know the issue. Fear, on the other hand,
is an inconstant pain also arising from the image of something
concerning which we are in doubt.* If the element of doubt
be removed from these emotions, hope becomes *Confidence*
and fear becomes *Despair.* In other words, *Pleasure or Pain
arising from the image of something concerning which we have
hoped or feared.* Again, *Joy* is *Pleasure arising from the image
of something past whereof we doubted the issue. Disappointment* is the *Pain opposed to Joy.*

PROP. XIX. *He who conceives that the object of his love is
destroyed will feel pain; if he conceives that it is preserved, he
will feel pleasure.*

Proof.—The mind, as far as possible, endeavours to conceive
those things which increase or help the body's power of activity (III. xii.); in other words (III. xii. note), those things
which it loves. But conception is helped by those things which
postulate the existence of a thing, and contrariwise is hindered
by those which exclude the existence of a thing (II. xvii.);
therefore the images of things, which postulate the existence
of an object of love, help the mind's endeavour to conceive

---

[1] *Conscientiæ morsus*—thus rendered by Mr. Pollock.

the object of love, in other words (III. xi. note), affect the mind pleasurably; contrariwise those things, which exclude the existence of an object of love, hinder the aforesaid mental endeavour; in other words, affect the mind painfully. He, therefore, who conceives that the object of his love is destroyed will feel pain, &c. *Q.E.D.*

PROP. XX. *He who conceives that the object of his hate is destroyed will feel pleasure.*

Proof.—The mind (III. xiii.) endeavours to conceive those things, which exclude the existence of things whereby the body's power of activity is diminished or constrained; that is (III. xiii. note), it endeavours to conceive such things as exclude the existence of what it hates; therefore the image of a thing, which excludes the existence of what the mind hates, helps the aforesaid mental effort, in other words (III. xi. note), affects the mind pleasurably. Thus he who conceives that the object of his hate is destroyed will feel pleasure. *Q.E.D.*

PROP. XXI. *He who conceives, that the object of his love is affected pleasurably or painfully, will himself be affected pleasurably or painfully; and the one or the other emotion will be greater or less in the lover according as it is greater or less in the thing loved.*

Proof.—The images of things (as we showed in III. xix.) which postulate the existence of the object of love, help the mind's endeavour to conceive the said object. But pleasure postulates the existence of something feeling pleasure, so much the more in proportion as the emotion of pleasure is greater; for it is (III. xi. note) a transition to a greater perfection; therefore the image of pleasure in the object of love helps the mental endeavour of the lover; that is, it affects the lover pleasurably, and so much the more, in proportion as this emotion may have been greater in the object of love. This was our first point. Further, in so far as a thing is affected with pain, it is to that extent destroyed, the extent being in proportion to the amount of pain (III. xi. note); therefore (III. xix.) he who conceives, that the object of his love is affected painfully, will himself be affected painfully, in proportion as the said emotion is greater or less in the object of love. *Q.E.D.*

PROP. XXII. *If we conceive that anything pleasurably affects some object of our love, we shall be affected with love towards that thing. Contrariwise, if we conceive that it affects an object of our love painfully, we shall be affected with hatred towards it.*

Proof.—He, who affects pleasurably or painfully the object of our love, affects us also pleasurably or painfully—that is, if we conceive the loved object as affected with the said pleasure or pain (III. xxi.). But this pleasure or pain is postulated to come to us accompanied by the idea of an external cause; therefore (III. xiii. note), if we conceive that anyone affects an object of our love pleasurably or painfully, we shall be affected with love or hatred towards him. *Q.E.D.*

Note.—Prop. xxi. explains to us the nature of *Pity*, which we may define as *pain arising from another's hurt.* What term we can use for pleasure arising from another's gain, I know not.

We will call the *love towards him who confers a benefit on another, Approval;* and the *hatred towards him who injures another,* we will call *Indignation.* We must further remark, that we not only feel pity for a thing which we have loved (as shown in III. xxi.), but also for a thing which we have hitherto regarded without emotion, provided that we deem that it resembles ourselves (as I will show presently). Thus, we bestow approval on one who has benefited anything resembling ourselves, and, contrariwise, are indignant with him who has done it an injury.

PROP. XXIII. *He who conceives, that an object of his hatred is painfully affected, will feel pleasure. Contrariwise, if he thinks that the said object is pleasurably affected, he will feel pain. Each of these emotions will be greater or less, according as its contrary is greater or less in the object of hatred.*

Proof.—In so far as an object of hatred is painfully affected, it is destroyed, to an extent proportioned to the strength of the pain (III. xi. note). Therefore, he (III. xx.) who conceives, that some object of his hatred is painfully affected, will feel pleasure, to an extent proportioned to the amount of pain he conceives in the object of his hatred. This was our first point. Again, pleasure postulates the existence of the pleasurably affected thing (III. xi. note), in proportion as the pleasure is greater or less. If anyone imagines that an object of his hatred is pleasurably affected, this conception (III. xiii.) will hinder his own endeavour to persist; in other words (III. xi. note), he who hates will be painfully affected. *Q.E.D.*

Note.—This pleasure can scarcely be felt unalloyed, and without any mental conflict. For (as I am about to show in Prop. xxvii.), in so far as a man conceives that something similar to himself is affected by pain, he will himself be affected in like manner; and he will have the contrary emotion in contrary circumstances. But here we are regarding hatred only.

PROP. XXIV. *If we conceive that anyone pleasurably affects an object of our hate, we shall feel hatred towards him also. If we conceive that he painfully affects the said object, we shall feel love towards him.*

Proof.—This proposition is proved in the same way as III. xxii., which see.

Note.—These and similar emotions of hatred are attributable to *envy*, which, accordingly, is nothing else but *hatred, in so far as it is regarded as disposing a man to rejoice in another's hurt, and to grieve at another's advantage.*

PROP. XXV. *We endeavour to affirm, concerning ourselves and concerning what we love, everything that we conceive to affect pleasurably ourselves, or the loved object. Contrariwise, we endeavour to negative everything, which we conceive to affect painfully ourselves or the loved object.*

Proof.—That, which we conceive to affect an object of our love pleasurably or painfully, affects us also pleasurably or painfully (III. xxi.). But the mind (III. xii.) endeavours, as far as possible, to conceive those things which affect us pleasurably; in other words (II. xvii. and Coroll.), it endeavours to regard them as present. And, contrariwise (III. xiii.), it endeavours to exclude the existence of such things as affect us painfully; therefore, we endeavour to affirm concerning ourselves, and concerning the loved object, whatever we conceive to affect ourselves, or the loved object pleasurably. *Q.E.D.*

PROP. XXVI. *We endeavour to affirm, concerning that which we hate, everything which we conceive to affect it painfully; and, contrariwise, we endeavour to deny, concerning it, everything which we conceive to affect it pleasurably.*

Proof.—This proposition follows from III. xxiii., as the foregoing proposition followed from III. xxi.

Note.—Thus we see that it may readily happen, that a man may easily think too highly of himself, or a loved object, and, contrariwise, too meanly of a hated object. This feeling is called *pride*, in reference to the man who thinks too highly of himself, and is a species of madness, wherein a man dreams with his eyes open, thinking that he can accomplish all things that fall within the scope of his conception, and thereupon accounting them real, and exulting in them, so long as he is unable to conceive anything which excludes their existence, and determines his own power of action. *Pride, therefore, is pleasure springing from a man thinking too highly of himself.* Again, the *pleasure which arises from a man thinking too highly of another* is called *over-esteem.* Whereas the *pleasure which arises from thinking too little of a man* is called *disdain.*

PROP. XXVII. *By the very fact that we conceive a thing, which is like ourselves, and which we have not regarded with any emotion, to be affected with any emotion, we are ourselves affected with a like emotion* (*affectus*).

Proof.—The images of things are modifications of the human body, whereof the ideas represent external bodies as present to us (II. xvii.); in other words (II. x.), whereof the ideas involve the nature of our body, and, at the same time, the nature of external bodies as present. If, therefore, the nature of the external body be similar to the nature of our body, then the idea which we form of the external body will involve a modification of our own body similar to the modification of the external body. Consequently, if we conceive anyone similar to ourselves as affected by any emotion, this conception will express a modification of our body similar to that emotion. Thus, from the fact of conceiving a thing like ourselves to be affected with any emotion, we are ourselves affected with a like emotion. If, however, we hate the said thing like ourselves, we shall, to that extent, be affected by a contrary, and not similar, emotion. *Q.E.D.*

Note I.—This imitation of emotions, when it is referred to pain, is called *compassion* (cf. III. xxii. note); when it is referred to desire, it is called *emulation*, which is nothing else but *the desire of anything, engendered in us by the fact that we conceive that others have the like desire*.

Corollary I.—If we conceive that anyone, whom we have hitherto regarded with no emotion, pleasurably affects something similar to ourselves, we shall be affected with love towards him. If, on the other hand, we conceive that he painfully affects the same, we shall be affected with hatred towards him.

Proof.—This is proved from the last proposition in the same manner as III. xxii. is proved from III. xxi.

Corollary II.—We cannot hate a thing which we pity, because its misery affects us painfully.

Proof.—If we could hate it for this reason, we should rejoice in its pain, which is contrary to the hypothesis.

Corollary III.—We seek to free from misery, as far as we can, a thing which we pity.

Proof.—That, which painfully affects the object of our pity, affects us also with similar pain (by the foregoing proposition); therefore, we shall endeavour to recall everything which removes its existence, or which destroys it (cf. III. xiii.); in other words (III. ix. note), we shall desire to destroy it, or we shall be determined for its destruction; thus, we shall endeavour to free from misery a thing which we pity. *Q.E.D.*

Note II.—This will or appetite for doing good, which arises from pity of the thing whereon we would confer a benefit, is called *benevolence*, and is nothing else but *desire arising from compassion*. Concerning love or hate towards him who has done good or harm to something, which we conceive to be like ourselves, see III. xxii. note.

PROP. XXVIII. *We endeavour to bring about whatsoever we conceive to conduce to pleasure; but we endeavour to remove or destroy whatsoever we conceive to be truly repugnant thereto, or to conduce to pain.*

Proof.—We endeavour, as far as possible, to conceive that which we imagine to conduce to pleasure (III. xii.); in other words (II. xvii.) we shall endeavour to conceive it as far as possible as present or actually existing. But the endeavour of the mind, or the mind's power of thought, is equal to, and simultaneous with, the endeavour of the body, or the body's power of action. (This is clear from II. vii. Coroll. and II. xi. Coroll.). Therefore we make an absolute endeavour for its existence, in other words (which by III. ix. note come to the same thing) we desire and strive for it; this was our first point. Again, if we conceive that something, which we believed to be the cause of pain, that is (III. xiii. note), which we hate, is destroyed, we shall rejoice (III. xx.). We shall, therefore (by the first part of this proof), endeavour to destroy the same, or (III. xiii.) to remove it from us, so that we may not regard it as present; this was our second point. Wherefore whatsoever conduces to pleasure, &c. Q.E.D.

PROP. XXIX. *We shall also endeavour to do whatsoever we conceive men[2] to regard with pleasure, and contrariwise we shall shrink from doing that which we conceive men to shrink from.*

Proof.—From the fact of imagining, that men love or hate anything, we shall love or hate the same thing (III. xxvii.). That is (III. xiii. note), from this mere fact we shall feel pleasure or pain at the thing's presence. And so we shall endeavour to do whatever we conceive men to love or regard with pleasure, etc. Q.E.D.

Note.—This endeavour to do a thing or leave it undone, solely in order to please men, we call *ambition*, especially when we so eagerly endeavour to please the vulgar, that we do or omit certain things to our own or another's hurt: in other cases it is generally called *kindliness*. Furthermore I give the name of *praise* to the *pleasure, with which we conceive the action of another, whereby he has endeavoured to please us;* but of *blame* to the *pain wherewith we feel aversion to his action.*

PROP. XXX. *If anyone has done something which he conceives as affecting other men pleasurably, he will be affected by pleasure, accompanied by the idea of himself as cause; in other words, he will regard himself with pleasure. On the other hand, if he has done anything which he conceives as affecting others painfully, he will regard himself with pain.*

Proof.—He who conceives, that he affects others with pleas-

[2] N.B. By "men" in this and the following propositions, I mean men whom we regard without any particular emotion.

ure or pain, will, by that very fact, himself be affected with
pleasure or pain (III. xxvii.), but, as a man (II. xix. and xxiii.)
is conscious of himself through the modifications whereby he
is determined to action, it follows that he who conceives, that
he affects others pleasurably, will be affected with pleasure
accompanied by the idea of himself as cause; in other words,
will regard himself with pleasure. And so *mutatis mutandis*
in the case of pain. *Q.E.D.*

Note.—As love (III. xiii.) is pleasure accompanied by the
idea of an external cause, and hatred is pain accompanied by
the idea of an external cause; the pleasure and pain in question will be a species of love and hatred. But, as the terms
love and hatred are used in reference to external objects, we
will employ other names for the emotions now under discussion: pleasure accompanied by the idea of an external cause[3]
we will style *Honour*, and the emotion contrary thereto we
will style *Shame:* I mean in such cases as where pleasure or
pain arises from a man's belief, that he is being praised or
blamed: otherwise pleasure accompanied by the idea of an
external cause[3] is called *self-complacency*, and its contrary
pain is called *repentance*. Again, as it may happen (II. xvii.
Coroll.) that the pleasure, wherewith a man conceives that he
affects others, may exist solely in his own imagination, and as
(III. xxv.) everyone endeavours to conceive concerning himself
that which he conceives will affect him with pleasure, it may
easily come to pass that a vain man may be proud and may
imagine that he is pleasing to all, when in reality he may be
an annoyance to all.

PROP. XXXI. *If we conceive that anyone loves, desires, or
hates anything which we ourselves love, desire, or hate, we
shall thereupon regard the thing in question with more stead-
fast love, &c. On the contrary, if we think that anyone shrinks
from something that we love, we shall undergo vacillation of
soul.*

Proof.—From the mere fact of conceiving that anyone loves
anything we shall ourselves love that thing (III. xxvii.): but
we are assumed to love it already; there is, therefore, a new

[3] So Van Vloten and Bruder. The Dutch version and Camerer
read, "an internal cause." "Honour" = *Gloria*.

cause of love, whereby our former emotion is fostered; hence we shall thereupon love it more steadfastly. Again, from the mere fact of conceiving that anyone shrinks from anything, we shall ourselves shrink from that thing (III. xxvii.). If we assume that we at the same time love it, we shall then simultaneously love it and shrink from it; in other words, we shall be subject to vacillation (III. xvii. note). *Q.E.D.*

Corollary.—From the foregoing, and also from III. xxviii. it follows that everyone endeavours, as far as possible, to cause others to love what he himself loves, and to hate what he himself hates: as the poet says: "As lovers let us share every hope and every fear: ironhearted were he who should love what the other leaves."[4]

Note.—This endeavour to bring it about, that our own likes and dislikes should meet with universal approval, is really ambition (see III. xxix. note); wherefore we see that everyone by nature desires (*appetere*), that the rest of mankind should live according to his own individual disposition: when such a desire is equally present in all, everyone stands in everyone else's way, and in wishing to be loved or praised by all, all become mutually hateful.

PROP. XXXII. *If we conceive that anyone takes delight in something which only one person can possess we shall endeavour to bring it about that the man in question shall not gain possession thereof.*

Proof.—From the mere fact of our conceiving that another person takes delight in a thing (III. xxvii. and Coroll.) we shall ourselves love that thing and desire to take delight therein. But we assumed that the pleasure in question would be prevented by another's delight in its object; we shall, therefore, endeavour to prevent his possession thereof (III. xxviii.). *Q.E.D.*

Note.—We thus see that man's nature is generally so constituted, that he takes pity on those who fare ill, and envies those who fare well with an amount of hatred proportioned to his own love for the goods in their possession. Further,

---

[4] Ovid. Amores, II. xix. 4, 5. Spinoza transposes the verses.

"Speremus pariter, pariter metuamus amantes;
     Ferreus est, si quis, quod sinit alter, amat."

we see that from the same property of human nature, whence it follows that men are merciful, it follows also that they are envious and ambitious. Lastly, if we make appeal to Experience, we shall find that she entirely confirms what we have said; more especially if we turn our attention to the first years of our life. We find that children, whose body is continually, as it were, in equilibrium, laugh or cry simply because they see others laughing or crying; moreover, they desire forthwith to imitate whatever they see others doing, and to possess themselves whatever they conceive as delighting others: inasmuch as the images of things are, as we have said, modifications of the human body, or modes wherein the human body is affected and disposed by external causes to act in this or that manner.

PROP. XXXIII. *When we love a thing similar to ourselves, we endeavour, as far as we can, to bring it about that it should love us in return.*

Proof.—That which we love we endeavour, as far as we can, to conceive in preference to anything else (III. xii.). If the thing be similar to ourselves, we shall endeavour to affect it pleasurably in preference to anything else (III. xxix.). In other words, we shall endeavour, as far as we can, to bring it about, that the thing should be affected with pleasure accompanied by the idea of ourselves, that is (III. xiii. note), that it should love us in return. *Q.E.D.*

PROP. XXXIV. *The greater the emotion with which we conceive a loved object to be affected towards us, the greater will be our complacency.*

Proof.—We endeavour (III. xxxiii.), as far as we can, to bring about, that what we love should love us in return: in other words, that what we love should be affected with pleasure accompanied by the idea of ourself as cause. Therefore, in proportion as the loved object is more pleasurably affected because of us, our endeavour will be assisted.—that is (III. xi. and note) the greater will be our pleasure. But when we take pleasure in the fact, that we pleasurably affect something similar to ourselves, we regard ourselves with pleasure (III. xxx.); therefore the greater the emotion with which we conceive a loved object to be affected, &c. *Q.E.D.*

PROP. XXXV. *If anyone conceives, that an object of his love joins itself to another with closer bonds of friendship than he himself has attained to, he will be affected with hatred towards the loved object and with envy towards his rival.*

Proof.—In proportion as a man thinks, that a loved object is well affected towards him, will be the strength of his self-approval (by the last Prop.), that is (III. xxx. note), of his pleasure; he will, therefore (III. xxviii.), endeavour, as far as he can, to imagine the loved object as most closely bound to him: this endeavour or desire will be increased, if he thinks that someone else has a similar desire (III. xxxi.). But this endeavour or desire is assumed to be checked by the image of the loved object in conjunction with the image of him whom the loved object has joined to itself; therefore (III. xi. note) he will for that reason be affected with pain, accompanied by the idea of the loved object as a cause in conjunction with the image of his rival; that is, he will be (III. xiii.) affected with hatred towards the loved object and also towards his rival (III. xv. Coroll.), which latter he will envy as enjoying the beloved object. *Q.E.D.*

Note.—This hatred towards an object of love joined with envy is called *Jealousy,* which accordingly is nothing else but a wavering of the disposition arising from combined love and hatred, accompanied by the idea of some rival who is envied. Further, this hatred towards the object of love will be greater, in proportion to the pleasure which the jealous man had been wont to derive from the reciprocated love of the said object; and also in proportion to the feelings he had previously entertained towards his rival. If he had hated him, he will forthwith hate the object of his love, because he conceives it is pleasurably affected by one whom he himself hates: and also because he is compelled to associate the image of his loved one with the image of him whom he hates. This condition generally comes into play in the case of love for a woman: for he who thinks, that a woman whom he loves prostitutes herself to another, will feel pain, not only because his own desire is restrained, but also because, being compelled to associate the image of her he loves with the parts of shame and the excreta of another, he therefore shrinks from her.

We must add, that a jealous man is not greeted by his beloved with the same joyful countenance as before, and this also gives him pain as a lover, as I will now show.

PROP. XXXVI. *He who remembers a thing, in which he has once taken delight, desires to possess it under the same circumstances as when he first took delight therein.*

Proof.—Everything, which a man has seen in conjunction with the object of his love, will be to him accidentally a cause of pleasure (III. xv.); he will, therefore, desire to possess it, in conjunction with that wherein he has taken delight; in other words, he will desire to possess the object of his love under the same circumstances as when he first took delight therein. *Q.E.D.*

Corollary.—A lover will, therefore, feel pain if one of the aforesaid attendant circumstances be missing.

Proof.—For, in so far as he finds some circumstance to be missing, he conceives something which excludes its existence. As he is assumed to be desirous for love's sake of that thing or circumstance (by the last Prop.), he will, in so far as he conceives it to be missing, feel pain (III. xix.). *Q.E.D.*

Note.—This pain, in so far as it has reference to the absence of the object of love, is called *Regret.*

PROP. XXXVII. *Desire arising through pain or pleasure, hatred or love, is greater in proportion as the emotion is greater.*

Proof.—Pain diminishes or constrains man's power of activity (III. xi. note), in other words (III. vii.), diminishes or constrains the effort, wherewith he endeavours to persist in his own being; therefore (III. v.) it is contrary to the said endeavour: thus all the endeavours of a man affected by pain are directed to removing that pain. But (by the definition of pain), in proportion as the pain is greater, so also is it necessarily opposed to a greater part of man's power of activity; therefore the greater the pain, the greater the power of activity employed to remove it; that is, the greater will be the desire or appetite in endeavouring to remove it. Again, since pleasure (III. xi. note) increases or aids a man's power of activity, it may easily be shown in like manner, that a man affected by pleasure has no desire further than to preserve it, and his desire will be in proportion to the magnitude of the pleasure.

Lastly, since hatred and love are themselves emotions of pain and pleasure, it follows in like manner that the endeavour, appetite, or desire, which arises through hatred or love, will be greater in proportion to the hatred or love. *Q.E.D.*

Prop. XXXVIII. *If a man has begun to hate an object of his love, so that love is thoroughly destroyed, he will, causes being equal, regard it with more hatred than if he had never loved it, and his hatred will be in proportion to the strength of his former love.*

Proof.—If a man begins to hate that which he had loved, more of his appetites are put under restraint than if he had never loved it. For love is a pleasure (III. xiii. note) which a man endeavours as far as he can to render permanent (III. xxviii.); he does so by regarding the object of his love as present, and by affecting it as far as he can pleasurably; this endeavour is greater in proportion as the love is greater, and so also is the endeavour to bring about that the beloved should return his affection (III. xxxiii.). Now these endeavours are constrained by hatred towards the object of love (III. xiii. Coroll. and III. xxiii.); wherefore the lover (III. xi. note) will for this cause also be affected with pain, the more so in proportion as his love has been greater; that is, in addition to the pain caused by hatred, there is a pain caused by the fact that he has loved the object; wherefore the lover will regard the beloved with greater pain, or in other words, will hate it more than if he had never loved it, and with the more intensity in proportion as his former love was greater. *Q.E.D.*

Prop. XXXIX. *He who hates anyone will endeavour to do him an injury, unless he fears that a greater injury will thereby accrue to himself; on the other hand, he who loves anyone will, by the same law, seek to benefit him.*

Proof.—To hate a man is (III. xiii. note) to conceive him as a cause of pain; therefore he who hates a man will endeavour to remove or destroy him. But if anything more painful, or, in other words, a greater evil, should accrue to the hater thereby—and if the hater thinks he can avoid such evil by not carrying out the injury, which he planned against the object of his hate—he will desire to abstain from inflicting that injury (III. xxviii.), and the strength of his endeavour (III. xxxvii.) will be greater than his former endeavour to do injury, and will therefore prevail over it, as we asserted. The second part of this proof proceeds in the same manner. Wherefore he who hates another, etc. *Q.E.D.*

Note.—By *good* I here mean every kind of pleasure, and all that conduces thereto, especially that which satisfies our longings, whatsoever they may be. By *evil,* I mean every kind of pain, especially that which frustrates our longings. For I have shown (III. ix. note) that we in no case desire a thing because we deem it good, but, contrariwise, we deem a thing good because we desire it: consequently we deem evil that which we shrink from; everyone, therefore, according to his particular emotions, judges or estimates what is good, what is bad, what is better, what is worse, lastly, what is best, and what is worst. Thus a miser thinks that abundance of money is the best, and want of money the worst; an ambitious man desires nothing so much as glory, and fears nothing so much as shame. To an envious man nothing is more delightful than another's misfortune, and nothing more painful than another's success. So every man, according to his emotions, judges a thing to be good or bad, useful or useless. The emotion, which induces a man to turn from that which he wishes, or to wish for that which he turns from, is called *timidity,* which may accordingly be defined as *the fear whereby a man is induced to avoid an evil which he regards as future by encountering a lesser evil* (III. xxviii.). But if the evil which he fears be shame, timidity becomes *bashfulness.* Lastly, if the desire to avoid a future evil be checked by the fear of another evil, so that the man knows not which to choose, fear becomes *consternation,* especially if both the evils feared be very great.

PROP. XL. *He, who conceives himself to be hated by another, and believes that he has given him no cause for hatred, will hate that other in return.*

Proof.—He who conceives another as affected with hatred, will thereupon be affected himself with hatred (III. xxvii.), that is, with pain, accompanied by the idea of an external cause. But, by the hypothesis, he conceives no cause for this pain except him who is his enemy; therefore, from conceiving that he is hated by some one, he will be affected with pain, accompanied by the idea of his enemy; in other words, he will hate his enemy in return. *Q.E.D.*

Note.—He who thinks that he has given just cause for hatred will (III. xxx. and note) be affected with shame; but this case (III. xxv.) rarely happens. This reciprocation of hatred may also arise from the hatred, which follows an endeavour to injure the object of our hate (III. xxxix.). He therefore who conceives that he is hated by another will conceive his enemy as the cause of some evil or pain; thus he will be affected with pain or fear, accompanied by the idea of his enemy as cause; in other words, he will be affected with hatred towards his enemy, as I said above.

Corollary I.—He who conceives, that one whom he loves hates him, will be a prey to conflicting hatred and love. For, in so far as he conceives that he is an object of hatred, he is determined to hate his enemy in return. But, by the hypothesis, he nevertheless loves him: wherefore he will be a prey to conflicting hatred and love.

Corollary II.—If a man conceives that one, whom he has hitherto regarded without emotion, has done him any injury from motives of hatred, he will forthwith seek to repay the injury in kind.

Proof.—He who conceives, that another hates him, will (by the last proposition) hate his enemy in return, and (III. xxvi.) will endeavour to recall everything which can affect him painfully; he will moreover endeavour to do him an injury (III. xxxix.). Now the first thing of this sort which he conceives is the injury done to himself; he will, therefore, forthwith endeavour to repay it in kind. *Q.E.D.*

Note.—The endeavour to injure one whom we hate is called *Anger;* the endeavour to repay in kind injury done to ourselves is called *Revenge.*

Prop. XLI. *If anyone conceives that he is loved by another, and believes that he has given no cause for such love, he will love that other in return.* (Cf. III. xv. Coroll., and III. xvi.)

Proof.—This proposition is proved in the same way as the preceding one. See also the note appended thereto.

Note.—If he believes that he has given just cause for the love, he will take pride therein (III. xxx. and note); this is what most often happens (III. xxv.), and we said that its contrary took place whenever a man conceives himself to be hated by another. (See note to preceding proposition.) This reciprocal love, and consequently the desire of benefiting him who loves us (III. xxxix.), and who endeavours to benefit us, is called *gratitude* or *thankfulness*. It thus appears that men are much more prone to take vengeance than to return benefits.

Corollary.—He who imagines, that he is loved by one whom he hates, will be a prey to conflicting hatred and love. This is proved in the same way as the first corollary of the preceding proposition.

Note.—If hatred be the prevailing emotion, he will endeavour to injure him who loves him; this emotion is called cruelty, especially if the victim be believed to have given no ordinary cause for hatred.

PROP. XLII. *He who has conferred a benefit on anyone from motives of love or honour will feel pain, if he sees that the benefit is received without gratitude.*

Proof.—When a man loves something similar to himself, he endeavours, as far as he can, to bring it about that he should be loved thereby in return (III. xxxiii.). Therefore he who has conferred a benefit confers it in obedience to the desire, which he feels of being loved in return; that is (III. xxxiv.) from the hope of honour or (III. xxx. note) pleasure; hence he will endeavour, as far as he can, to conceive this cause of honour, or to regard it as actually existing. But, by the hypothesis, he conceives something else, which excludes the existence of the said cause of honour: wherefore he will thereat feel pain (III. xix.). *Q.E.D.*

PROP. XLIII. *Hatred is increased by being reciprocated, and can on the other hand be destroyed by love.*

Proof.—He who conceives, that an object of his hate hates him in return, will thereupon feel a new hatred, while the former hatred (by hypothesis) still remains (III. xl.). But if, on the other hand, he conceives that the object of hate loves him, he will to this extent (III. xxxviii.) regard himself with pleasure, and (III. xxix.) will endeavour to please the cause of his emotion. In other words, he will endeavour not to hate him (III. xli.), and not to affect him painfully; this endeavour (III. xxxvii.) will be greater or less in proportion to the emotion from which it arises. Therefore, if it be greater than that which arises from hatred, and through which the man endeavours to affect painfully the thing which he hates, it will get the better of it and banish the hatred from his mind. *Q.E.D.*

PROP. XLIV. *Hatred which is completely vanquished by love passes into love: and love is thereupon greater than if hatred had not preceded it.*

Proof.—The proof proceeds in the same way as Prop. xxxviii. of this Part: for he who begins to love a thing, which he was wont to hate or regard with pain, from the very fact of loving feels pleasure. To this pleasure involved in love is added the pleasure arising from aid given to the endeavour to remove the pain involved in hatred (III. xxxvii.), accompanied by the idea of the former object of hatred as cause.

Note.—Though this be so, no one will endeavour to hate anything, or to be affected with pain, for the sake of enjoying this greater pleasure; that is, no one will desire that he should be injured, in the hope of recovering from the injury, nor long to be ill for the sake of getting well. For everyone will always endeavour to persist in his being, and to ward off pain as far as he can. If the contrary is conceivable, namely, that a man should desire to hate someone, in order that he might love him the more thereafter, he will always desire to hate him. For the strength of the love is in proportion to the strength of the hatred, wherefore the man would desire, that the hatred be continually increased more and more, and, for a similar reason, he would desire to become more and more ill, in order that he might take a greater pleasure in being restored to health: in such a case he would always endeavour to be ill, which (III. vi.) is absurd.

PROP. XLV. *If a man conceives, that anyone similar to him-*

self hates anything also similar to himself, which he loves, he will hate that person.

Proof.—The beloved object feels reciprocal hatred towards him who hates it (III. xl.); therefore the lover, in conceiving that anyone hates the beloved object, conceives the beloved thing as affected by hatred, in other words (III. xiii.), by pain; consequently he is himself affected by pain accompanied by the idea of the hater of the beloved thing as cause; that is, he will hate him who hates anything which he himself loves (III. xiii. note). *Q.E.D.*

PROP. XLVI. *If a man has been affected pleasurably or painfully by anyone of a class or nation different from his own, and if the pleasure or pain has been accompanied by the idea of the said stranger as cause, under the general category of the class or nation: the man will feel love or hatred, not only to the individual stranger, but also to the whole class or nation whereto he belongs.*

Proof.—This is evident from III. xvi.

PROP. XLVII. *Joy arising from the fact that anything we hate is destroyed or suffers other injury is never unaccompanied by a certain pain in us.*

Proof.—This is evident from III. xxvii. For in so far as we conceive a thing similar to ourselves to be affected with pain, we ourselves feel pain.

Note.—This proposition can also be proved from the Corollary to II. xvii. Whenever we remember anything, even if it does not actually exist, we regard it only as present, and the body is affected in the same manner; wherefore, in so far as the remembrance of the thing is strong, a man is determined to regard it with pain; this determination, while the image of the thing in question lasts, is indeed checked by the remembrance of other things excluding the existence of the aforesaid thing, but is not destroyed: hence, a man only feels pleasure in so far as the said determination is checked: for this reason the joy arising from the injury done to what we hate is repeated, every time we remember that object of hatred. For, as we have said, when the image of the thing in question is aroused, inasmuch as it involves the thing's existence, it determines the man to regard the thing with the same pain as he was wont to do, when it actually did exist. However, since he has joined to the image of the thing other images, which exclude its existence, this determination to pain is forthwith checked, and the man rejoices afresh as often as the repetition takes place. This is the cause of men's pleasure in recalling past evils, and delight in narrating dangers from which they have escaped. For when men conceive a danger, they conceive it as still future, and are determined to fear it; this determination is checked afresh by the idea of freedom, which became associated with the idea of the danger when they escaped therefrom: this renders them secure afresh: therefore they rejoice afresh.

PROP. XLVIII. *Love or hatred towards, for instance, Peter is destroyed, if the pleasure involved in the former, or the pain involved in the latter emotion, be associated with the idea of another cause; and will be diminished in proportion as we conceive Peter not to have been the sole cause of either emotion.*

Proof.—This Prop. is evident from the mere definition of love and hatred (III. xiii. note). For pleasure is called love towards Peter, and pain is called hatred towards Peter, simply in so far as Peter is regarded as the cause of one emotion or the other. When this condition of causality is either wholly or partly removed, the emotion towards Peter also wholly or in part vanishes. *Q.E.D.*

PROP. XLIX. *Love or hatred towards a thing which we conceive to be free must, other conditions being similar, be greater than if it were felt towards a thing acting by necessity.*

Proof.—A thing which we conceive as free must (I. Def. vii.) be perceived through itself without anything else. If, therefore, we conceive it as the cause of pleasure or pain, we shall therefore (III. xiii. note) love it or hate it, and shall do so with the utmost love or hatred that can arise from the given emotion. But if the thing which causes the emotion be conceived as acting by necessity, we shall then (by the same Def. vii. Part I.) conceive it not as the sole cause, but as one of the causes of the emotion, and therefore our love or hatred towards it will be less. *Q.E.D.*

Note.—Hence it follows, that men, thinking themselves to

be free, feel more love or hatred towards one another than towards anything else: to this consideration we must add the imitation of emotions treated of in III. xxvii. xxxiv. xl. and xliii.

PROP. L. *Anything whatever can be, accidentally, a cause of hope or fear.*

Proof.—This proposition is proved in the same way as III. xv., which see, together with the note to III. xviii.

Note.—Things which are accidentally the causes of hope or fear are called good or evil omens. Now, in so far as such omens are the cause of hope or fear, they are (by the definitions of hope and fear given in III. xviii. note) the causes also of pleasure and pain; consequently we, to this extent, regard them with love or hatred, and endeavour either to invoke them as means towards that which we hope for, or to remove them as obstacles, or causes of that which we fear. It follows, further, from III. xxv., that we are naturally so constituted as to believe readily in that which we hope for, and with difficulty in that which we fear; moreover, we are apt to estimate such objects above or below their true value. Hence there have arisen superstitions, whereby men are everywhere assailed. However, I do not think it worth while to point out here the vacillations springing from hope and fear; it follows from the definition of these emotions, that there can be no hope without fear, and no fear without hope, as I will duly explain in the proper place. Further, in so far as we hope for or fear anything, we regard it with love or hatred; thus everyone can apply by himself to hope and fear what we have said concerning love and hatred.

PROP. LI. *Different men may be differently affected by the same object, and the same man may be differently affected at different times by the same object.*

Proof.—The human body is affected by external bodies in a variety of ways (II. Post. iii.). Two men may therefore be differently affected at the same time, and therefore (by Ax. i. after Lemma iii. after II. xiii.) may be differently affected by one and the same object. Further (by the same Post.) the human body can be affected sometimes in one way, sometimes in another; consequently (by the same Axiom) it may be differently affected at different times by one and the same object. *Q.E.D.*

Note.—We thus see that it is possible, that what one man loves another may hate, and that what one man fears another may not fear; or, again, that one and the same man may love what he once hated, or may be bold where he once was timid, and so on. Again, as everyone judges according to his emotions what is good, what bad, what better, and what worse (III. xxxix. note), it follows that men's judgments may vary no less than their emotions,[5] hence when we compare some with others, we distinguish them solely by the diversity of their emotions, and style some intrepid, others timid, others by some other epithet. For instance, I shall call a man *intrepid,* if he despises an evil which I am accustomed to fear; if I further take into consideration that, in his desire to injure his enemies and to benefit those whom he loves, he is not restrained by the fear of an evil which is sufficient to restrain me, I shall call him *daring.* Again, a man will appear *timid* to me, if he fears an evil which I am accustomed to despise; and if I further take into consideration that his desire is restrained by the fear of an evil, which is not sufficient to restrain me, I shall say that he is *cowardly;* and in like manner will everyone pass judgment.

Lastly, from this inconstancy in the nature of human judgment, inasmuch as a man often judges of things solely by his emotions, and inasmuch as the things which he believes cause pleasure or pain, and therefore endeavours to promote or prevent, are often purely imaginary, not to speak of the uncertainty of things alluded to in III. xxviii.; we may readily conceive that a man may be at one time affected with pleasure, and at another with pain, accompanied by the idea of himself as cause. Thus we can easily understand what are *Repentance* and *Self-complacency. Repentance is pain, accompanied by the idea of one's self as cause; Self-complacency is pleasure accompanied by the idea of one's self as cause,* and these emotions are most intense because men believe themselves to be free (III. xlix.).

[5] This is possible, though the human mind is part of the divine intellect, as I have shown in II. xiii. note.

Prop. LII. *An object which we have formerly seen in conjunction with others, and which we do not conceive to have any property that is not common to many, will not be regarded by us for so long as an object which we conceive to have some property peculiar to itself.*

Proof.—As soon as we conceive an object which we have seen in conjunction with others, we at once remember those others (II. xviii. and note), and thus we pass forthwith from the contemplation of one object to the contemplation of another object. And this is the case with the object, which we conceive to have no property that is not common to many. For we thereupon assume that we are regarding therein nothing, which we have not before seen in conjunction with other objects. But when we suppose that we conceive in an object something special, which we have never seen before, we must needs say that the mind, while regarding that object, has in itself nothing which it can fall to regarding instead thereof; therefore it is determined to the contemplation of that object only. Therefore an object, &c. *Q.E.D.*

Note.—This mental modification, or imagination of a particular thing, in so far as it is alone in the mind, is called *Wonder;* but if it be excited by an object of fear, it is called *Consternation,* because wonder at an evil keeps a man so engrossed in the simple contemplation thereof, that he has no power to think of anything else whereby he might avoid the evil. If, however, the object of wonder be a man's prudence, industry, or anything of that sort, inasmuch as the said man is thereby regarded as far surpassing ourselves, wonder is called *Veneration;* otherwise, if a man's anger, envy, &c., be what we wonder at, the emotion is called *Horror.* Again, if it be the prudence, industry, or what not, of a man we love, that we wonder at, our love will on this account be the greater (III. xii.), and when joined to wonder or veneration is called *Devotion.* We may in like manner conceive hatred, hope, confidence, and the other emotions, as associated with wonder; and we should thus be able to deduce more emotions than those which have obtained names in ordinary speech. Whence it is evident, that the names of the emotions have been applied in accordance rather with their ordinary manifestations than with an accurate knowledge of their nature.

To wonder is opposed *Contempt,* which generally arises from the fact that, because we see someone wondering at, loving, or fearing something, or because something, at first sight, appears to be like things, which we ourselves wonder at, love, fear, &c., we are, in consequence (III. xv. Coroll. and iii. xxvii.), determined to wonder at, love, or fear that thing. But if from the presence, or more accurate contemplation of the said thing, we are compelled to deny concerning it all that can be the cause of wonder, love, fear, &c., the mind then, by the presence of the thing, remains determined to think rather of those qualities which are not in it, than of those which are in it; whereas, on the other hand, the presence of the object would cause it more particularly to regard that which is therein. As devotion springs from wonder at a thing which we love, so does *Derision* spring from contempt of a thing which we hate or fear, and *Scorn* from contempt of folly, as veneration from wonder at prudence. Lastly, we can conceive the emotions of love, hope, honour, &c., in association with contempt, and can thence deduce other emotions, which are not distinguished one from another by any recognized name.

PROP. LIII. *When the mind regards itself and its own power of activity, it feels pleasure; and that pleasure is greater in proportion to the distinctness wherewith it conceives itself and its own power of activity.*

Proof.—A man does not know himself except through the modifications of his body, and the ideas thereof (II. xix. and xxiii.). When, therefore, the mind is able to contemplate itself, it is thereby assumed to pass to a greater perfection, or (III. xi. note) to feel pleasure; and the pleasure will be greater in proportion to the distinctness, wherewith it is able to conceive itself and its own power of activity. *Q.E.D.*

Corollary.—This pleasure is fostered more and more, in proportion as a man conceives himself to be praised by others. For the more he conceives himself as praised by others, the more will he imagine them to be affected with pleasure, accompanied by the idea of himself (III. xxix. note); thus he is (III. xxvii.) himself affected with greater pleasure, accompanied by the idea of himself. *Q.E.D.*

PROP. LIV. *The mind endeavours to conceive only such things as assert its power of activity.*

Proof.—The endeavour or power of the mind is the actual essence thereof (III. vii.); but the essence of the mind obviously only affirms that which the mind is and can do; not that which it neither is nor can do; therefore the mind endeavours to conceive only such things as assert or affirm its power of activity. *Q.E.D.*

PROP. LV. *When the mind contemplates its own weakness, it feels pain thereat.*

Proof.—The essence of the mind only affirms that which the mind is, or can do; in other words, it is the mind's nature to conceive only such things as assert its power of activity (last Prop.). Thus, when we say that the mind contemplates its own weakness, we are merely saying that while the mind is attempting to conceive something which asserts its power of activity, it is checked in its endeavour—in other words (III. xi. note), it feels pain. *Q.E.D.*

Corollary.—This pain is more and more fostered, if a man conceives that he is blamed by others; this may be proved in the same way as the corollary to III. liii.

Note.—This pain, accompanied by the idea of our own weakness, is called *humility;* the pleasure, which springs from the contemplation of ourselves, is called *self-love* or *self-complacency.* And inasmuch as this feeling is renewed as often as a man contemplates his own virtues, or his own power of activity, it follows that everyone is fond of narrating his own exploits, and displaying the force both of his body and mind, and also that, for this reason, men are troublesome one to another. Again, it follows that men are naturally envious (III. xxiv. note, and III. xxxii. note), rejoicing in the shortcomings of their equals, and feeling pain at their virtues. For whenever a man conceives his own actions, he is affected with pleasure (III. liii.), in proportion as his actions display more perfection, and he conceives them more distinctly—that is (II. xl. note), in proportion as he can distinguish them from others, and regard them as something special. Therefore, a man will take most pleasure in contemplating himself, when he contemplates some quality which he denies to others. But, if that which he affirms of himself be attributable to the idea of man or animals in general, he will not be so greatly pleased: he will, on the contrary, feel pain, if he conceives that his own actions fall short when compared with those of others. This pain (III. xxviii.) he will endeavour to remove, by putting a wrong construction on the actions of his equals, or by, as far as he can, embellishing his own.

It is thus apparent that men are naturally prone to hatred and envy, which latter is fostered by their education. For parents are accustomed to incite their children to virtue solely by the spur of honour and envy. But, perhaps, some will scruple to assent to what I have said, because we not seldom admire men's virtues, and venerate their possessors. In order to remove such doubts, I append the following corollary.

Corollary.—No one envies the virtue of anyone who is not his equal.

Proof.—Envy is a species of hatred (III. xxiv. note) or (III. xiii. note) pain, that is (III. xi. note), a modification whereby a man's power of activity, or endeavour towards activity, is checked. But a man does not endeavour or desire to do anything, which cannot follow from his nature as it is given; therefore a man will not desire any power of activity or virtue (which is the same thing) to be attributed to him, that is appropriate to another's nature and foreign to his own; hence his desire cannot be checked, nor he himself pained by the contemplation of virtue in some one unlike himself, consequently he cannot envy such an one. But he can envy his equal, who is assumed to have the same nature as himself. Q.E.D.

Note.—When, therefore, as we said in the note to III. lii., we venerate a man, through wonder at his prudence, fortitude, &c., we do so, because we conceive those qualities to be peculiar to him, and not as common to our nature; we, therefore, no more envy their possessor, than we envy trees for being tall, or lions for being courageous.

PROP. LVI. *There are as many kinds of pleasure, of pain, of desire, and of every emotion compounded of these, such as vacillations of spirit, or derived from these, such as love, hatred, hope, fear, &c., as there are kinds of objects whereby we are affected.*

Proof.—Pleasure and pain, and consequently the emotions compounded thereof, or derived therefrom, are passions, or passive states (III. xi. note); now we are necessarily passive (III. i.), in so far as we have inadequate ideas; and only in so far as we have such ideas are we passive (III. iii.); that is, we are only necessarily passive (II. xl. note), in so far as we conceive, or (II. xvii. and note) in so far as we are affected by an emotion, which involves the nature of our own body, and the nature of an external body. Wherefore the nature of every passive state must necessarily be so explained, that the nature of the object whereby we are affected be expressed. Namely, the pleasure, which arises from, say, the object A, involves the nature of that object A, and the pleasure, which arises from the object B, involves the nature of the object B; wherefore these two pleasurable emotions are by nature different, inasmuch as the causes whence they arise are by nature different. So again the emotion of pain, which arises from one object, is by nature different from the pain arising from another object, and, similarly, in the case of love, hatred, hope, fear, vacillation, &c.

Thus, there are necessarily as many kinds of pleasure, pain, love, hatred, &c., as there are kinds of objects whereby we are affected. Now desire is each man's essence or nature, in so far as it is conceived as determined to a particular action by any given modification of itself (III. ix. note); therefore, according as a man is affected through external causes by this or that kind of pleasure, pain, love, hatred, &c., in other words, according as his nature is disposed in this or that manner, so will his desire be of one kind or another, and the nature of one desire must necessarily differ from the nature of another desire, as widely as the emotions differ, wherefrom each desire arose. Thus there are as many kinds of desire, as there are kinds of pleasure, pain, love, &c., consequently (by what has been shown) there are as many kinds of desire, as there are kinds of objects whereby we are affected. *Q.E.D.*

Note.—Among the kinds of emotions, which, by the last proposition, must be very numerous, the chief are *luxury, drunkenness, lust, avarice,* and *ambition,* being merely species of love or desire, displaying the nature of those emotions in a manner varying according to the object, with which they are concerned. For by luxury, drunkenness, lust, avarice, ambition, &c., we simply mean the immoderate love of feasting, drinking, venery, riches, and fame. Furthermore, these emotions, in so far as we distinguish them from others merely by the objects wherewith they are concerned, have no contraries. For *temperance, sobriety,* and *chastity,* which we are wont to oppose to luxury, drunkenness, and lust, are not emotions or passive states, but indicate a power of the mind which moderates the last-named emotions. However, I cannot here explain the remaining kinds of emotions (seeing that they are as numerous as the kinds of objects), nor, if I could, would it be necessary. It is sufficient for our purpose, namely, to determine the strength of the emotions, and the mind's power over them, to have a general definition of each emotion. It is sufficient, I repeat, to understand the general properties of the emotions and the mind, to enable us to determine the quality and extent of the mind's power in moderating and checking the emotions. Thus, though there is a great difference between various emotions of love, hatred, or desire, for instance between love felt towards children, and love felt towards a wife, there is no need for us to take cognizance of such differences, or to track out further the nature and origin of the emotions.

PROP. LVII. *Any emotion of a given individual differs from the emotion of another individual, only in so far as the essence of the one individual differs from the essence of the other.*

Proof.—This proposition is evident from Ax. i. (which see after Lemma iii. Prop. xiii. Part ii.). Nevertheless, we will prove it from the nature of the three primary emotions.

All emotions are attributable to desire, pleasure, or pain, as their definitions above given show. But desire is each man's nature or essence (III. ix. note); therefore desire in one individual differs from desire in another individual, only in so far as the nature or essence of the one differs from the nature or essence

of the other. Again, pleasure and pain are passive states or
passions, whereby every man's power or endeavour to persist
in his being is increased or diminished, helped or hindered
(III. xi. and note). But by the endeavour to persist in its being, in so far as it is attributable to mind and body in conjunction, we mean appetite and desire (III. ix. note); therefore pleasure and pain are identical with desire or appetite,
in so far as by external causes they are increased or diminished, helped or hindered, in other words, they are every
man's nature; wherefore the pleasure and pain felt by one
man differ from the pleasure and pain felt by another man,
only in so far as the nature or essence of the one man differs
from the essence of the other; consequently, any emotion of
one individual only differs, &c. *Q.E.D.*

Note.—Hence it follows, that the emotions of the animals
which are called irrational (for after learning the origin of
mind we cannot doubt that brutes feel) only differ from
man's emotions, to the extent that brute nature differs from
human nature. Horse and man are alike carried away by
the desire of procreation; but the desire of the former is equine,
the desire of the latter is human. So also the lusts and appetites of insects, fishes, and birds must needs vary according to
the several natures. Thus, although each individual lives content and rejoices in that nature belonging to him wherein
he has his being, yet the life, wherein each is content and
rejoices, is nothing else but the idea, or soul, of the said individual, and hence the joy of one only differs in nature from
the joy of another, to the extent that the essence of one differs from the essence of another. Lastly, it follows from the
foregoing proposition, that there is no small difference between the joy which actuates, say, a drunkard, and the joy
possessed by a philosopher, as I just mention here by the way.
Thus far I have treated of the emotions attributable to man,
in so far as he is passive. It remains to add a few words on
those attributable to him in so far as he is active.

PROP. LVIII. *Besides pleasure and desire, which are passivi-
ties or passions, there are other emotions derived from pleasure and desire which are attributable to us in so far as we
are active.*

Proof.—When the mind conceives itself and its power of activity, it feels pleasure (III. liii.): now the mind necessarily contemplates itself, when it conceives a true or adequate idea (II. xliii.). But the mind does conceive certain adequate ideas (II. xl. note ii.). Therefore, it feels pleasure in so far as it conceives adequate ideas; that is, in so far as it is active (III. i.). Again, the mind, both in so far as it has clear and distinct ideas, and in so far as it has confused ideas, endeavours to persist in its own being (III. ix.); but by such an endeavour we mean desire (by the note to the same Prop.); therefore, desire is also attributable to us, in so far as we understand, or (III. i.) in so far as we are active. *Q.E.D.*

PROP. LIX. *Among all the emotions attributable to the mind as active, there are none which cannot be referred to pleasure or pain.*

Proof.—All emotions can be referred to desire, pleasure, or pain, as their definitions, already given, show. Now by pain we mean that the mind's power of thinking is diminished or checked (III. xi. and note); therefore, in so far as the mind feels pain, its power of understanding, that is, of activity, is diminished or checked (III. i.); therefore, no painful emotions can be attributed to the mind in virtue of its being active, but only emotions of pleasure and desire, which (by the last Prop.) are attributable to the mind in that condition. *Q.E.D.*

Note.—All actions following from emotion, which are attributable to the mind in virtue of its understanding, I set down to *strength of character* (*fortitudo*), which I divide into *courage* (*animositas*) and *highmindedness* (*generositas*). By *courage* I mean *the desire whereby every man strives to preserve his own being in accordance solely with the dictates of reason.* By *highmindedness* I mean *the desire whereby every man endeavours, solely under the dictates of reason, to aid other men and to unite them to himself in friendship.* Those actions, therefore, which have regard solely to the good of the agent I set down to courage, those which aim at the good of others I set down to highmindedness. Thus temperance, sobriety, and presence of mind in danger, &c., are varieties of courage; courtesy, mercy, &c., are varieties of highmindedness.

I think I have thus explained, and displayed through

their primary causes the principal emotions and vacillations of spirit, which arise from the combination of the three primary emotions, to wit, desire, pleasure, and pain. It is evident from what I have said, that we are in many ways driven about by external causes, and that like waves of the sea driven by contrary winds we toss to and fro unwitting of the issue and of our fate. But I have said, that I have only set forth the chief conflicting emotions, not all that might be given. For, by proceeding in the same way as above, we can easily show that love is united to repentance, scorn, shame, &c. I think everyone will agree from what has been said, that the emotions may be compounded one with another in so many ways, and so many variations may arise therefrom, as to exceed all possibility of computation. However, for my purpose, it is enough to have enumerated the most important; to reckon up the rest which I have omitted would be more curious than profitable. It remains to remark concerning love, that it very often happens that while we are enjoying a thing which we longed for, the body, from the act of enjoyment, acquires a new disposition, whereby it is determined in another way, other images of things are aroused in it, and the mind begins to conceive and desire something fresh. For example, when we conceive something which generally delights us with its flavour, we desire to enjoy, that is, to eat it. But whilst we are thus enjoying it, the stomach is filled and the body is otherwise disposed. If, therefore, when the body is thus otherwise disposed, the image of the food which is present be stimulated, and consequently the endeavour or desire to eat it be stimulated also, the new disposition of the body will feel repugnance to the desire or attempt, and consequently the presence of the food which we formerly longed for will become odious. This revulsion of feeling is called *satiety* or weariness. For the rest, I have neglected the outward modifications of the body observable in emotions, such, for instance, as trembling, pallor, sobbing, laughter, &c., for these are attributable to the body only, without any reference to the mind. Lastly, the definitions of the emotions require to be supplemented in a few points; I will therefore repeat them, interpolating such observations as I think should here and there be added.

DEFINITIONS OF THE EMOTIONS

I. *Desire* is the actual essence of man, in so far as it is conceived, as determined to a particular activity by some given modification of itself.

Explanation.—We have said above, in the note to Prop. ix. of this part, that desire is appetite, with consciousness thereof; further, that appetite is the essence of man, in so far as it is determined to act in a way tending to promote its own persistence. But, in the same note, I also remarked that, strictly speaking, I recognize no distinction between appetite and desire. For whether a man be conscious of his appetite or not, it remains one and the same appetite. Thus, in order to avoid the appearance of tautology, I have refrained from explaining desire by appetite; but I have taken care to define it in such a manner, as to comprehend, under one head, all those endeavours of human nature, which we distinguish by the terms appetite, will, desire, or impulse. I might, indeed, have said, that desire is the essence of man, in so far as it is conceived as determined to a particular activity; but from such a definition (cf. II. xxiii.) it would not follow that the mind can be conscious of its desire or appetite. Therefore, in order to imply the cause of such consciousness, it was necessary to add, *in so far as it is determined by some given modification,* &c. For, by a modification of man's essence, we understand every disposition of the said essence, whether such disposition be innate, or whether it be conceived solely under the attribute of thought, or solely under the attribute of extension, or whether, lastly, it be referred simultaneously to both these attributes. By the term desire, then, I here mean all man's endeavours, impulses, appetites, and volitions, which vary according to each man's disposition, and are, therefore, not seldom opposed one to another, according as a man is drawn in different directions, and knows not where to turn.

II. *Pleasure* is the transition of a man from a less to a greater perfection.

III. *Pain* is the transition of a man from a greater to a less perfection.

Explanation.—I say transition: for pleasure is not perfection itself. For, if man were born with the perfection to which he passes, he would possess the same, without the emotion of pleasure. This appears more clearly from the consideration of the contrary emotion, pain. No one can deny, that pain consists in the transition to a less perfection, and not in the less perfection itself: for a man cannot be pained, in so far as he partakes of perfection of any degree. Neither can we say, that pain consists in the absence of a greater perfection. For absence is nothing, whereas the emotion of pain is an activity; wherefore this activity can only be the activity of transition from a greater to a less perfection—in other words, it is an activity whereby a man's power of action is lessened or constrained (cf. III. xi. note). I pass over the definitions of merriment, stimulation, melancholy, and grief, because these terms are generally used in reference to the body, and are merely kinds of pleasure or pain.

IV. *Wonder* is the conception (*imaginatio*) of anything, wherein the mind comes to a stand, because the particular concept in question has no connection with other concepts (cf. III. lii. and note).

Explanation.—In the note to II. xviii. we showed the reason, why the mind, from the contemplation of one thing, straightway falls to the contemplation of another thing, namely, because the images of the two things are so associated and arranged, that one follows the other. This state of association is impossible, if the image of the thing be new; the mind will then be at a stand in the contemplation thereof, until it is determined by other causes to think of something else.

Thus the conception of a new object, considered in itself, is of the same nature as other conceptions; hence, I do not include wonder among the emotions, nor do I see why I should so include it, inasmuch as this distraction of the mind arises from no positive cause drawing away the mind from other objects, but merely from the absence of a cause, which should determine the mind to pass from the contemplation of one object to the contemplation of another.

I, therefore, recognize only three primitive or primary emotions (as I said in the note to III. xi.), namely, pleasure, pain,

and desire. I have spoken of wonder, simply because it is customary to speak of certain emotions springing from the three
primitive ones by different names, when they are referred to
the objects of our wonder. I am led by the same motive to
add a definition of contempt.

V. *Contempt* is the conception of anything which touches
the mind so little, that its presence leads the mind to imagine
those qualities which are not in it rather than such as are in
it (cf. III. lii. note).

The definitions of veneration and scorn I here pass over, for
I am not aware that any emotions are named after them.

VI. *Love* is pleasure, accompanied by the idea of an external
cause.

Explanation.—This definition explains sufficiently clearly
the essence of love; the definition given by those authors who
say that love is *the lover's wish to unite himself to the loved
object* expresses a property, but not the essence of love; and,
as such authors have not sufficiently discerned love's essence,
they have been unable to acquire a true conception of its properties, accordingly their definition is on all hands admitted to
be very obscure. It must, however, be noted, that when I say
that it is a property of love, that the lover should wish to unite
himself to the beloved object, I do not here mean by *wish*
consent, or conclusion, or a free decision of the mind (for I
have shown such, in II. xlviii., to be fictitious); neither do I
mean a desire of being united to the loved object when it is
absent, or of continuing in its presence when it is at hand;
for love can be conceived without either of these desires; but
by *wish* I mean the contentment, which is in the lover, on
account of the presence of the beloved object, whereby the
pleasure of the lover is strengthened, or at least maintained.

VII. *Hatred* is pain, accompanied by the idea of an external
cause.

Explanation.—These observations are easily grasped after
what has been said in the explanation of the preceding definition (cf. also III. xiii. note).

VIII. *Inclination* is pleasure, accompanied by the idea of
something which is accidentally a cause of pleasure.

IX. *Aversion* is pain, accompanied by the idea of something which is accidentally the cause of pain (cf. III. xv. note).

X. *Devotion* is love towards one whom we admire.

Explanation.—Wonder (*admiratio*) arises (as we have shown, III. lii.) from the novelty of a thing. If, therefore, it happens that the object of our wonder is often conceived by us, we shall cease to wonder at it; thus we see, that the emotion of devotion readily degenerates into simple love.

XI. *Derision* is pleasure arising from our conceiving the presence of a quality, which we despise, in an object which we hate.

Explanation.—In so far as we despise a thing which we hate, we deny existence thereof (III. lii. note), and to that extent rejoice (III. xx.). But since we assume that man hates that which he derides, it follows that the pleasure in question is not without alloy (cf. III. xlvii. note).

XII. *Hope* is an inconstant pleasure, arising from the idea of something past or future, whereof we to a certain extent doubt the issue.

XIII. *Fear* is an inconstant pain arising from the idea of something past or future, whereof we to a certain extent doubt the issue (cf. III. xviii. note).

Explanation.—From these definitions it follows, that there is no hope unmingled with fear, and no fear unmingled with hope. For he, who depends on hope and doubts concerning the issue of anything, is assumed to conceive something, which excludes the existence of the said thing in the future; therefore he, to this extent, feels pain (cf. III. xix.); consequently, while dependent on hope, he fears for the issue. Contrariwise he, who fears, in other words doubts, concerning the issue of something which he hates, also conceives something which excludes the existence of the thing in question; to this extent he feels pleasure, and consequently to this extent he hopes that it will turn out as he desires (III. xx.).

XIV. *Confidence* is pleasure arising from the idea of something past or future, wherefrom all cause of doubt has been removed.

XV. *Despair* is pain arising from the idea of something past or future, wherefrom all cause of doubt has been removed.

Explanation.—Thus confidence springs from hope, and despair from fear, when all cause for doubt as to the issue of an event has been removed: this comes to pass, because man conceives something past or future as present and regards it as such, or else because he conceives other things, which exclude the existence of the causes of his doubt. For, although we can never be absolutely certain of the issue of any particular event (II. xxxi. Coroll.), it may nevertheless happen that we feel no doubt concerning it. For we have shown, that to feel no doubt concerning a thing is not the same as to be quite certain of it (II. xlix. note). Thus it may happen that we are affected by the same emotion of pleasure or pain concerning a thing past or future, as concerning the conception of a thing present; this I have already shown in III. xviii., to which, with its note, I refer the reader.

XVI. *Joy* is pleasure accompanied by the idea of something past, which has had an issue beyond our hope.

XVII. *Disappointment* is pain accompanied by the idea of something past, which has had an issue contrary to our hope.

XVIII. *Pity* is pain accompanied by the idea of evil, which has befallen someone else whom we conceive to be like ourselves (cf. III. xxii. note, and III. xxvii. note).

Explanation.—Between pity and sympathy (*misericordia*) there seems to be no difference, unless perhaps that the former term is used in reference to a particular action, and the latter in reference to a disposition.

XIX. *Approval* is love towards one who has done good to another.

XX. *Indignation* is hatred towards one who has done evil to another.

Explanation.—I am aware that these terms are employed in senses somewhat different from those usually assigned. But my purpose is to explain, not the meaning of words, but the nature of things. I therefore make use of such terms, as may convey my meaning without any violent departure from their ordinary signification. One statement of my method will suffice. As for the cause of the above-named emotions see III. xxvii. Coroll. i., and III. xxii. note.

XXI. *Partiality* is thinking too highly of anyone because of the love we bear him.

XXII. *Disparagement* is thinking too meanly of anyone, because we hate him.

Explanation.—Thus partiality is an effect of love, and disparagement an effect of hatred: so that *partiality* may also be defined as *love, in so far as it induces a man to think too highly of a beloved object.* Contrariwise, *disparagement* may be defined as *hatred, in so far as it induces a man to think too meanly of a hated object.* Cf. III. xxvi. note.

XXIII. *Envy* is hatred, in so far as it induces a man to be pained by another's good fortune, and to rejoice in another's evil fortune.

Explanation.—Envy is generally opposed to sympathy, which, by doing some violence to the meaning of the word, may therefore be thus defined:

XXIV. *Sympathy* (*misericordia*) is love, in so far as it induces a man to feel pleasure at another's good fortune, and pain at another's evil fortune.

Explanation.—Concerning envy see the notes to III. xxiv. and xxxii. These emotions also arise from pleasure or pain accompanied by the idea of something external, as cause either in itself or accidentally. I now pass on to other emotions, which are accompanied by the idea of something within as a cause.

XXV. *Self-approval* is pleasure arising from a man's contemplation of himself and his own power of action.

XXVI. *Humility* is pain arising from a man's contemplation of his own weakness of body or mind.

Explanation.—Self-complacency is opposed to humility, in so far as we thereby mean pleasure arising from a contemplation of our own power of action; but, in so far as we mean thereby pleasure accompanied by the idea of any action which we believe we have performed by the free decision of our mind, it is opposed to repentance, which we may thus define:

XXVII. *Repentance* is pain accompanied by the idea of some action, which we believe we have performed by the free decision of our mind.

Explanation.—The causes of these emotions we have set forth in III. li. note, and in III. liii. liv. lv. and note. Concerning the free decision of the mind see II. xxxv. note. This is perhaps the place to call attention to the fact, that it is nothing wonderful that all those actions, which are commonly called *wrong*, are followed by pain, and all those, which are called *right*, are followed by pleasure. We can easily gather from what has been said, that this depends in great measure on education. Parents, by reprobating the former class of actions, and by frequently chiding their children because of them, and also by persuading to and praising the latter class, have brought it about, that the former should be associated with pain and the latter with pleasure. This is confirmed by experience. For custom and religion are not the same among all men, but that which some consider sacred others consider profane, and what some consider honourable others consider disgraceful. According as each man has been educated, he feels repentance for a given action or glories therein.

XXVIII. *Pride* is thinking too highly of one's self from self-love.

Explanation.—Thus pride is different from partiality, for the latter term is used in reference to an external object, but pride is used of a man thinking too highly of himself. However, as partiality is the effect of love, so is pride the effect or property of *self-love*, which may therefore be thus defined, *love of self or self-approval, in so far as it leads a man to think too highly of himself.* To this emotion there is no contrary. For no one thinks too meanly of himself because of self-hatred; I say that no one thinks too meanly of himself, in so far as he conceives that he is incapable of doing this or that. For whatsoever a man imagines that he is incapable of doing, he imagines this of necessity, and by that notion he is so disposed, that he really cannot do that which he conceives that he cannot do. For, so long as he conceives that he cannot do it, so long is he not determined to do it, and consequently so long is it impossible for him to do it. However, if we consider such matters as only depend on opinion, we shall find it conceivable that a man may think too meanly of himself; for it may happen, that a man, sorrowfully regarding his own weakness, should imagine that he is despised by all men, while the rest of the world are thinking of nothing less than of despising him. Again, a man may think too meanly of himself, if he deny of himself in the present something in relation to a future time of which he is uncertain. As, for instance, if he should say that he is unable to form any clear conceptions, or that he can desire and do nothing but what is wicked and base, &c. We may also say, that a man thinks too meanly of himself, when we see him from excessive fear of shame refusing to do things which others, his equals, venture. We can, therefore, set down as a contrary to pride an emotion which I will call self-abasement, for as from self-complacency springs pride, so from humility springs self-abasement, which I will accordingly thus define:

XXIX. *Self-abasement* is thinking too meanly of one's self by reason of pain.

Explanation.—We are nevertheless generally accustomed to oppose pride to humility, but in that case we pay more attention to the effect of either emotion than to its nature. We are wont to call *proud* the man who boasts too much (III. xxx. note), who talks of nothing but his own virtues and other people's faults, who wishes to be first; and lastly who goes through life with a style and pomp suitable to those far above him in station. On the other hand, we call *humble* the man who too often blushes, who confesses his faults, who sets forth other men's virtues, and who, lastly, walks with bent head and is negligent of his attire. However, these emotions, humility and self-abasement, are extremely rare. For human nature, considered in itself, strives against them as much as it can (see III. xiii. liv.); hence those, who are believed to be most self-abased and humble, are generally in reality the most ambitious and envious.

XXX. *Honour*[6] is pleasure accompanied by the idea of some action of our own, which we believe to be praised by others.

XXXI. *Shame* is pain accompanied by the idea of some action of our own, which we believe to be blamed by others.

Explanation.—On this subject see the note to III. xxx. But we should here remark the difference which exists between shame and modesty. Shame is the pain following the deed whereof we are ashamed. Modesty is the fear or dread of

[6] *Gloria.*

shame, which restrains a man from committing a base action. Modesty is usually opposed to shamelessness, but the latter is not an emotion, as I will duly show; however, the names of the emotions (as I have remarked already) have regard rather to their exercise than to their nature.

I have now fulfilled my task of explaining the emotions arising from pleasure and pain. I therefore proceed to treat of those which I refer to desire.

XXXII. *Regret* is the desire or appetite to possess something, kept alive by the remembrance of the said thing, and at the same time constrained by the remembrance of other things which exclude the existence of it.

Explanation.—When we remember a thing, we are by that very fact, as I have already said more than once, disposed to contemplate it with the same emotion as if it were something present; but this disposition or endeavour, while we are awake, is generally checked by the images of things which exclude the existence of that which we remember. Thus when we remember something which affected us with a certain pleasure, we by that very fact endeavour to regard it with the same emotion of pleasure as though it were present, but this endeavour is at once checked by the remembrance of things which exclude the existence of the thing in question. Wherefore regret is, strictly speaking, a pain opposed to that pleasure, which arises from the absence of something we hate (cf. III. xlvii. note). But, as the name regret seems to refer to desire, I set this emotion down, among the emotions springing from desire.

XXXIII. *Emulation* is the desire of something, engendered in us by our conception that others have the same desire.

Explanation.—He who runs away, because he sees others running away, or he who fears, because he sees others in fear; or again, he who, on seeing that another man has burnt his hand, draws towards him his own hand, and moves his body as though his own hand were burnt; such an one can be said to imitate another's emotion, but not to emulate him; not because the causes of emulation and imitation are different, but because it has become customary to speak of emulation only in him, who imitates that which we deem to be honourable, useful, or pleasant. As to the cause of emulation, cf.

III. xxvii. and note. The reason why this emotion is generally coupled with envy may be seen from III. xxxii. and note.

XXXIV. *Thankfulness* or *Gratitude* is the desire or zeal springing from love, whereby we endeavour to benefit him, who with similar feelings of love has conferred a benefit on us. Cf. III. xxxix. note and xl.

XXXV. *Benevolence* is the desire of benefiting one whom we pity. Cf. III. xxvii. note.

XXXVI. *Anger* is the desire, whereby through hatred we are induced to injure one whom we hate, III. xxxix.

XXXVII. *Revenge* is the desire whereby we are induced, through mutual hatred, to injure one who, with similar feelings, has injured us. (See III. xl. Coroll. ii. and note.)

XXXVIII. *Cruelty* or *savageness* is the desire, whereby a man is impelled to injure one whom we love or pity.

Explanation.—To cruelty is opposed clemency, which is not a passive state of the mind, but a power whereby man restrains his anger and revenge.

XXXIX. *Timidity* is the desire to avoid a greater evil, which we dread, by undergoing a lesser evil. Cf. III. xxxix. note.

XL. *Daring* is the desire, whereby a man is set on to do something dangerous which his equals fear to attempt.

XLI. *Cowardice* is attributed to one, whose desire is checked by the fear of some danger which his equals dare to encounter.

Explanation.—Cowardice is, therefore, nothing else but the fear of some evil, which most men are wont not to fear; hence I do not reckon it among the emotions springing from desire. Nevertheless, I have chosen to explain it here, because, in so far as we look to the desire, it is truly opposed to the emotion of daring.

XLII. *Consternation* is attributed to one, whose desire of avoiding evil is checked by amazement at the evil which he fears.

Explanation.—Consternation is, therefore, a species of cowardice. But, inasmuch as consternation arises from a double fear, it may be more conveniently defined as a fear which keeps a man so bewildered and wavering, that he is not able to remove the evil. I say bewildered, in so far as we understand his desire of removing the evil to be constrained by his amazement. I say wavering, in so far as we understand the said desire to be constrained by the fear of another evil, which equally torments him: whence it comes to pass that he knows not, which he may avert of the two. On this subject, see III. xxxix. note, and III. lii. note. Concerning cowardice and daring, see III. li. note.

XLIII. *Courtesy*, or *deference* (*Humanitas seu modestia*), is the desire of acting in a way that should please men, and refraining from that which should displease them.

XLIV. *Ambition* is the immoderate desire of power.

Explanation.—Ambition is the desire, whereby all the emotions (cf. III. xxvii. and xxxi.) are fostered and strengthened; therefore this emotion can with difficulty be overcome. For, so long as a man is bound by any desire, he is at the same time necessarily bound by this. "The best men," says Cicero, "are especially led by honour. Even philosophers, when they write a book contemning honour, sign their names thereto," and so on.

XLV. *Luxury* is excessive desire, or even love of living sumptuously.

XLVI. *Intemperance* is the excessive desire and love of drinking.

XLVII. *Avarice* is the excessive desire and love of riches.

XLVIII. *Lust* is desire and love in the matter of sexual intercourse.

Explanation.—Whether this desire be excessive or not, it is still called lust. These last five emotions (as I have shown in III. lvi.) have no contraries. For deference is a species of ambition. Cf. III. xxix. note.

Again, I have already pointed out, that temperance, sobriety, and chastity indicate rather a power than a passivity of the mind. It may, nevertheless, happen, that an avaricious, an ambitious, or a timid man may abstain from excess in eating, drinking, or sexual indulgence, yet avarice, ambition, and fear are not contraries to luxury, drunkenness, and debauchery. For an avaricious man often is glad to gorge himself with food and drink at another man's expense. An ambitious man will restrain himself in nothing, so long as he thinks his indulgences are secret; and if he lives among drunkards and debauchees, he will, from the mere fact of being ambitious, be more prone to those vices. Lastly, a timid man does that which he would not. For though an avaricious man should, for the sake of avoiding death, cast his riches into the sea, he will none the less remain avaricious; so, also, if a lustful man is downcast, because he cannot follow his bent, he does not, on the ground of abstention, cease to be lustful. In fact, these emotions are not so much concerned with the actual feasting, drinking, &c., as with the appetite and love of such. Nothing, therefore, can be opposed to these emotions, but highmindedness and valour, whereof I will speak presently.

The definitions of jealousy and other waverings of the mind I pass over in silence, first, because they arise from the compounding of the emotions already described; secondly, because many of them have no distinctive names, which shows that it is sufficient for practical purposes to have merely a general knowledge of them. However, it is established from the definitions of the emotions, which we have set forth, that they all spring from desire, pleasure, or pain, or, rather, that there is nothing besides these three; wherefore each is wont to be called by a variety of names in accordance with its various relations and extrinsic tokens. If we now direct our attention to these primitive emotions, and to what has been said concerning the nature of the mind, we shall be able thus to define the emotions, in so far as they are referred to the mind only.

GENERAL DEFINITION OF THE EMOTIONS

Emotion, which is called a passivity of the soul, is a confused idea, whereby the mind affirms concerning its body, or any part thereof, a force for existence (*existendi vis*) greater or less than before, and by the presence of which the mind is determined to think of one thing rather than another.

Explanation.—I say, first, that emotion or passion of the soul is *a confused idea*. For we have shown that the mind is only passive, in so far as it has inadequate or confused ideas. (III. iii.) I say, further, *whereby the mind affirms concerning its body or any part thereof a force for existence greater than be-*

fore. For all the ideas of bodies, which we possess, denote rather the actual disposition of our own body (II. xvi. Coroll. ii.) than the nature of an external body. But the idea which constitutes the reality of an emotion must denote or express the disposition of the body, or of some part thereof, which is possessed by the body, or some part thereof, because its power of action or force for existence is increased or diminished, helped or hindered. But it must be noted that, when I say *a greater or less force for existence* than before, I do not mean that the mind compares the present with the past disposition of the body, but that the idea which constitutes the reality of an emotion affirms something of the body, which, in fact, involves more or less of reality than before.

And inasmuch as the essence of mind consists in the fact (II. xi. xiii.), that it affirms the actual existence of its own body, and inasmuch as we understand by perfection the very essence of a thing, it follows that the mind passes to greater or less perfection, when it happens to affirm concerning its own body, or any part thereof, something involving more or less reality than before.

When, therefore, I said above that the power of the mind is increased or diminished, I merely meant that the mind had formed of its own body, or of some part thereof, an idea involving more or less of reality, than it had already affirmed concerning its own body. For the excellence of ideas, and the actual power of thinking are measured by the excellence of the object. Lastly, I have added *by the presence of which the mind is determined to think of one thing rather than another*, so that, besides the nature of pleasure and pain, which the first part of the definition explains, I might also express the nature of desire.

PART IV OF HUMAN BONDAGE
OR THE STRENGTH OF THE EMOTIONS

PREFACE

Human infirmity in moderating and checking the emotions I name bondage: for, when a man is a prey to his emotions, he is not his own master, but lies at the mercy of fortune: so much so, that he is often compelled, while seeing that which is better for him, to follow that which is worse. Why this is so, and what is good or evil in the emotions, I propose to show in this part of my treatise. But, before I begin, it would be well to make a few prefatory observations on perfection and imperfection, good and evil.

When a man has purposed to make a given thing, and has brought it to perfection, his work will be pronounced perfect, not only by himself, but by everyone who rightly knows, or thinks that he knows, the intention and aim of its author. For instance, suppose anyone sees a work (which I assume to be not yet completed), and knows that the aim of the author of that work is to build a house, he will call the work imperfect; he will, on the other hand, call it perfect, as soon as he sees that it is carried through to the end, which its author had purposed for it. But if a man sees a work, the like whereof he has never seen before, and if he knows not the intention of the artificer, he plainly cannot know, whether that work be perfect or imperfect. Such seems to be the primary meaning of these terms.

But, after men began to form general ideas, to think out types of houses, buildings, towers, &c., and to prefer certain types to others, it came about, that each man called perfect that which he saw agree with the general idea he had formed of the thing in question, and called imperfect that which he saw agree less with his own preconceived type, even though it had evidently been completed in accordance with the idea of its artificer. This seems to be the only reason for calling natural phenomena, which, indeed, are not made with human hands, perfect or imperfect: for men are wont to form general ideas of things natural, no less than of things artificial, and such ideas they hold as types, believing that Nature (who they think does nothing without an object) has them in view, and has set them as types before herself. Therefore, when they behold something in Nature, which does not wholly conform to the preconceived type which they have formed of the thing in question, they say that Nature has fallen short or has blundered, and has left her work incomplete. Thus we see that men are wont to style natural phenomena perfect or imperfect rather from their own prejudices, than from true knowledge of what they pronounce upon.

Now we showed in the Appendix to Part I., that Nature does not work with an end in view. For the eternal and infinite Being, which we call God or Nature, acts by the same necessity as that whereby it exists. For we have shown, that by the same necessity of its nature, whereby it exists, it likewise works (I. xvi.). The reason or cause why God or Nature exists, and the reason why he acts, are one and the same. Therefore, as he does not exist for the sake of an end, so neither does he act for the sake of an end; of his existence and of his action there is neither origin nor end. Wherefore, a cause which is called final is nothing else but human desire, in so far as it is considered as the origin or cause of anything. For example, when we say that to be inhabited is the final cause of this or that house, we mean nothing more than that a man, conceiving the conveniences of household life, had a desire to build a house. Wherefore, the being inhabited, in so far as it is regarded as a final cause, is nothing else but this particular desire, which is really the efficient cause; it is regarded as the primary cause, because men are generally ignorant of the causes of their desires. They are, as I have often said already, conscious of their own actions and appetites, but ignorant of the causes whereby they are determined to any particular desire. Therefore, the common saying that Nature sometimes falls short, or blunders, and produces things which are imperfect, I set down among the glosses treated of in the Appendix to Part I. Perfection and imperfection, then, are in reality merely modes of thinking, or notions which we form from a comparison among one another of individuals of the same species; hence I said above (II. Def. vi.), that by reality and perfection I mean the same thing. For we are wont to refer all the individual things in nature to one genus, which is called the highest genus, namely, to the category of Being, whereto absolutely all individuals in nature belong. Thus, in so far as we refer the individuals in nature to this category, and comparing them one with another, find that some possess more of being or reality than others, we, to this extent, say that some are more perfect than others. Again, in so far as we attribute to them anything implying negation—as term, end, infirmity, etc.,—we, to this extent, call them imperfect, because they do not affect our mind so much as the things which we call perfect, not because they have any intrinsic deficiency, or because Nature has blundered. For nothing lies within the scope of a thing's nature, save that which follows from the necessity of the nature of its efficient cause, and whatsoever follows from the necessity of the nature of its efficient cause necessarily comes to pass.

As for the terms *good* and *bad*, they indicate no positive quality in things regarded in themselves, but are merely modes of thinking, or notions which we form from the comparison of things one with another. Thus one and the same thing can be at the same time good, bad, and indifferent. For instance, music is good for him that is melancholy, bad for him that mourns; for him that is deaf, it is neither good nor bad.

Nevertheless, though this be so, the terms should still be retained. For, inasmuch as we desire to form an idea of man as a type of human nature which we may hold in view, it will be useful for us to retain the terms in question, in the sense I have indicated.

In what follows, then, I shall mean by "good" that which

we certainly know to be a means of approaching more nearly to the type of human nature, which we have set before ourselves; by "bad," that which we certainly know to be a hindrance to us in approaching the said type. Again, we shall say that men are more perfect, or more imperfect, in proportion as they approach more or less nearly to the said type. For it must be specially remarked that, when I say that a man passes from a lesser to a greater perfection, or *vice versâ*, I do not mean that he is changed from one essence or reality to another; for instance, a horse would be as completely destroyed by being changed into a man, as by being changed into an insect. What I mean is, that we conceive the thing's power of action, in so far as this is understood by its nature, to be increased or diminished. Lastly, by perfection in general I shall, as I have said, mean reality—in other words, each thing's essence, in so far as it exists, and operates in a particular manner, and without paying any regard to its duration. For no given thing can be said to be more perfect, because it has passed a longer time in existence. The duration of things cannot be determined by their essence, for the essence of things involves no fixed and definite period of existence; but everything, whether it be more perfect or less perfect, will always be able to persist in existence with the same force wherewith it began to exist; wherefore, in this respect, all things are equal.

DEFINITIONS

I. By *good* I mean that which we certainly know to be useful to us.

II. By *evil* I mean that which we certainly know to be a hindrance to us in the attainment of any good.

(Concerning these terms see the foregoing preface towards the end.)

III. Particular things I call *contingent* in so far as, while regarding their essence only, we find nothing therein, which necessarily asserts their existence or excludes it.

IV. Particular things I call *possible* in so far as, while regarding the causes whereby they must be produced, we know not, whether such causes be determined for producing them.

(In I. xxxiii. note i., I drew no distinction between possible and contingent, because there was in that place no need to distinguish them accurately.)

V. By *conflicting emotions* I mean those which draw a man in different directions, though they are of the same kind, such as luxury and avarice, which are both species of love, and are contraries, not by nature, but by accident.

VI. What I mean by emotion felt towards a thing, future, present, and past, I explained in III. xviii., notes i. and ii., which see.

(But I should here also remark, that we can only distinctly conceive distance of space or time up to a certain definite limit; that is, all objects distant from us more than two hundred feet, or whose distance from the place where we are exceeds that which we can distinctly conceive, seem to be an equal distance from us, and all in the same plane; so also objects, whose time of existing is conceived as removed from the present by a longer interval than we can distinctly conceive, seem to be all equally distant from the present, and are set down, as it were, to the same moment of time.)

VII. By an *end,* for the sake of which we do something, I mean a desire.

VIII. By *virtue* (*virtus*) and *power* I mean the same thing; that is (III. vii.), virtue, in so far as it is referred to man, is a man's nature or essence, in so far as it has the power of effecting what can only be understood by the laws of that nature.

AXIOM

There is no individual thing in nature, than which there is not another more powerful and strong. Whatsoever thing be given, there is something stronger whereby it can be destroyed.

PROP. I. *No positive quality possessed by a false idea is removed by the presence of what is true in virtue of its being true.*

Proof.—Falsity consists solely in the privation of knowledge which inadequate ideas involve (II. xxxv.), nor have they

any positive quality on account of which they are called false
(II. xxxiii.); contrariwise, in so far as they are referred to
God, they are true (II. xxxii.). Wherefore, if the positive qual-
ity possessed by a false idea were removed by the pres-
ence of what is true, in virtue of its being true, a true idea
would then be removed by itself, which (IV. iii.) is absurd.
Therefore, no positive quality possessed by a false idea, &c.
Q.E.D.

Note.—This proposition is more clearly understood from II.
xvi. Coroll. ii. For imagination is an idea, which indicates
rather the present disposition of the human body than the
nature of the external body; not indeed distinctly, but confusedly; whence it comes to pass, that the mind is said to err.
For instance, when we look at the sun, we conceive that it
is distant from us about two hundred feet; in this judgment
we err, so long as we are in ignorance of its true distance;
when its true distance is known, the error is removed, but not
the imagination; or, in other words, the idea of the sun, which
only explains the nature of that luminary, in so far as the body
is affected thereby: wherefore, though we know the real distance, we shall still nevertheless imagine the sun to be near
us. For, as we said in II. xxxv. note, we do not imagine the
sun to be so near us, because we are ignorant of its true
distance, but because the mind conceives the magnitude of
the sun to the extent that the body is affected thereby. Thus,
when the rays of the sun falling on the surface of water are
reflected into our eyes, we imagine the sun as if it were in the
water, though we are aware of its real position; and similarly
other imaginations, wherein the mind is deceived, whether
they indicate the natural disposition of the body, or that its
power of activity is increased or diminished, are not contrary
to the truth, and do not vanish at its presence. It happens
indeed that, when we mistakenly fear an evil, the fear vanishes when we hear the true tidings; but the contrary also
happens, namely, that we fear an evil which will certainly
come, and our fear vanishes when we hear false tidings; thus
imaginations do not vanish at the presence of the truth, in
virtue of its being true, but because other imaginations,
stronger than the first, supervene and exclude the present ex-

istence of that which we imagined, as I have shown in II. xvii.

PROP. II. *We are only passive in so far as we are a part of Nature, which cannot be conceived by itself without other parts.*

Proof.—We are said to be passive, when something arises in us, whereof we are only a partial cause (III. Def. ii.), that is (III. Def. i.), something which cannot be deduced solely from the laws of our nature. We are passive therefore, in so far as we are a part of Nature, which cannot be conceived by itself without other parts. *Q.E.D.*

PROP. III. *The force whereby a man persists in existing is limited, and is infinitely surpassed by the power of external causes.*

Proof.—This is evident from the axiom of this part. For, when man is given, there is something else—say A—more powerful; when A is given, there is something else—say B—more powerful than A, and so on to infinity; thus the power of man is limited by the power of some other thing, and is infinitely surpassed by the power of external causes. *Q.E.D.*

PROP. IV. *It is impossible, that man should not be a part of Nature, or that he should be capable of undergoing no changes, save such as can be understood through his nature only as their adequate cause.*

Proof.—The power, whereby each particular thing, and consequently man, preserves his being, is the power of God or of Nature (I. xxiv. Coroll.); not in so far as it is infinite, but in so far as it can be explained by the actual human essence (III. vii.). Thus the power of man, in so far as it is explained through his own actual essence, is a part of the infinite power of God or Nature, in other words, of the essence thereof (I. xxxiv.). This was our first point. Again, if it were possible, that man should undergo no changes save such as can be understood solely through the nature of man, it would follow that he would not be able to die, but would always necessarily exist; this would be the necessary consequence of a cause whose power was either finite or infinite; namely, either of man's power only, inasmuch as he would be capable of removing from himself all changes which could spring from external causes; or of the infinite power of Nature, whereby all individual things would be so ordered, that man should be incapable of undergoing any changes save such as tended towards his own preservation. But the first alternative is absurd (by the last Prop., the proof of which is universal, and can be applied to all individual things). Therefore, if it be possible, that man should not be capable of undergoing any changes, save such as can be explained solely through his own nature, and consequently that he must always (as we have shown) necessarily exist; such a result must follow from the infinite power of God, and consequently (I. xvi.) from the necessity of the divine nature, in so far as it is regarded as affected by the idea of any given man, the whole order of nature as conceived under the attributes of extension and thought must be deducible. It would therefore follow (I. xxi.) that man is infinite, which (by the first part of this proof) is absurd. It is, therefore, impossible, that man should not undergo any changes save those whereof he is the adequate cause. *Q.E.D.*

Corollary.—Hence it follows, that man is necessarily always a prey to his passions, that he follows and obeys the general order of nature, and that he accommodates himself thereto, as much as the nature of things demands.

PROP. V. *The power and increase of every passion, and its persistence in existing are not defined by the power, whereby we ourselves endeavour to persist in existing, but by the power of an external cause compared with our own.*

Proof.—The essence of a passion cannot be explained through our essence alone (III. Deff. i. and ii.), that is (III. vii.), the power of a passion cannot be defined by the power, whereby we ourselves endeavour to persist in existing, but (as is shown in II. xvi.) must necessarily be defined by the power of an external cause compared with our own. *Q.E.D.*

PROP. VI. *The force of any passion or emotion can overcome the rest of a man's activities or power, so that the emotion becomes obstinately fixed to him.*

Proof.—The force and increase of any passion and its persistence in existing are defined by the power of an external cause compared with our own (by the foregoing Prop.);

therefore (IV. iii.) it can overcome a man's power, &c.
Q.E.D.

PROP. VII. *An emotion can only be controlled or destroyed by another emotion contrary thereto, and with more power for controlling emotion.*

Proof.—Emotion, in so far as it is referred to the mind, is an idea, whereby the mind affirms of its body a greater or less force of existence than before (cf. the general Definition of the Emotions at the end of Part III.). When, therefore, the mind is assailed by any emotion, the body is at the same time affected with a modification whereby its power of activity is increased or diminished. Now this modification of the body (IV. v.) receives from its cause the force for persistence in its being; which force can only be checked or destroyed by a bodily cause (II. vi.), in virtue of the body being affected with a modification contrary to (III. v.) and stronger than itself (IV. Ax.); wherefore (II. xii.) the mind is affected by the idea of a modification contrary to, and stronger than the former modification, in other words, (by the general Definition of the Emotions) the mind will be affected by an emotion contrary to and stronger than the former emotion, which will exclude or destroy the existence of the former emotion; thus an emotion cannot be destroyed nor controlled except by a contrary and stronger emotion. Q.E.D.

Corollary.—An emotion, in so far as it is referred to the mind, can only be controlled or destroyed through an idea of a modification of the body contrary to, and stronger than, that which we are undergoing. For the emotion which we undergo can only be checked or destroyed by an emotion contrary to, and stronger than, itself, in other words, (by the general Definition of the Emotions) only by an idea of a modification of the body contrary to, and stronger than, the modification which we undergo.

PROP. VIII. *The knowledge of good and evil is nothing else but the emotions of pleasure or pain in so far as we are conscious thereof.*

Proof.—We call a thing good or evil, when it is of service or the reverse in preserving our being (IV. Deff. i. and ii.),

that is (III. vii.), when it increases or diminishes, helps or
hinders, our power of activity. Thus, in so far as we perceive
that a thing affects us with pleasure or pain, we call it good
or evil; wherefore the knowledge of good and evil is nothing
else but the idea of the pleasure or pain, which necessarily
follows from that pleasurable or painful emotion (II. xxii.).
But this idea is united to the emotion in the same way as
mind is united to body (II. xxi.); that is, there is no real
distinction between this idea and the emotion or idea of the
modification of the body, save in conception only. Therefore
the knowledge of good and evil is nothing else but the emotion, in so far as we are conscious thereof. *Q.E.D.*

Prop. IX. *An emotion, whereof we conceive the cause to
be with us at the present time, is stronger than if we did not
conceive the cause to be with us.*

Proof.—Imagination or conception is the idea, by which the
mind regards a thing as present (II. xvii. note), but which
indicates the disposition of the mind rather than the nature
of the external thing (II. xvi. Coroll. ii.). An emotion is therefore a conception, in so far as it indicates the disposition of
the body. But a conception (by II. xvii.) is stronger, so long
as we conceive nothing which excludes the present existence
of the external object; wherefore an emotion is also stronger
or more intense, when we conceive the cause to be with us
at the present time, than when we do not conceive the cause
to be with us. *Q.E.D.*

Note.—When I said above in III. xviii. that we are affected
by the image of what is past or future with the same emotion
as if the thing conceived were present, I expressly stated, that
this is only true in so far as we look solely to the image of the
thing in question itself; for the thing's nature is unchanged,
whether we have conceived it or not; I did not deny that the
image becomes weaker, when we regard as present to us other
things which exclude the present existence of the future object: I did not expressly call attention to the fact, because I
purposed to treat of the strength of the emotions in this part
of my work.

Corollary.—The image of something past or future, that is,
of a thing which we regard as in relation to time past or time

future, to the exclusion of time present, is, when other conditions are equal, weaker than the image of something present; consequently an emotion felt towards what is past or future is less intense, other conditions being equal, than an emotion felt towards something present.

PROP. X. *Towards something future, which we conceive as close at hand, we are affected more intensely, than if we conceive that its time for existence is separated from the present by a longer interval; so too by the remembrance of what we conceive to have not long passed away we are affected more intensely, than if we conceive that it has long passed away.*

Proof.—In so far as we conceive a thing as close at hand, or not long passed away, we conceive that which excludes the presence of the object less, than if its period of future existence were more distant from the present, or if it had long passed away (this is obvious); therefore (by the foregoing Prop.) we are, so far, more intensely affected towards it. Q.E.D.

Corollary.—From the remarks made in Def. vi. of this part it follows that, if objects are separated from the present by a longer period than we can define in conception, though their dates of occurrence be widely separated one from the other, they all affect us equally faintly.

PROP. XI. *An emotion towards that which we conceive as necessary is, when other conditions are equal, more intense than an emotion towards that which is possible, or contingent, or non-necessary.*

Proof.—In so far as we conceive a thing to be necessary, we, to that extent, affirm its existence; on the other hand we deny a thing's existence, in so far as we conceive it not to be necessary (I. xxxiii. note i.); wherefore (IV. ix.) an emotion towards that which is necessary is, other conditions being equal, more intense than an emotion towards that which is non-necessary. Q.E.D.

PROP. XII. *An emotion towards a thing, which we know not to exist at the present time, and which we conceive as possible, is more intense, other conditions being equal, than an emotion towards a thing contingent.*

Proof.—In so far as we conceive a thing as contingent, we

are affected by the conception of some further thing, which would assert the existence of the former (IV. Def. iii.); but, on the other hand, we (by hypothesis) conceive certain things, which exclude its present existence. But, in so far as we conceive a thing to be possible in the future, we thereby conceive things which assert its existence (IV. iv.), that is (III. xviii.), things which promote hope or fear: wherefore an emotion towards something possible is more vehement. *Q.E.D.*

Corollary.—An emotion towards a thing, which we know not to exist in the present, and which we conceive as contingent, is far fainter, than if we conceive the thing to be present with us.

Proof.—Emotion towards a thing, which we conceive to exist, is more intense than it would be, if we conceived the thing as future (IV. ix. Coroll.), and is much more vehement, than if the future time be conceived as far distant from the present (IV. x.). Therefore an emotion towards a thing, whose period of existence we conceive to be far distant from the present, is far fainter, than if we conceive the thing as present; it is, nevertheless, more intense, than if we conceived the thing as contingent, wherefore an emotion towards a thing, which we regard as contingent, will be far fainter, than if we conceived the thing to be present with us. *Q.E.D.*

PROP. XIII. *Emotion towards a thing contingent, which we know not to exist in the present, is, other conditions being equal, fainter than an emotion towards a thing past.*

Proof.—In so far as we conceive a thing as contingent, we are not affected by the image of any other thing, which asserts the existence of the said thing (IV. Def. iii.), but, on the other hand (by hypothesis), we conceive certain things excluding its present existence. But, in so far as we conceive it in relation to time past, we are assumed to conceive something, which recalls the thing to memory, or excites the image thereof (II. xviii. and note), which is so far the same as regarding it as present (II. xvii. Coroll.). Therefore (IV. ix.) an emotion towards a thing contingent, which we know does not exist in the present, is fainter, other conditions being equal, than an emotion towards a thing past. *Q.E.D.*

PROP. XIV. *A true knowledge of good and evil cannot check any emotion by virtue of being true, but only in so far as it is considered as an emotion.*

Proof.—An emotion is an idea, whereby the mind affirms of its body a greater or less force of existing than before (by the general Definition of the Emotions); therefore it has no positive quality, which can be destroyed by the presence of what is true; consequently the knowledge of good and evil cannot, by virtue of being true, restrain any emotion. But, in so far as such knowledge is an emotion (IV. viii.) if it have more strength for restraining emotion, it will to that extent be able to restrain the given emotion. *Q.E.D.*

PROP. XV. *Desire arising from the knowledge of good and bad can be quenched or checked by many of the other desires arising from the emotions whereby we are assailed.*

Proof.—From the true knowledge of good and evil, in so far as it is an emotion, necessarily arises desire (Def. of the Emotions, i.), the strength of which is proportioned to the strength of the emotion wherefrom it arises (III. xxxvii.). But, inasmuch as this desire arises (by hypothesis) from the fact of our truly understanding anything, it follows that it is also present with us, in so far as we are active (III. i.), and must therefore be understood through our essence only (III. Def. ii.); consequently (III. vii.) its force and increase can be defined solely by human power. Again, the desires arising from the emotions whereby we are assailed are stronger, in proportion as the said emotions are more vehement; wherefore their force and increase must be defined solely by the power of external causes, which, when compared with our own power, indefinitely surpass it (IV. iii.); hence the desires arising from like emotions may be more vehement, than the desire which arises from a true knowledge of good and evil, and may, consequently, control or quench it. *Q.E.D.*

PROP. XVI. *Desire arising from the knowledge of good and evil, in so far as such knowledge regards what is future, may be more easily controlled or quenched, than the desire for what is agreeable at the present moment.*

Proof.—Emotion towards a thing, which we conceive as future, is fainter than emotion towards a thing that is present

(IV. ix. Coroll.). But desire, which arises from the true knowledge of good and evil, though it be concerned with things which are good at the moment, can be quenched or controlled by any headstrong desire (by the last Prop., the proof whereof is of universal application). Wherefore desire arising from such knowledge, when concerned with the future, can be more easily controlled or quenched, &c. *Q.E.D.*

PROP. XVII. *Desire arising from the true knowledge of good and evil, in so far as such knowledge is concerned with what is contingent, can be controlled far more easily still, than desire for things that are present.*

Proof.—This Prop. is proved in the same way as the last Prop. from IV. xii. Coroll.

Note.—I think I have now shown the reason, why men are moved by opinion more readily than by true reason, why it is that the true knowledge of good and evil stirs up conflicts in the soul, and often yields to every kind of passion. This state of things gave rise to the exclamation of the poet:[1]—

> "The better path I gaze at and approve,
> The worse—I follow."

Ecclesiastes seems to have had the same thought in his mind, when he says, "He who increaseth knowledge increaseth sorrow." I have not written the above with the object of drawing the conclusion, that ignorance is more excellent than knowledge, or that a wise man is on a par with a fool in controlling his emotions, but because it is necessary to know the power and the infirmity of our nature, before we can determine what reason can do in restraining the emotions, and what is beyond her power. I have said, that in the present part I shall merely treat of human infirmity. The power of reason over the emotions I have settled to treat separately.

PROP. XVIII. *Desire arising from pleasure is, other conditions being equal, stronger than desire arising from pain.*

Proof.—Desire is the essence of a man (Def. of the Emotions, i.), that is, the endeavour whereby a man endeavours to persist in his own being. Wherefore desire arising from pleasure is, by the fact of pleasure being felt, increased or

[1] Ov. Met. vii. 20, "Video meliora proboque, Deteriora sequor."

helped; on the contrary, desire arising from pain is, by the fact of pain being felt, diminished or hindered; hence the force of desire arising from pleasure must be defined by human power together with the power of an external cause, whereas desire arising from pain must be defined by human power only. Thus the former is the stronger of the two. *Q.E.D.*

Note.—In these few remarks I have explained the causes of human infirmity and inconstancy, and shown why men do not abide by the precepts of reason. It now remains for me to show what course is marked out for us by reason, which of the emotions are in harmony with the rules of human reason, and which of them are contrary thereto. But, before I begin to prove my propositions in detailed geometrical fashion, it is advisable to sketch them briefly in advance, so that everyone may more readily grasp my meaning.

As reason makes no demands contrary to nature, it demands, that every man should love himself, should seek that which is useful to him—I mean, that which is really useful to him, should desire everything which really brings man to greater perfection, and should, each for himself, endeavour as far as he can to preserve his own being. This is as necessarily true, as that a whole is greater than its part. (Cf. III. iv.)

Again, as virtue is nothing else but action in accordance with the laws of one's own nature (IV. Def. viii.), and as no one endeavours to preserve his own being, except in accordance with the laws of his own nature, it follows, *first,* that the foundation of virtue is the endeavour to preserve one's own being, and that happiness consists in man's power of preserving his own being; *secondly,* that virtue is to be desired for its own sake, and that there is nothing more excellent or more useful to us, for the sake of which we should desire it; *thirdly* and lastly, that suicides are weak-minded, and are overcome by external causes repugnant to their nature. Further, it follows from Postulate iv. Part II., that we can never arrive at doing without all external things for the preservation of our being or living, so as to have no relations with things which are outside ourselves. Again, if we consider our mind, we see that our intellect would be more imperfect, if mind were alone, and could understand nothing besides itself. There are, then, many things outside ourselves, which are useful to us, and are, therefore, to be desired. Of such none can be discerned more excellent, than those which are in entire agreement with our nature. For if, for example, two individuals of entirely the same nature are united, they form a combination twice as powerful as either of them singly.

Therefore, to man there is nothing more useful than man —nothing, I repeat, more excellent for preserving their being can be wished for by men, than that all should so in all points agree, that the minds and bodies of all should form, as it were, one single mind and one single body, and that all should, with one consent, as far as they are able, endeavour to preserve their being, and all with one consent seek what is useful to them all. Hence, men who are governed by reason—that is, who seek what is useful to them in accordance with reason,—desire for themselves nothing, which they do not also desire for the rest of mankind, and, consequently, are just, faithful, and honourable in their conduct.

Such are the dictates of reason, which I purposed thus briefly to indicate, before beginning to prove them in greater detail. I have taken this course, in order, if possible, to gain the attention of those who believe, that the principle that every man is bound to seek what is useful for himself is the foundation of impiety, rather than of piety and virtue.

Therefore, after briefly showing that the contrary is the case, I go on to prove it by the same method, as that whereby I have hitherto proceeded.

PROP. XIX. *Every man, by the laws of his nature, necessarily desires or shrinks from that which he deems to be good or bad.*

Proof.—The knowledge of good and evil is (IV. viii.) the emotion of pleasure or pain, in so far as we are conscious thereof; therefore, every man necessarily desires what he thinks good, and shrinks from what he thinks bad. Now this appetite is nothing else but man's nature or essence (cf. the Definition of Appetite, III. ix. note, and Def. of the Emotions, i.). Therefore, every man, solely by the laws of his nature, desires the one, and shrinks from the other, &c. *Q.E.D.*

PROP. XX. *The more every man endeavours and is able to seek what is useful to him—in other words, to preserve his own being—the more is he endowed with virtue; on the contrary, in proportion as a man neglects to seek what is useful to him, that is, to preserve his own being, he is wanting in power.*

Proof.—Virtue is human power, which is defined solely by man's essence (IV. Def. viii.), that is, which is defined solely by the endeavour made by man to persist in his own being. Wherefore, the more a man endeavours, and is able to preserve his own being, the more is he endowed with virtue, and, consequently (III. iv. and vi.), in so far as a man neglects to preserve his own being, he is wanting in power. Q.E.D.

Note.—No one, therefore, neglects seeking his own good, or preserving his own being, unless he be overcome by causes external and foreign to his nature. No one, I say, from the necessity of his own nature, or otherwise than under compulsion from external causes, shrinks from food, or kills himself: which latter may be done in a variety of ways. A man, for instance, kills himself under the compulsion of another man, who twists round his right hand, wherewith he happened to have taken up a sword, and forces him to turn the blade against his own heart; or, again, he may be compelled, like Seneca, by a tyrant's command, to open his own veins—that is, to escape a greater evil by incurring a lesser; or, lastly, latent external causes may so disorder his imagination, and so affect his body, that it may assume a nature contrary to its former one, and whereof the idea cannot exist in the mind (III. x.). But that a man, from the necessity of his own nature, should endeavour to become non-existent, is as impossible as that something should be made out of nothing, as everyone will see for himself, after a little reflection.

PROP. XXI. *No one can desire to be blessed, to act rightly, and to live rightly, without at the same time wishing to be, to act, and to live, in other words, to actually exist.*

Proof.—The proof of this proposition, or rather the proposition itself, is self-evident, and is also plain from the definition of desire. For the desire of living, acting, &c., blessedly or rightly, is (Def. of the Emotions, i.) the essence of man— that is (III. vii.), the endeavour made by everyone to preserve his own being. Therefore, no one can desire, &c. *Q.E.D.*

PROP. XXII. *No virtue can be conceived as prior to this endeavour to preserve one's own being.*

Proof.—The effort for self-preservation is the essence of a thing (III. vii.); therefore, if any virtue could be conceived as prior thereto, the essence of a thing would have to be conceived as prior to itself, which is obviously absurd. Therefore no virtue, &c. *Q.E.D.*

Corollary.—The effort for self-preservation is the first and only foundation of virtue. For prior to this principle nothing can be conceived, and without it no virtue can be conceived.

PROP. XXIII. *Man, in so far as he is determined to a particular action because he has inadequate ideas, cannot be absolutely said to act in obedience to virtue; he can only be so described in so far as he is determined for the action because he understands.*

Proof.—In so far as a man is determined to an action through having inadequate ideas, he is passive (III. i.), that is (III. Deff. i. and iii.), he does something, which cannot be perceived solely through his essence, that is (by IV. Def. viii.), which does not follow from his virtue. But, in so far as he is determined for an action because he understands, he is active; that is, he does something, which is perceived through his essence alone, or which adequately follows from his virtue. *Q.E.D.*

PROP. XXIV. *To act absolutely in obedience to virtue is in us the same thing as to act, to live, or to preserve one's being (these three terms are identical in meaning) in accordance with the dictates of reason on the basis of seeking what is useful to one's self.*

Proof.—To act absolutely in obedience to virtue is nothing else but to act according to the laws of one's own nature. But we only act, in so far as we understand (III. iii.): therefore to act in obedience to virtue is in us nothing else but to act, to live, or to preserve one's being in obedience to reason and that on the basis of seeking what is useful for us (IV. xxii. Coroll.). *Q.E.D.*

PROP. XXV. *No one wishes to preserve his being for the sake of anything else.*

Proof.—The endeavour, wherewith everything endeavours to persist in its being, is defined solely by the essence of the thing itself (III. vii.); from this alone, and not from the essence of anything else, it necessarily follows (III. vi.) that everyone endeavours to preserve his being. Moreover, this proposition is plain from IV. xxii. Coroll., for if a man should endeavour to preserve his being for the sake of anything else, the last-named thing would obviously be the basis of virtue, which, by the foregoing corollary, is absurd. Therefore no one, &c. *Q.E.D.*

PROP. XXVI. *Whatsoever we endeavour in obedience to reason is nothing further than to understand; neither does the mind, in so far as it makes use of reason, judge anything to be useful to it, save such things as are conducive to understanding.*

Proof.—The effort for self-preservation is nothing else but the essence of the thing in question (III. vii.), which, in so far as it exists such as it is, is conceived to have force for continuing in existence (III. vi.) and doing such things as necessarily follow from its given nature (see the Def. of Appetite, III. ix. note). But the essence of reason is nought else but our mind, in so far as it clearly and distinctly understands (see the definition in II. xl. note ii.); therefore (II. xl.) whatsoever we endeavour in obedience to reason is nothing else but to understand. Again, since this effort of the mind wherewith the mind endeavours, in so far as it reasons, to preserve its own being is nothing else but understanding; this effort at understanding is (IV. xxii. Coroll.) the first and single basis of virtue, nor shall we endeavour to understand things for the sake of any ulterior object (IV. xxv.); on the other hand, the mind, in so far as it reasons, will not be able to conceive any good for itself, save such things as are conducive to understanding.

PROP. XXVII. *We know nothing to be certainly good or evil, save such things as really conduce to understanding, or such as are able to hinder us from understanding.*

Proof.—The mind, in so far as it reasons, desires nothing beyond understanding, and judges nothing to be useful to itself, save such things as conduce to understanding (by the foregoing Prop.). But the mind (II. xli. xliii. and note) cannot possess certainty concerning anything, except in so far as it has adequate ideas, or (what by II. xl. note, is the same thing) in so far as it reasons. Therefore we know nothing to be good or evil save such things as really conduce, &c. *Q.E.D.*

PROP. XXVIII. *The mind's highest good is the knowledge of God, and the mind's highest virtue is to know God.*

Proof.—The mind is not capable of understanding anything higher than God, that is (I. Def. vi.), than a Being absolutely infinite, and without which (I. xv.) nothing can either be or be conceived; therefore (IV. xxvi. and xxvii.), the mind's highest utility or (IV. Def. i.) good is the knowledge of God. Again, the mind is active, only in so far as it understands, and only to the same extent can it be said absolutely to act virtuously. The mind's absolute virtue is therefore to understand. Now, as we have already shown, the highest that the mind can understand is God; therefore the highest virtue of the mind is to understand or to know God. *Q.E.D.*

PROP. XXIX. *No individual thing, which is entirely different from our own nature, can help or check our power of activity, and absolutely nothing can do us good or harm, unless it has something in common with our nature.*

Proof.—The power of every individual thing, and consequently the power of man, whereby he exists and operates, can only be determined by an individual thing (I. xxviii.), whose nature (II. vi.) must be understood through the same nature as that, through which human nature is conceived. Therefore our power of activity, however it be conceived, can be determined and consequently helped or hindered by the power of any other individual thing, which has something in common with us, but not by the power of anything, of which the nature is entirely different from our own; and since we call good or evil that which is the cause of pleasure or pain (IV. viii.), that is (III. xi. note), which increases or diminishes, helps or hinders, our power of activity; therefore, that which is entirely different from our nature can neither be to us good nor bad. *Q.E.D.*

PROP. XXX. *A thing cannot be bad for us through the quality which it has in common with our nature, but it is bad for us in so far as it is contrary to our nature.*

Proof.—We call a thing bad when it is the cause of pain (IV. viii.), that is (by the Def., which see in III. xi. note), when it diminishes or checks our power of action. Therefore, if anything were bad for us through that quality which it has in common with our nature, it would be able itself to diminish or check that which it has in common with our nature, which (III. iv.) is absurd. Wherefore nothing can be bad for us through that quality which it has in common with us, but, on the other hand, in so far as it is bad for us, that is (as we have just shown), in so far as it can diminish or check our power of action, it is contrary to our nature. *Q.E.D.*

PROP. XXXI. *In so far as a thing is in harmony with our nature, it is necessarily good.*

Proof.—In so far as a thing is in harmony with our nature, it cannot be bad for it. It will therefore necessarily be either good or indifferent. If it be assumed that it be neither good nor bad, nothing will follow from its nature (IV. Def. i.), which tends to the preservation of our nature, that is (by the hypothesis), which tends to the preservation of the thing itself; but this (III. vi.) is absurd; therefore, in so far as a thing is in harmony with our nature, it is necessarily good. *Q.E.D.*

Corollary.—Hence it follows, that, in proportion as a thing is in harmony with our nature, so is it more useful or better for us, and *vice versâ*, in proportion as a thing is more useful for us, so is it more in harmony with our nature. For, in so far as it is not in harmony with our nature, it will necessarily be different therefrom or contrary thereto. If different, it can neither be good nor bad (IV. xxix); if contrary, it will be contrary to that which is in harmony with our nature, that is, contrary to what is good—in short, bad. Nothing, therefore, can be good, except in so far as it is in harmony with our nature; and hence a thing is useful, in proportion as it is in harmony with our nature, and *vice versâ. Q.E.D.*

PROP. XXXII. *In so far as men are a prey to passion, they*

cannot, in that respect, be said to be naturally in harmony.

Proof.—Things, which are said to be in harmony naturally, are understood to agree in power (III. vii.), not in want of power or negation, and consequently not in passion (III. iii. note); wherefore men, in so far as they are a prey to their passions, cannot be said to be naturally in harmony. *Q.E.D.*

Note.—This is also self-evident; for, if we say that white and black only agree in the fact that neither is red, we absolutely affirm that they do not agree in any respect. So, if we say that a man and a stone only agree in the fact that both are finite—wanting in power, not existing by the necessity of their own nature, or, lastly, indefinitely surpassed by the power of external causes—we should certainly affirm that a man and a stone are in no respect alike; therefore, things which agree only in negation, or in qualities which neither possess, really agree in no respect.

PROP. XXXIII. *Men can differ in nature, in so far as they are assailed by those emotions which are passions or passive states; and to this extent one and the same man is variable and inconstant.*

Proof.—The nature or essence of the emotions cannot be explained solely through our essence or nature (III. Deff. i. ii.), but it must be defined by the power, that is (III. vii.), by the nature of external causes in comparison with our own; hence it follows, that there are as many kinds of each emotion as there are external objects whereby we are affected (III. lvi.), and that men may be differently affected by one and the same object (III. li.), and to this extent differ in nature; lastly, that one and the same man may be differently affected towards the same object, and may therefore be variable and inconstant. *Q.E.D.*

PROP. XXXIV. *In so far as men are assailed by emotions which are passions, they can be contrary one to another.*

Proof.—A man, for instance Peter, can be the cause of Paul's feeling pain, because he (Peter) possesses something similar to that which Paul hates (III. xvi.), or because Peter has sole possession of a thing which Paul also loves (III. xxxii. and note), or for other causes (of which the chief are enumerated in III. lv. note); it may therefore happen that Paul should hate Peter (Def. of Emotions, vii.), consequently it may easily happen also, that Peter should hate Paul in return, and that each should endeavour to do the other an injury (III. xxxix.), that is (IV. xxx.), that they should be contrary one to another. But the emotion of pain is always a passion or passive state (III. lix.); hence men, in so far as they are assailed by emotions which are passions, can be contrary one to another. Q.E.D.

Note.—I said that Paul may hate Peter, because he conceives that Peter possesses something which he (Paul) also loves; from this it seems, at first sight, to follow, that these two men, through both loving the same thing, and, consequently, through agreement of their respective natures, stand in one another's way; if this were so, Props. xxx. and xxxi. of this Part would be untrue. But if we give the matter our unbiassed attention, we shall see that the discrepancy vanishes. For the two men are not in one another's way in virtue of the agreement of their natures, that is, through both loving the same thing, but in virtue of one differing from the other. For, in so far as each loves the same thing, the love of each is fostered thereby (III. xxxi.), that is (Def. of the Emotions, vi.) the pleasure of each is fostered thereby. Wherefore it is far from being the case, that they are at variance through both loving the same thing, and through the agreement in their natures. The cause for their opposition lies, as I have said, solely in the fact that they are assumed to differ. For we assume that Peter has the idea of the loved object as already in his possession, while Paul has the idea of the loved object as lost. Hence the one man will be affected with pleasure, the other will be affected with pain, and thus they will be at variance one with another. We can easily show in like manner, that all other causes of hatred depend solely on differences, and not on the agreement between men's natures.

PROP. XXXV. *In so far only as men live in obedience to reason, do they always necessarily agree in nature.*

Proof.—In so far as men are assailed by emotions that are passions, they can be different in nature (IV. xxxiii.), and at variance one with another. But men are only said to be active, in so far as they act in obedience to reason (III. iii.); there-

fore, whatsoever follows from human nature in so far as it is
defined by reason must (III. Def. ii.) be understood solely
through human nature as its proximate cause. But, since every
man by the laws of his nature desires that which he deems
good, and endeavours to remove that which he deems bad
(IV. xix.); and further, since that which we, in accordance
with reason, deem good or bad, necessarily is good or bad (II.
xli.); it follows that men, in so far as they live in obedience
to reason, necessarily do only such things as are necessarily
good for human nature, and consequently for each individual
man (IV. xxxi. Coroll.); in other words, such things as are in
harmony with each man's nature. Therefore, men in so far as
they live in obedience to reason, necessarily live always in
harmony one with another. *Q.E.D.*

Corollary I.—There is no individual thing in nature, which
is more useful to man, than a man who lives in obedience to
reason. For that thing is to man most useful, which is most
in harmony with his nature (IV. xxxi. Coroll.); that is, obviously, man. But man acts absolutely according to the laws of
his nature, when he lives in obedience to reason (III. Def. ii.),
and to this extent only is always necessarily in harmony with
the nature of another man (by the last Prop.); wherefore
among individual things nothing is more useful to man, than
a man who lives in obedience to reason. *Q.E.D.*

Corollary II.—As every man seeks most that which is useful
to him, so are men most useful one to another. For the more
a man seeks what is useful to him and endeavours to preserve
himself, the more is he endowed with virtue (IV. xx.), or,
what is the same thing (IV. Def. viii.), the more is he endowed with power to act according to the laws of his own nature, that is to live in obedience to reason. But men are most
in natural harmony, when they live in obedience to reason
(by the last Prop.); therefore (by the foregoing Coroll.) men
will be most useful one to another, when each seeks most that
which is useful to him. *Q.E.D.*

Note.—What we have just shown is attested by experience
so conspicuously, that it is in the mouth of nearly everyone:
"Man is to man a God." Yet it rarely happens that men live
in obedience to reason, for things are so ordered among them,

that they are generally envious and troublesome one to another. Nevertheless they are scarcely able to lead a solitary life, so that the definition of man as a social animal has met with general assent; in fact, men do derive from social life much more convenience than injury. Let satirists then laugh their fill at human affairs, let theologians rail, and let misanthropes praise to their utmost the life of untutored rusticity, let them heap contempt on men and praises on beasts; when all is said, they will find that men can provide for their wants much more easily by mutual help, and that only by uniting their forces can they escape from the dangers that on every side beset them: not to say how much more excellent and worthy of our knowledge it is, to study the actions of men than the actions of beasts. But I will treat of this more at length elsewhere.

PROP. XXXVI. *The highest good of those who follow virtue is common to all, and therefore all can equally rejoice therein.*

Proof.—To act virtuously is to act in obedience with reason (IV. xxiv.), and whatsoever we endeavour to do in obedience to reason is to understand (IV. xxvi.); therefore (IV. xxviii.) the highest good for those who follow after virtue is to know God; that is (II. xlvii. and note) a good which is common to all and can be possessed by all men equally, in so far as they are of the same nature. *Q.E.D.*

Note.—Someone may ask how it would be, if the highest good of those who follow after virtue were not common to all? Would it not then follow, as above (IV. xxxiv.), that men living in obedience to reason, that is (IV. xxxv.), men in so far as they agree in nature, would be at variance one with another? To such an inquiry I make answer, that it follows not accidentally but from the very nature of reason, that man's highest good is common to all, inasmuch as it is deduced from the very essence of man, in so far as defined by reason; and that a man could neither be, nor be conceived without the power of taking pleasure in this highest good. For it belongs to the essence of the human mind (II. xlvii.), to have an adequate knowledge of the eternal and infinite essence of God.

PROP. XXXVII. *The good which every man who follows after virtue desires for himself, he will also desire for other men, and so much the more, in proportion as he has a greater knowledge of God.*

Proof.—Men, in so far as they live in obedience to reason, are most useful to their fellow-men (IV. xxxv. Coroll. i.); therefore (IV. xix.), we shall in obedience to reason necessarily endeavour to bring about that men should live in obedience to reason. But the good which every man, in so far as he is guided by reason, or, in other words, follows after virtue, desires for himself, is to understand (IV. xxvi.); wherefore the good, which each follower of virtue seeks for himself, he will desire also for others. Again, desire, in so far as it is referred to the mind, is the very essence of the mind (Def. of the Emotions, i.); now the essence of the mind consists in knowledge (II. xi.), which involves the knowledge of God (II. xlvii.), and without it (I. xv.), can neither be, nor be conceived; therefore, in proportion as the mind's essence involves a greater knowledge of God, so also will be greater the desire of the follower of virtue, that other men should possess that which he seeks as good for himself. *Q.E.D.*

Another Proof.—The good, which a man desires for himself and loves, he will love more constantly, if he sees that others love it also (III. xxxi.); he will therefore endeavour that others should love it also; and as the good in question is common to all, and therefore all can rejoice therein, he will endeavour, for the same reason, to bring about that all should rejoice therein, and this he will do the more (III. xxxvii.), in proportion as his own enjoyment of the good is greater.

Note I.—He who, guided by emotion only, endeavours to cause others to love what he loves himself, and to make the rest of the world live according to his own fancy, acts solely by impulse, and is, therefore, hateful, especially to those who take delight in something different, and accordingly study and, by similar impulse, endeavour, to make men live in accordance with what pleases themselves. Again, as the highest good sought by men under the guidance of emotion is often such, that it can only be possessed by a single individual, it follows that those who love it are not consistent in their intentions, but, while they delight to sing its praises, fear to be believed. But he, who endeavours to lead men by reason, does not act by impulse but courteously and kindly, and his intention is always consistent. Again, whatsoever we desire and do, whereof we are the cause in so far as we possess the idea of God, or know God, I set down to *Religion*. The desire of well-doing, which is engendered by a life according to reason, I call *piety*. Further, the desire, whereby a man living according to reason is bound to associate others with himself in friendship, I call *honour*;[2] by *honourable* I mean that which is praised by men living according to reason, and by *base* I mean that which is repugnant to the gaining of friendship. I have also shown in addition what are the foundations of a state; and the difference between true virtue and infirmity may be readily gathered from what I have said; namely, that true virtue is nothing else but living in accordance with reason; while infirmity is nothing else but man's allowing himself to be led by things which are external to himself, and to be by them determined to act in a manner demanded by the general disposition of things rather than by his own nature considered solely in itself.

Such are the matters which I engaged to prove in Prop. xviii. of this Part, whereby it is plain that the law against the slaughtering of animals is founded rather on vain superstition and womanish pity than on sound reason. The rational quest of what is useful to us further teaches us the necessity of associating ourselves with our fellow-men, but not with beasts, or things, whose nature is different from our own; we have the same rights in respect to them as they have in respect to us. Nay, as everyone's right is defined by his virtue, or power, men have far greater rights over beasts than beasts have over men. Still I do not deny that beasts feel: what I deny is, that we may not consult our own advantage and use them as we please, treating them in the way which best suits us; for their nature is not like ours, and their emotions are naturally different from human emotions (III. lvii. note). It remains for me to explain what I mean by just and unjust, sin and merit. On these points see the following note.

[2] *Honestas*.

Note II.—In the Appendix to Part I. I undertook to explain praise and blame, merit and sin, justice and injustice.

Concerning praise and blame I have spoken in III. xxix. note: the time has now come to treat of the remaining terms. But I must first say a few words concerning man in the state of nature and in society.

Every man exists by sovereign natural right, and, consequently, by sovereign natural right performs those actions which follow from the necessity of his own nature; therefore by sovereign natural right every man judges what is good and what is bad, takes care of his own advantage according to his own disposition (IV. xix. and xx.), avenges the wrongs done to him (III. xl. Coroll. ii.), and endeavours to preserve that which he loves and to destroy that which he hates (III. xxviii.). Now, if men lived under the guidance of reason, everyone would remain in possession of this his right, without any injury being done to his neighbour (IV. xxxv. Coroll. i.). But seeing that they are a prey to their emotions, which far surpass human power or virtue (IV. vi.), they are often drawn in different directions, and being at variance one with another (IV. xxxiii. xxxiv.), stand in need of mutual help (IV. xxxv. note). Wherefore, in order that men may live together in harmony, and may aid one another, it is necessary that they should forego their natural right, and, for the sake of security, refrain from all actions which can injure their fellow-men. The way in which this end can be attained, so that men who are necessarily a prey to their emotions (IV. iv. Coroll.), inconstant, and diverse, should be able to render each other mutually secure, and feel mutual trust, is evident from IV. vii. and III. xxxix. It is there shown, that an emotion can only be restrained by an emotion stronger than, and contrary to itself, and that men avoid inflicting injury through fear of incurring a greater injury themselves.

On this law society can be established, so long as it keeps in its own hand the right, possessed by everyone, of avenging injury, and pronouncing on good and evil; and provided it also possesses the power to lay down a general rule of conduct, and to pass laws sanctioned, not by reason, which is powerless in restraining emotion, but by threats (IV. xvii. note). Such a society established with laws and the power of preserving itself is called a *State*, while those who live under its protection are called *citizens*. We may readily understand that there is in the state of nature nothing, which by universal consent is pronounced good or bad; for in the state of nature everyone thinks solely of his own advantage, and according to his disposition, with reference only to his individual advantage, decides what is good or bad, being bound by no law to anyone besides himself.

In the state of nature, therefore, sin is inconceivable; it can only exist in a state, where good and evil are pronounced on by common consent, and where everyone is bound to obey the State authority. *Sin*, then, is nothing else but disobedience, which is therefore punished by the right of the State only. Obedience, on the other hand, is set down as *merit*, inasmuch as a man is thought worthy of merit, if he takes delight in the advantages which a State provides.

Again, in the state of nature, no one is by common consent master of anything, nor is there anything in nature, which can be said to belong to one man rather than another: all things are common to all. Hence, in the state of nature, we can conceive no wish to render to every man his own, or to deprive a man of that which belongs to him; in other words, there is nothing in the state of nature answering to justice and injustice. Such ideas are only possible in a social state, when it is decreed by common consent what belongs to one man and what to another.

From all these considerations it is evident, that justice and injustice, sin and merit, are extrinsic ideas, and not attributes which display the nature of the mind. But I have said enough.

PROP. XXXVIII. *Whatsoever disposes the human body, so as to render it capable of being affected in an increased number of ways, or of affecting external bodies in an increased number of ways, is useful to man; and is so, in proportion as the body is thereby rendered more capable of being affected or affecting other bodies in an increased number of ways; contrariwise, whatsoever renders the body less capable in this respect is hurtful to man.*

Proof.—Whatsoever thus increases the capabilities of the

body increases also the mind's capability of perception (II. xiv.); therefore, whatsoever thus disposes the body and thus renders it capable, is necessarily good or useful (IV. xxvi. xxvii.); and is so in proportion to the extent to which it can render the body capable; contrariwise (II. xiv. IV. xxvi. xxvii.), it is hurtful, if it renders the body in this respect less capable. Q.E.D.

PROP. XXXIX. *Whatsoever brings about the preservation of the proportion of motion and rest, which the parts of the human body mutually possess, is good; contrariwise, whatsoever causes a change in such proportion is bad.*

Proof.—The human body needs many other bodies for its preservation (II. Post. iv.). But that which constitutes the specific reality (*forma*) of a human body is, that its parts communicate their several motions one to another in a certain fixed proportion (Def. before Lemma iv. after II. xiii.). Therefore, whatsoever brings about the preservation of the proportion between motion and rest, which the parts of the human body mutually possess, preserves the specific reality of the human body, and consequently renders the human body capable of being affected in many ways and of affecting external bodies in many ways; consequently it is good (by the last Prop.). Again, whatsoever brings about a change in the aforesaid proportion causes the human body to assume another specific character, in other words (see Preface to this Part towards the end, though the point is indeed self-evident), to be destroyed, and consequently totally incapable of being affected in an increased number of ways; therefore it is bad. Q.E.D.

Note.—The extent to which such causes can injure or be of service to the mind will be explained in the Fifth Part. But I would here remark that I consider that a body undergoes death, when the proportion of motion and rest which obtained mutually among its several parts is changed. For I do not venture to deny that a human body, while keeping the circulation of the blood and other properties, wherein the life of a body is thought to consist, may none the less be changed into another nature totally different from its own. There is no reason, which compels me to maintain that a body does not die, unless it becomes a corpse; nay, experience would seem to point to the opposite conclusion. It sometimes happens, that a man undergoes such changes, that I should hardly call him the same. As I have heard tell of a certain Spanish poet, who had been seized with sickness, and though he recovered therefrom yet remained so oblivious of his past life, that he would not believe the plays and tragedies he had written to be his own: indeed, he might have been taken for a grown-up child, if he had also forgotten his native tongue. If this instance seems incredible, what shall we say of infants? A man of ripe age deems their nature so unlike his own, that he can only be persuaded that he too has been an infant by the analogy of other men. However, I prefer to leave such questions undiscussed, lest I should give ground to the superstitious for raising new issues.

PROP. XL. *Whatsoever conduces to man's social life, or causes men to live together in harmony, is useful, whereas whatsoever brings discord into a State is bad.*

Proof.—For whatsoever causes men to live together in harmony also causes them to live according to reason (IV. xxxv.), and is therefore (IV. xxvi. and xxvii.) good, and (for the same reason) whatsoever brings about discord is bad. *Q.E.D.*

PROP. XLI. *Pleasure in itself is not bad but good; contrariwise, pain in itself is bad.*

Proof.—Pleasure (III. xi. and note) is emotion, whereby the body's power of activity is increased or helped; pain is emotion, whereby the body's power of activity is diminished or checked; therefore (IV. xxxviii.) pleasure in itself is good, &c. *Q.E.D.*

PROP. XLII. *Mirth cannot be excessive, but is always good; contrariwise, Melancholy is always bad.*

Proof.—Mirth (see its Def. in III. xi. note) is pleasure, which, in so far as it is referred to the body, consists in all parts of the body being affected equally: that is (III. xi.), the body's power of activity is increased or aided in such a manner, that the several parts maintain their former proportion of motion and rest; therefore Mirth is always good (IV. xxxix.), and cannot be excessive. But Melancholy (see its Def. in the same note to III. xi.) is pain, which, in so far as it is referred to the body, consists in the absolute decrease or hindrance of the body's power of activity; therefore (IV. xxxviii.) it is always bad. *Q.E.D.*

Prop. XLIII. *Stimulation may be excessive and bad; on the other hand, grief may be good, in so far as stimulation or pleasure is bad.*

Proof.—Localized pleasure or stimulation (*titillatio*) is pleasure, which, in so far as it is referred to the body, consists in one or some of its parts being affected more than the rest (see its Definition, III. xi. note); the power of this emotion may be sufficient to overcome other actions of the body (IV. vi.), and may remain obstinately fixed therein, thus rendering it incapable of being affected in a variety of other ways: therefore (IV. xxxviii.) it may be bad. Again, grief, which is pain, cannot as such be good (IV. xli.). But, as its force and increase is defined by the power of an external cause compared with our own (IV. v.), we can conceive infinite degrees and modes of strength in this emotion (IV. iii.); we can, therefore, conceive it as capable of restraining stimulation, and preventing its becoming excessive, and hindering the body's capabilities; thus, to this extent, it will be good. *Q.E.D.*

Prop. XLIV. *Love and desire may be excessive.*

Proof.—Love is pleasure, accompanied by the idea of an external cause (Def. of Emotions, vi.); therefore stimulation, accompanied by the idea of an external cause is love (III. xi. note); hence love may be excessive. Again, the strength of desire varies in proportion to the emotion from which it arises (III. xxxvii.). Now emotion may overcome all the rest of men's actions (IV. vi.); so, therefore, can desire, which arises from the same emotion, overcome all other desires, and become excessive, as we showed in the last proposition concerning stimulation.

Note.—Mirth, which I have stated to be good, can be conceived more easily than it can be observed. For the emotions, whereby we are daily assailed, are generally referred to some part of the body which is affected more than the rest; hence the emotions are generally excessive, and so fix the mind in the contemplation of one object, that it is unable to think of others; and although men, as a rule, are a prey to many emotions—and very few are found who are always assailed by one and the same—yet there are cases, where one and the same emotion remains obstinately fixed. We sometimes see men so absorbed in one object, that, although it be not present, they think they have it before them; when this is the case with a man who is not asleep, we say he is delirious or mad; nor are those persons who are inflamed with love, and who dream all night and all day about nothing but their mistress, or some woman, considered as less mad, for they are made objects of ridicule. But when a miser thinks of nothing but gain or money, or when an ambitious man thinks of nothing but glory, they are not reckoned to be mad, because they are generally harmful, and are thought worthy of being hated. But, in reality, Avarice, Ambition, Lust, &c., are species of madness, though they may not be reckoned among diseases.

Prop. XLV. *Hatred can never be good.*

Proof.—When we hate a man, we endeavour to destroy him (III. xxxix.), that is (IV. xxxvii.), we endeavour to do something that is bad. Therefore, &c. *Q.E.D.*

N.B. Here, and in what follows, I mean by hatred only hatred towards men.

Corollary I.—Envy, derision, contempt, anger, revenge, and other emotions attributable to hatred, or arising therefrom, are bad; this is evident from III. xxxix. and IV. xxxvii.

Corollary II.—Whatsoever we desire from motives of hatred is base, and in a State unjust. This also is evident from III. xxxix., and from the definitions of baseness and injustice in IV. xxxvii. note.

Note.—Between derision (which I have in Coroll. I. stated to be bad) and laughter I recognize a great difference. For laughter, as also jocularity, is merely pleasure; therefore, so long as it be not excessive, it is in itself good (IV. xli.). Assuredly nothing forbids man to enjoy himself, save grim and gloomy superstition. For why is it more lawful to satiate one's hunger and thirst than to drive away one's melancholy? I reason, and have convinced myself as follows: No deity, nor anyone else, save the envious, takes pleasure in my infirmity and discomfort, nor sets down to my virtue the tears, sobs, fear, and the like, which are signs of infirmity of spirit; on the contrary, the greater the pleasure wherewith we are affected, the greater the perfection whereto we pass; in other words, the more must we necessarily partake of the divine nature. Therefore, to make use of what comes in our way, and to enjoy it as much as possible (not to the point of satiety, for that would not be enjoyment) is the part of a wise man. I say it is the part of a wise man to refresh and recreate himself with moderate and pleasant food and drink, and also with perfumes, with the soft beauty of growing plants, with dress, with music, with many sports, with theatres, and the like, such as every man may make use of without injury to his neighbour. For the human body is composed of very numerous parts, of diverse nature, which continually stand in need of fresh and varied nourishment, so that the whole body may be equally capable of performing all the actions, which follow from the necessity of its own nature; and, consequently, so that the mind may also be equally capable of understanding many things simultaneously. This way of life, then, agrees best with our principles, and also with general practice; therefore, if there be any question of another plan, the plan we have mentioned is the best, and in every way to be commended. There is no need for me to set forth the matter more clearly or in more detail.

PROP. XLVI. *He, who lives under the guidance of reason, endeavours, as far as possible, to render back love, or kindness, for other men's hatred, anger, contempt, &c., towards him.*

Proof.—All emotions of hatred are bad (IV. xlv. Coroll. i.); therefore he who lives under the guidance of reason will endeavour, as far as possible, to avoid being assailed by such emotions (IV. xix.); consequently, he will also endeavour to prevent others being so assailed (IV. xxxvii.). But hatred is increased by being reciprocated, and can be quenched by love (III. xliii.), so that hatred may pass into love (III. xliv.); therefore he who lives under the guidance of reason will endeavour to repay hatred with love, that is, with kindness. Q.E.D.

Note.—He who chooses to avenge wrongs with hatred is assuredly wretched. But he, who strives to conquer hatred with love, fights his battle in joy and confidence; he withstands many as easily as one, and has very little need of fortune's aid. Those whom he vanquishes yield joyfully, not through failure, but through increase in their powers; all these consequences follow so plainly from the mere definitions of love and understanding, that I have no need to prove them in detail.

PROP. XLVII. *Emotions of hope and fear cannot be in themselves good.*

Proof.—Emotions of hope and fear cannot exist without pain. For fear is pain (Def. of the Emotions, xiii.), and hope (Def. of the Emotions, Explanation xii. and xiii.) cannot exist without fear; therefore (IV. xli.) these emotions cannot be good in themselves, but only in so far as they can restrain excessive pleasure (IV. xliii.). *Q.E.D.*

Note.—We may add, that these emotions show defective knowledge and an absence of power in the mind; for the same reason confidence, despair, joy, and disappointment are signs of a want of mental power. For although confidence and joy are pleasurable emotions, they nevertheless imply a preceding pain, namely, hope and fear. Wherefore the more we endeavour to be guided by reason, the less do we depend on hope; we endeavour to free ourselves from fear, and, as far as we can, to dominate fortune, directing our actions by the sure counsels of wisdom.

PROP. XLVIII. *The emotions of over-esteem and disparagement are always bad.*

Proof.—These emotions (see Def. of the Emotions, xxi. xxii.) are repugnant to reason; and are therefore (IV. xxvi. xxvii.) bad. *Q.E.D.*

PROP. XLIX. *Over-esteem is apt to render its object proud.*

Proof.—If we see that any one rates us too highly, for love's sake, we are apt to become elated (III. xli.), or to be pleasurably affected (Def. of the Emotions, xxx.); the good which we hear of ourselves we readily believe (III. xxv.); and therefore, for love's sake, rate ourselves too highly; in other words, we are apt to become proud. *Q.E.D.*

PROP. L. *Pity, in a man who lives under the guidance of reason, is in itself bad and useless.*

Proof.—Pity (Def. of the Emotions, xviii.) is a pain, and therefore (IV. xli.) is in itself bad. The good effect which

follows, namely, our endeavour to free the object of our pity
from misery, is an action which we desire to do solely at the
dictation of reason (IV. xxxvii.); only at the dictation of reason are we able to perform any action, which we know for
certain to be good (IV. xxvii.); thus, in a man who lives under
the guidance of reason, pity in itself is useless and bad. *Q.E.D.*

Note.—He who rightly realizes, that all things follow from
the necessity of the divine nature, and come to pass in accordance with the eternal laws and rules of nature, will not find
anything worthy of hatred, derision, or contempt, nor will he
bestow pity on anything, but to the utmost extent of human
virtue he will endeavour to do well, as the saying is, and to
rejoice. We may add, that he, who is easily touched with compassion, and is moved by another's sorrow or tears, often does
something which he afterwards regrets; partly because we can
never be sure that an action caused by emotion is good, partly
because we are easily deceived by false tears. I am in this
place expressly speaking of a man living under the guidance
of reason. He who is moved to help others neither by reason
nor by compassion, is rightly styled inhuman, for (III. xxvii.)
he seems unlike a man.

PROP. LI. *Approval is not repugnant to reason, but can
agree therewith and arise therefrom.*

Proof.—Approval is love towards one who has done good
to another (Def. of the Emotions, xix.); therefore it may be
referred to the mind, in so far as the latter is active (III. lix.),
that is (III. iii.), in so far as it understands; therefore, it is
in agreement with reason, &c. *Q.E.D.*

Another Proof.—He, who lives under the guidance of reason, desires for others the good which he seeks for himself
(IV. xxxvii.); wherefore from seeing someone doing good
to his fellow his own endeavour to do good is aided; in
other words, he will feel pleasure (III. xi. note) accompanied
by the idea of the benefactor. Therefore he approves of him.
Q.E.D.

Note.—Indignation as we defined it (Def. of the Emotions,
xx.) is necessarily evil (IV. xlv.); we may, however, remark
that, when the sovereign power for the sake of preserving
peace punishes a citizen who has injured another, it should

not be said to be indignant with the criminal, for it is not incited by hatred to ruin him, it is led by a sense of duty to punish him.

PROP. LII. *Self-approval may arise from reason, and that which arises from reason is the highest possible.*

Proof.—Self-approval is pleasure arising from a man's contemplation of himself and his own power of action (Def. of the Emotions, xxv.). But a man's true power of action or virtue is reason herself (III. iii.), as the said man clearly and distinctly contemplates her (II. xl. xliii.); therefore self-approval arises from reason. Again, when a man is contemplating himself, he only perceives clearly and distinctly or adequately, such things as follow from his power of action (III. Def. ii.), that is (III. iii.), from his power of understanding; therefore in such contemplation alone does the highest possible self-approval arise. *Q.E.D.*

Note.—Self-approval is in reality the highest object for which we can hope. For (as we showed in IV. xxv.) no one endeavours to preserve his being for the sake of any ulterior object, and, as this approval is more and more fostered and strengthened by praise (III. liii. Coroll.), and on the contrary (III. lv. Coroll.) is more and more disturbed by blame, fame becomes the most powerful of incitements to action, and life under disgrace is almost unendurable.

PROP. LIII. *Humility is not a virtue, or does not arise from reason.*

Proof.—Humility is pain arising from a man's contemplation of his own infirmities (Def. of the Emotions, xxvi.). But, in so far as a man knows himself by true reason, he is assumed to understand his essence, that is, his power (III. vii.). Wherefore, if a man in self-contemplation perceives any infirmity in himself, it is not by virtue of his understanding himself, but (III. lv.) by virtue of his power of activity being checked. But, if we assume that a man perceives his own infirmity by virtue of understanding something stronger than himself, by the knowledge of which he determines his own power of activity, this is the same as saying that we conceive that a man understands himself distinctly (IV. xxvi.), because[3] his power of activity is aided. Wherefore humility, or the pain which arises from a man's contemplation of his own infirmity, does not arise from the contemplation or reason, and is not a virtue but a passion. *Q.E.D.*

PROP. LIV. *Repentance is not a virtue, or does not arise from reason; but he who repents of an action is doubly wretched or infirm.*

Proof.—The first part of this proposition is proved like the foregoing one. The second part is proved from the mere definition of the emotion in question (Def. of the Emotions, xxvii.). For the man allows himself to be overcome, first, by evil desires; secondly, by pain.

Note.—As men seldom live under the guidance of reason, these two emotions, namely, Humility and Repentance, as also Hope and Fear, bring more good than harm; hence, as we must sin, we had better sin in that direction. For, if all men who are a prey to emotion were all equally proud, they would shrink from nothing, and would fear nothing; how then could they be joined and linked together in bonds of union? The crowd plays the tyrant, when it is not in fear; hence we need not wonder that the prophets, who consulted the good, not of a few, but of all, so strenuously commended Humility, Repentance, and Reverence. Indeed those who are a prey to these emotions may be led much more easily than others to live under the guidance of reason, that is, to become free and to enjoy the life of the blessed.

PROP. LV. *Extreme pride or dejection indicates extreme ignorance of self.*

Proof.—This is evident from Def. of the Emotions, xxviii. and xxix.

PROP. LVI. *Extreme pride or dejection indicates extreme infirmity of spirit.*

Proof.—The first foundation of virtue is self-preservation (IV. xxii. Coroll.) under the guidance of reason (IV. xxiv.). He, therefore, who is ignorant of himself, is ignorant of the foundation of all virtues, and consequently of all virtues.

---

[3] Land reads: "Quod ipsius agendi potentia juvatur"—which I have translated above. He suggests as alternative readings to 'quod' 'quo' (= whereby) and 'quodque' (= and that).

Again, to act virtuously is merely to act under the guidance of reason (IV. xxiv.): now he, that acts under the guidance of reason, must necessarily know that he so acts (II. xliii.). Therefore he who is in extreme ignorance of himself, and consequently of all virtues, acts least in obedience to virtue; in other words (IV. Def. viii.), is most infirm of spirit. Thus extreme pride or dejection indicates extreme infirmity of spirit. *Q.E.D.*

Corollary.—Hence it most clearly follows, that the proud and the dejected specially fall a prey to the emotions.

Note.—Yet dejection can be more easily corrected than pride; for the latter being a pleasurable emotion, and the former a painful emotion, the pleasurable is stronger than the painful (IV. xviii.).

PROP. LVII. *The proud man delights in the company of flatterers and parasites, but hates the company of the high-minded.*

Proof.—Pride is pleasure arising from a man's over-estimation of himself (Def. of the Emotions, xxviii. and vi.); this estimation the proud man will endeavour to foster by all the means in his power (III. xiii. note); he will therefore delight in the company of flatterers and parasites (whose character is too well known to need definition here), and will avoid the company of high-minded men, who value him according to his deserts. *Q.E.D.*

Note.—It would be too long a task to enumerate here all the evil results of pride, inasmuch as the proud are a prey to all the emotions, though to none of them less than to love and pity. I cannot, however, pass over in silence the fact, that a man may be called proud from his under-estimation of other people; and, therefore, pride in this sense may be defined as pleasure arising from the false opinion, whereby a man may consider himself superior to his fellows. The dejection, which is the opposite quality to this sort of pride, may be defined as pain arising from the false opinion, whereby a man may think himself inferior to his fellows. Such being the case, we can easily see that a proud man is necessarily envious (III. xli. note), and only takes pleasure in the company, who fool his weak mind to the top of his bent, and make him insane instead of merely foolish.

Though dejection is the emotion contrary to pride, yet is the dejected man very near akin to the proud man. For, inasmuch as his pain arises from a comparison between his own infirmity and other men's power or virtue, it will be removed, or, in other words, he will feel pleasure, if his imagination be occupied in contemplating other men's faults; whence arises the proverb, "The unhappy are comforted by finding fellow-sufferers." Contrariwise, he will be the more pained in proportion as he thinks himself inferior to others; hence none are so prone to envy as the dejected, they are specially keen in observing men's actions, with a view to fault-finding rather than correction, in order to reserve their praises for dejection, and to glory therein, though all the time with a dejected air. These effects follow as necessarily from the said emotion, as it follows from the nature of a triangle, that the three angles are equal to two right angles. I have already said that I call these and similar emotions bad, solely in respect to what is useful to man. The laws of nature have regard to nature's general order, whereof man is but a part. I mention this, in passing, lest any should think that I have wished to set forth the faults and irrational deeds of men rather than the nature and properties of things. For, as I said in the preface to the Third Part, I regard human emotions and their properties as on the same footing with other natural phenomena. Assuredly human emotions indicate the power and ingenuity of nature, if not of human nature, quite as fully as other things which we admire, and which we delight to contemplate. But I pass on to note those qualities in the emotions, which bring advantage to man, or inflict injury upon him.

PROP. LVIII. *Honour (gloria) is not repugnant to reason, but may arise therefrom.*

Proof.—This is evident from Def. of the Emotions, xxx., and also from the definition of an honourable man (IV. xxxvii. note i.).

Note.—Empty honour, as it is styled, is self-approval, fostered only by the good opinion of the populace; when this good opinion ceases there ceases also the self-approval, in other words, the highest object of each man's love (IV. lii. note); consequently, he whose honour is rooted in popular approval must, day by day, anxiously strive, act, and scheme in order to retain his reputation. For the populace is variable and inconstant, so that, if a reputation be not kept up, it quickly withers away. Everyone wishes to catch popular applause for himself, and readily represses the fame of others. The object of the strife being estimated as the greatest of all goods, each combatant is seized with a fierce desire to put down his rivals in every possible way, till he who at last comes out victorious is more proud of having done harm to others than of having done good to himself. This sort of honour, then, is really empty, being nothing.

The points to note concerning shame may easily be inferred from what was said on the subject of mercy and repentance. I will only add that shame, like compassion, though not a virtue, is yet good, in so far as it shows, that the feeler of shame is really imbued with the desire to live honourably; in the same way as suffering is good, as showing that the injured part is not mortified. Therefore, though a man who feels shame is sorrowful, he is yet more perfect than he, who is shameless, and has no desire to live honourably.

Such are the points which I undertook to remark upon concerning the emotions of pleasure and pain; as for the desires, they are good or bad according as they spring from good or evil emotions. But all, in so far as they are engendered in us by emotions wherein the mind is passive, are blind (as is evident from what was said in IV. xliv. note), and would be useless, if men could easily be induced to live by the guidance of reason only, as I will now briefly show.

PROP. LIX. *To all the actions whereto we are determined by emotions, wherein the mind is passive, we can be determined without emotion by reason.*

Proof.—To act rationally is nothing else (III. iii. and Def. ii.) but to perform those actions, which follow from the necessity of our nature considered in itself alone. But pain is bad, in so far as it diminishes or checks the power of action (IV. xli.); wherefore we cannot by pain be determined to any action, which we should be unable to perform under the guidance of reason. Again, pleasure is bad only in so far as it hinders a man's capability for action (IV. xli. xliii.); therefore to this extent we could not be determined by it to any action, which we could not perform under the guidance of reason. Lastly, pleasure, in so far as it is good, is in harmony with reason (for it consists in the fact that a man's capability for action is increased or aided); nor is the mind passive therein, except in so far as a man's power of action is not increased to the extent of affording him an adequate conception of himself and his actions (III. iii. and note).

Wherefore, if a man who is pleasurably affected be brought to such a state of perfection, that he gains an adequate conception of himself and his own actions, he will be equally, nay more, capable of those actions, to which he is determined by emotion wherein the mind is passive. But all emotions are attributable to pleasure, to pain, or to desire (Def. of the Emotions, iv. explanation); and desire (Def. of the Emotions, i.) is nothing else but the attempt to act; therefore, to all actions, &c. *Q.E.D.*

Another Proof.—A given action is called bad, in so far as it arises from one being affected by hatred or any evil emotion. But no action, considered in itself alone, is either good or bad (as we pointed out in the preface to Pt. IV.), one and the same action being sometimes good, sometimes bad; wherefore to the action which is sometimes bad, or arises from some evil emotion, we may be led by reason (IV. xix.). *Q.E.D.*

Note.—An example will put this point in a clearer light. The action of striking, in so far as it is considered physically, and in so far as we merely look to the fact that a man raises his arm, clenches his fist, and moves his whole arm violently downwards, is a virtue or excellence which is conceived as proper to the structure of the human body. If, then, a man, moved by anger or hatred, is led to clench his fist or to move his arm, this result takes place (as we showed in Pt. II.), because one and the same action can be associated with various mental images of things; therefore we may be determined to the performance of one and the same action by confused ideas, or by clear and distinct ideas. Hence it is evident that every desire which springs from emotion, wherein the mind is passive, would become useless, if men could be guided by reason. Let us now see why desire which arises from emotion, wherein the mind is passive, is called by us blind.

PROP. LX. *Desire arising from a pleasure or pain that is not attributable to the whole body, but only to one or certain parts thereof, is without utility in respect to a man as a whole.*

Proof.—Let it be assumed, for instance, that A, a part of a body, is so strengthened by some external cause, that it prevails over the remaining parts (IV. vi.). This part will not endeavour to do away with its own powers, in order that the other parts of the body may perform its office; for this it would be necessary for it to have a force or power of doing away with its own powers, which (III. vi.) is absurd. The said part, and, consequently, the mind also, will endeavour to preserve its condition. Wherefore desire arising from a pleasure of the kind aforesaid has no utility in reference to a man as a whole. If it be assumed, on the other hand, that the part, A, be checked so that the remaining parts prevail, it may be proved in the same manner that desire arising from pain has no utility in respect to a man as a whole. *Q.E.D.*

Note.—As pleasure is generally (IV. xliv. note) attributed to one part of the body, we generally desire to preserve our being without taking into consideration our health as a whole: to which it may be added, that the desires which have most hold over us (IV. ix.) take account of the present and not of the future.

PROP. LXI. *Desire which springs from reason cannot be excessive.*

Proof.—Desire (Def. of the Emotions, i.) considered absolutely is the actual essence of man, in so far as it is conceived as in any way determined to a particular activity by some given modification of itself. Hence desire, which arises from reason, that is (III. iii.), which is engendered in us in so far as we act, is the actual essence or nature of man, in so far as it is conceived as determined to such activities as are adequately conceived through man's essence only (III. Def. ii.). Now, if such desire could be excessive, human nature considered in itself alone would be able to exceed itself, or would be able to do more than it can, a manifest contradiction. Therefore, such desire cannot be excessive. *Q.E.D.*

PROP. LXII. *In so far as the mind conceives a thing under the dictates of reason, it is affected equally, whether the idea be of a thing future, past, or present.*

Proof.—Whatsoever the mind conceives under the guidance of reason, it conceives under the form of eternity or necessity (II. xliv. Coroll. ii.), and is therefore affected with the same certitude (II. xliii. and note). Wherefore, whether the thing be present, past, or future, the mind conceives it under the same necessity and is affected with the same certitude; and whether the idea be of something present, past, or future, it will in all cases be equally true (II. xli.); that is, it will always possess the same properties of an adequate idea (II. Def. iv.); therefore, in so far as the mind conceives things under the dictates of reason, it is affected in the same manner, whether the idea be of a thing future, past, or present. *Q.E.D.*

Note.—If we could possess an adequate knowledge of the duration of things, and could determine by reason their periods of existence, we should contemplate things future with the same emotion as things present; and the mind would desire as though it were present the good which it conceived as future; consequently it would necessarily neglect a lesser good in the present for the sake of a greater good in the future, and would in no wise desire that which is good in the present but a source of evil in the future, as we shall presently show. However, we can have but a very inadequate knowledge of the duration of things (II. xxxi.); and the periods of their existence (II. xliv. note) we can only determine by imagination, which is not so powerfully affected by the future as by the present. Hence such true knowledge of good and evil as we possess is merely abstract or general, and the judgment which we pass on the order of things and the connection of causes, with a view to determining what is good or bad for us in the present, is rather imaginary than real.

Therefore it is nothing wonderful, if the desire arising from such knowledge of good and evil, in so far as it looks on into the future, be more readily checked than the desire of things which are agreeable at the present time. (Cf. IV. xvi.)

PROP. LXIII. *He who is led by fear, and does good in order to escape evil, is not led by reason.*

Proof.—All the emotions which are attributable to the mind as active, or in other words to reason, are emotions of pleasure and desire (III. lix.); therefore, he who is led by fear, and does good in order to escape evil, is not led by reason.

Note.—Superstitious persons, who know better how to rail at vice than how to teach virtue, and who strive not to guide men by reason, but so to restrain them that they would rather escape evil than love virtue, have no other aim but to make others as wretched as themselves; wherefore it is nothing wonderful, if they be generally troublesome and odious to their fellow-men.

Corollary.—Under desire which springs from reason, we seek good directly, and shun evil indirectly.

Proof.—Desire which springs from reason can only spring from a pleasurable emotion, wherein the mind is not passive (III. lix.), in other words, from a pleasure which cannot be excessive (IV. lxi.), and not from pain; wherefore this desire springs from the knowledge of good, not of evil (IV. viii.); hence under the guidance of reason we seek good directly and only by implication shun evil. *Q.E.D.*

Note.—This Corollary may be illustrated by the example of a sick and a healthy man. The sick man through fear of death eats what he naturally shrinks from, but the healthy man takes pleasure in his food, and thus gets a better enjoyment out of life, than if he were in fear of death, and desired directly to avoid it. So a judge, who condemns a criminal to death, not from hatred or anger but from love of the public well-being, is guided solely by reason.

PROP. LXIV. *The knowledge of evil is an inadequate knowledge.*

Proof.—The knowledge of evil (IV. viii.) is pain, in so far as we are conscious thereof. Now pain is the transition to a lesser perfection (Def. of the Emotions, iii.) and therefore cannot be understood through man's nature (III. vi. and vii.); therefore it is a passive state (III. Def. ii.) which (III. iii.) depends on inadequate ideas; consequently the knowledge thereof (II. xxix.), namely, the knowledge of evil, is inadequate. *Q.E.D.*

Corollary.—Hence it follows that, if the human mind possessed only adequate ideas, it would form no conception of evil.

PROP. LXV. *Under the guidance of reason we should pursue the greater of two goods and the lesser of two evils.*

Proof.—A good which prevents our enjoyment of a greater good is in reality an evil; for we apply the terms good and bad to things, in so far as we compare them one with another (see preface to this Part); therefore, evil is in reality a lesser good; hence under the guidance of reason we seek or pursue only the greater good and the lesser evil. *Q.E.D.*

Corollary.—We may, under the guidance of reason, pursue the lesser evil as though it were the greater good, and we may shun the lesser good, which would be the cause of the greater evil. For the evil, which is here called the lesser, is really good, and the lesser good is really evil, wherefore we may seek the former and shun the latter. *Q.E.D.*

PROP. LXVI. *We may, under the guidance of reason, seek a greater good in the future in preference to a lesser good in the present, and we may seek a lesser evil in the present in preference to a greater evil in the future.*[4]

Proof.—If the mind could have an adequate knowledge of things future, it would be affected towards what is future in the same way as towards what is present (IV. lxii.); wherefore, looking merely to reason, as in this proposition we are assumed to do, there is no difference, whether the greater good or evil be assumed as present, or assumed as future; hence (IV. lxv.) we may seek a greater good in the future in preference to a lesser good in the present, &c. *Q.E.D.*

---

[4] "Malum præsens minus præ majori futuro." (Van Vloten). Bruder reads: "Malum præsens minus, quod causa est futuri alicujus mali." The last word of the latter is an obvious misprint, and is corrected by the Dutch translator into "majoris boni." (Pollock, p. 268, note.)

Corollary.—We may, under the guidance of reason, seek a lesser evil in the present, because it is the cause of a greater good in the future, and we may shun a lesser good in the present, because it is the cause of a greater evil in the future. This Corollary is related to the foregoing Proposition as the Corollary to IV. lxv. is related to the said IV. lxv.

Note.—If these statements be compared with what we have pointed out concerning the strength of the emotions in this Part up to Prop. xviii., we shall readily see the difference between a man, who is led solely by emotion or opinion, and a man, who is led by reason. The former, whether he will or no, performs actions whereof he is utterly ignorant; the latter is his own master and only performs such actions, as he knows are of primary importance in life, and therefore chiefly desires; wherefore I call the former a slave, and the latter a free man, concerning whose disposition and manner of life it will be well to make a few observations.

PROP. LXVII. *A free man thinks of death least of all things; and his wisdom is a meditation not of death but of life.*

Proof.—A free man is one who lives under the guidance of reason, who is not led by fear (IV. lxiii.), but who directly desires that which is good (IV. lxiii. Coroll.), in other words (IV. xxiv.), who strives to act, to live, and to preserve his being on the basis of seeking his own true advantage; wherefore such an one thinks of nothing less than of death, but his wisdom is a meditation of life. *Q.E.D.*

PROP. LXVIII. *If men were born free, they would, so long as they remained free, form no conception of good and evil.*

Proof.—I call free him who is led solely by reason; he, therefore, who is born free, and who remains free, has only adequate ideas; therefore (IV. lxiv. Coroll.) he has no conception of evil, or consequently (good and evil being correlative) of good. *Q.E.D.*

Note.—It is evident, from IV. iv., that the hypothesis of this Proposition is false and inconceivable, except in so far as we look solely to the nature of man, or rather to God; not in so far as the latter is infinite, but only in so far as he is the cause of man's existence.

This, and other matters which we have already proved,

seem to have been signified by Moses in the history of the
first man. For in that narrative no other power of God is conceived, save that whereby he created man, that is the power
wherewith he provided solely for man's advantage; it is
stated that God forbade man, being free, to eat of the tree
of the knowledge of good and evil, and that, as soon as man
should have eaten of it, he would straightway fear death
rather than desire to live. Further, it is written that when
man had found a wife, who was in entire harmony with
his nature, he knew that there could be nothing in nature
which could be more useful to him; but that after he believed
the beasts to be like himself, he straightway began to imitate their emotions (III. xxvii.), and to lose his freedom; this
freedom was afterwards recovered by the patriarchs, led by
the spirit of Christ; that is, by the idea of God, whereon alone
it depends, that man may be free, and desire for others the
good which he desires for himself, as we have shown above
(IV. xxxvii.).

PROP. LXIX. *The virtue of a free man is seen to be as
great, when it declines dangers, as when it overcomes them.*

Proof.—Emotion can only be checked or removed by an
emotion contrary to itself, and possessing more power in restraining emotion (IV. vii.). But blind daring and fear are
emotions, which can be conceived as equally great (IV. v.
and iii.): hence, no less virtue or firmness is required in
checking daring than in checking fear (III. lix. note); in
other words (Def. of the Emotions, xl. and xli.), the free
man shows as much virtue, when he declines dangers, as
when he strives to overcome them. *Q.E.D.*

Corollary.—The free man is as courageous in timely retreat
as in combat; or, a free man shows equal courage or presence
of mind, whether he elect to give battle or to retreat.

Note.—What courage (*animositas*) is, and what I mean
thereby, I explained in III. lix. note. By danger I mean everything, which can give rise to any evil, such as pain, hatred,
discord, &c.

PROP. LXX. *The free man, who lives among the ignorant,
strives, as far as he can, to avoid receiving favours from them.*

Proof.—Everyone judges what is good according to his

disposition (III. xxxix. note); wherefore an ignorant man, who has conferred a benefit on another, puts his own estimate upon it, and, if it appears to be estimated less highly by the receiver, will feel pain (III. xlii.). But the free man only desires to join other men to him in friendship (IV. xxxvii.), not repaying their benefits with others reckoned as of like value, but guiding himself and others by the free decision of reason, and doing only such things as he knows to be of primary importance. Therefore the free man, lest he should become hateful to the ignorant, or follow their desires rather than reason, will endeavour, as far as he can, to avoid receiving their favours.

Note.—I say, *as far as he can.* For though men be ignorant, yet are they men, and in cases of necessity could afford us human aid, the most excellent of all things: therefore it is often necessary to accept favours from them, and consequently to repay such favours in kind; we must, therefore, exercise caution in declining favours, lest we should have the appearance of despising those who bestow them, or of being, from avaricious motives, unwilling to requite them, and so give ground for offence by the very fact of striving to avoid it. Thus, in declining favours, we must look to the requirements of utility and courtesy.

PROP. LXXI. *Only free men are thoroughly grateful, one to another.*

Proof.—Only free men are thoroughly useful one to another, and associated among themselves by the closest necessity of friendship (IV. xxxv. and Coroll. i.), only such men endeavour, with mutual zeal of love, to confer benefits on each other (IV. xxxvii.), and, therefore, only they are thoroughly grateful one to another. *Q.E.D.*

Note.—The goodwill, which men who are led by blind desire have for one another, is generally a bargaining or enticement, rather than pure goodwill. Moreover, ingratitude is not an emotion. Yet it is base, inasmuch as it generally shows, that a man is affected by excessive hatred, anger, pride, avarice, &c. He who, by reason of his folly, knows not how to return benefits, is not ungrateful, much less he who is not gained over by the gifts of a courtesan to serve her lust, or by a thief to conceal his thefts, or by any similar persons. Contrariwise, such an one shows a constant mind, inasmuch as he cannot by any gifts be corrupted, to his own or the general hurt.

PROP. LXXII. *The free man never acts fraudulently, but always in good faith.*

Proof.—If it be asked: What should a man's conduct be in a case where he could by breaking faith free himself from the danger of present death? Would not his plan of self-preservation completely persuade him to deceive? this may be answered by pointing out that, if reason persuaded him to act thus, it would persuade all men to act in a similar manner, in which case reason would persuade men not to agree in good faith to unite their forces, or to have laws in common, that is, not to have any general laws, which is absurd.

PROP. LXXIII. *The man, who is guided by reason, is more free in a State, where he lives under a general system of law, than in solitude, where he is independent.*

Proof.—The man, who is guided by reason, does not obey through fear (IV. lxiii.): but, in so far as he endeavours to preserve his being according to the dictates of reason, that is (IV. lxvi. note), in so far as he endeavours to live in freedom, he desires to order his life according to the general good (IV. xxxvii.), and, consequently (as we showed in IV. xxxvii. note ii.), to live according to the laws of his country. Therefore the free man, in order to enjoy greater freedom, desires to possess the general rights of citizenship. *Q.E.D.*

Note.—These and similar observations, which we have made on man's true freedom, may be referred to strength, that is, to courage and nobility of character (III. lix. note). I do not think it worth while to prove separately all the properties of strength; much less need I show, that he that is strong hates no man, is angry with no man, envies no man, is indignant with no man, despises no man, and least of all things is proud. These propositions, and all that relate to the true way of life and religion, are easily proved from IV. xxxvii. and xlvi.; namely, that hatred should be overcome with love, and that every man should desire for others the good which he seeks for himself. We may also repeat what we drew attention to in the note to IV. l., and in other places; namely, that the strong man has ever first in his thoughts, that all things follow from the necessity of the divine nature; so that whatsoever he deems to be hurtful and evil, and whatsoever, accordingly, seems to him impious, horrible, unjust, and base, assumes that appearance owing to his own disordered, fragmentary, and confused view of the universe. Wherefore he strives before all things to conceive things as they really are, and to remove the hindrances to true knowledge, such as are hatred, anger, envy, derision, pride, and similar emotions, which I have mentioned above. Thus he endeavours, as we said before, as far as in him lies, to do good, and to go on his way rejoicing. How far human virtue is capable of attaining to such a condition, and what its powers may be, I will prove in the following Part.

APPENDIX

What I have said in this Part concerning the right way of life has not been arranged, so as to admit of being seen at one view, but has been set forth piece-meal, according as I thought each Proposition could most readily be deduced from what preceded it. I propose, therefore, to rearrange my remarks and to bring them under leading heads.

I. All our endeavours or desires so follow from the necessity of our nature, that they can be understood either through it alone, as their proximate cause, or by virtue of our being a part of nature, which cannot be adequately conceived through itself without other individuals.

II. Desires, which follow from our nature in such a manner, that they can be understood through it alone, are those which are referred to the mind, in so far as the latter is conceived to consist of adequate ideas: the remaining desires are only referred to the mind, in so far as it conceives things inadequately, and their force and increase are generally defined not by the power of man, but by the power of things external to us: wherefore the former are rightly called actions, the latter passions, for the former always indicate our power, the latter, on the other hand, show our infirmity and fragmentary knowledge.

III. Our actions, that is, those desires which are defined by man's power or reason, are always good. The rest may be either good or bad.

IV. Thus in life it is before all things useful to perfect the understanding, or reason, as far as we can, and in this alone man's highest happiness or blessedness consists, indeed blessedness is nothing else but the contentment of spirit, which arises from the intuitive knowledge of God: now, to perfect the understanding is nothing else but to understand God, God's attributes, and the actions which follow from the necessity of his nature. Wherefore of a man, who is led by reason, the ultimate aim or highest desire, whereby he seeks to govern all his fellows, is that whereby he is brought to the adequate conception of himself and of all things within the scope of his intelligence.

V. Therefore, without intelligence there is not rational life: and things are only good, in so far as they aid man in his enjoyment of the intellectual life, which is defined by intelligence. Contrariwise, whatsoever things hinder man's perfecting of his reason, and capability to enjoy the rational life, are alone called evil.

VI. As all things whereof man is the efficient cause are necessarily good, no evil can befall man except through external causes; namely, by virtue of man being a part of universal nature, whose laws human nature is compelled to obey, and to conform to in almost infinite ways.

VII. It is impossible, that man should not be a part of nature, or that he should not follow her general order; but if he be thrown among individuals whose nature is in harmony with his own, his power of action will thereby be aided and fostered, whereas, if he be thrown among such as are but very little in harmony with his nature, he will hardly be able to accommodate himself to them without undergoing a great change himself.

VIII. Whatsoever in nature we deem to be evil, or to be capable of injuring our faculty for existing and enjoying the rational life, we may endeavour to remove in whatever way seems safest to us; on the other hand, whatsoever we deem to be good or useful for preserving our being, and enabling us to enjoy the rational life, we may appropriate to our use and employ as we think best. Everyone without exception may, by sovereign right of nature, do whatsoever he thinks will advance his own interest.

IX. Nothing can be in more harmony with the nature of any given thing than other individuals of the same species; therefore (cf. vii.) for man in the preservation of his being and the enjoyment of the rational life there is nothing more useful than his fellow-man who is led by reason. Further, as we know not anything among individual things which is more excellent than a man led by reason, no man can better display the power of his skill and disposition, than in so training men, that they come at last to live under the dominion of their own reason.

X. In so far as men are influenced by envy or any kind of hatred, one towards another, they are at variance, and are therefore to be feared in proportion, as they are more powerful than their fellows.

XI. Yet minds are not conquered by force, but by love and high-mindedness.

XII. It is before all things useful to men to associate their ways of life, to bind themselves together with such bonds as they think most fitted to gather them all into unity, and generally to do whatsoever serves to strengthen friendship.

XIII. But for this there is need of skill and watchfulness. For men are diverse (seeing that those who live under the guidance of reason are few), yet are they generally envious and more prone to revenge than to sympathy. No small force of character is therefore required to take everyone as he is, and to restrain one's self from imitating the emotions of others. But those who carp at mankind, and are more skilled in railing at vice than in instilling virtue, and who break rather than strengthen men's dispositions, are hurtful both to themselves and others. Thus many from too great impatience of spirit, or from misguided religious zeal, have preferred to live among brutes rather than among men; as boys or youths, who cannot peaceably endure the chidings of their parents, will enlist as soldiers and choose the hardships of war and the despotic discipline in preference to the comforts of home and the admonitions of their father: suffering any burden to be put upon them, so long as they may spite their parents.

XIV. Therefore, although men are generally governed in everything by their own lusts, yet their association in common brings many more advantages than drawbacks. Wherefore it is better to bear patiently the wrongs they may do us, and to strive to promote whatsoever serves to bring about harmony and friendship.

XV. Those things, which beget harmony, are such as are attributable to justice, equity, and honourable living. For men brook ill not only what is unjust or iniquitous, but also what is reckoned disgraceful, or that a man should slight the received customs of their society. For winning love those qualities are especially necessary which have regard to religion and piety (cf. IV. xxxvii. notes, i. ii.; xlvi. note; and lxxiii. note).

XVI. Further, harmony is often the result of fear: but such harmony is insecure. Further, fear arises from infirmity of spirit, and moreover belongs not to the exercise of reason: the same is true of compassion, though this latter seems to bear a certain resemblance to piety.

XVII. Men are also gained over by liberality, especially such as have not the means to buy what is necessary to sustain life. However, to give aid to every poor man is far beyond the power and the advantage of any private person. For the riches of any private person are wholly inadequate to meet such a call. Again, an individual man's resources of character are too limited for him to be able to make all men his friends. Hence providing for the poor is a duty, which falls on the State as a whole, and has regard only to the general advantage.

XVIII. In accepting favours, and in returning gratitude our duty must be wholly different (cf. IV. lxx. note; lxxi. note).

XIX. Again, meretricious love, that is, the lust of generation arising from bodily beauty, and generally every sort of love, which owns anything save freedom of soul as its cause, readily passes into hate; unless indeed, what is worse, it is a species of madness; and then it promotes discord rather than harmony (cf. III. xxxi. Coroll.).

XX. As concerning marriage, it is certain that this is in

harmony with reason, if the desire for physical union be not engendered solely by bodily beauty, but also by the desire to beget children and to train them up wisely; and moreover, if the love of both, to wit, of the man and of the woman, is not caused by bodily beauty only, but also by freedom of soul.

XXI. Furthermore, flattery begets harmony; but only by means of the vile offence of slavishness or treachery. None are more readily taken with flattery than the proud, who wish to be first, but are not.

XXII. There is in abasement a spurious appearance of piety and religion. Although abasement is the opposite to pride, yet is he that abases himself most akin to the proud (IV. lvii. note).

XXIII. Shame also brings about harmony, but only in such matters as cannot be hid. Further, as shame is a species of pain, it does not concern the exercise of reason.

XXIV. The remaining emotions of pain towards men are directly opposed to justice, equity, honour, piety, and religion; and, although indignation seems to bear a certain resemblance to equity, yet is life but lawless, where every man may pass judgment on another's deeds, and vindicate his own or other men's rights.

XXV. Correctness of conduct (*modestia*), that is, the desire of pleasing men which is determined by reason, is attributable to piety (as we said in IV. xxxvii. note i.). But, if it spring from emotion, it is ambition, or the desire whereby men, under the false cloak of piety, generally stir up discords and seditions. For he who desires to aid his fellows either in word or in deed, so that they may together enjoy the highest good, he, I say, will before all things strive to win them over with love: not to draw them into admiration, so that a system may be called after his name, nor to give any cause for envy. Further, in his conversation he will shrink from talking of men's faults, and will be careful to speak but sparingly of human infirmity: but he will dwell at length on human virtue or power, and the way whereby it may be perfected. Thus will men be stirred not by fear, nor by aversion, but only by the emotion of joy, to endeavour, so far as in them lies, to live in obedience to reason.

XXVI. Besides men, we know of no particular thing in nature in whose mind we may rejoice, and whom we can associate with ourselves in friendship or any sort of fellowship; therefore, whatsoever there be in nature besides man, a regard for our advantage does not call on us to preserve, but to preserve or destroy according to its various capabilities, and to adapt to our use as best we may.

XXVII. The advantage which we derive from things external to us, besides the experience and knowledge which we acquire from observing them, and from recombining their elements in different forms, is principally the preservation of the body; from this point of view, those things are most useful which can so feed and nourish the body, that all its parts may rightly fulfil their functions. For, in proportion as the body is capable of being affected in a greater variety of ways, and of affecting external bodies in a great number of ways, so much the more is the mind capable of thinking (IV. xxxviii. xxxix.). But there seem to be very few things of this kind in nature; wherefore for the due nourishment of the body we must use many foods of diverse nature. For the human body is composed of very many parts of different nature, which stand in continual need of varied nourishment, so that the whole body may be equally capable of doing everything that can follow from its own nature, and consequently that the mind also may be equally capable of forming many perceptions.

XXVIII. Now for providing these nourishments the strength of each individual would hardly suffice, if men did not lend one another mutual aid. But money has furnished us with a token for everything: hence it is with the notion of money, that the mind of the multitude is chiefly engrossed: nay, it can hardly conceive any kind of pleasure, which is not accompanied with the idea of money as cause.

XXIX. This result is the fault only of those, who seek money, not from poverty or to supply their necessary wants, but because they have learned the arts of gain, wherewith they bring themselves to great splendour. Certainly they nourish their bodies, according to custom, but scantily, believing that they lose as much of their wealth as they spend on the preservation of their body. But they who know the true use of money, and who fix the measure of wealth solely with regard to their actual needs, live content with little.

XXX. As, therefore, those things are good which assist the various parts of the body, and enable them to perform their functions; and as pleasure consists in an increase of, or aid to, man's power, in so far as he is composed of mind and body; it follows that all those things which bring pleasure are good. But seeing that things do not work with the object of giving us pleasure, and that their power of action is not tempered to suit our advantage, and, lastly, that pleasure is generally referred to one part of the body more than to the other parts; therefore most emotions of pleasure (unless reason and watchfulness be at hand), and consequently the desires arising therefrom, may become excessive. Moreover we may add that emotion leads us to pay most regard to what is agreeable in the present, nor can we estimate what is future with emotions equally vivid. (IV. xliv. note, and lx. note.)

XXXI. Superstition, on the other hand, seems to account as good all that brings pain, and as bad all that brings pleasure. However, as we said above (IV. xlv. note), none but the envious take delight in my infirmity and trouble. For the greater the pleasure whereby we are affected, the greater is the perfection whereto we pass, and consequently the more do we partake of the divine nature: no pleasure can ever be evil, which is regulated by a true regard for our advantage. But contrariwise he, who is led by fear and does good only to avoid evil, is not guided by reason.

XXXII. But human power is extremely limited, and is infinitely surpassed by the power of external causes; we have not, therefore, an absolute power of shaping to our use those things which are without us. Nevertheless, we shall bear with an equal mind all that happens to us in contravention to the claims of our own advantage, so long as we are conscious, that we have done our duty, and that the power which we possess is not sufficient to enable us to protect ourselves completely; remembering that we are a part of universal nature, and that we follow her order. If we have a clear and distinct understanding of this, that part of our nature which is defined by intelligence, in other words the better part of ourselves, will assuredly acquiesce in what befalls us, and in such acquiescence will endeavour to persist. For, in so far as we are intelligent beings, we cannot desire anything save that which is necessary, nor yield absolute acquiescence to anything, save to that which is true: wherefore, in so far as we have a right understanding of these things, the endeavour of the better part of ourselves is in harmony with the order of nature as a whole.

PART V OF THE POWER OF THE UNDERSTANDING, OR OF HUMAN FREEDOM

PREFACE

At length I pass to the remaining portion of my Ethics, which is concerned with the way leading to freedom. I shall therefore treat therein of the power of the reason, showing how far the reason can control the emotions, and what is the nature of Mental Freedom or Blessedness; we shall then be able to see, how much more powerful the wise man is than the ignorant. It is no part of my design to point out the method and means whereby the understanding may be perfected, nor to show the skill whereby the body may be so tended, as to be capable of the due performance of its functions. The latter question lies in the province of Medicine, the former in the province of Logic. Here, therefore, I repeat, I shall treat only of the power of the mind, or of reason; and I shall mainly show the extent and nature of its dominion over the emotions, for their control and moderation. That we do not possess absolute dominion over them, I have already shown. Yet the Stoics have thought, that the emotions depended absolutely on our will, and that we could absolutely govern them. But these philosophers were compelled, by the protest of experience, not from their own principles, to confess, that no slight practice and zeal is needed to control and moderate them: and this someone endeavoured to illustrate by the example (if I remember rightly) of two dogs, the one a house-dog and the other a hunting-dog. For by long training it could be brought about, that the house-dog should become accustomed to hunt, and the hunting-dog to cease from run-

ning after hares. To this opinion Descartes not a little inclines.
For he maintained, that the soul or mind is specially united
to a particular part of the brain, namely, to that part called
the pineal gland, by the aid of which the mind is enabled to
feel all the movements which are set going in the body, and
also external objects, and which the mind by a simple act of
volition can put in motion in various ways. He asserted, that
this gland is so suspended in the midst of the brain, that it
could be moved by the slightest motion of the animal spirits:
further, that this gland is suspended in the midst of the brain
in as many different manners, as the animal spirits can impinge thereon; and, again, that as many different marks are
impressed on the said gland, as there are different external
objects which impel the animal spirits towards it; whence it
follows, that if the will of the soul suspends the gland in a
position, wherein it has already been suspended once before
by the animal spirits driven in one way or another, the gland
in its turn reacts on the said spirits, driving and determining
them to the condition wherein they were, when repulsed before by a similar position of the gland. He further asserted,
that every act of mental volition is united in nature to a certain given motion of the gland. For instance, whenever anyone desires to look at a remote object, the act of volition
causes the pupil of the eye to dilate, whereas, if the person
in question had only thought of the dilatation of the pupil,
the mere wish to dilate it would not have brought about the
result, inasmuch as the motion of the gland, which serves to
impel the animal spirits towards the optic nerve in a way
which would dilate or contract the pupil, is not associated in
nature with the wish to dilate or contract the pupil, but with
the wish to look at remote or very near objects. Lastly, he
maintained that, although every motion of the aforesaid gland
seems to have been united by nature to one particular thought
out of the whole number of our thoughts from the very beginning of our life, yet it can nevertheless become through
habituation associated with other thoughts; this he endeavours
to prove in the *Passions de l'âme*, I. 50. He thence concludes,
that there is no soul so weak, that it cannot, under proper
direction, acquire absolute power over its passions. For pas-

sions as defined by him are "perceptions, or feelings, or disturbances of the soul, which are referred to the soul as species, and which (mark the expression) are produced, preserved, and strengthened through some movement of the spirits." (*Passions de l'âme*, I. 27.) But, seeing that we can join any motion of the gland, or consequently of the spirits, to any volition, the determination of the will depends entirely on our own powers; if, therefore, we determine our will with sure and firm decisions in the direction to which we wish our actions to tend, and associate the motions of the passions which we wish to acquire with the said decisions, we shall acquire an absolute dominion over our passions. Such is the doctrine of this illustrious philosopher (in so far as I gather it from his own words); it is one which, had it been less ingenious, I could hardly believe to have proceeded from so great a man. Indeed, I am lost in wonder, that a philosopher, who had stoutly asserted, that he would draw no conclusions which do not follow from self-evident premisses, and would affirm nothing which he did not clearly and distinctly perceive, and who had so often taken to task the scholastics for wishing to explain obscurities through occult qualities, could maintain a hypothesis, beside which occult qualities are commonplace. What does he understand, I ask, by the union of the mind and the body? What clear and distinct conception has he got of thought in most intimate union with a certain particle of extended matter? Truly I should like him to explain this union through its proximate cause. But he had so distinct a conception of mind being distinct from body, that he could not assign any particular cause of the union between the two, or of the mind itself, but was obliged to have recourse to the cause of the whole universe, that is to God. Further, I should much like to know, what degree of motion the mind can impart to this pineal gland, and with what force can it hold it suspended? For I am in ignorance, whether this gland can be agitated more slowly or more quickly by the mind than by the animal spirits, and whether the motions of the passions, which we have closely united with firm decisions, cannot be again disjoined therefrom by physical causes; in which case it would follow that, although the mind firmly intended to face a given

danger, and had united to this decision the motions of bold-
ness, yet at the sight of the danger the gland might become
suspended in a way, which would preclude the mind thinking
of anything except running away. In truth, as there is no common standard of volition and motion, so is there no comparison possible between the powers of the mind and the power
or strength of the body; consequently the strength of one cannot in any wise be determined by the strength of the other.
We may also add, that there is no gland discoverable in the
midst of the brain, so placed that it can thus easily be set in
motion in so many ways, and also that all the nerves are not
prolonged so far as the cavities of the brain. Lastly, I omit all
the assertions which he makes concerning the will and its
freedom, inasmuch as I have abundantly proved that his premisses are false. Therefore, since the power of the mind, as I
have shown above, is defined by the understanding only, we
shall determine solely by the knowledge of the mind the remedies against the emotions, which I believe all have had experience of, but do not accurately observe or distinctly see, and
from the same basis we shall deduce all those conclusions,
which have regard to the mind's blessedness.

AXIOMS

I. If two contrary actions be started in the same subject,
a change must necessarily take place, either in both, or in one
of the two, and continue until they cease to be contrary.

II. The power of an effect is defined by the power of its
cause, in so far as its essence is explained or defined by the
essence of its cause.

(This axiom is evident from III. vii.)

PROP. I. *Even as thoughts and the ideas of things are arranged and associated in the mind, so are the modifications
of body or the images of things precisely in the same way
arranged and associated in the body.*

Proof.—The order and connection of ideas is the same (II.
vii.) as the order and connection of things, and *vice versâ* the
order and connection of things is the same (II. vi. Coroll. and
vii.) as the order and connection of ideas. Wherefore, even

as the order and connection of ideas in the mind takes place according to the order and association of modifications of the body (II. xviii.), so *vice versâ* (III. ii.) the order and connection of modifications of the body takes place in accordance with the manner, in which thoughts and the ideas of things are arranged and associated in the mind. *Q.E.D.*

PROP. II. *If we remove a disturbance of the spirit, or emotion, from the thought of an external cause, and unite it to other thoughts, then will the love or hatred towards that external cause, and also the vacillations of spirit which arise from these emotions, be destroyed.*

Proof.—That, which constitutes the reality of love or hatred, is pleasure or pain, accompanied by the idea of an external cause (Def. of the Emotions, vi. vii.); wherefore, when this cause is removed, the reality of love or hatred is removed with it; therefore these emotions and those which arise therefrom are destroyed. *Q.E.D.*

PROP. III. *An emotion, which is a passion, ceases to be a passion, as soon as we form a clear and distinct idea thereof.*

Proof.—An emotion, which is a passion, is a confused idea (by the general Def. of the Emotions). If, therefore, we form a clear and distinct idea of a given emotion, that idea will only be distinguished from the emotion, in so far as it is referred to the mind only, by reason (II. xxi. and note); therefore (III. iii.), the emotion will cease to be a passion. *Q.E.D.*

Corollary.—An emotion therefore becomes more under our control, and the mind is less passive in respect to it, in proportion as it is more known to us.

PROP. IV. *There is no modification of the body, whereof we cannot form some clear and distinct conception.*

Proof.—Properties which are common to all things can only be conceived adequately (II. xxxviii.); therefore (II. xii. and Lemma ii. after II. xiii.) there is no modification of the body, whereof we cannot form some clear and distinct conception. *Q.E.D.*

Corollary.—Hence it follows that there is no emotion, whereof we cannot form some clear and distinct conception. For an emotion is the idea of a modification of the body (by the general Def. of the Emotions), and must therefore (by the preceding Prop.) involve some clear and distinct conception.

Note.—Seeing that there is nothing which is not followed by an effect (I. xxxvi.), and that we clearly and distinctly understand whatever follows from an idea, which in us is adequate (II. xl.), it follows that everyone has the power of clearly and distinctly understanding himself and his emotions, if not absolutely, at any rate in part, and consequently of bringing it about, that he should become less subject to them. To attain this result, therefore, we must chiefly direct our efforts to acquiring, as far as possible, a clear and distinct knowledge of every emotion, in order that the mind may thus, through emotion, be determined to think of those things which it clearly and distinctly perceives, and wherein it fully acquiesces: and thus that the emotion itself may be separated from the thought of an external cause, and may be associated with true thoughts; whence it will come to pass, not only that love, hatred, &c. will be destroyed (V. ii.), but also that the appetites or desires, which are wont to arise from such emotion, will become incapable of being excessive (IV. lxi.). For it must be especially remarked, that the appetite through which a man is said to be active, and that through which he is said to be passive is one and the same. For instance, we have shown that human nature is so constituted, that everyone desires his fellow-men to live after his own fashion (III. xxxi. note); in a man, who is not guided by reason, this appetite is a passion which is called ambition, and does not greatly differ from pride; whereas in a man, who lives by the dictates of reason, it is an activity or virtue which is called piety (IV. xxxvii. note i. and second proof). In like manner all appetites or desires are only passions, in so far as they spring from inadequate ideas; the same results are accredited to virtue, when they are aroused or generated by adequate ideas. For all desires, whereby we are determined to any given action, may arise as much from adequate as from inadequate ideas (IV. lix.). Than this remedy for the emotions (to return to the point from which I started), which consists in a true knowledge thereof, nothing more excellent, being within our power, can be devised. For the mind has no other power save that of thinking and of forming adequate ideas, as we have shown above (III. iii.).

PROP. V. *An emotion towards a thing which we conceive simply, and not as necessary, or as contingent, or as possible, is, other conditions being equal, greater than any other emotion.*

Proof.—An emotion towards a thing, which we conceive to be free, is greater than one towards what we conceive to be necessary (III. xlix.), and, consequently, still greater than one towards what we conceive as possible, or contingent (IV. xi.). But to conceive a thing as free can be nothing else than to conceive it simply, while we are in ignorance of the causes whereby it has been determined to action (II. xxxv. note); therefore, an emotion towards a thing which we conceive simply is, other conditions being equal, greater than one, which we feel towards what is necessary, possible, or contingent, and, consequently, it is the greatest of all. *Q.E.D.*

PROP. VI. *The mind has greater power over the emotions and is less subject thereto, in so far as it understands all things as necessary.*

Proof.—The mind understands all things to be necessary (I. xxix.) and to be determined to existence and operation by an infinite chain of causes; therefore (by the foregoing Proposition), it thus far brings it about, that it is less subject to the emotions arising therefrom, and (III. xlviii.) feels less emotion towards the things themselves. *Q.E.D.*

Note.—The more this knowledge, that things are necessary, is applied to particular things, which we conceive more distinctly and vividly, the greater is the power of the mind over the emotions, as experience also testifies. For we see, that the pain arising from the loss of any good is mitigated, as soon as the man who has lost it perceives, that it could not by any means have been preserved. So also we see that no one pities an infant, because it cannot speak, walk, or reason, or lastly, because it passes so many years, as it were, in unconsciousness. Whereas, if most people were born full-grown and only one here and there as an infant, everyone would pity the infants; because infancy would not then be looked on as a state natural and necessary, but as a fault or delinquency in Nature; and we may note several other instances of the same sort.

PROP. VII. *Emotions which are aroused or spring from reason, if we take account of time, are stronger than those which are attributable to particular objects that we regard as absent.*

Proof.—We do not regard a thing as absent, by reason of the emotion wherewith we conceive it, but by reason of the body being affected by another emotion excluding the existence of the said thing (II. xvii.). Wherefore, the emotion, which is referred to the thing which we regard as absent, is not of a nature to overcome the rest of a man's activities and power (IV. vi.), but is, on the contrary, of a nature to be in some sort controlled by the emotions, which exclude the existence of its external cause (IV. ix.). But an emotion which springs from reason is necessarily referred to the common properties of things (see the def. of reason in II. xl. note ii.), which we always regard as present (for there can be nothing to exclude their present existence), and which we always conceive in the same manner (II. xxxviii.). Wherefore an emotion of this kind always remains the same; and consequently (V. Ax. i.) emotions, which are contrary thereto and are not kept going by their external causes, will be obliged to adapt themselves to it more and more, until they are no longer contrary to it; to this extent the emotion which springs from reason is more powerful. *Q.E.D.*

PROP. VIII. *An emotion is stronger in proportion to the number of simultaneous concurrent causes whereby it is aroused.*

Proof.—Many simultaneous causes are more powerful than a few (III. vii.): therefore (IV. v.), in proportion to the increased number of simultaneous causes whereby it is aroused, an emotion becomes stronger. *Q.E.D.*

Note.—This proposition is also evident from V. Ax. ii.

PROP. IX. *An emotion which is attributable to many and diverse causes which the mind regards as simultaneous with the emotion itself is less hurtful, and we are less subject thereto and less affected towards each of its causes, than if it were a different and equally powerful emotion attributable to fewer causes or to a single cause.*

Proof.—An emotion is only bad or hurtful, in so far as it hinders the mind from being able to think (IV. xxvi. xxvii.); therefore, an emotion, whereby the mind is determined to the contemplation of several things at once, is less hurtful than another equally powerful emotion, which so engrosses the mind in the single contemplation of a few objects or of one, that it is unable to think of anything else; this was our first point. Again, as the mind's essence, in other words, its power (III. vii.), consists solely in thought (II. xi.), the mind is less passive in respect to an emotion, which causes it to think of several things at once, than in regard to an equally strong emotion, which keeps it engrossed in the contemplation of a few or of a single object: this was our second point. Lastly, this emotion (III. xlviii.), in so far as it is attributable to several causes, is less powerful in regard to each of them. *Q.E.D.*

PROP. X. *So long as we are not assailed by emotions contrary to our nature, we have the power of arranging and associating the modifications of our body according to the intellectual order.*

Proof.—The emotions, which are contrary to our nature, that is (IV. xxx.), which are bad, are bad in so far as they impede the mind from understanding (IV. xxvii.). So long, therefore, as we are not assailed by emotions contrary to our nature, the mind's power, whereby it endeavours to understand things (IV. xxvi.), is not impeded, and therefore it is able to form clear and distinct ideas and to deduce them one from another (II. xl. note ii. and xlvii. note); consequently we have in such cases the power of arranging and associating the modifications of the body according to the intellectual order. *Q.E.D.*

Note.—By this power of rightly arranging and associating the bodily modifications we can guard ourselves from being easily affected by evil emotions. For (V. vii.) a greater force is needed for controlling the emotions, when they are arranged and associated according to the intellectual order, than when they are uncertain and unsettled. The best we can do, therefore, so long as we do not possess a perfect knowledge of our emotions, is to frame a system of right conduct, or fixed practical precepts, to commit it to memory, and to apply it forth-with[1] to the particular circumstances which now and again meet us in life, so that our imagination may become fully imbued therewith, and that it may be always ready to our hand. For instance, we have laid down among the rules of life (IV. xlvi. and note), that hatred should be overcome with love or high-mindedness, and not requited with hatred in return. Now, that this precept of reason may be always ready to our hand in time of need, we should often think over and reflect upon the wrongs generally committed by men, and in what manner and way they may be best warded off by high-mindedness: we shall thus associate the idea of wrong with the idea of this precept, which accordingly will always be ready for use when a wrong is done to us (II. xviii.). If we keep also in readiness the notion of our true advantage, and of the good which follows from mutual friendships, and common fellow-ships; further, if we remember that complete acquiescence is the result of the right way of life (IV. lii.), and that men, no less than everything else, act by the necessity of their nature: in such case I say the wrong, or the hatred, which commonly arises therefrom, will engross a very small part of our imagination and will be easily overcome; or, if the anger which springs from a grievous wrong be not overcome easily, it will neverthe-less be overcome, though not without a spiritual conflict, far sooner than if we had not thus reflected on the subject before-hand. As is indeed evident from V. vi. vii. viii. We should, in the same way, reflect on courage as a means of overcoming fear; the ordinary dangers of life should frequently be brought to mind and imagined, together with the means whereby through readiness of resource and strength of mind we can avoid and overcome them. But we must note, that in arrang-ing our thoughts and conceptions we should always bear in mind that which is good in every individual thing (IV. lxiii. Coroll. and III. lix.), in order that we may always be deter-mined to action by an emotion of pleasure. For instance, if a

---

[1] *Continuo.* Rendered "constantly" by Mr. Pollock on the ground that the classical meaning of the word does not suit the context. I venture to think, however, that a tolerable sense may be obtained without doing violence to Spinoza's scholarship.

man sees that he is too keen in the pursuit of honour, let him think over its right use, the end for which it should be pursued, and the means whereby he may attain it. Let him not think of its misuse, and its emptiness, and the fickleness of mankind, and the like, whereof no man thinks except through a morbidness of disposition; with thoughts like these do the most ambitious most torment themselves, when they despair of gaining the distinctions they hanker after, and in thus giving vent to their anger would fain appear wise. Wherefore it is certain that those, who cry out the loudest against the misuse of honour and the vanity of the world, are those who most greedily covet it. This is not peculiar to the ambitious, but is common to all who are ill-used by fortune, and who are infirm in spirit. For a poor man also, who is miserly, will talk incessantly of the misuse of wealth and of the vices of the rich; whereby he merely torments himself, and shows the world that he is intolerant, not only of his own poverty, but also of other people's riches. So, again, those who have been ill received by a woman they love think of nothing but the inconstancy, treachery, and other stock faults of the fair sex; all of which they consign to oblivion, directly they are again taken into favour by their sweetheart. Thus he who would govern his emotions and appetite solely by the love of freedom strives, as far as he can, to gain a knowledge of the virtues and their causes, and to fill his spirit with the joy which arises from the true knowledge of them: he will in no wise desire to dwell on men's faults, or to carp at his fellows, or to revel in a false show of freedom. Whosoever will diligently observe and practise these precepts (which indeed are not difficult) will verily, in a short space of time, be able, for the most part, to direct his actions according to the commandments of reason.

PROP. XI. *In proportion as a mental image is referred to more objects, so is it more frequent, or more often vivid, and occupies the mind more.*

Proof.—In proportion as a mental image or an emotion is referred to more objects, so are there more causes whereby it can be aroused and fostered, all of which (by hypothesis) the mind contemplates simultaneously in association with the given emotion; therefore the emotion is more frequent, or is more often in full vigour, and (V. viii.) occupies the mind more. *Q.E.D.*

PROP. XII. *The mental images of things are more easily associated with the images referred to things which we clearly and distinctly understand, than with others.*

Proof.—Things, which we clearly and distinctly understand, are either the common properties of things or deductions therefrom (see definition of Reason, II. xl. note ii.), and are consequently (by the last Prop.) more often aroused in us. Wherefore it may more readily happen, that we should contemplate other things in conjunction with these than in conjunction with something else, and consequently (II. xviii.) that the images of the said things should be more often associated with the images of these than with the images of something else. *Q.E.D.*

PROP. XIII. *A mental image is more often vivid, in proportion as it is associated with a greater number of other images.*

Proof.—In proportion as an image is associated with a greater number of other images, so (II. xviii.) are there more causes whereby it can be aroused. *Q.E.D.*

PROP. XIV. *The mind can bring it about, that all bodily modifications or images of things may be referred to the idea of God.*

Proof.—There is no modification of the body, whereof the mind may not form some clear and distinct conception (V. iv.); wherefore it can bring it about, that they should all be referred to the idea of God (I. xv.). *Q.E.D.*

PROP. XV. *He who clearly and distinctly understands himself and his emotions loves God, and so much the more in proportion as he more understands himself and his emotions.*

Proof.—He who clearly and distinctly understands himself and his emotions feels pleasure (III. liii.), and this pleasure is (by the last Prop.) accompanied by the idea of God; therefore (Def. of the Emotions, vi.) such an one loves God, and (for the same reason) so much the more in proportion as he more understands himself and his emotions. *Q.E.D.*

PROP. XVI. *This love towards God must hold the chief place in the mind.*

Proof.—For this love is associated with all the modifications of the body (V. xiv.) and is fostered by them all (V. xv.); therefore (V. xi.), it must hold the chief place in the mind. *Q.E.D.*

PROP. XVII. *God is without passions, neither is he affected by any emotion of pleasure or pain.*

Proof.—All ideas, in so far as they are referred to God, are true (II. xxxii.), that is (II. Def. iv.) adequate; and therefore (by the general Def. of the Emotions) God is without passions. Again, God cannot pass either to a greater or to a lesser perfection (I. xx. Coroll. ii.); therefore (by Def. of the Emotions, ii. iii.) he is not affected by any emotion of pleasure or pain.

Corollary.—Strictly speaking, God does not love or hate anyone. For God (by the foregoing Prop.) is not affected by any emotion of pleasure or pain, consequently (Def. of the Emotions, vi. vii.) he does not love or hate anyone.

PROP. XVIII. *No one can hate God.*

Proof.—The idea of God which is in us is adequate and perfect (II. xlvi. xlvii.); wherefore, in so far as we contemplate God, we are active (III. iii.); consequently (III. lix.) there can be no pain accompanied by the idea of God, in other words (Def. of the Emotions, vii.), no one can hate God. *Q.E.D.*

Corollary.—Love towards God cannot be turned into hate.

Note.—It may be objected that, as we understand God as the cause of all things, we by that very fact regard God as the cause of pain. But I make answer, that, in so far as we understand the causes of pain, it to that extent (V. iii.) ceases to be a passion, that is, it ceases to be pain (III. lix.); therefore, in so far as we understand God to be the cause of pain, we to that extent feel pleasure.

PROP. XIX. *He who loves God cannot endeavour that God should love him in return.*

Proof.—For, if a man should so endeavour, he would desire (V. xvii. Coroll.) that God, whom he loves, should not be God, and consequently he would desire to feel pain (III. xix.); which is absurd (III. xxviii.). Therefore, he who loves God, &c. *Q.E.D.*

Prop. XX. *This love towards God cannot be stained by the emotion of envy or jealousy; contrariwise, it is the more fostered in proportion as we conceive a greater number of men to be joined to God by the same bond of love.*

Proof.—This love towards God is the highest good which we can seek for under the guidance of reason (IV. xxviii.), it is common to all men (IV. xxxvi.), and we desire that all should rejoice therein (IV. xxxvii.); therefore (Def. of the Emotions, xxiii.), it cannot be stained by the emotion of envy, nor by the emotion of jealousy (V. xviii. see definition of Jealousy, III. xxxv. note); but, contrariwise, it must needs be the more fostered, in proportion as we conceive a greater number of men to rejoice therein. *Q.E.D.*

Note.—We can in the same way show, that there is no emotion directly contrary to this love, whereby this love can be destroyed; therefore we may conclude, that this love towards God is the most constant of all the emotions, and that, in so far as it is referred to the body, it cannot be destroyed, unless the body be destroyed also. As to its nature, in so far as it is referred to the mind only, we shall presently inquire.

I have now gone through all the remedies against the emotions, or all that the mind, considered in itself alone, can do against them. Whence it appears that the mind's power over the emotions consists:—

I. In the actual knowledge of the emotions (V. iv. note).

II. In the fact that it separates the emotions from the thought of an external cause, which we conceive confusedly (V. ii. and iv. note).

III. In the fact, that, in respect to time, the emotions referred to things, which we distinctly understand, surpass those referred to what we conceive in a confused and fragmentary manner (V. vii.).

IV. In the number of causes whereby those modifications[2] are fostered, which have regard to the common properties of things or to God (V. ix. xi.).

V. Lastly, in the order wherein the mind can arrange and

---

[2] *Affectiones.* Camerer reads *affectus*—emotions.

associate, one with another, its own emotions (V. x. note and xii. xiii. xiv.).

But, in order that this power of the mind over the emotions may be better understood, it should be specially observed that the emotions are called by us strong, when we compare the emotion of one man with the emotion of another, and see that one man is more troubled than another by the same emotion; or when we are comparing the various emotions of the same man one with another, and find that he is more affected or stirred by one emotion than by another. For the strength of every emotion is defined by a comparison of our own power with the power of an external cause. Now the power of the mind is defined by knowledge only, and its infirmity or passion is defined by the privation of knowledge only: it therefore follows, that that mind is most passive, whose greatest part is made up of inadequate ideas, so that it may be characterized more readily by its passive states than by its activities: on the other hand, that mind is most active, whose greatest part is made up of adequate ideas, so that, although it may contain as many inadequate ideas as the former mind, it may yet be more easily characterized by ideas attributable to human virtue, than by ideas which tell of human infirmity. Again, it must be observed, that spiritual unhealthiness and misfortunes can generally be traced to excessive love for something which is subject to many variations, and which we can never become masters of. For no one is solicitous or anxious about anything, unless he loves it; neither do wrongs, suspicions, enmities, &c. arise, except in regard to things whereof no one can be really master.

We may thus readily conceive the power which clear and distinct knowledge, and especially that third kind of knowledge (II. xlvii. note), founded on the actual knowledge of God, possesses over the emotions: if it does not absolutely destroy them, in so far as they are passions (V. iii. and iv. note); at any rate, it causes them to occupy a very small part of the mind (V. xiv.). Further, it begets a love towards a thing immutable and eternal (V. xv.), whereof we may really enter into possession (II. xlv.); neither can it be defiled with those faults which are inherent in ordinary love; but it may grow from strength to strength, and may engross the greater part of the mind, and deeply penetrate it.

And now I have finished with all that concerns this present life: for, as I said in the beginning of this note, I have briefly described all the remedies against the emotions. And this everyone may readily have seen for himself, if he has attended to what is advanced in the present note, and also to the definitions of the mind and its emotions, and, lastly, to Propositions i. and iii. of Part III. It is now, therefore, time to pass on to those matters, which appertain to the duration of the mind, without relation to the body.

PROP. XXI. *The mind can only imagine anything, or remember what is past, while the body endures.*

Proof.—The mind does not express the actual existence of its body, nor does it imagine the modifications of the body as actual, except while the body endures (II. viii. Coroll.); and, consequently (II. xxvi.), it does not imagine any body as actually existing, except while its own body endures. Thus it cannot imagine anything (for definition of Imagination, see II. xvii. note), or remember things past, except while the body endures (see definition of Memory, II. xviii. note). *Q.E.D.*

PROP. XXII. *Nevertheless in God there is necessarily an idea, which expresses the essence of this or that human body under the form of eternity.*

Proof.—God is the cause, not only of the existence of this or that human body, but also of its essence (I. xxv.). This essence, therefore, must necessarily be conceived through the very essence of God (I. Ax. iv.), and be thus conceived by a certain eternal necessity (I. xvi.); and this conception must necessarily exist in God (II. iii.). *Q.E.D.*

PROP. XXIII. *The human mind cannot be absolutely destroyed with the body, but there remains of it something which is eternal.*

Proof.—There is necessarily in God a concept or idea, which expresses the essence of the human body (last Prop.), which, therefore, is necessarily something appertaining to the essence of the human mind (II. xiii.). But we have not assigned to the human mind any duration, definable by time, except in so far as it expresses the actual existence of the body, which is explained through duration, and may be defined by time—that is (II. viii. Coroll.), we do not assign to it duration, except while the body endures. Yet, as there is something, notwithstanding, which is conceived by a certain eternal necessity through the very essence of God (last Prop.); this something, which appertains to the essence of the mind, will necessarily be eternal. *Q.E.D.*

Note.—This idea, which expresses the essence of the body under the form of eternity, is, as we have said, a certain mode of thinking, which belongs to the essence of the mind, and is necessarily eternal. Yet it is not possible that we should remember that we existed before our body, for our body can bear no trace of such existence, neither can eternity be defined in terms of time, or have any relation to time. But, notwithstanding, we feel and know that we are eternal. For the mind feels those things that it conceives by understanding, no less than those things that it remembers. For the eyes of the mind, whereby it sees and observes things, are none other than proofs. Thus, although we do not remember that we existed before the body, yet we feel that our mind, in so far as it involves the essence of the body, under the form of eternity, is eternal, and that thus its existence cannot be defined in terms of time, or explained through duration. Thus our mind can only be said to endure, and its existence can only be defined by a fixed time, in so far as it involves the actual existence of the body. Thus far only has it the power of determining the existence of things by time, and conceiving them under the category of duration.

PROP. XXIV. *The more we understand particular things, the more do we understand God.*

Proof.—This is evident from I. xxv. Coroll.

PROP. XXV. *The highest endeavour of the mind, and the highest virtue, is to understand things by the third kind of knowledge.*

Proof.—The third kind of knowledge proceeds from an adequate idea of certain attributes of God to an adequate knowledge of the essence of things (see its definition II. xl. note ii.); and, in proportion as we understand things more in this way, we better understand God (by the last Prop.); therefore (IV.

xxviii.) the highest virtue of the mind, that is (IV. Def. viii.) the power, or nature, or (III. vii.) highest endeavour of the mind, is to understand things by the third kind of knowledge. Q.E.D.

PROP. XXVI. *In proportion as the mind is more capable of understanding things by the third kind of knowledge, it desires more to understand things by that kind.*

Proof.—This is evident. For, in so far as we conceive the mind to be capable of conceiving things by this kind of knowledge, we, to that extent, conceive it as determined thus to conceive things; and consequently (Def. of the Emotions, i.), the mind desires so to do, in proportion as it is more capable thereof. Q.E.D.

PROP. XXVII. *From this third kind of knowledge arises the highest possible mental acquiescence.*

Proof.—The highest virtue of the mind is to know God (IV. xxviii.), or to understand things by the third kind of knowledge (V. xxv.), and this virtue is greater in proportion as the mind knows things more by the said kind of knowledge (V. xxiv.): consequently, he who knows things by this kind of knowledge passes to the summit of human perfection, and is therefore (Def. of the Emotions, ii.) affected by the highest pleasure, such pleasure being accompanied by the idea of himself and his own virtue; thus (Def. of the Emotions, xxv.), from this kind of knowledge arises the highest possible acquiescence. Q.E.D.

PROP. XXVIII. *The endeavour or desire to know things by the third kind of knowledge cannot arise from the first, but from the second kind of knowledge.*

Proof.—This proposition is self-evident. For whatsoever we understand clearly and distinctly, we understand either through itself, or through that which is conceived through itself; that is, ideas which are clear and distinct in us, or which are referred to the third kind of knowledge (II. xl. note ii.) cannot follow from ideas that are fragmentary and confused, and are referred to knowledge of the first kind, but must follow from adequate ideas, or ideas of the second and third kind of knowledge; therefore (Def. of the Emotions, i.), the desire of knowing things by the third kind of knowledge cannot arise from the first, but from the second kind. *Q.E.D.*

PROP. XXIX. *Whatsoever the mind understands under the form of eternity, it does not understand by virtue of conceiving the present actual existence of the body, but by virtue of conceiving the essence of the body under the form of eternity.*

Proof.—In so far as the mind conceives the present existence of its body, it to that extent conceives duration which can be determined by time, and to that extent only has it the power of conceiving things in relation to time (V. xxi. II. xxvi.). But eternity cannot be explained in terms of duration (I. Def. viii. and explanation). Therefore to this extent the mind has not the power of conceiving things under the form of eternity, but it possesses such power, because it is of the nature of reason to conceive things under the form of eternity (II. xliv. Coroll. ii.), and also because it is of the nature of the mind to conceive the essence of the body under the form of eternity (V. xxiii.), for besides these two there is nothing which belongs to the essence of mind (II. xiii.). Therefore this power of conceiving things under the form of eternity only belongs to the mind in virtue of the mind's conceiving the essence of the body under the form of eternity. *Q.E.D.*

Note.—Things are conceived by us as actual in two ways; either as existing in relation to a given time and place, or as contained in God and following from the necessity of the divine nature. Whatsoever we conceive in this second way as true or real, we conceive under the form of eternity, and their ideas involve the eternal and infinite essence of God, as we showed in II. xlv. and note, which see.

PROP. XXX. *Our mind, in so far as it knows itself and the body under the form of eternity, has to that extent necessarily a knowledge of God, and knows that it is in God, and is conceived through God.*

Proof.—Eternity is the very essence of God, in so far as this involves necessary existence (I. Def. viii.). Therefore to conceive things under the form of eternity, is to conceive things in so far as they are conceived through the essence of God as real entities, or in so far as they involve existence through the essence of God; wherefore our mind, in so far as it conceives itself and the body under the form of eternity, has to that extent necessarily a knowledge of God, and knows, &c. *Q.E.D.*

Prop. XXXI. *The third kind of knowledge depends on the mind, as its formal cause, in so far as the mind itself is eternal.*

Proof.—The mind does not conceive anything under the form of eternity, except in so far as it conceives its own body under the form of eternity (V. xxix.); that is, except in so far as it is eternal (V. xxi. xxiii.); therefore (by the last Prop.), in so far as it is eternal, it possesses the knowledge of God, which knowledge is necessarily adequate (II. xlvi.); hence the mind, in so far as it is eternal, is capable of knowing everything which can follow from this given knowledge of God (II. xl.), in other words, of knowing things by the third kind of knowledge (see Def. in II. xl. note ii.), whereof accordingly the mind (III. Def. i.), in so far as it is eternal, is the adequate or formal cause of such knowledge. *Q.E.D.*

Note.—In proportion, therefore, as a man is more potent in this kind of knowledge, he will be more completely conscious of himself and of God; in other words, he will be more perfect and blessed, as will appear more clearly in the sequel. But we must here observe that, although we are already certain that the mind is eternal, in so far as it conceives things under the form of eternity, yet, in order that what we wish to show may be more readily explained and better understood, we will consider the mind itself, as though it had just begun to exist and to understand things under the form of eternity, as indeed we have done hitherto; this we may do without any danger of error, so long as we are careful not to draw any conclusion, unless our premisses are plain.

Prop. XXXII. *Whatsoever we understand by the third kind of knowledge, we take delight in, and our delight is accompanied by the idea of God as cause.*

Proof.—From this kind of knowledge arises the highest possible mental acquiescence, that is (Def. of the Emotions, xxv.), pleasure, and this acquiescence is accompanied by the idea of the mind itself (V. xxvii.), and consequently (V. xxx.) the idea also of God as cause. *Q.E.D.*

Corollary.—From the third kind of knowledge necessarily arises the intellectual love of God. From this kind of knowledge arises pleasure accompanied by the idea of God as cause, that is (Def. of the Emotions, vi.), the love of God; not in so far as we imagine him as present (V. xxix.), but in so far as we understand him to be eternal; this is what I call the intellectual love of God.

PROP. XXXIII. *The intellectual love of God, which arises from the third kind of knowledge, is eternal.*

Proof.—The third kind of knowledge is eternal (V. xxxi. I. Ax. iii.); therefore (by the same Axiom) the love which arises therefrom is also necessarily eternal. *Q.E.D.*

Note.—Although this love towards God has (by the foregoing Prop.) no beginning, it yet possesses all the perfections of love, just as though it had arisen as we feigned in the Coroll. of the last Prop. Nor is there here any difference, except that the mind possesses as eternal those same perfections which we feigned to accrue to it, and they are accompanied by the idea of God as eternal cause. If pleasure consists in the transition to a greater perfection, assuredly blessedness must consist in the mind being endowed with perfection itself.

PROP. XXXIV. *The mind is, only while the body endures, subject to those emotions which are attributable to passions.*

Proof.—Imagination is the idea wherewith the mind contemplates a thing as present (II. xvii. note); yet this idea indicates rather the present disposition of the human body than the nature of the external thing (II. xvi. Coroll. ii.). Therefore emotion (see general Def. of Emotions) is imagination, in so far as it indicates the present disposition of the body; therefore (V. xxi.) the mind is, only while the body endures, subject to emotions which are attributable to passions. *Q.E.D.*

Corollary.—Hence it follows that no love save intellectual love is eternal.

Note.—If we look to men's general opinion, we shall see that they are indeed conscious of the eternity of their mind, but that they confuse eternity with duration, and ascribe it to the imagination or the memory which they believe to remain after death.

PROP. XXXV. *God loves himself with an infinite intellectual love.*

Proof.—God is absolutely infinite (I. Def. vi.), that is (II. Def. vi.), the nature of God rejoices in infinite perfection; and such rejoicing is (II. iii.) accompanied by the idea of himself, that is (I. xi. and Def. i.), the idea of his own cause: now this is what we have (in V. xxxii. Coroll.) described as intellectual love.

PROP. XXXVI. *The intellectual love of the mind towards God is that very love of God whereby God loves himself, not in so far as he is infinite, but in so far as he can be explained through the essence of the human mind regarded under the form of eternity; in other words, the intellectual love of the mind towards God is part of the infinite love wherewith God loves himself.*

Proof.—This love of the mind must be referred to the activities of the mind (V. xxxii. Coroll. and III. iii.); it is itself, indeed, an activity whereby the mind regards itself accompanied by the idea of God as cause (V. xxxii. and Coroll.); that is (I. xxv. Coroll. and II. xi. Coroll.), an activity whereby God, in so far as he can be explained through the human mind, regards himself accompanied by the idea of himself; therefore (by the last Prop.), this love of the mind is part of the infinite love wherewith God loves himself. *Q.E.D.*

Corollary.—Hence it follows that God, in so far as he loves himself, loves man, and, consequently, that the love of God towards men, and the intellectual love of the mind towards God are identical.

Note.—From what has been said we clearly understand, wherein our salvation, or blessedness, or freedom, consists: namely, in the constant and eternal love towards God, or in God's love towards men. This love or blessedness is, in the Bible, called Glory, and not undeservedly. For whether this love be referred to God or to the mind, it may rightly be called acquiescence of spirit, which (Def. of the Emotions, xxv. xxx.) is not really distinguished from glory. In so far as it is referred to God, it is (V. xxxv.) pleasure, if we may still use that term, accompanied by the idea of itself, and, in so far as it is referred to the mind, it is the same (V. xxvii.).

Again, since the essence of our mind consists solely in knowledge, whereof the beginning and the foundation is God

(I. xv. and II. xlvii. note), it becomes clear to us, in what manner and way our mind, as to its essence and existence, follows from the divine nature and constantly depends on God. I have thought it worth while here to call attention to this, in order to show by this example how the knowledge of particular things, which I have called intuitive or of the third kind (II. xl. note ii.), is potent, and more powerful than the universal knowledge, which I have styled knowledge of the second kind. For, although in Part I. I showed in general terms, that all things (and consequently, also, the human mind) depend as to their essence and existence on God, yet that demonstration, though legitimate and placed beyond the chances of doubt, does not affect our mind so much, as when the same conclusion is derived from the actual essence of some particular thing, which we say depends on God.

PROP. XXXVII. *There is nothing in nature, which is contrary to this intellectual love, or which can take it away.*

Proof.—This intellectual love follows necessarily from the nature of the mind, in so far as the latter is regarded through the nature of God as an eternal truth (V. xxxiii. and xxix.). If, therefore, there should be anything which would be contrary to this love, that thing would be contrary to that which is true; consequently, that, which should be able to take away this love, would cause that which is true to be false; an obvious absurdity. Therefore there is nothing in nature which, &c. *Q.E.D.*

Note.—The Axiom of Part IV. has reference to particular things, in so far as they are regarded in relation to a given time and place: of this, I think, no one can doubt.

PROP. XXXVIII. *In proportion as the mind understands more things by the second and third kind of knowledge, it is less subject to those emotions which are evil, and stands in less fear of death.*

Proof.—The mind's essence consists in knowledge (II. xi.); therefore, in proportion as the mind understands more things by the second and third kinds of knowledge, the greater will be the part of it that endures (V. xxix. and xxiii.), and, consequently (by the last Prop.), the greater will be the part that is not touched by the emotions, which are contrary to our nature, or in other words, evil (IV. xxx.). Thus, in proportion as the mind understands more things by the second and third kinds of knowledge, the greater will be the part of it, that remains unimpaired, and, consequently, less subject to emotions, &c. *Q.E.D.*

Note.—Hence we understand that point which I touched on in IV. xxxix. note, and which I promised to explain in this Part; namely, that death becomes less hurtful, in proportion as the mind's clear and distinct knowledge is greater, and, consequently, in proportion as the mind loves God more. Again, since from the third kind of knowledge arises the highest possible acquiescence (V. xxvii.), it follows that the human mind can attain to being of such a nature, that the part thereof which we have shown to perish with the body (V. xxi.) should be of little importance when compared with the part which endures. But I will soon treat of the subject at greater length.

PROP. XXXIX. *He, who possesses a body capable of the greatest number of activities, possesses a mind whereof the greatest part is eternal.*

Proof.—He, who possesses a body capable of the greatest number of activities, is least agitated by those emotions which are evil (IV. xxxviii.)—that is (IV. xxx.), by those emotions which are contrary to our nature; therefore (V. x.), he possesses the power of arranging and associating the modifications of the body according to the intellectual order, and, consequently, of bringing it about, that all the modifications of the body should be referred to the idea of God; whence it will come to pass that (V. xv.) he will be affected with love towards God, which (V. xvi.) must occupy or constitute the chief part of the mind; therefore (V. xxxiii.), such a man will possess a mind whereof the chief part is eternal. *Q.E.D.*

Note.—Since human bodies are capable of the greatest number of activities, there is no doubt but that they may be of such a nature, that they may be referred to minds possessing a great knowledge of themselves and of God, and whereof the greatest or chief part is eternal, and, therefore, that they should scarcely fear death. But, in order that this may be understood more clearly, we must here call to mind, that we live in a state of perpetual variation, and, according as we are changed for the better or the worse, we are called happy or unhappy.

For he, who, from being an infant or a child, becomes a corpse, is called unhappy; whereas it is set down to happiness, if we have been able to live through the whole period of life with a sound mind in a sound body. And, in reality, he, who, as in the case of an infant or a child, has a body capable of very few activities, and depending, for the most part, on external causes, has a mind which, considered in itself alone, is scarcely conscious of itself, or of God, or of things; whereas, he, who has a body capable of very many activities, has a mind which, considered in itself alone, is highly conscious of itself, of God, and of things. In this life, therefore, we primarily endeavour to bring it about, that the body of a child, in so far as its nature allows and conduces thereto, may be changed into something else capable of very many activities, and referable to a mind which is highly conscious of itself, of God, and of things; and we desire so to change it, that what is referred to its imagination and memory may become insignificant, in comparison with its intellect, as I have already said in the note to the last Proposition.

PROP. XL. *In proportion as each thing possesses more of perfection, so is it more active, and less passive; and, vice versâ, in proportion as it is more active, so is it more perfect.*

Proof.—In proportion as each thing is more perfect, it possesses more of reality (II. Def. vi.), and, consequently (III. iii. and note), it is to that extent more active and less passive. This demonstration may be reversed, and thus prove that, in proportion as a thing is more active, so is it more perfect. *Q.E.D.*

Corollary.—Hence it follows that the part of the mind which endures, be it great or small, is more perfect than the rest. For the eternal part of the mind (V. xxiii. xxix.) is the understanding, through which alone we are said to act (III. iii.); the part which we have shown to perish is the imagination (V. xxi.), through which only we are said to be passive (III. iii. and general Def. of the Emotions); therefore, the former, be it great or small, is more perfect than the latter. *Q.E.D.*

Note.—Such are the doctrines which I had purposed to set forth concerning the mind, in so far as it is regarded without relation to the body; whence, as also from I. xxi. and other places, it is plain that our mind, in so far as it understands, is an eternal mode of thinking, which is determined by another eternal mode of thinking, and this other by a third, and so on to infinity; so that all taken together at once constitute the eternal and infinite intellect of God.

PROP. XLI. *Even if we did not know that our mind is eternal, we should still consider as of primary importance piety and religion, and generally all things which, in Part IV., we showed to be attributable to courage and high-mindedness.*

Proof.—The first and only foundation of virtue, or the rule of right living is (IV. xxii. Coroll. and xxiv.) seeking one's own true interest. Now, while we determined what reason prescribes as useful, we took no account of the mind's eternity, which has only become known to us in this Fifth Part. Although we were ignorant at that time that the mind is eternal, we nevertheless stated that the qualities attributable to courage and high-mindedness are of primary importance. Therefore, even if we were still ignorant of this doctrine, we should yet put the aforesaid precepts of reason in the first place. *Q.E.D.*

Note.—The general belief of the multitude seems to be different. Most people seem to believe that they are free, in so far as they may obey their lusts, and that they cede their rights, in so far as they are bound to live according to the commandments of the divine law. They therefore believe that piety, religion, and, generally, all things attributable to firmness of mind, are burdens, which, after death, they hope to lay aside, and to receive the reward for their bondage, that is, for their piety and religion; it is not only by this hope, but also, and chiefly, by the fear of being horribly punished after death, that they are induced to live according to the divine commandments, so far as their feeble and infirm spirit will carry them.

If men had not this hope and this fear, but believed that the mind perishes with the body, and that no hope of prolonged life remains for the wretches who are broken down with the burden of piety, they would return to their own inclinations, controlling everything in accordance with their lusts, and desiring to obey fortune rather than themselves. Such a course appears to me not less absurd than if a man, because he does not believe that he can by wholesome food sustain his body for ever, should wish to cram himself with poisons and deadly fare; or if, because he sees that the mind is not eternal or immortal, he should prefer to be out of his mind altogether, and to live without the use of reason; these ideas are so absurd as to be scarcely worth refuting.

PROP. XLII. *Blessedness is not the reward of virtue, but virtue itself; neither do we rejoice therein, because we control our lusts, but, contrariwise, because we rejoice therein, we are able to control our lusts.*

Proof.—Blessedness consists in love towards God (V. xxxvi. and note), which love springs from the third kind of knowledge (V. xxxii. Coroll.); therefore this love (III. iii. lix.) must be referred to the mind, in so far as the latter is active; therefore (IV. Def. viii.) it is virtue itself. This was our first point. Again, in proportion as the mind rejoices more in this divine love or blessedness, so does it the more understand (V. xxxii.); that is (V. iii. Coroll.), so much the more power has it over the emotions, and (V. xxxviii.) so much the less is it subject to those emotions which are evil; therefore, in proportion as the mind rejoices in this divine love or blessedness, so has it the power of controlling lusts. And, since human power in controlling the emotions consists solely in the understanding, it follows that no one rejoices in blessedness, because he has controlled his lusts, but, contrariwise, his power of controlling his lusts arises from this blessedness itself. Q.E.D.

Note.—I have thus completed all I wished to set forth touching the mind's power over the emotions and the mind's freedom. Whence it appears, how potent is the wise man, and how much he surpasses the ignorant man, who is driven only by his lusts. For the ignorant man is not only distracted in various ways by external causes without ever gaining the true acquiescence of his spirit, but moreover lives, as it were un-

THE RATIONALISTS

witting of himself, and of God, and of things, and as soon as he ceases to suffer, ceases also to be.

Whereas the wise man, in so far as he is regarded as such, is scarcely at all disturbed in spirit, but, being conscious of himself, and of God, and of things, by a certain eternal necessity, never ceases to be, but always possesses true acquiescence of his spirit.

If the way which I have pointed out as leading to this result seems exceedingly hard, it may nevertheless be discovered. Needs must it be hard, since it is so seldom found. How would it be possible, if salvation were ready to our hand, and could without great labour be found, that it should be by almost all men neglected? But all things excellent are as difficult as they are rare.

GOTTFRIED WILHELM FREIHERR VON LEIBNIZ

DISCOURSE ON METAPHYSICS

THE MONADOLOGY

DISCOURSE ON METAPHYSICS

I. Concerning the divine perfection and that God does everything in the most desirable way.

The conception of God which is the most common and the most full of meaning is expressed well enough in the words: God is an absolutely perfect being. The implications, however, of these words fail to receive sufficient consideration. For instance, there are many different kinds of perfection, all of which God possesses, and each one of them pertains to him in the highest degree.

We must also know what perfection is. One thing which can surely be affirmed about it is that those forms or natures which are not susceptible of it to the highest degree, say the nature of numbers or of figures, do not permit of perfection. This is because the number which is the greatest of all (that is, the sum of all the numbers), and likewise the greatest of all figures, imply contradictions. The greatest knowledge, however, and omnipotence contain no impossibility. Consequently power and knowledge do admit of perfection, and in so far as they pertain to God they have no limits.

Whence it follows that God who possesses supreme and infinite wisdom acts in the most perfect manner not only metaphysically, but also from the moral standpoint. And with respect to ourselves it can be said that the more we are enlightened and informed in regard to the works of God the more will we be disposed to find them excellent and conforming entirely to that which we might desire.

II. Against those who hold that there is in the works of God no goodness, or that the principles of goodness and beauty are arbitrary.

Therefore I am far removed from the opinion of those who maintain that there are no principles of goodness or perfection in the nature of things, or in the ideas which God has about them, and who say that the works of God are good only through the formal reason that God has made them. If this position were true, God, knowing that he is the author of things, would not have to regard them afterwards and find them good, as the Holy Scripture witnesses. Such anthropological expressions are used only to let us know that excellence is recognized in regarding the works themselves, even if we do not consider their evident dependence on their author. This is confirmed by the fact that it is in reflecting upon the works that we are able to discover the one who wrought. They must therefore bear in themselves his character. I confess that the contrary opinion seems to me extremely dangerous and closely approaches that of recent innovators who hold that the beauty of the universe and the goodness which we attribute to the works of God are chimeras of human beings who think of God in human terms. In saying, therefore, that things are not good according to any standard of goodness, but simply by the will of God, it seems to me that one destroys, without realizing it, all the love of God and all his glory; for why praise him for what he has done, if he would be equally praiseworthy in doing the contrary? Where will be his justice and his wisdom if he has only a certain despotic power, if arbitrary will takes the place of reasonableness, and if in accord with the definition of tyrants, justice consists in that which is pleasing to the most powerful? Besides it seems that every act of willing supposes some reason for the willing and this reason, of course, must precede the act. This is why, accordingly, I find so strange those expressions of certain philosophers who say that the eternal truths of metaphysics and Geometry, and consequently the principles of goodness, of justice, and of perfection, are effects only of the will of God. To me it seems that all these follow from his understanding, which does not depend upon his will any more than does his essence.

III. Against those who think that God might have made things better than he has.

Neither am I able to approve of the opinion of certain modern writers who boldly maintain that that which God has made is not perfect in the highest degree, and that he might have done better. It seems to me that the consequences of such an opinion are wholly inconsistent with the glory of God. *Uti minus malum habet rationem boni, ita minus bonum habet rationem mali.* I think that one acts imperfectly if he acts with less perfection than he is capable of. To show that an architect could have done better is to find fault with his work. Furthermore this opinion is contrary to the Holy Scriptures when they assure us of the goodness of God's work. For if comparative perfection were sufficient, then in whatever way God had accomplished his work, since there is an infinitude of possible imperfections, it would always have been good in comparison with the less perfect; but a thing is little praiseworthy when it can be praised only in this way.

I believe that a great many passages from the divine writings and from the holy fathers will be found favoring my position, while hardly any will be found in favor of that of these modern thinkers. Their opinion is, in my judgment, foreign to the writers of antiquity and is a deduction based upon the too slight acquaintance which we have with the general harmony of the universe and with the hidden reasons for God's conduct. In our ignorance, therefore, we are tempted to decide audaciously that many things might have been done better.

These modern thinkers insist upon certain hardly tenable subtleties, for they imagine that nothing is so perfect that there might not have been something more perfect. This is an error. They think, indeed, that they are thus safeguarding the liberty of God. As if it were not the highest liberty to act in perfection according to the sovereign reason. For to think that God acts in anything without having any reason for his willing, even if we overlook the fact that such action seems impossible, is an opinion which conforms little to God's glory. For example, let us suppose that God chooses between A and B, and that he takes A without any reason for preferring it to B. I say that this action on the part of God is at least not praiseworthy, for all praise ought to be founded upon reason which *ex hypothesi* is not present here. My opinion is that God does nothing for which he does not deserve to be glorified.

IV. That love for God demands on our part complete satisfaction with and acquiescence in that which he has done.

The general knowledge of this great truth that God acts always in the most perfect and most desirable manner possible, is in my opinion the basis of the love which we owe to God in all things; for he who loves seeks his satisfaction in the felicity or perfection of the subject loved and in the perfection of his actions. *Idem velle et idem nolle vera amicitia est.* I believe that it is difficult to love God truly when one, having the power to change his disposition, is not disposed to wish for that which God desires. In fact those who are not satisfied with what God does seem to me like dissatisfied subjects whose attitude is not very different from that of rebels. I hold, therefore, that on these principles, to act conformably to the love of God it is not sufficient to force oneself to be patient, we must be really satisfied with all that comes to us according to his will. I mean this acquiescence in regard to the past; for as regards the future one should not be a quietist with the arms folded, open to ridicule, awaiting that which God will do; according to the sophism which the ancients called λόγον ἄεργον, the lazy reason. It is necessary to act conformably to the presumptive will of God as far as we are able to judge of it, trying with all our might to contribute to the general welfare and particularly to the ornamentation and the perfection of that which touches us, or of that which is nigh and so to speak at our hand. For if the future shall perhaps show that God has not wished our good intention to have its way, it does not follow that he has not wished us to act as we have; on the contrary, since he is the best of all masters, he ever demands only the right intentions, and it is for him to know the hour and the proper place to let good designs succeed.

V. In what the principles of the divine perfection consist, and that the simplicity of the means counterbalances the richness of the effects.

It is sufficient, therefore, to have this confidence in God, that he has done everything for the best and that nothing will be able to injure those who love him. To know in particular, however, the reasons which have moved him to choose this order of the universe, to permit sin, to dispense his salutary grace in a certain manner—this passes the capacity of a finite mind, above all when such a mind has not come into the joy of the vision of God. Yet it is possible to make some general remarks touching the course of providence in the government of things. One is able to say, therefore, that he who acts perfectly is like an excellent Geometer who knows how to find the best construction for a problem; like a good architect who utilizes his location and the funds destined for the building in the most advantageous manner, leaving nothing which shocks or which does not display that beauty of which it is capable; like a good householder who employs his property in such a way that there shall be nothing uncultivated or sterile; like a clever machinist who makes his production in the least difficult way possible; and like an intelligent author who encloses the most of reality in the least possible compass.

Of all beings those which are the most perfect and occupy the least possible space, that is to say those which interfere with one another the least, are the spirits whose perfections are the virtues. That is why we may not doubt that the felicity of the spirits is the principal aim of God and that he puts this purpose into execution, as far as the general harmony will permit. We will recur to this subject again.

When the simplicity of God's way is spoken of, reference is specially made to the means which he employs, and on the other hand when the variety, richness and abundance are referred to, the ends or effects are had in mind. Thus one ought to be proportioned to the other, just as the cost of a building

should balance the beauty and grandeur which is expected.
It is true that nothing costs God anything, just as there is no
cost for a philosopher who makes hypotheses in constructing
his imaginary world, because God has only to make decrees in
order that a real world come into being; but in matters of
wisdom the decrees or hypotheses meet the expenditure in
proportion as they are more independent of one another. Reason wishes to avoid multiplicity in hypotheses or principles very
much as the simplest system is preferred in Astronomy.

VI. *That God does nothing which is not orderly, and that
it is not even possible to conceive of events which are not
regular.*

The activities or the acts of will of God are commonly divided into ordinary and extraordinary. But it is well to bear in
mind that God does nothing out of order. Therefore, that
which passes for extraordinary is so only with regard to a particular order established among the created things, for as regards the universal order, everything conforms to it. This is so
true that not only does nothing occur in this world which is
absolutely irregular, but it is even impossible to conceive of
such an occurrence. Because, let us suppose for example that
some one jots down a quantity of points upon a sheet of paper
helter skelter, as do those who exercise the ridiculous art of
Geomancy; now I say that it is possible to find a geometrical
line whose concept shall be uniform and constant, that is, in
accordance with a certain formula, and which line at the same
time shall pass through all of those points, and in the same
order in which the hand jotted them down; also if a continuous
line be traced, which is now straight, now circular, and now
of any other description, it is possible to find a mental equivalent, a formula or an equation common to all the points of this
line by virtue of which formula the changes in the direction
of the line must occur. There is no instance of a face whose
contour does not form part of a geometric line and which can
not be traced entire by a certain mathematical motion. But
when the formula is very complex, that which conforms to it
passes for irregular. Thus we may say that in whatever manner

God might have created the world, it would always have been regular and in a certain order. God, however, has chosen the most perfect, that is to say the one which is at the same time the simplest in hypotheses and the richest in phenomena, as might be the case with a geometric line, whose construction was easy, but whose properties and effects were extremely remarkable and of great significance. I use these comparisons to picture a certain imperfect resemblance to the divine wisdom, and to point out that which may at least raise our minds to conceive in some sort what cannot otherwise be expressed. I do not pretend at all to explain thus the great mystery upon which the whole universe depends.

VII. *That miracles conform to the regular order although they go against the subordinate regulations; concerning that which God desires or permits and concerning general and particular intentions.*

Now since nothing is done which is not orderly, we may say that miracles are quite within the order of natural operations. We use the term natural of these operations because they conform to certain subordinate regulations which we call the nature of things. For it can be said that this nature is only a custom of God's which he can change on the occasion of a stronger reason than that which moved him to use these regulations. As regards general and particular intentions, according to the way in which we understand the matter, it may be said on the one hand that everything is in accordance with his most general intention, or that which best conforms to the most perfect order he has chosen; on the other hand, however, it is also possible to say that he has particular intentions which are exceptions to the subordinate regulations above mentioned. Of God's laws, however, the most universal, i. e., that which rules the whole course of the universe, is without exceptions.

It is possible to say that God desires everything which is an object of his particular intention. When we consider the objects of his general intentions, however, such as are the modes of activities of created things and especially of the reasoning creatures with whom God wishes to co-operate, we must make a

distinction; for if the action is good in itself, we may say that
God wishes it and at times commands it, even though it does
not take place; but if it is bad in itself and becomes good only
by accident through the course of events and especially after
chastisement and satisfaction have corrected its malignity and
rewarded the ill with interest in such a way that more perfection results in the whole train of circumstances than would
have come if that ill had not occurred,—if all this takes place
we must say that God permits the evil, and not that he desired it, although he has co-operated by means of the laws of
nature which he has established. He knows how to produce
the greatest good from them.

VIII. *In order to distinguish between the activities of God
and the activities of created things we must explain the conception of an individual substance.*

It is quite difficult to distinguish God's actions from those
of his creatures. Some think that God does everything; others
imagine that he only conserves the force that he has given to
created things. How far can we say either of these opinions is
right?

In the first place since activity and passivity pertain properly
to individual substances (*actiones sunt suppositorum*) it will
be necessary to explain what such a substance is. It is indeed
true that when several predicates are attributes of a single subject and this subject is not an attribute of another, we speak
of it as an individual substance, but this is not enough, and
such an explanation is merely nominal. We must therefore inquire what it is to be an attribute in reality of a certain subject. Now it is evident that every true predication has some
basis in the nature of things, and even when a proposition is
not identical, that is, when the predicate is not expressly contained in the subject, it is still necessary that it be virtually
contained in it, and this is what the philosophers call *inesse*,
saying thereby that the predicate is in the subject. Thus the
content of the subject must always include that of the predicate
in such a way that if one understands perfectly the concept
of the subject, he will know that the predicate appertains to

it also. This being so, we are able to say that this is the nature of an individual substance or of a complete being, namely, to afford a conception so complete that the concept shall be sufficient for the understanding of it and for the deduction of all the predicates of which the substance is or may become the subject. Thus the quality of king, which belonged to Alexander the Great, an abstraction from the subject, is not sufficiently determined to constitute an individual, and does not contain the other qualities of the same subject, nor everything which the idea of this prince includes. God, however, seeing the individual concept, or hæcceity, of Alexander, sees there at the same time the basis and the reason of all the predicates which can be truly uttered regarding him; for instance that he will conquer Darius and Porus, even to the point of knowing *a priori* (and not by experience) whether he died a natural death or by poison,—facts which we can learn only through history. When we carefully consider the connection of things we see also the possibility of saying that there was always in the soul of Alexander marks of all that had happened to him and evidences of all that would happen to him and traces even of everything which occurs in the universe, although God alone could recognize them all.

IX. That every individual substance expresses the whole universe in its own manner and that in its full concept are included all its experiences together with all the attendant circumstances and the whole sequence of exterior events.

There follow from these considerations several noticeable paradoxes; among others that it is not true that two substances may be exactly alike and differ only numerically, *solo numero*, and that what St. Thomas says on this point regarding angels and intelligences (*quod ibi omne individuum sit species infima*) is true of all substances, provided that the specific difference is understood as Geometers understand it in the case of figures; again that a substance will be able to commence only through creation and perish only through annihilation; that a substance cannot be divided into two nor can one be made out of two, and that thus the number of substances neither aug-

ments nor diminishes through natural means, although they
are frequently transformed. Furthermore every substance is
like an entire world and like a mirror of God, or indeed of the
whole world which it portrays, each one in its own fashion;
almost as the same city is variously represented according to
the various viewpoints from which it is regarded. Thus the
universe is multiplied in some sort as many times as there are
substances, and the glory of God is multiplied in the same way
by as many wholly different representations of his works. It
can indeed be said that every substance bears in some sort the
character of God's infinite wisdom and omnipotence, and imitates him as much as it is able to; for it expresses, although
confusedly, all that happens in the universe, past, present and
future, deriving thus a certain resemblance to an infinite perception or power of knowing. And since all other substances
express this particular substance and accommodate themselves
to it, we can say that it exerts its power upon all the others
in imitation of the omnipotence of the creator.

X. *That the belief in substantial forms has a certain basis
in fact, but that these forms effect no changes in the phenomena and must not be employed for the explanation of particular events.*

It seems that the ancients, able men, who were accustomed
to profound meditations and taught theology and philosophy
for several centuries and some of whom recommend themselves to us on account of their piety, had some knowledge
of that which we have just said and this is why they introduced and maintained the substantial forms so much decried
to-day. But they were not so far from the truth nor so open to
ridicule as the common run of our new philosophers imagine.
I grant that the consideration of these forms is of no service
in the details of physics and ought not to be employed in the
explanation of particular phenomena. In regard to this last
point, the schoolmen were at fault, as were also the physicists
of times past who followed their example, thinking they had
given the reason for the properties of a body in mentioning
the forms and qualities without going to the trouble of ex-

amining the manner of operation; as if one should be content to say that a clock had a certain amount of clockness derived from its form, and should not inquire in what that clockness consisted. This is indeed enough for the man who buys it, provided he surrenders the care of it to someone else. The fact, however, that there was this misunderstanding and misuse of the substantial forms should not bring us to throw away something whose recognition is so necessary in metaphysics. Since without these we will not be able, I hold, to know the ultimate principles nor to lift our minds to the knowledge of the incorporeal natures and of the marvels of God. Yet as the geometer does not need to encumber his mind with the famous puzzle of the composition of the continuum, and as no moralist, and still less a jurist or a statesman has need to trouble himself with the great difficulties which arise in conciliating free will with the providential activity of God (since the geometer is able to make all his demonstrations and the statesman can complete all his deliberations without entering into these discussions which are so necessary and important in Philosophy and Theology), so in the same way the physicist can explain his experiments, now using simpler experiments already made, now employing geometrical and mechanical demonstrations without any need of the general considerations which belong to another sphere, and if he employs the co-operation of God, or perhaps of some soul or animating force, or something else of a similar nature, he goes out of his path quite as much as that man who, when facing an important practical question, would wish to enter into profound argumentations regarding the nature of destiny and of our liberty; a fault which men quite frequently commit without realizing it when they cumber their minds with considerations regarding fate, and thus they are even sometimes turned from a good resolution or from some necessary provision.

XI. *That the opinions of the theologians and of the so-called scholastic philosophers are not to be wholly despised.*

I know that I am advancing a great paradox in pretending to resuscitate in some sort the ancient philosophy, and to recall *postliminio* the substantial forms almost banished from our modern thought. But perhaps I will not be condemned lightly when it is known that I have long meditated over the modern philosophy and that I have devoted much time to experiments in physics and to the demonstrations of geometry and that I, too, for a long time was persuaded of the baselessness of those "beings" which, however, I was finally obliged to take up again in spite of myself and as though by force. The many investigations which I carried on compelled me to recognize that our moderns do not do sufficient justice to Saint Thomas and to the other great men of that period and that there is in the theories of the scholastic philosophers and theologians far more solidity than is imagined, provided that these theories are employed *à propos* and in their place. I am persuaded that if some careful and meditative mind were to take the trouble to clarify and direct their thoughts in the manner of analytic geometers, he would find a great treasure of very important truths, wholly demonstrable.

XII. That the conception of the extension of a body is in a way imaginary and does not constitute the substance of the body.

But to resume the thread of our discussion, I believe that he who will meditate upon the nature of substance, as I have explained it above, will find that the whole nature of bodies is not exhausted in their extension, that is to say, in their size, figure and motion, but that we must recognize something which corresponds to soul, something which is commonly called substantial form, although these forms effect no change in the phenomena, any more than do the souls of beasts, that is if they have souls. It is even possible to demonstrate that the ideas of size, figure and motion are not so distinctive as is imagined, and that they stand for something imaginary relative to our perceptions as do, although to a greater extent, the ideas of color, heat, and the other similar qualities in regard to which we may doubt whether they are actually to be found in the nature of the things outside of us. This is why these latter qualities are unable to constitute "substance" and if there is no other principle of identity in bodies than that which has just been referred to a body would not subsist more than for a moment.

The souls and the substance-forms of other bodies are entirely different from intelligent souls which alone know their actions, and not only do not perish through natural means but indeed always retain the knowledge of what they are; a fact which makes them alone open to chastisement or recompense, and makes them citizens of the republic of the universe whose monarch is God. Hence it follows that all the other creatures should serve them, a point which we shall discuss more amply later.

XIII. As the individual concept of each person includes once for all everything which can ever happen to him, in it can be seen the a priori evidences or the reasons for the reality of each event, and why one happened sooner than the other. But these events, however certain, are nevertheless contingent, being based on the free choice of God and of his creatures. It is true that their choices always have their reasons, but they incline to the choices under no compulsion of necessity.

But before going further it is necessary to meet a difficulty which may arise regarding the principles which we have set forth in the preceding. We have said that the concept of an individual substance includes once for all everything which can ever happen to it and that in considering this concept one will be able to see everything which can truly be said concerning the individual, just as we are able to see in the nature of a circle all the properties which can be derived from it. But does it not seem that in this way the difference between contingent and necessary truths will be destroyed, that there will be no place for human liberty, and that an absolute fatality will rule as well over all our actions as over all the rest of the events of the world? To this I reply that a distinction must be made between that which is certain and that which is necessary. Every one grants that future contingencies are assured since God foresees them, but we do not say just because of that that they are necessary. But it will be objected, that if any conclusion can be deduced infallibly from some definition or concept, it is necessary; and now since we have maintained that everything which is to happen to anyone is already virtually included in his nature or concept, as all the properties are contained in the definition of a circle, therefore, the difficulty still remains. In order to meet the objection completely, I say that the connection or sequence is of two kinds: the one, absolutely necessary, whose contrary implies contradiction, occurs in the eternal verities like the truths of geometry; the other is necessary only *ex hypothesi*, and so to speak by accident, and in itself it is contingent since the contrary is not implied. This latter sequence is not founded upon ideas wholly pure and upon the pure understanding of God, but upon his free decrees and upon the processes of the universe. Let us give an example. Since Julius Caesar will become perpetual Dictator and master of the Republic and will overthrow the liberty of Rome, this action is contained in his concept, for we have supposed that it is the nature of such a perfect concept of a subject to involve everything, in fact so that the predicate may be included in the subject *ut possit inesse subjecto*. We may say that it is not in virtue of this concept or idea that he is obliged to perform this action, since it pertains to him only because God knows everything. But it will be insisted in reply that his nature or form responds to this concept, and since God imposes upon him this personality, he is compelled henceforth to live up to it. I could reply by instancing the similar case of the future contingencies which as yet have no reality save in the understanding and will of God, and which, because God has given them in advance this form, must needs correspond to it. But I prefer to overcome a difficulty rather than to excuse it by instancing other difficulties, and what I am about to say will serve to clear up the one as well as the other. It is here that must be applied the distinction in the kind of relation, and I say that that which happens conformably to these decrees is assured, but that it is not therefore necessary, and if anyone did the contrary, he would do nothing impossible in itself, although it is impossible *ex hypothesi* that that other happen. For if anyone were capable of carrying out a complete demonstration by virtue of which he could prove this connection of the subject, which is Caesar, with the predicate, which is his successful enterprise, he would bring us to see in fact that the future dictatorship of Caesar had its basis in his concept or nature, so that one would see there a reason why he resolved to cross the Rubicon rather than to stop, and why he gained instead of losing the day at Pharsalus, and that it was reasonable and by consequence assured that this would occur, but one would not prove that it was necessary in itself, nor that the contrary implied a contradiction, almost in the same way in which it is reasonable and assured that God will always do what is best although that which is less perfect is not thereby implied. For it would be found that this demonstration of this predicate as belonging to Caesar is not as absolute as are those of numbers or of geometry, but that this predicate supposes a sequence of things which God has shown by his free will. This sequence is based on the first free decree of God which was to do always that which is the most perfect and upon the decree which God made following the first one, regarding human nature, which is that men should always do, although freely, that which appears to be the best. Now every truth which is founded upon this kind of decree is contingent, although certain, for the decrees of God do not change the possibilities of things and, as I have already said, although God assuredly chooses the best, this does not prevent that which is less perfect from being possible in itself. Although it will never happen, it is not its impossibility but its imperfection which causes him to reject it. Now nothing is necessitated whose opposite is possible. One will then be in a position to satisfy these kinds of difficulties, however great they may appear (and in fact they have not been less vexing to all other thinkers who have ever treated this matter), provided that he considers well that all contingent propositions have reasons why they are thus, rather than otherwise, or indeed (what is the same thing) that they have proof *a priori* of their truth, which render them certain and show that the connection of the subject and predicate in these propositions has its basis in the nature of the one and of the other, but he must further remember that such contingent propositions have not the demonstrations of necessity, since their reasons are founded only on the principle of contingency or of the existence of things, that is to say, upon that which is, or which appears to be the best among several things equally possible. Necessary truths, on the other hand, are founded upon the principle of contradiction, and upon the possibility or impossibility of the essences themselves, without regard here to the free will of God or of creatures.

XIV. *God produces different substances according to the different views which he has of the world, and by the intervention of God, the appropriate nature of each substance brings it about that what happens to one corresponds to what happens to all the others, without, however, their acting upon one another directly.*

After having seen, to a certain extent, in what the nature of substances consists, we must try to explain the dependence they have upon one another and their actions and passions. Now it is first of all very evident that created substances depend upon God who preserves them and can produce them continually by a kind of emanation just as we produce our thoughts, for when God turns, so to say, on all sides and in all fashions, the general system of phenomena which he finds it good to produce for the sake of manifesting his glory, and when he regards all the aspects of the world in all possible manners, since there is no relation which escapes his omniscience, the result of each view of the universe as seen from a different position is a substance which expresses the universe conformably to this view, provided God sees fit to render his thought effective and to produce the substance, and since God's vision is always true, our perceptions are always true and that which deceives us are our judgments, which are of us. Now we have said before, and it follows from what we have just said that each substance is a world by itself, independent of everything else excepting God; therefore, all our phenomena that is all things which are ever able to happen to us, are only consequences of our being. Now as the phenomena maintain a certain order conformably to our nature, or so to speak to the world which is in us (from whence it follows that we can, for the regulation of our conduct, make useful observations which are justified by the outcome of the future phenomena) and as we are thus able often to judge the future by the past without deceiving ourselves, we have sufficient grounds for saying that these phenomena are true and we will not be put to the task of inquiring whether they are outside of us, and whether others perceive them also.

Nevertheless it is most true that the perceptions and expressions of all substances intercorrespond, so that each one following independently certain reasons or laws which he has noticed meets others which are doing the same, as when several have agreed to meet together in a certain place on a set day, they are able to carry out the plan if they wish. Now although all express the same phenomena, this does not bring it about that their expressions are exactly alike. It is sufficient if they are proportional. As when several spectators think they see the same thing and are agreed about it, although each one sees or speaks according to the measure of his vision. It is God alone (from whom all individuals emanate continually, and who sees the universe not only as they see it, but besides in a very different way from them) who is the cause of this correspondence in their phenomena and who brings it about that that which is particular to one, is also common to all, otherwise there would be no relation. In a way, then, we might properly say, although it seems strange, that a particular substance never acts upon another particular substance nor is it acted upon by it. That which happens to each one is only the consequence of its complete idea or concept, since this idea already includes all the predicates and expresses the whole universe. In fact nothing can happen to us except thoughts and perceptions, and all our thoughts and perceptions are but the consequence, contingent it is true, of our precedent thoughts and perceptions, in such a way that were I able to consider directly all that happens or appears to me at the present time, I should be able to see all that will happen to me or that will ever appear to me. This future will not fail me, and will surely appear to me even if all that which is outside of me were destroyed, save only that God and myself were left.

Since, however, we ordinarily attribute to other things an

action upon us which brings us to perceive things in a certain manner, it is necessary to consider the basis of this judgment and to inquire what there is of truth in it.

XV. *The action of one finite substance upon another consists only in the increase in the degrees of the expression of the first combined with a decrease in that of the second, in so far as God has in advance fashioned them so that they shall act in accord.*

Without entering into a long discussion it is sufficient for reconciling the language of metaphysics with that of practical life to remark that we preferably attribute to ourselves, and with reason, the phenomena which we express the most perfectly, and that we attribute to other substances those phenomena which each one expresses the best. Thus a substance, which is of an infinite extension in so far as it expresses all, becomes limited in proportion to its more or less perfect manner of expression. It is thus then that we may conceive of substances as interfering with and limiting one another, and hence we are able to say that in this sense they act upon one another, and that they, so to speak, accommodate themselves to one another. For it can happen that a single change which augments the expression of the one may diminish that of the other. Now the virtue of a particular substance is to express well the glory of God, and the better it expresses it, the less is it limited. Everything when it expresses its virtue or power, that is to say, when it acts, changes to better, and expands just in so far as it acts. When therefore a change occurs by which several substances are affected (in fact every change affects them all) I think we may say that those substances, which by this change pass immediately to a greater degree of perfection, or to a more perfect expression, exert power and act, while those which pass to a lesser degree disclose their weakness and suffer. I also hold that every activity of a substance which has perception implies some pleasure, and every passion some pain, except that it may very well happen that a present advantage will be eventually destroyed by a greater evil, whence it comes that one may sin in acting or exerting his power and in finding pleasure.

XVI. The extraordinary intervention of God is not excluded in that which our particular essences express, because their expression includes everything. Such intervention, however, goes beyond the power of our natural being or of our distinct expression, because these are finite, and follow certain subordinate regulations.

There remains for us at present only to explain how it is possible that God has influence at times upon men or upon other substances by an extraordinary or miraculous intervention, since it seems that nothing is able to happen which is extraordinary or supernatural inasmuch as all the events which occur to the other substances are only the consequences of their natures. We must recall what was said above in regard to the miracles in the universe. These always conform to the universal law of the general order, although they may contravene the subordinate regulations, and since every person or substance is like a little world which expresses the great world, we can say that this extraordinary action of God upon this substance is nevertheless miraculous, although it is comprised in the general order of the universe in so far as it is expressed by the individual essence or concept of this substance. This is why, if we understand in our natures all that they express, nothing is supernatural in them, because they reach out to everything, an effect always expressing its cause, and God being the veritable cause of the substances. But as that which our natures express the most perfectly pertains to them in a particular manner, that being their special power, and since they are limited, as I have just explained, many things there are which surpass the powers of our natures and even of all limited natures. As a consequence, to speak more clearly, I say that the miracles and the extraordinary interventions of God have this peculiarity that they cannot be foreseen by any created mind however enlightened. This is because the distinct comprehension of the fundamental order surpasses them all, while on the other hand, that which is called natural depends upon less fundamental regulations which the creatures are able to understand. In order then that my words may be as irreprehensible as the meaning I am trying to convey, it will be well to associate certain words with certain significations. We may call that which includes everything that we express and which expresses our union with God himself, nothing going beyond it, our essence. But that which is limited in us may be designated as our nature or our power, and in accordance with this terminology that which goes beyond the natures of all created substances is supernatural.

XVII. An example of a subordinate regulation in the law of nature which demonstrates that God always preserves the same amount of force but not the same quantity of motion: —against the Cartesians and many others.

I have frequently spoken of subordinate regulations, or of the laws of nature, and it seems that it will be well to give an example. Our new philosophers are unanimous in employing that famous law that God always preserves the same amount of motion in the universe. In fact it is a very plausible law, and in times past I held it as indubitable. But since then I have learned in what its fault consists. Monsieur Descartes and many other clever mathematicians have thought that the quantity of motion, that is to say the velocity multiplied by the bulk of the moving body, is exactly equivalent to the moving force, or to speak in mathematical terms that the force varies as the velocity multiplied by the bulk. Now it is reasonable that the same force is always preserved in the universe. So also, looking to phenomena, it will be readily seen that a mechanical perpetual motion is impossible, because the force in such a machine, being always diminished a little by friction and so ultimately destined to be entirely spent, would necessarily have to recoup its losses, and consequently would keep on increasing of itself without any new impulsion from without; and we see furthermore that the force of a body is diminished only in proportion as it gives up force, either to a contiguous body or to its own parts, in so far as they have a separate movement. The mathematicians to whom I have referred think that what can be said of force can be said of the quantity of motion. In order, however, to show the difference I make two suppositions: in the first place, that a body falling from a certain height acquires a force enabling it to remount to the same height, provided that its direction is turned that way, or provided that there are no hindrances. For instance, a pendulum will rise exactly to the height from which it has fallen, provided the resistance of the air and of certain other small particles do not diminish a little its acquired force.

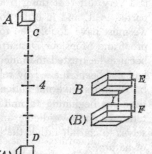

I suppose in the second place that it will take as much force to lift a body A weighing one pound to the height CD, four feet, as to raise a body B weighing four pounds to the height EF, one foot. These two suppositions are granted by our new philosophers. It is therefore manifest that the body A falling from the height CD acquires exactly as much force as the body B falling from the height EF, for the body B at F, having by the first supposition sufficient force to return to E, has therefore the force to carry a body of four pounds to the distance of one foot, EF. And likewise the body A at D, having the force to return to C, has also the force required to carry a body weighing one pound, its own weight, back to C, a distance of four feet. Now by the second supposition the force of these two bodies is equal. Let us now see if the quantity of motion is the same in each case. It is here that we will be surprised to find a very great difference, for it has been proved by Galileo that the velocity acquired by the fall CD is double the velocity acquired by the fall EF, although the height is four times as great. Multiplying, therefore, the body A, whose bulk is 1, by its velocity, which is 2, the product or the quantity of movement will be 2, and on the other hand, if we multiply the body B, whose bulk is 4, by its velocity, which is 1, the product or quantity of motion will be 4. Hence the quantity of the motion of the body A at the point D is half the quantity of motion of the body B at the point F, yet their forces are equal, and there is therefore a great difference between the quantity of motion and the force. This is what we set out to show. We can see therefore how the force ought to be estimated by the quantity of the effect which it is able to produce, for example by the height to which a body of certain weight can be raised. This is a very different thing from the velocity which can be imparted to it, and in order to impart to it double the velocity we must have double the force. Nothing is simpler than this proof and Monsieur Descartes has fallen into error here, only because he trusted too much to his thoughts even when they had not been ripened by reflection. But it astonishes me that his disciples have not noticed this error, and I am afraid that they are beginning to imitate little by little certain Peripatetics whom they ridicule, and that they are accustoming themselves to consult rather the books of their master, than reason or nature.

XVIII. The distinction between force and the quantity of motion is, among other reasons, important as showing that we must have recourse to metaphysical considerations in addition to discussions of extension if we wish to explain the phenomena of matter.

This consideration of the force, distinguished from the quantity of motion, is of importance, not only in physics and mechanics for finding the real laws of nature and the principles of motion, and even for correcting many practical errors which have crept into the writings of certain able mathematicians, but also in metaphysics it is of importance for the better understanding of principles. Because motion, if we regard only its exact and formal meaning, that is, change of place, is not something really absolute, and when several bodies change their places reciprocally, it is not possible to determine by considering the bodies alone to which among them movement or repose is to be attributed, as I could demonstrate geometrically, if I wished to stop for it now. But the force, or the proximate cause of these changes is something more real, and there are sufficient grounds for attributing it to one body rather than to another, and it is only through this latter investigation that we can determine to which one the movement must appertain. Now this force is something different from size, from form or from motion, and it can be seen from this consideration that the whole meaning of a body is not exhausted in its extension together with its modifications as our moderns persuade themselves. We are therefore obliged to restore certain beings or forms which they have banished. It appears more and more clear that although all the particular phenomena of nature can be explained mathematically or mechanically by those who understand them, yet nevertheless, the general principles of corporeal nature and even of mechanics are metaphysical rather than geometric, and belong rather to certain indivisible forms or natures as the causes of the appearances, than to the corporeal mass or to extension. In this way we are able to reconcile the mechanical philosophy of the moderns with the circumspection of those intelligent and well-meaning persons who, with a certain justice, fear that we are becoming too far removed from immaterial beings and that we are thus prejudicing piety.

XIX. The utility of final causes in Physics.

As I do not wish to judge people in ill part I bring no accusation against our new philosophers who pretend to banish final causes from physics, but I am nevertheless obliged to avow that the consequences of such a banishment appear to me dangerous, especially when joined to that position which I refuted at the beginning of this treatise. That position seemed to go the length of discarding final causes entirely as though God proposed no end and no good in his activity, or as if good were not to be the object of his will. I hold on the contrary that it is just in this that the principle of all existences and of the laws of nature must be sought, hence God always proposes the best and most perfect. I am quite willing to grant that we are liable to err when we wish to determine the purposes or councils of God, but this is the case only when we try to limit them to some particular design, thinking that he has had in view only a single thing, while in fact he regards everything at once. As for instance, if we think that God has made the world only for us, it is a great blunder, although it may be quite true that he has made it entirely for us, and that there is nothing in the universe which does not touch us and which does not accommodate itself to the regard which he has for us according to the principle laid down above. Therefore when we see some good effect or some perfection which happens or which follows from the works of God we are able to say assuredly that God has purposed it, for he does nothing by chance, and is not like us who sometimes fail to do well. Therefore, far from being able to fall into error in this respect as do the extreme statesmen who postulate too much foresight in the designs of Princes, or as do commentators who seek for too much erudition in their authors, it will be impossible to attribute too much reflection to God's infinite wisdom, and there is no matter in which error is less to be feared provided we confine ourselves to affirmations and provided we avoid negative statements which limit the designs of God. All those who see the admirable structure of animals find themselves led to recognize the wisdom of the author of things and I advise those who have any sentiment of piety and indeed of true philosophy to hold aloof from the expressions of certain pretentious minds who instead of saying that eyes were made for seeing, say that we see because we find ourselves having eyes. When one seriously holds such opinions which hand everything over to material necessity or to a kind of chance (although either alternative ought to appear ridiculous to those who understand what we have explained above) it is difficult to recognize an intelligent author of nature. The effect should correspond to its cause and indeed it is best known through the recognition of its cause, so that it is reasonable to introduce a sovereign intelligence ordering things, and in place of making use of the wisdom of this sovereign being, to employ only the properties of matter to explain phenomena. As if in order to account for the capture of an important place by a prince, the historian should say it was because the particles of powder in the cannon having been touched by a spark of fire expanded with a rapidity capable of pushing a hard solid body against the walls of the place, while the little particles which composed the brass of the cannon were so well interlaced that they did not separate under this impact,—as if he should account for it in this way instead of making us see how the foresight of the conqueror brought him to choose the time and the proper means and how his ability surmounted all obstacles.

XX. A noteworthy disquisition in Plato's Phaedo against the philosophers who were too materialistic.

This reminds me of a fine disquisition by Socrates in Plato's Phaedo, which agrees perfectly with my opinion on this subject and seems to have been uttered expressly for our too materialistic philosophers. This agreement has led me to a desire to translate it although it is a little long. Perhaps this example will give some of us an incentive to share in many of the other beautiful and well balanced thoughts which are found in the writings of this famous author.

XXI. If the mechanical laws depended upon Geometry alone without metaphysical influences, the phenomena would be very different from what they are.

Now since the wisdom of God has always been recognized in the details of the mechanical structures of certain particular bodies, it should also be shown in the general economy of the world and in the constitution of the laws of nature. This is so true that even in the laws of motion in general, the plans of this wisdom have been noticed. For if bodies were only extended masses, and motion were only a change of place, and if everything ought to be and could be deduced by geometric necessity from these two definitions alone, it would follow, as I have shown elsewhere, that the smallest body on contact with a very large one at rest would impart to it its own velocity, yet without losing any of the velocity that it had. A quantity of other rules wholly contrary to the formation of a system would also have to be admitted. But the decree of the divine wisdom in preserving always the same force and the same total direction has provided for a system. I find indeed that many of the effects of nature can be accounted for in a twofold way, that is to say by a consideration of efficient causes, and again independently by a consideration of final causes. An example of the latter is God's decree always to carry out his plan by the easiest and most determined way. I have shown this elsewhere in accounting for the catoptric and dioptric laws, and I will speak more at length about it in what follows.

XXII. Reconciliation of the two methods of explanation, the one using final causes, and the other efficient causes, thus satisfying both those who explain nature mechanically and those who have recourse to incorporeal natures.

It is worth while to make the preceding remark in order to reconcile those who hope to explain mechanically the formation of the first tissue of an animal and all the interrelation of the parts, with those who account for the same structure by referring to final causes. Both explanations are good; both are useful not only for the admiring of the work of a great artificer, but also for the discovery of useful facts in physics and medicine. And writers who take these diverse routes should not speak ill of each other. For I see that those who attempt to explain beauty by the divine anatomy ridicule those who imagine that the apparently fortuitous flow of certain liquids has been able to produce such a beautiful variety and that they regard them as overbold and irreverent. These others on the contrary treat the former as simple and superstitious, and compare them to those ancients who regarded the physicists as impious when they maintained that not Jupiter thundered but some material which is found in the clouds. The best plan would be to join the two ways of thinking. To use a practical comparison, we recognize and praise the ability of a workman not only when we show what designs he had in making the parts of his machine, but also when we explain the instruments which he employed in making each part, especially if these instruments are simple and ingeniously contrived. God is also a workman able enough to produce a machine still a thousand times more ingenious than is our body, by employing only certain quite simple liquids purposely composed in such a way that ordinary laws of nature alone are required to develop them so as to produce such a marvellous effect. But it is also true that this development would not take place if God were not the author of nature. Yet I find that the method of efficient causes, which goes much deeper and is in a measure more immediate and *a priori,* is also more difficult when we come to details, and I think that our philosophers are still very frequently far removed from making the most of this method. The method of final causes, however, is easier and can be frequently employed to find out important and useful truths which we should have to seek for a long time, if we were confined to that other more physical method of which anatomy is able to furnish many examples. It seems to me that Snellius, who was the first discoverer of the laws of refraction, would have waited a long time before finding them if he had wished to seek out first how light was formed. But he apparently followed that method which the ancients employed for Catoptrics, that is, the method of final causes. Because, while seeking for the easiest way in which to conduct a ray of light from one given point to another given point by reflection from a given plane (supposing that that was the design of nature) they discovered the equality of the angles of incidence and reflection, as can be seen from a little treatise by Heliodorus of Larissa and also elsewhere. This principle Mons. Snellius, I believe, and afterwards independently of him, M. Fermat, applied most ingeniously to refraction. For since the rays while in the same media always maintain the same proportion of sines, which in turn corresponds to the resistance of the media, it appears that they follow the easiest way, or at least that way which is the most determinate for passing from a given point in one medium to a given point in another medium. That demonstration of this same theorem which M. Descartes has given, using efficient causes, is much less satisfactory. At least we have grounds to think that he would never have found the principle by that means if he had not learned in Holland of the discovery of Snellius.

XXIII. Returning to immaterial substances we explain how God acts upon the understanding of spirits and ask whether one always keeps the idea of what he thinks about.

I have thought it well to insist a little upon final causes, upon incorporeal natures and upon an intelligent cause with respect to bodies so as to show the use of these conceptions in physics and in mathematics. This for two reasons, first to purge from mechanical philosophy the impiety that is imputed to it, second, to elevate to nobler lines of thought the thinking of our philosophers who incline to materialistic considerations alone. Now, however, it will be well to return from corporeal substances to the consideration of immaterial natures and particularly of spirits, and to speak of the methods which God uses to enlighten them and to act upon them. Although we must not forget that there are here at the same time certain laws of nature in regard to which I can speak more amply elsewhere. It will be enough for now to touch upon ideas and to inquire if we see everything in God and how God is our light. First of all it will be in place to remark that the wrong use of ideas occasions many errors. For when one reasons in regard to anything, he imagines that he has an idea of it and this is the foundation upon which certain philosophers, ancient and modern, have constructed a demonstration of God that is extremely imperfect. It must be, they say, that I have an idea of God, or of a perfect being, since I think of him and we cannot think without having ideas; now the idea of this being includes all perfections and since existence is one of these perfections, it follows that he exists. But I reply, inasmuch as we often think of impossible chimeras, for example of the highest degree of swiftness, of the greatest number, of the meeting of the conchoid with its base or determinant, such reasoning is not sufficient. It is therefore in this sense that we can say that there are true and false ideas according as the thing which is in question is possible or not. And it is when he is assured of the possibility of a thing, that one can boast of having an idea of it. Therefore, the aforesaid argument proves that God exists, if he is possible. This is in fact an excellent privilege of the divine nature, to have need only of a possibility or an essence in order to actually exist, and it is just this which is called self-sufficient being, *ens a se.*

XXIV. What clear and obscure, distinct and confused, adequate and inadequate, intuitive and assumed knowledge is, and the definition of nominal, real, causal and essential.

In order to understand better the nature of ideas it is necessary to touch somewhat upon the various kinds of knowledge. When I am able to recognize a thing among others, without being able to say in what its differences or characteristics consist, the knowledge is confused. Sometimes indeed we may know clearly, that is without being in the slightest doubt, that a poem or a picture is well or badly done because there is in it an "I know not what" which satisfies or shocks us. Such knowledge is not yet distinct. It is when I am able to explain the peculiarities which a thing has, that the knowledge is called distinct. Such is the knowledge of an assayer who discerns the true gold from the false by means of certain tests or marks which make up the definition of gold. But distinct knowledge has degrees, because ordinarily the conceptions which enter into the definitions will themselves be in need of definition, and are only known confusedly. When at length everything which enters into a definition or into distinct knowledge is known distinctly, even back to the primitive conception, I call that knowledge adequate. When my mind understands at once and distinctly all the primitive ingredients of a conception, then we have intuitive knowledge. This is extremely rare as most human knowledge is only confused or indeed assumed. It is well also to distinguish nominal from real definition. I call a definition nominal when there is doubt whether an exact conception of it is possible; as for instance, when I say that an endless screw is a line in three dimensional space whose parts are congruent or fall one upon another. Now although this is one of the reciprocal properties of an endless screw, he who did not know by other means what an endless screw was could doubt if such a line were possible, because the other lines whose ends are congruent (there are only two:

the circumference of a circle and the straight line) are plane figures, that is to say they can be described *in plano*. This instance enables us to see that any reciprocal property can serve as a nominal definition, but when the property brings us to see the possibility of a thing it makes the definition real, and as long as one has only a nominal definition he cannot be sure of the consequences which he draws, because if it conceals a contradiction or an impossibility he would be able to draw the opposite conclusions. That is why truths do not depend upon names and are not arbitrary, as some of our new philosophers think. There is also a considerable difference among real definitions, for when the possibility proves itself only by experience, as in the definition of quicksilver, whose possibility we know because such a body, which is both an extremely heavy fluid and quite volatile, actually exists, the definition is merely real and nothing more. If, however, the proof of the possibility is *a priori*, the definition is not only real but also causal as for instance when it contains the possible generation of a thing. Finally, when the definition, without assuming anything which requires a proof *a priori* of its possibility, carries the analysis clear to the primitive conception, the definition is perfect or essential.

XXV. In what cases knowledge is added to mere contemplation of the idea.

Now it is manifest that we have no idea of a conception when it is impossible. And in case the knowledge, where we have the idea of it, is only assumed, we do not visualize it because such a conception is known only in like manner as conceptions internally impossible. And if it be in fact possible, it is not by this kind of knowledge that we learn its possibility. For instance, when I am thinking of a thousand or of a chiliagon, I frequently do it without contemplating the idea. Even if I say a thousand is ten times a hundred, I frequently do not trouble to think what ten and a hundred are, because I assume that I know, and I do not consider it necessary to stop just at present to conceive of them. Therefore it may well happen, as it in fact does happen often enough, that

I am mistaken in regard to a conception which I assume that I understand, although it is an impossible truth or at least is incompatible with others with which I join it, and whether I am mistaken or not, this way of assuming our knowledge remains the same. It is, then, only when our knowledge is clear in regard to confused conceptions, and when it is intuitive in regard to those which are distinct, that we see its entire idea.

XXVI. Ideas are all stored up within us. Plato's doctrine of reminiscence.

In order to see clearly what an idea is, we must guard ourselves against a misunderstanding. Many regard the idea as the form or the differentiation of our thinking, and according to this opinion we have the idea in our mind, in so far as we are thinking of it, and each separate time that we think of it anew we have another idea although similar to the preceding one. Some, however, take the idea as the immediate object of thought, or as a permanent form which remains even when we are no longer contemplating it. As a matter of fact our soul has the power of representing to itself any form or nature whenever the occasion comes for thinking about it, and I think that this activity of our soul is, so far as it expresses some nature, form or essence, properly the idea of the thing. This is in us, and is always in us, whether we are thinking of it or no. (Our soul expresses God and the universe and all essences as well as all existences.) This position is in accord with my principles that naturally nothing enters into our minds from outside.

It is a bad habit we have of thinking as though our minds receive certain messengers, as it were, or as if they had doors or windows. We have in our minds all those forms for all periods of time because the mind at every moment expresses all its future thoughts and already thinks confusedly of all that of which it will ever think distinctly. Nothing can be taught us of which we have not already in our minds the idea. This idea is as it were the material out of which the thought will form itself. This is what Plato has excellently brought out in his doctrine of reminiscence, a doctrine which contains a great deal of truth, provided that it is properly understood and purged of the error of pre-existence, and provided that one does not conceive of the soul as having already known and thought at some other time what it learns and thinks now. Plato has also confirmed his position by a beautiful experiment. He introduces [*Meno*] a boy, whom he leads by short steps, to extremely difficult truths of geometry bearing on incommensurables, all this without teaching the boy anything, merely drawing out replies by a well arranged series of questions. This shows that the soul virtually knows those things, and needs only to be reminded (animadverted) to recognize the truths. Consequently it possesses at least the idea upon which those truths depend. We may say even that it already possesses those truths, if we consider them as the relations of the ideas.

XXVII. In what respect our souls can be compared to blank tablets and how conceptions are derived from the senses.

Aristotle preferred to compare our souls to blank tablets prepared for writing, and he maintained that nothing is in the understanding which does not come through the senses. This position is in accord with the popular conceptions, as Aristotle's approach usually is. Plato thinks more profoundly. Such tenets or practicologies are nevertheless allowable in ordinary use somewhat in the same way as those who accept the Copernican theory still continue to speak of the rising and setting of the sun. I find indeed that these usages can be given a real meaning containing no error, quite in the same way as I have already pointed out that we may truly say particular substances act upon one another. In this same sense we may say that knowledge is received from without through the medium of the senses because certain exterior things contain or express more particularly the causes which determine us to certain thoughts. Because in the ordinary uses of life we attribute to the soul only that which belongs to it most manifestly and particularly, and there is no advantage in going further. When, however, we are dealing with the exactness of metaphysical truths, it is important to recognize the powers and independence of the soul which extend infinitely further than is commonly supposed. In order, therefore, to avoid misunderstandings it would be well to choose separate terms for the two. These expressions which are in the soul whether one is conceiving of them or not may be called ideas, while those which one conceives of or constructs may be called conceptions, *conceptus*. But whatever terms are used, it is always false to say that all our conceptions come from the so-called external senses, because those conceptions which I have of myself and of my thoughts, and consequently of being, of substance, of action, of identity, and of many others come from an inner experience.

XXVIII. The only immediate object of our perceptions which exists outside of us is God, and in him alone is our light.

In the strictly metaphysical sense no external cause acts upon us excepting God alone, and he is in immediate relation with us only by virtue of our continual dependence upon him. Whence it follows that there is absolutely no other external object which comes into contact with our souls and directly excites perceptions in us. We have in our souls ideas of everything, only because of the continual action of God upon us, that is to say, because every effect expresses its cause and therefore the essences of our souls are certain expressions, imitations or images of the divine essence, divine thought and divine will, including all the ideas which are there contained. We may say, therefore, that God is for us the only immediate external object, and that we see things through him. For example, when we see the sun or the stars, it is God who gives to us and preserves in us the ideas and whenever our senses are affected according to his own laws in a certain manner, it is he, who by his continual concurrence, determines our thinking. God is the sun and the light of souls, *lumen illuminans omnem hominem venientem in hunc mundum,* although this is not the current conception. I think I have already remarked that during the scholastic period many believed God to be the light of the soul, *intellectus agens animæ rationalis,* following in this the Holy Scriptures and the fathers who were always more Platonic than Aristotelian in their mode of thinking. The Averroists misused this conception, but others, among whom were several mystic theologians, and William of Saint Amour also, I think, understood this conception in a manner which assured the dignity of God and was able to raise the soul to a knowledge of its welfare.

XXIX. Yet we think directly by means of our own ideas and not through God's.

Nevertheless I cannot approve of the position of certain able philosophers who seem to hold that our ideas themselves are in God and not at all in us. I think that in taking this position they have neither sufficiently considered the nature of substance, which we have just explained, nor the complete purview and independence of the soul which includes all that happens to it, and expresses God, and with him all possible and actual beings in the same way that an effect expresses its cause. It is indeed inconceivable that the soul should think using the ideas of something else. The soul when it thinks of anything must be affected dynamically in a certain manner, and it must needs have in itself in advance not only the passive capacity of being thus affected, a capacity already wholly determined, but it must have besides an active power by virtue of which it has always had in its nature the marks of the future production of this thought, and the disposition to produce it at its proper time. All of this shows that the soul already includes the idea which is comprised in any particular thought.

XXX. How God inclines our souls without necessitating them; that there are no grounds for complaint; that we must not ask why Judas sinned because this free act is contained in his concept, the only question being why Judas the sinner is admitted to existence, preferably to other possible persons; concerning the original imperfection or limitation before the fall and concerning the different degrees of grace.

Regarding the action of God upon the human will there are many quite different considerations which it would take too long to investigate here. Nevertheless the following is what can be said in general. God in co-operating with ordinary actions only follows the laws which he has established, that is to say, he continually preserves and produces our being so that the ideas come to us spontaneously or with freedom in that order which the concept of our individual substance carries with itself. In this concept they can be foreseen for all eternity. Furthermore, by virtue of the decree which God has made that the will shall always seek the apparent good in certain particular respects (in regard to which this apparent good always has in it something of reality expressing or imitating God's will), he, without at all necessitating our choice, determines it by that which appears most desirable. For absolutely speaking, our will as contrasted with necessity, is in a state of indifference, being able to act otherwise, or wholly to suspend its action, either alternative being and remaining possible. It therefore devolves upon the soul to be on guard against appearances, by means of a firm will, to reflect and to refuse to act or decide in certain circumstances, except after mature deliberation. It is, however, true and has been assured from all eternity that certain souls will not employ their power upon certain occasions.

But who could do more than God has done, and can such a soul complain of anything except itself? All these complaints after the deed are unjust, inasmuch as they would have been unjust before the deed. Would this soul shortly before committing the sin have had the right to complain of God as though he had determined the sin? Since the determinations of God in these matters cannot be foreseen, how would the soul know that it was preordained to sin unless it had already committed the sin? It is merely a question of wishing to or not wishing to, and God could not have set an easier or juster condition. Therefore all judges without asking the reasons which have disposed a man to have an evil will, consider only how far this will is wrong. But, you object, perhaps it is ordained from all eternity that I will sin. Find your own answer. Perhaps it has not been. Now then, without asking for what you are unable to know and in regard to which you can have no light, act according to your duty and your knowledge. But, some one will object; whence comes it then that this man will assuredly do this sin? The reply is easy. It is that otherwise he would not be a man. For God foresees from all time that there will be a certain Judas, and in the concept or idea of him which God has, is contained this future free act. The only question, therefore, which remains is why this certain Judas, the betrayer who is possible only because of the idea of God, actually exists. To this question, however, we can expect no answer here on earth excepting to say in general that it is because God has found it good that he should exist notwithstanding that sin which he foresaw. This evil will be more than overbalanced. God will derive a greater good from it, and it will finally turn out that this series of events in which is included the existence of this sinner, is the most perfect among all the possible series of events. An explanation in every case of the admirable economy of this choice cannot be given while we are sojourners on earth. It is enough to know the excellence without understanding it. It is here that we must recognize the unfathomable depth of the divine wisdom, without hesitating at a detail which involves an infinite number of considerations. It is clear, however, that God is not the cause of ill. For not only after the loss of innocence by men, has original sin possessed the soul, but even before that there was an original limitation or imperfection in the very nature of all creatures, which rendered them open to sin and able to fall. There is, therefore, no more difficulty in the supralapsarian view than there is in the other views of sin. To this also, it seems to me, can be reduced the opinion of Saint Augustine and of other authors: that the root of evil is in the privation, that is to say, in the lack or limitation of creatures which God graciously remedies by whatever degree of perfection it pleases him to give. This grace of God, whether ordinary or extraordinary, has its degrees and its measures. It is always efficacious in itself to produce a certain proportionate effect and furthermore it is always sufficient not only to keep one from sin but even to effect his salvation, provided that the man co-operates with that which is in him. It has not always, however, sufficient power to overcome the inclination, for, if it did, it would no longer be limited in any way, and this superiority to limitations is reserved to that unique grace which is absolutely efficacious. This grace is always victorious whether through its own self or through the congruity of circumstances.

XXXI. Concerning the motives of election; concerning faith foreseen and the absolute decree and that it all reduces to the question why God has chosen and resolved to admit to existence just such a possible person, whose concept includes just such a sequence of free acts and of free gifts of grace. This at once puts an end to all difficulties.

Finally, the grace of God is wholly unprejudiced and creatures have no claim upon it. Just as it is not sufficient in accounting for God's choice in his dispensations of grace to refer to his absolute or conditional prevision of men's future actions, so it is also wrong to imagine his decrees as absolute with no reasonable motive. As concerns foreseen faith and good works, it is very true that God has elected none but those whose faith and charity he foresees, *quos se fide donaturum praescivit*. The same question, however, arises again as to why God gives to some rather than to others the grace of faith or of good works. As concerns God's ability to foresee not only the faith and good deeds, but also their content and predisposition, or that which a man on his part contributes to them (since there are as truly diversities on the part of men as on the part of grace, and a man although he needs to be aroused to good and needs to become converted, yet acts in accordance with his temperament)—as regards his ability to foresee there are many who say that God, knowing what a particular man will do without grace, that is without his extraordinary assistance, or knowing at least what will be the human contribution, resolves to give grace to those whose natural dispositions are the best, or at any rate are the least imperfect and evil. But if this were the case then the natural dispositions in so far as they were good would be like gifts of grace, since God would have given advantages to some over others; and therefore, since he would well know that the natural advantages which he had given would serve as motives for his grace or for his extraordinary assistance, would not everything be reduced to his mercy? I think, therefore, that since we do not know how much and in what way God regards natural dispositions in the dispensations of his grace, it would be safest and most exact to say, in accordance with our principles and as I have already remarked, that there must needs be among possible beings the person Peter or John whose concept or idea contains all that particular sequence of ordinary and extraordinary manifestations of grace together with the rest of the accompanying events and circumstances, and that it has pleased God to choose him among an infinite number of persons equally possible for actual existence. When we have said this there seems nothing left to ask, and all difficulties vanish. For in regard to that great and ultimate question why it has pleased God to choose him among so great a number of possible persons, it is surely unreasonable to demand more than the general reasons which we have given. The reasons in detail surpass our ken. Therefore, instead of postulating an absolute decree, which being without reason would be unreasonable, and instead of postulating reasons which do not succeed in solving the difficulties and in turn have need themselves of reasons, it will be best to say with St. Paul that there are for God's choice certain great reasons of wisdom and congruity which he follows, which reasons, however, are unknown to mortals and are founded upon the general order, whose goal is the greatest perfection of the world. This is what is meant when the motives of God's glory and of the manifestation of his justice are spoken of, as well as when men speak of his mercy, and his perfection in general; that immense vastness of wealth, in fine, with which the soul of the same St. Paul was to be thrilled.

XXXII. Usefulness of these principles in matters of piety and of religion.

In addition it seems that the thoughts which we have just explained and particularly the great principle of the perfection of God's operations and the concept of substance which includes all its changes with all its accompanying circumstances, far from injuring, serve rather to confirm religion, serve to dissipate great difficulties, to inflame souls with a divine love and to raise the mind to a knowledge of incorporeal substances much more than the present-day hypotheses. For it appears clearly that all other substances depend upon God just as our thoughts emanate from our own substances; that God is all in all and that he is intimately united to all created things, in proportion however to their perfection; that it is he alone who determines them from without by his influence, and if to act is to determine directly, it may be said in metaphysical language that God alone acts upon me and he alone causes me to do good or ill, other substances contributing only because of his determinations; because God, who takes all things into consideration, distributes his bounties and compels created beings to accommodate themselves to one another. Thus God alone constitutes the relation or communication between substances. It is through him that the phenomena of the one meet and accord with the phenomena of the others, so that there may be a reality in our perceptions. In common parlance, however, an action is attributed to particular causes in the sense that I have explained above because it is not necessary to make continual mention of the universal cause when speaking of particular cases. It can be seen also that every substance has a perfect spontaneity (which becomes liberty with intelligent substances). Everything which happens to it is a consequence of its idea or its being and nothing determines it except God only. It is for this reason that a person of exalted mind and revered saintliness may say that the soul ought often to think as if there were only God and itself in the world. Nothing can make us hold to immortality more firmly than this independence and vastness of the soul which protects it completely against exterior things, since it alone constitutes our universe and together with God is sufficient for itself. It is as impossible for it to perish save through annihilation as it is impossible for the universe to destroy itself, the universe whose animate and perpetual expression it is. Furthermore, the changes in this extended mass which is called our body cannot possibly affect the soul nor can the dissipation of the body destroy that which is indivisible.

XXXIII. Explanation of the relation between the soul and the body, a matter which has been regarded as inexplicable or else as miraculous; concerning the origin of confused perceptions.

We can also see the explanation of that great mystery "the union of the soul and the body," that is to say how it comes about that the passions and actions of the one are accompanied by the actions and passions or else the appropriate phenomena of the other. For it is not possible to conceive how one can have an influence upon the other and it is unreasonable to have recourse at once to the extraordinary intervention of the universal cause in an ordinary and particular case. The following, however, is the true explanation. We have said that everything which happens to a soul or to any substance is a consequence of its concept; hence the idea itself or the essence of the soul brings it about that all of its appearances or perceptions should be born out of its nature and precisely in such a way that they correspond of themselves to that which happens in the universe at large, but more particularly and more perfectly to that which happens in the body associated with it, because it is in a particular way and only for a certain time according to the relation of other bodies to its own body that the soul expresses the state of the universe. This last fact enables us to see how our body belongs to us, without, however, being attached to our essence. I believe that those who are careful thinkers will decide favorably for our principles because of this single reason, viz., that they are able to see in what consists the relation between the soul and the body, a parallelism which appears inexplicable in any other way. We can also see that the perceptions of our senses even when they are clear must necessarily contain certain confused elements, for as all the bodies in the universe are in sympathy, ours receives the impressions of all the others, and while our senses respond to everything, our soul cannot pay attention to every particular. That is why our confused sensations are the result of a variety of perceptions. This variety is infinite. It is almost like the confused murmuring which is heard by those who approach the shore of a sea. It comes from the continual beatings of innumerable waves. If now, out of many perceptions which do not at all fit together to make one, no particular one perception surpasses the others, and if they make impressions about equally strong or equally capable of holding the attention of the soul, they can be perceived only confusedly.

XXXIV. Concerning the difference between spirits and other substances, souls or substantial forms; that the immortality which men desire includes memory.

Supposing that the bodies which constitute a *unum per se*, as human bodies, are substances, and have substantial forms, and supposing that animals have souls, we are obliged to grant that these souls and these substantial forms cannot entirely perish, any more than can the atoms or the ultimate elements of matter, according to the position of other philosophers; for no substance perishes, although it may become very different. Such substances also express the whole universe, although more imperfectly than do spirits. The principal difference, however, is that they do not know that they are, nor what they are. Consequently, not being able to reason, they are unable to discover necessary and universal truths. It is also because they do not reflect regarding themselves that they have no moral qualities, whence it follows that they undergo myriad transformations—as we see a caterpillar change into a butterfly; the result from a moral or practical standpoint is the same as if we said that they perished in each case, and we can indeed say it from the physical standpoint in the same way that we say bodies perish in their dissolution. But the intelligent soul, knowing that it exists, having the ability to say that word "I" so full of meaning, not only continues and exists, metaphysically far more certainly than do the others, but it remains the same from the moral standpoint, and constitutes the same personality, for it is its memory or knowledge of this ego which renders it open to punishment and reward. Also the immortality which is required in morals and in religion does not consist merely in this perpetual existence, which pertains to all substances, for if in addition there were no remembrance of what one had been, immortality would not be at all desirable. Suppose that some individual could suddenly become King of China on condition, however, of forgetting what he had been, as though being born again, would it not amount to the same practically, or as far as the effects could be perceived, as if the individual were annihilated, and a king of China were the same instant created in his place? The individual would have no reason to desire this.

XXXV. The excellence of spirits; that God considers them preferable to other creatures; that the spirits express God rather than the world, while other simple substances express the world rather than God.

In order, however, to prove by natural reasons that God will preserve forever not only our substance, but also our personality, that is to say the recollection and knowledge of what we are (although the distinct knowledge is sometimes suspended during sleep and in swoons) it is necessary to join to metaphysics moral considerations. God must be considered not only as the principle and the cause of all substances and of all existing things, but also as the chief of all persons or intelligent substances, as the absolute monarch of the most perfect city or republic, such as is constituted by all the spirits together in the universe, God being the most complete of all spirits at the same time that he is greatest of all beings. For assuredly the spirits are the most perfect of substances and best express the divinity. Since all the nature, purpose, virtue and function of substances is, as has been sufficiently explained, to express God and the universe, there is no room for doubting that those substances which give the expression, knowing what they are doing and which are able to understand the great truths about God and the universe, do express God and the universe incomparably better than do those natures which are either brutish and incapable of recognizing truths, or are wholly destitute of sensation and knowledge. The difference between intelligent substances and those which are not intelligent is quite as great as between a mirror and one who sees. As God is himself the greatest and wisest of spirits it is easy to understand that the spirits with which he can, so to speak, enter into conversation and even into social relations by communicating to them in particular ways his feelings and his will so that they are able to know and love their benefactor, must be much nearer to him than the rest of created things which may be regarded as the instruments of spirits. In the same way we see that all wise persons consider far more the condition of a man than of anything else however precious it may be; and it seems that the greatest satisfaction which a soul, satisfied in other respects, can have is to see itself loved by others. However, with respect to God there is this difference that his glory and our worship can add nothing to his satisfaction, the recognition of creatures being nothing but a consequence of his sovereign and perfect felicity and being far from contributing to it or from causing it even in part. Nevertheless, that which is reasonable in finite spirits is found eminently in him and as we praise a king who prefers to preserve the life of a man before that of the most precious and rare of his animals, we should not doubt that the most enlightened and most just of all monarchs has the same preference.

XXXVI. *God is the monarch of the most perfect republic composed of all the spirits, and the happiness of this city of God is his principal purpose.*

Spirits are of all substances the most capable of perfection and their perfections are different in this that they interfere with one another the least, or rather they aid one another the most, for only the most virtuous can be the most perfect friends. Hence it follows that God who in all things has the greatest perfection will have the greatest care for spirits and will give not only to all of them in general, but even to each one in particular the highest perfection which the universal harmony will permit. We can even say that it is because he is a spirit that God is the originator of existences, for if he had lacked the power of will to choose what is best, there would have been no reason why one possible being should exist rather than any other. Therefore God's being a spirit himself dominates all the consideration which he may have toward created things.

Spirits alone are made in his image, being as it were of his blood or as children in the family, since they alone are able to serve him of free will, and to act consciously imitating the divine nature. A single spirit is worth a whole world, because it not only expresses the whole world, but it also knows it and governs itself as does God. In this way we may say that though every substance expresses the whole universe, yet the other substances express the world rather than God, while spirits express God rather than the world. This nature of spirits, so noble that it enables them to approach divinity as much as is possible for created things, has as a result that God derives infinitely more glory from them than from the other beings, or rather the other beings furnish to spirits the material for glorifying him. This moral quality of God which constitutes him Lord and Monarch of spirits influences him so to speak personally and in a unique way. It is through this that he humanizes himself, that he is willing to suffer anthropologies, and that he enters into social relations with us; and this consideration is so dear to him that the happy and prosperous condition of his empire which consists in the greatest possible felicity of its inhabitants, becomes supreme among his laws. Happiness is to persons what perfection is to beings. And if the dominant principle in the existence of the physical world is the decree to give it the greatest possible perfection, the primary purpose in the moral world or in the city of God which constitutes the noblest part of the universe ought to be to extend the greatest happiness possible. We must not therefore doubt that God has so ordained everything that spirits not only shall live forever, because this is unavoidable, but that they shall also preserve forever their moral quality, so that his city may never lose a person, quite in the same way that the world never loses a substance. Consequently they will always be conscious of their being, otherwise they would be open to neither reward nor punishment, a condition which is the essence of a republic, and above all of the most perfect republic where nothing can be neglected. In fine, God being at the same time the most just and the most debonnaire of monarchs, and requiring only a good will on the part of men, provided that it be sincere and intentional, his subjects cannot desire a better condition. To render them perfectly happy he desires only that they love him.

XXXVII. Jesus Christ has revealed to men the mystery and the admirable laws of the kingdom of heaven, and the greatness of the supreme happiness which God has prepared for those who love him.

The ancient philosophers knew very little of these important truths. Jesus Christ alone has expressed them divinely well, and in a way so clear and simple that the dullest minds have understood them. His gospel has entirely changed the face of human affairs. It has brought us to know the kingdom of heaven, or that perfect republic of spirits which deserves to be called the city of God. He it is who has discovered to us its wonderful laws. He alone has made us see how much God loves us and with what care everything that concerns us has been provided for; how God, inasmuch as he cares for the sparrows, will not neglect reasoning beings, who are infinitely more dear to him; how all the hairs of our heads are numbered; how heaven and earth may pass away but the word of God and that which belongs to the means of our salvation will not pass away; how God has more regard for the least one among intelligent souls than for the whole machinery of the world; how we ought not to fear those who are able to destroy the body but are unable to destroy the soul, since God alone can render the soul happy or unhappy; and how the souls of the righteous are protected by his hand against all the upheavals of the universe, since God alone is able to act upon them; how none of our acts are forgotten; how everything is to be accounted for; even careless words and even a spoonful of water which is well used; in fact how everything must result in the greatest welfare of the good, for then shall the righteous become like suns and neither our sense nor our minds have ever tasted of anything approaching the joys which God has laid up for those that love him.

THE MONADOLOGY

1. The Monad, of which we will speak here, is nothing else than a simple substance, which goes to make up composites; by simple, we mean without parts.

2. There must be simple substances because there are composites; for a composite is nothing else than a collection or *aggregatum* of simple substances.

3. Now, where there are no constituent parts there is possible neither extension, nor form, nor divisibility. These Monads are the true Atoms of nature, and, in fact, the Elements of things.

4. Their dissolution, therefore, is not to be feared and there is no way conceivable by which a simple substance can perish through natural means.

5. For the same reason there is no way conceivable by which a simple substance might, through natural means, come into existence, since it can not be formed by composition.

6. We may say then, that the existence of Monads can begin or end only all at once, that is to say, the Monad can begin only through creation and end only through annihilation. Composites, however, begin or end gradually.

7. There is also no way of explaining how a Monad can be altered or changed in its inner being by any other created thing, since there is no possibility of transposition within it, nor can we conceive of any internal movement which can be produced, directed, increased or diminished there within the substance, such as can take place in the case of composites where a change can occur among the parts. The Monads have no windows through which anything may come in or go out.

The Attributes are not liable to detach themselves and make an excursion outside the substance, as could *sensible species* of the Schoolmen. In the same way neither substance nor attribute can enter from without into a Monad.

8. Still Monads must needs have some qualities, otherwise they would not even be existences. And if simple substances did not differ at all in their qualities, there would be no means of perceiving any change in things. Whatever is in a composite can come into it only through its simple elements and the Monads, if they were without qualities, since they do not differ at all in quantity, would be indistinguishable one from another. For instance, if we imagine *a plenum* or completely filled space, where each part receives only the equivalent of its own previous motion, one state of things would not be distinguishable from another.

9. Each Monad, indeed, must be different from every other. For there are never in nature two beings which are exactly alike, and in which it is not possible to find a difference either internal or based on an intrinsic property.

10. I assume it as admitted that every created being, and consequently the created Monad, is subject to change, and indeed that this change is continuous in each.

11. It follows from what has just been said, that the natural changes of the Monad come from an internal principle, because an external cause can have no influence upon its inner being.

12. Now besides this principle of change there must also be in the Monad a manifoldness which changes. This manifoldness constitutes, so to speak, the specific nature and the variety of the simple substances.

13. This manifoldness must involve a multiplicity in the unity or in that which is simple. For since every natural change takes place by degrees, there must be something which changes and something which remains unchanged, and consequently there must be in the simple substance a plurality of conditions and relations, even though it has no parts.

14. The passing condition which involves and represents a multiplicity in the unity, or in the simple substance, is nothing else than what is called Perception. This should be carefully

distinguished from Apperception or Consciousness, as will appear in what follows. In this matter the Cartesians have fallen into a serious error, in that they treat as nonexistent those perceptions of which we are not conscious. It is this also which has led them to believe that spirits alone are Monads and that there are no souls of animals or other Entelechies, and it has led them to make the common confusion between a protracted period of unconsciousness and actual death. They have thus adopted the Scholastic error that souls can exist entirely separated from bodies, and have even confirmed ill-balanced minds in the belief that souls are mortal.

15. The action of the internal principle which brings about the change or the passing from one perception to another may be called Appetition. It is true that the desire (*l'appetit*) is not always able to attain to the whole of the perception which it strives for, but it always attains a portion of it and reaches new perceptions.

16. We, ourselves, experience a multiplicity in a simple substance, when we find that the most trifling thought of which we are conscious involves a variety in the object. Therefore all those who acknowledge that the soul is a simple substance ought to grant this multiplicity in the Monad, and Monsieur Bayle should have found no difficulty in it, as he has done in his *Dictionary*, article "Rorarius."

17. It must be confessed, however, that Perception, and that which depends upon it, are inexplicable by mechanical causes, that is to say, by figures and motions. Supposing that there were a machine whose structure produced thought, sensation, and perception, we could conceive of it as increased in size with the same proportions until one was able to enter into its interior, as he would into a mill. Now, on going into it he would find only pieces working upon one another, but never would he find anything to explain Perception. It is accordingly in the simple substance, and not in the composite nor in a machine that the Perception is to be sought. Furthermore, there is nothing besides perceptions and their changes to be found in the simple substance. And it is in these alone that all the internal activities of the simple substance can consist.

18. All simple substances or created Monads may be called

Entelechies, because they have in themselves a certain perfection (ἔχουσι τὸ ἐντελές). There is in them a sufficiency (αὐτάρκεια) which makes them the source of their internal activities, and renders them, so to speak, incorporeal Automatons.

19. If we wish to designate as soul everything which has perceptions and desires in the general sense that I have just explained, all simple substances or created Monads could be called souls. But since feeling is something more than a mere perception I think that the general name of Monad or Entelechy should suffice for simple substances which have only perception, while we may reserve the term Soul for those whose perception is more distinct and is accompanied by memory.

20. We experience in ourselves a state where we remember nothing and where we have no distinct perception, as in periods of fainting, or when we are overcome by a profound, dreamless sleep. In such a state the soul does not sensibly differ at all from a simple Monad. As this state, however, is not permanent and the soul can recover from it, the soul is something more.

21. Nevertheless it does not follow at all that the simple substance is in such a state without perception. This is so because of the reasons given above; for it cannot perish, nor on the other hand would it exist without some affection and the affection is nothing else than its perception. When, however, there are a great number of weak perceptions where nothing stands out distinctively, we are stunned; as when one turns around and around in the same direction, a dizziness comes on, which makes him swoon and makes him able to distinguish nothing. Among animals, death can occasion this state for quite a period.

22. Every present state of a simple substance is a natural consequence of its preceding state, in such a way that its present is big with its future.

23. Therefore, since on awakening after a period of unconsciousness we become conscious of our perceptions, we must, without having been conscious of them, have had perceptions immediately before; for one perception can come in a natural

way only from another perception, just as a motion can come in a natural way only from a motion.

24. It is evident from this that if we were to have nothing distinctive, or so to speak prominent, and of a higher flavor in our perceptions, we should be in a continual state of stupor. This is the condition of Monads which are wholly bare.

25. We see that nature has given to animals heightened perceptions, having provided them with organs which collect numerous rays of light or numerous waves of air and thus make them more effective in their combination. Something similar to this takes place in the case of smell, in that of taste and of touch, and perhaps in many other senses which are unknown to us. I shall have occasion very soon to explain how that which occurs in the soul represents that which goes on in the sense-organs.

26. The memory furnishes a sort of consecutiveness which imitates reason but is to be distinguished from it. We see that animals when they have the perception of something which they notice and of which they have had a similar previous perception, are led by the representation of their memory to expect that which was associated in the preceding perception, and they come to have feelings like those which they had before. For instance, if a stick be shown to a dog, he remembers the pain which it has caused him and he whines or runs away.

27. The vividness of the picture, which comes to him or moves him, is derived either from the magnitude or from the number of the previous perceptions. For, oftentimes, a strong impression brings about, all at once, the same effect as a long-continued habit or as a great many re-iterated, moderate perceptions.

28. Men act in like manner as animals, in so far as the sequence of their perceptions is determined only by the law of memory, resembling the *empirical physicians* who practice simply, without any theory, and we are empiricists in three-fourths of our actions. For instance, when we expect that there will be day-light to-morrow, we do so empirically, because it has always happened so up to the present time. It is only the astronomer who uses his reason in making such an affirmation.

29. But the knowledge of eternal and necessary truths is

that which distinguishes us from mere animals and gives us reason and the sciences, thus raising us to a knowledge of ourselves and of God. This is what is called in us the Rational Soul or the Mind.

30. It is also through the knowledge of necessary truths and through abstractions from them that we come to perform Reflective Acts, which cause us to think of what is called the I, and to decide that this or that is within us. It is thus, that in thinking upon ourselves we think of *being*, of *substance*, of the *simple* and *composite*, of a *material* thing and of *God* himself, conceiving that what is limited in us is in him without limits. These Reflective Acts furnish the principal objects of our reasonings.

31. Our reasoning is based upon two great principles: first, that of Contradiction, by means of which we decide that to be false which involves contradiction and that to be true which contradicts or is opposed to the false.

32. And second, the principle of Sufficient Reason, in virtue of which we believe that no fact can be real or existing and no statement true unless it has a sufficient reason why it should be thus and not otherwise. Most frequently, however, these reasons cannot be known by us.

33. There are also two kinds of Truths: those of Reasoning and those of Fact. The Truths of Reasoning are necessary, and their opposite is impossible. Those of Fact, however, are contingent, and their opposite is possible. When a truth is necessary, the reason can be found by analysis in resolving it into simpler ideas and into simpler truths until we reach those which are primary.

34. It is thus that with mathematicians the Speculative Theorems and the practical Canons are reduced by analysis to Definitions, Axioms, and Postulates.

35. There are finally simple ideas of which no definition can be given. There are also the Axioms and Postulates or, in a word, the primary principles which cannot be proved and, indeed, have no need of proof. These are identical propositions whose opposites involve express contradictions.

36. But there must be also a sufficient reason for contingent truths or truths of fact; that is to say, for the sequence of the

things which extend throughout the universe of created beings, where the analysis into more particular reasons can be continued into greater detail without limit because of the immense variety of the things in nature and because of the infinite division of bodies. There is an infinity of figures and of movements, present and past, which enter into the efficient cause of my present writing, and in its final cause there are an infinity of slight tendencies and dispositions of my soul, present and past.

37. And as all this detail again involves other and more detailed contingencies, each of which again has need of a similar analysis in order to find its explanation, no real advance has been made. Therefore, the sufficient or ultimate reason must needs be outside of the sequence or series of these details of contingencies, however infinite they may be.

38. It is thus that the ultimate reason for things must be a necessary substance, in which the detail of the changes shall be present merely potentially, as in the fountain-head, and this substance we call God.

39. Now, since this substance is a sufficient reason for all the above mentioned details, which are linked together throughout, *there is but one God, and this God is sufficient.*

40. We may hold that the supreme substance, which is unique, universal and necessary with nothing independent outside of it, which is further a pure sequence of possible being, must be incapable of limitation and must contain as much reality as possible.

41. Whence it follows that God is absolutely perfect, perfection being understood as the magnitude of positive reality in the strict sense, when the limitations or the bounds of those things which have them are removed. There where there are no limits, that is to say, in God, perfection is absolutely infinite.

42. It follows also that created things derive their perfections through the influence of God, but their imperfections come from their own natures, which cannot exist without limits. It is in this latter that they are distinguished from God. An example of this original imperfection of created things is to be found in the natural inertia of bodies.

43. It is true, furthermore, that in God is found not only

the source of existences, but also that of essences, in so far as they are real. In other words, he is the source of whatever there is real in the possible. This is because the Understanding of God is in the region of eternal truths or of the ideas upon which they depend, and because without him there would be nothing real in the possibilities of things, and not only would nothing be existent, nothing would be even possible.

44. For it must needs be that if there is a reality in essences or in possibilities or indeed in the eternal truths, this reality is based upon something existent and actual, and, consequently, in the existence of the necessary Being in whom essence includes existence or in whom possibility is sufficient to produce actuality.

45. Therefore God alone (or the Necessary Being) has this prerogative that if he be possible he must necessarily exist, and, as nothing is able to prevent the possibility of that which involves no bounds, no negation, and consequently, no contradiction, this alone is sufficient to establish *a priori* his existence. We have, therefore, proved his existence through the reality of eternal truths. But a little while ago we also proved it *a posteriori,* because contingent beings exist which can have their ultimate and sufficient reason only in the necessary being which, in turn, has the reason for existence in itself.

46. Yet we must not think that the eternal truths being dependent upon God are therefore arbitrary and depend upon his will, as Descartes seems to have held, and after him M. Poiret. This is the case only with contingent truths which depend upon fitness or the choice of the greatest good; necessarily truths on the other hand depend solely upon his understanding and are the inner objects of it.

47. God alone is the ultimate unity or the original simple substance, of which all created or derivative monads are the products, and arise, so to speak, through the continual out-flashings (fulgurations) of the divinity from moment to moment, limited by the receptivity of the creature to whom limitation is an essential.

48. In God are present: power, which is the source of everything; knowledge, which contains the details of the ideas; and, finally, will, which changes or produces things in accordance

with the principle of the greatest good. To these correspond in the created monad, the subject or basis, the faculty of perception, and the faculty of appetition. In God these attributes are absolutely infinite or perfect, while in the created monads or in the entelechies (*perfectihabies*, as Hermolaus Barbarus translates this word), they are imitations approaching him in proportion to the perfection.

49. A created thing is said to act outwardly in so far as it has perfection, and to be acted upon by another in so far as it is imperfect. Thus action is attributed to the monad in so far as it has distinct perceptions, and passion or passivity is attributed in so far as it has confused perceptions.

50. One created thing is more perfect than another when we find in the first that which gives an *a priori* reason for what occurs in the second. This is why we say that one acts upon the other.

51. In the case of simple substances, the influence which one monad has upon another is only ideal. It can have its effect only through the mediation of God, in so far as in the ideas of God each monad can rightly demand that God, in regulating the others from the beginning of things, should have regarded it also. For since one created monad cannot have a physical influence upon the inner being of another, it is only through the primal regulation that one can have dependence upon another.

52. It is thus that among created things action and passivity are reciprocal. For God, in comparing two simple substances, finds in each one reasons obliging him to adapt the other to it; and consequently what is active in certain respects is passive from another point of view, active in so far as what we distinctly know in it serves to give a reason for what occurs in another, and passive in so far as the reason for what occurs in it is found in what is distinctly known in another.

53. Now as there are an infinity of possible universes in the ideas of God, and but one of them can exist, there must be a sufficient reason for the choice of God which determines him to select one rather than another.

54. And this reason is to be found only in the fitness or in the degree of perfection which these worlds possess, each pos-

sible thing having the right to claim existence in proportion to the perfection which it involves.

55. This is the cause for the existence of the greatest good; namely, that the wisdom of God permits him to know it, his goodness causes him to choose it, and his power enables him to produce it.

56. Now this interconnection, relationship, or this adaptation of all things to each particular one, and of each one to all the rest, brings it about that every simple substance has relations which express all the others and that it is consequently a perpetual living mirror of the universe.

57. And as the same city regarded from different sides appears entirely different, and is, as it were multiplied respectively, so, because of the infinite number of simple substances, there are a similar infinite number of universes which are, nevertheless, only the aspects of a single one as seen from the special point of view of each monad.

58. Through this means has been obtained the greatest possible variety, together with the greatest order that may be; that is to say, through this means has been obtained the greatest possible perfection.

59. This hypothesis, moreover, which I venture to call demonstrated, is the only one which fittingly gives proper prominence to the greatness of God. M. Bayle recognized this when in his dictionary (article "Rorarius") he raised objections to it; indeed, he was inclined to believe that I attributed too much to God, and more than it is possible to attribute to him: But he was unable to bring forward any reason why this universal harmony which causes every substance to express exactly all others through the relation which it has with them is impossible.

60. Besides, in what has just been said can be seen the *a priori* reasons why things cannot be otherwise than they are. It is because God, in ordering the whole, has had regard to every part and in particular to each monad; and since the monad is by its very nature *representative*, nothing can limit it to represent merely a part of things. It is nevertheless true that this representation is, as regards the details of the whole universe, only a confused representation, and is distinct only

as regards a small part of them, that is to say, as regards those things which are nearest or greatest in relation to each monad. If the representation were distinct as to the details of the entire universe, each monad would be a Deity. It is not in the object represented that the monads are limited, but in the modifications of their knowledge of the object. In a confused way they reach out to infinity or to the whole, but are limited and differentiated in the degree of their distinct perceptions.

61. In this respect composites are like simple substances, for all space is filled up; therefore, all matter is connected. And in a plenum or filled space every movement has an effect upon bodies in proportion to this distance, so that not only is every body affected by those which are in contact with it and responds in some way to whatever happens to them, but also by means of them the body responds to those bodies adjoining them, and their intercommunication reaches to any distance whatsoever. Consequently every body responds to all that happens in the universe, so that he who saw all could read in each one what is happening everywhere, and even what has happened and what will happen. He can discover in the present what is distant both as regards space and as regards time; σύμπνοια πάντα,[1] as Hippocrates said. A soul can, however, read in itself only what is there represented distinctly. It cannot all at once open up all its folds, because they extend to infinity.

62. Thus although each created monad represents the whole universe, it represents more distinctly the body which specially pertains to it and of which it constitutes the entelechy. And as this body expresses all the universe through the interconnection of all matter in the plenum, the soul also represents the whole universe in representing this body, which belongs to it in a particular way.

63. The body belonging to a monad, which is its entelechy or soul, constitutes together with the entelechy what may be called a *living being*, and with a soul what is called an *animal*. Now this body of a living being or of an animal is always or-

---

[1] "All things conspire" is what Leibniz means. See note in Latta's edition.—A. R. C.

ganic, because every monad is a mirror of the universe is regulated with perfect order there must needs be order also in what represents it, that is to say in the perceptions of the soul and consequently in the body through which the universe is represented in the soul.

64. Therefore every organic body of a living being is a kind of divine machine or natural automaton, infinitely surpassing all artificial automatons. Because a machine constructed by man's skill is not a machine in each of its parts; for instance, the teeth of a brass wheel have parts or bits which to us are not artificial products and contain nothing in themselves to show the use to which the wheel was destined in the machine. The machines of nature, however, that is to say, living bodies, are still machines in their smallest parts *ad infinitum*. Such is the difference between nature and art, that is to say, between divine art and ours.

65. The author of nature has been able to employ this divine and infinitely marvelous artifice, because each portion of matter is not only, as the ancients recognized, infinitely divisible, but also because it is really divided without end, every part into other parts, each one of which has its own proper motion. Otherwise it would be impossible for each portion of matter to express all the universe.

66. Whence we see that there is a world of created things, of living beings, of animals, of entelechies, of souls, in the minutest particle of matter.

67. Every portion of matter may be conceived as like a garden full of plants and like a pond full of fish. But every branch of a plant, every member of an animal, and every drop of the fluids within it, is also such a garden or such a pond.

68. And although the ground and air which lies between the plants of the garden, and the water which is between the fish in the pond, are not themselves plants or fish, yet they nevertheless contain these, usually so small however as to be imperceptible to us.

69. There is, therefore, nothing uncultivated, or sterile or dead in the universe, no chaos, no confusion, save in appearance; somewhat as a pond would appear at a distance when

we could see in it a confused movement, and so to speak, a swarming of the fish, without however discerning the fish themselves.

70. It is evident, then, that every living body has a dominating entelechy, which in animals is the soul. The parts, however, of this living body are full of other living beings, plants and animals, which in turn have each one its entelechy or dominating soul.

71. This does not mean, as some who have misunderstood my thought have imagined, that each soul has a quantity or portion of matter appropriated to it or attached to itself for ever, and that it consequently owns other inferior living beings destined to serve it always; because all bodies are in a state of perpetual flux like rivers, and the parts are continually entering in or passing out.

72. The soul, therefore, changes its body only gradually and by degrees, so that it is never deprived all at once of all its organs. There is frequently a metamorphosis in animals, but never metempsychosis or a transmigration of souls. Neither are there souls wholly separate from bodies, nor bodiless spirits. God alone is without body.

73. This is also why there is never absolute generation or perfect death in the strict sense, consisting in the separation of the soul from the body. What we call generation is development and growth, and what we call death is envelopment and diminution.

74. Philosophers have been much perplexed in accounting for the origin of forms, entelechies, or souls. To-day, however, when it has been learned through careful investigations made in plant, insect and animal life, that the organic bodies of nature are never the product of chaos or putrefaction, but always come from seeds in which there was without doubt some preformation, it has been decided that not only is the organic body already present before conception, but also a soul in this body, in a word, the animal itself; and it has been decided that, by means of conception the animal is merely made ready for a great transformation, so as to become an animal of another sort. We can see cases somewhat similar outside

of generation when grubs become flies and caterpillars butter-flies.

75. These little animals, some of which by conception be-come large animals, may be called spermatic. Those among them which remain in their species, that is to say, the greater part, are born, multiply, and are destroyed, like the larger ani-mals. There are only a few chosen ones which come out upon a greater stage.

76. This, however, is only half the truth. I believe, there-fore, that if the animal never actually commences by natural means, no more does it by natural means come to an end. Not only is there no generation, but also there is no entire destruction or absolute death. These reasonings, carried on *a posteriori* and drawn from experience, accord perfectly with the principles which I have above deduced *a priori*.

77. Therefore we may say that not only the soul (the mir-ror of the indestructible universe) is indestructible, but also the animal itself is, although its mechanism is frequently de-stroyed in parts and although it puts off and takes on organic coatings.

78. These principles have furnished me the means of ex-plaining on natural grounds the union, or rather the conform-ity between the soul and the organic body. The soul follows its own laws, and the body likewise follows its own laws. They are fitted to each other in virtue of the preestablished harmony between all substances, since they are all representations of one and the same universe.

79. Souls act in accordance with the laws of final causes through their desires, ends and means. Bodies act in accord-ance with the laws of efficient causes or of motion. The two realms, that of efficient causes and that of final causes, are in harmony, each with the other.

80. Descartes saw that souls cannot at all impart force to bodies, because there is always the same quantity of force in matter. Yet he thought that the soul could change the direc-tion of bodies. This was, however, because at that time the law of nature which affirms also that conservation of the same total direction in the motion of matter was not known. If he

had known that law, he would have fallen upon my system of preestablished harmony.

81. According to this system bodies act as if (to suppose the impossible) there were no souls at all, and souls act as if there were no bodies, and yet both body and soul act as if the one were influencing the other.

82. Although I find that essentially the same thing is true of all living things and animals, which we have just said (namely, that animals and souls begin from the very commencement of the world and that they no more come to an end than does the world) nevertheless, rational animals have this peculiarity, that their little spermatic animals, as long as they remain such, have only ordinary or sensuous souls, but those of them which are, so to speak, elected, attain by actual conception to human nature, and their sensuous souls are raised to the rank of reason and to the prerogative of spirits.

83. Among the differences that there are between ordinary souls and spirits, some of which I have already instanced, there is also this, that while souls in general are living mirrors or images of the universe of created things, spirits are also images of the Deity himself or of the author of nature. They are capable of knowing the system of the universe, and of imitating some features of it by means of artificial models, each spirit being like a small divinity in its own sphere.

84. Therefore, spirits are able to enter into a sort of social relationship with God, and with respect to them he is not only what an inventor is to his machine (as in his relation to the other created things), but he is also what a prince is to his subjects, and even what a father is to his children.

85. Whence it is easy to conclude that the totality of all spirits must compose the city of God, that is to say, the most perfect state that is possible under the most perfect monarch.

86. This city of God, this truly universal monarchy, is a moral world within the natural world. It is what is noblest and most divine among the works of God. And in it consists in reality the glory of God, because he would have no glory were not his greatness and goodness known and wondered at by spirits. It is also in relation to this divine city that God

properly has goodness. His wisdom and his power are shown everywhere.

87. As we established above that there is a perfect harmony between the two natural realms of efficient and final causes, it will be in place here to point out another harmony which appears between the physical realm of nature and the moral realm of grace, that is to say, between God considered as the architect of the mechanism of the world and God considered as the monarch of the divine city of spirits.

88. This harmony brings it about that things progress of themselves toward grace along natural lines, and that this earth, for example, must be destroyed and restored by natural means at those times when the proper government of spirits demands it, for chastisement in the one case and for a reward in the other.

89. We can say also that God, the Architect, satisfies in all respects God the Law-Giver, that therefore sins will bring their own penalty with them through the order of nature, and because of the very structure of things, mechanical though it is. And in the same way the good actions will attain their rewards in mechanical way through their relation to bodies, although this cannot and ought not always to take place without delay.

90. Finally, under this perfect government, there will be no good action unrewarded and no evil action unpunished; everything must turn out for the well-being of the good; that is to say, of those who are not disaffected in this great state, who, after having done their duty, trust in Providence and who love and imitate, as is meet, the Author of all Good, delighting in the contemplation of his perfections according to the nature of that genuine, pure love which finds pleasure in the happiness of those who are loved. It is for this reason that wise and virtuous persons work in behalf of everything which seems comformable to presumptive or antecedent will of God, and are, nevertheless, content with what God actually brings to pass through his secret, consequent and determining will, recognizing that if we were able to understand sufficiently well the order of the universe, we should find that it surpasses all the desires of the wisest of us, and that it is impossible to render it better than it is, not only for all in general, but also